SOCIAL PSYCHOLOGY RESEARCH PROGRESS

SOCIAL PSYCHOLOGY AND COUNSELING

ISSUES AND APPLICATIONS

Social Psychology Research Progress

Additional books and e-books in this series can be found on Nova's website under the Series tab.

SOCIAL PSYCHOLOGY RESEARCH PROGRESS

SOCIAL PSYCHOLOGY AND COUNSELING

ISSUES AND APPLICATIONS

DOUGLAS A. KLEIBER
AND
EDWARD DELGADO-ROMERO
EDITORS

nova
science publishers
New York

Library of Congress Cataloging-in-Publication Data

Names: Kleiber, Douglas A., editor.
Title: Social psychology and counseling: issues and applications / [edited by] Douglas A. Kleiber.
Identifiers: LCCN 2019045983 (print) | LCCN 2019045984 (ebook) | ISBN 9781536165487 (hardcover) | ISBN 9781536165494 (ebook)
Subjects: LCSH: Social psychology. | Social media--Psychological aspects. | Counseling.
Classification: LCC HM1033 .S6383 2020 (print) | LCC HM1033 (ebook) | DDC 302--dc23
LC record available at https://lccn.loc.gov/2019045983
LC ebook record available at https://lccn.loc.gov/2019045984

Published by Nova Science Publishers, Inc. † New York

CONTENTS

FOREWORD

Arthur M. Horne

Reading *Social Psychology and Counseling: Issues and Applications*, by Douglas Kleiber and Edward Delgado-Romero and their co-authors provided me with a wonderful opportunity for reflecting on the past, thinking of the present, and imagining the future. Their presentations on the interaction of the variety of areas of social psychology and counseling psychology today led me to reflect on the journey of learning that, for me, began in a very different world of counseling than their excellent text represents today. My first counseling course occurred 53 years ago. At that time the emphasis of training was on learning to understand the experience of individuals in conflict and distress and to provide a relational engagement that would allow them to explore personal avenues for resolving their interpersonal conflicts and lifestyle challenges, ideally helping them to establish more fulfilling and personally enriching lives. The emphasis was on the individual and how clients were experiencing their world and their circumstances while fostering ways to manage those areas more effectively. While that is certainly an oversimplification of the training of those days, very few of the concepts addressing social context and social influence used by the authors in this volume were particularly evident then.

For example, *social justice* was implied as a concern in various ways in the 1970s and 80s but was not identified as a counseling concern until relatively recently. There was an emphasis on psychological development and self-actualization but, with the exception of fostering respect for others, there was little focus on the social factors that undermined such growth and development. Oh, there was an awareness of the importance of the broader culture and community, but cultural issues were addressed more as issues or obstacles that the individual would be expected to examine, challenge, and overcome, if they were even brought up at all, rather than recognized as indicators for leaving the office or clinic and instigating community, regional, national, and international change to mitigate negative effects on clients. The focus of the training was on the individual, and while social change rather than adaptation could be indicated, it was usually examined as an individual responsibility. For example, consider the social problems associated with the issue of apartheid in South Africa in the past. In some cases whites were assisted in managing their guilt over the problem, while in some other cases blacks were taught to manage their anger in less hostile ways. The individuals may have coped better, but apartheid was not addressed as a systemic influence requiring social action to alleviate the problems that were manifested by individuals in complex ways. Similarly, in the United States laws were in effect that were discriminatory, including legal segregation. A conflict for counselors was whether to facilitate accommodation to unjust laws as a way of managing emotional stress, or challenge the laws and advocate for change. Clearly, supporting the civil rights movement was an imperative for those committed to healthy lifestyles for all, but that required a different level of engagement with individuals and the community. The emphasis began to change, though, as the training programs became more diverse in their makeup, the faculty developed greater heterogeneity, and the increasing awareness of the toxicity of many situations became more evident. It also become more evident that simply helping people adapt to adverse situations was not health promoting or advancing human rights and human potential. As civil rights activity demonstrated the potential for changing laws, rules, and customs, counselors become more inclined to address transformation through addressing changing systems at the local, regional, and national levels. Helping seeds develop in a harsh environment is not as effective as helping those healthy seeds flourish in a fulfilling and supportive and encouraging world.

In reading the chapters of the current book, it is clear that the authors, some new professionals and some yet to fully complete their doctoral programs, have nevertheless demonstrated a broad and diverse appreciation of the factors of influence in the lives of people of different ages and contexts in ways that will provoke readers to make contributions of their own. The authors are also clearly adept at understanding both the breadth and depth of the interventions necessary to help individuals, groups, and entire communities create change. It is very encouraging to read of the variety of concerns and problems being addressed, the scope of the settings and circumstances that are experienced by the services, and the efficacy and efficiency of the interventions being described and implemented. The world is very complex, and the mental health and emotional concerns counselors address (both in offices and beyond in the communities) require expertise in technical skills but also a commitment to impacting the harmful social structures that result in so much pain and emotional conflict. The young authors and psychologists demonstrate in their chapters their background and preparation, their awareness and maturity related to the problems, and their creativity and enthusiasm for being impactful in their work to positively impact the lives of those seeking and needing their support.

The future is also worthy of consideration at this point. While discussing the narrower training model I experienced decades ago, there is still an awareness of the commitment to change, to helping people establish better lives, and to move toward a world of respect and dignity. That process is more sophisticated and advanced today and the social justice commitment manifests itself in more diverse and challenging ways than previously, and best practices continue to enable people to live lives of respect and dignity.

And for the future? It seems it will only continue to be better in the promotion of human health and wellness. The Society of Counseling Psychology and the Prevention Section of the Society have recently launched a new journal, *The Journal of Prevention and Health Promotion.* The journal is an example of a commitment to advancing social justice by providing publication of manuscripts focusing on the practice, theory, research, and training in prevention efforts – a commitment to the recognition that it is truly better to prevent mental health problems than it is to treat them through therapy. Therapy will still be essential, necessary, and a given in our world, but just as lifeguards are still necessary at waterfronts, so prevention of problems from developing is akin to teaching young people to swim so that less intervention will be necessary in the future. There is also an implied commitment with *JPHP* that the future will require becoming more involved outside the office – through activism, engagement, and communication – with improving the quality of life for all people. We already have extensive knowledge of how to promote health and wellness – it is going to take activism to make it happen. Some of the greatest problems facing our lives today include topics that were once essential for our living, for our existence: salt, calories, aggression. Today we have too much of each in our lives, and we know this – which is why as we move forward into the future our emphasis will go beyond just providing knowledge (eat less salt; eat fewer calories, be less aggressive) and, instead, will need to embrace the human values and lifestyle characteristics that knowledge alone cannot address. That is our role as we move forward.

On a personal note, it is so very gratifying to read these materials. I've devoted a lifetime to the teaching, research, and practice of counseling, and it is with great pride that I see the process continuing in such enriching and creative ways. I finished my career as the Dean of the College of Education at the University of Georgia. Seeing the talented faculty and students of today continue the excellent tradition of bringing knowledge to practice, to advancing awareness and appreciation of the intricacies of the field of counseling psychology, and to demonstrating a commitment to social justice and the advancement of opportunity and positive life-experiences is so very gratifying and encouraging. I am most appreciative of my current and future colleagues for their efforts and leadership. We've had a rich past and an impressive present, and we certainly have a most promising future. This text is a worthy professional contribution to that future.

Arthur M. Horne
Athens, GA, US
September, 2019

PREFACE

The authors of the chapters of this book are, with few exceptions, emerging professional counselors who are academically trained through doctoral degrees programs in counseling psychology. Most have their PhDs (see author appendix), while some are very close, with only more practice experience in the way. Even though they are relatively young and new scholars, they have been trained to use the best of psychology to execute the best of practices in the field of counseling.

The editors (Kleiber & Delgado Romero) and three of the other authors (Geoff Bathje, Alan Stewart, and Elizabeth Stewart) are academics for at least part of their working time, but nearly all of the others are currently practicing psychologists with occasional teaching and research opportunities and responsibilities. I'm the one exception, having *only* academic experience, and that in social, developmental and educational psychology rather than counseling. But having taught social psychology to a good number of the authors, and having them teach me a bit of 'the ropes' around their craft, we developed a good shared purpose…to apply theory and research in social psychology to the purpose of counseling. And it is our collective understanding that in so doing we are offering perspectives that will be useful to all those in counseling and mental health services who have a need for a better grasp of the social psychological aspects of mental health practice.

But thanks to my co-editor, Edward Delgado Romero, a leader in the field of counseling psychology with plenty of professional experience (and now associate dean of a college of education), we have also decided to take the other perspective and see how contemporary counseling practice and related sensibilities might inform social psychology as well. Despite what might be expected of him as associate editor of the *Journal of Latina/o Psychology,* "D-R," as his students call him, has let his students past and present make the case for the extent to which counseling psychology has become multicultural and for the value of that perspective to society and to an evolving social psychology that has only relatively recently become so attuned.

It is our intent with this volume to provide a companion reader for a graduate course that uses a social psychology text or stands on its own as a text for a seminar on counseling and social psychology, applied social psychology, allied perspectives in social work, educational and school counseling and other mental health services. Given the range and complexity of those domain, the chapters that follow here must by necessity be regarded as partial assessments with limited reach, well-grounded though they are. Thus, it would be reasonable to expect a sequel, or a 'Volume II,' with different issues, or different, updated, and revised perspectives on the same issues in the near future. Nevertheless, we offer this volume as a useful way to jump into the intersection of social and counseling psychology.

Doug A. Kleiber

INTRODUCTION

Social psychology has been applied to many subjects such as work, leisure, and family studies but rarely to counseling. And yet, the issues commonly addressed as part of social psychology – obedience, persuasion, conformity, aggression, interpersonal attraction and love, and prejudice, among the more common -- have obvious importance to mental health and to the problems commonly faced by therapists with their clients. For example, social cognition and attribution are readily addressed in the cognitive behavioral therapy (CBT) approach of professional counseling. The following chapters in this volume represent a progression of thought within the context of doctoral training, where an understanding of social psychology is required as part of counseling programs accredited by the American Psychological Association, where practice is informed by theory and research. Authors are thus current and former doctoral students, with varying degrees of professional experience with which to interpret some of the principles and research findings from social psychology, along with professional colleagues and academic researchers who have made contributions related to the subjects in the past. The book is organized in a way generally consistent with the contents of *The Social Animal* by Eliot Aronson (2012), one of the most popular books in academic social psychology more generally.

It is also the case that a consideration of practical applications of social psychology has the advantage of informing the perspectives and positions commonly embraced and may even suggest revisions of previously accepted "truths." This is consistent with the general trend in social psychology to be increasingly receptive to multiple truths and the critical assessment of findings that reflect the world of largely privileged western cultures (and, one might argue, even narrowly those of white male European college students most of all). Thus, in keeping with the post-modern critiques of Kenneth Gergen (2001) and others, the authors of this volume treat existing social psychological research as working "intelligibilities" to be tested across boundaries of culture, gender, race and ethnicity among other important factors. Practically speaking, this neglect of alternative truths and realities has often led to the acceptance of patterns of injustice whereas most contemporary counseling psychology training programs are dedicated to redressing issues of social injustice. It is our view that contemporary social psychology, its methods and its premises, offer tools for that redress at the same time that research findings – including minority effects – argue for the refinement of those tools.

Additionally, this volume addresses another shortcoming in social psychology and psychology more generally, that there has been insufficient attention to the *positive* aspects of human experience. Thus, positive psychology was born in ways that conjured some of the orientations of humanistic psychology but with greater attention to social relatedness and also to the principle that even with deficiencies and pathologies, positive experience may be therapeutic and developmental. Maslow's paradigm-setting (1943) humanistic view asserted that needs were satisfied hierarchically with deficiency needs having to be addressed before positive growth needs can be served. Positive psychology shows its relevance to counseling and therapy by recognizing the value of the positive for prevention of mental illness but also for treating mental health issues in recognizing that individuals generally have strengths to build on.

The first full chapter takes this perspective in introducing the reader to the value of recognizing the positive motives that drive an individual's behavior in *Self Determination Theory* and applying them to processes of self-regulation and motivational interviewing. Varley and Zito thus mine Ryan and Deci's writings (e.g., 2000) for promoting of self-regulation in ways that are sustainable well beyond the confines of psychotherapy, using motivational interviewing as the mechanism for getting clients to that point.

In the first unit on social influence, Stamateris-Flaherty and Perkins address the ways in which the two most common motives for conformity – being right and being liked – influence adolescent risk-taking. Offering a case study as an example, these authors demonstrate that counseling clients with problems of substance abuse, promiscuity and other forms of risky behavior may make good use of an understanding of the dynamics of conformity. Conformity is also at play in the impact of *social media* involvement on mental health, as Nevels and Vazquez demonstrate. They use a case study to wade into that controversy in showing that conformity may be a key mediator in the impact of social media involvement on both lower self-esteem and depression in the cases where those effects occur. Nevels and Vazquez refer to techniques of psychoeducation to manage tendencies toward conformity and invidious comparison prompted by social media involvement.

The second section on social influence demonstrates the relevance of empirically supported principles of persuasion and mass communication for counseling practice. In examining the factors that make a message more or less convincing, Hoyle and Hansen take on issues of body dissatisfaction as a result of media exposure and gender orientation and offer ways to combat such influences in the therapeutic milieu while also recognizing that therapy itself utilizes such principles and practices of persuasion. Perlman and

Delgado-Romero analyze the ways in which mainstream media are biased and prejudicial in reporting on matters of immigration, creating significant challenges for treating clients from other countries in the United States with or without documentation. Certainly, this issue has never been more serious than it is currently in contemporary politics.

Speaking of the subject of attribution a bit more generally, patterns of social cognition are an essential subject of social psychology in person perception and interpretation of cause, effect and responsibility for one's own and others' behavior. It is also a critical part of psychotherapy in *Cognitive Behavior Therapy* and other approaches. Edner and Cassiello-Robbins open the next section with an analysis that digs into some of the neurobehavioral underpinnings of common cognitive "heuristics" and self-serving biases that may need redressing in the context of therapy. The research on cognitive dissonance and self-justification – some of it done by Aronson (2012) himself – is a particularly significant part of the typical biases of social cognition that lead to self-deception. Britton demonstrates that the self-justifying resolution of cognitive dissonance may be maladaptive in some cases, but that treatment can actually *generate* dissonance in a constructive way to create attitude and behavior change.

The presumably positive objective of *hazing* – building commitment to a particular group, cause or point of view – is usually overmatched by the negative impacts of such manipulations. While some of the most egregious effects of hazing – the death of a fraternity "pledge" for example – are especially newsworthy, Bigham focuses on the pattern of hazing in sport, especially, to illustrate how the use of hazing can be psychologically destructive, warranting intervention at both policy and practice levels, especially for those requiring counseling as a result. And as an ongoing reminder that faulty assumptions of universal generalizability of patterns of social behavior may even apply to social cognition, Wu and Bathje show that patterns of dissonance reduction and self-justification show contrasting effects in Eastern and Western cultures which has implications for mental health management.

The "self" in self-justification, self-evaluation social comparison, self-regulation and other social process involving a reflective cognitive process begs a deeper understanding of self and identity particularly as such constructs are influenced by social context and cultural difference. Oh does a careful analysis of how *self-discrepancy*, where real and ideal selves diverge, is a particularly significant source of self-esteem loss and depression. His treatment recommendations draw heavily from Acceptance and Commitment Therapy which uses a more reflective approach to resolution than others (e.g., Baumeister, 1991) that recommend activity as a way of reducing the impact of self-awareness though focusing attention elsewhere. Williams addresses issues of self-awareness and self-discrepancy with respect to race and body image in particular, while Ringdahl digs deeper into issues of masculinity, examining problems of masculinity as amenable to the cultivation of prosocial behavior in much the same way that Williams incorporates prosocial behavior as part of group interventions to diffuse the toxic impact of invidious social comparisons on the body images of young Black women.

Several chapters address the always very relevant issue of aggression and violence. Field and Robinson explore how adjudicated clients, offenders, both normalize to their aggression and attempt to attenuate that which is pathological and self- and socially-destructive. Their biopsychosocial perspective offers an especially comprehensive approach to treatment. Nevels focuses more specifically on the emotional regulation issues that affect adolescent and young adult girls' tendency to be aggressive in non-physical ways. Relational aggression can be every bit as destructive to mental health as physical aggression and in some cases more impactful. Nevels deals with the roots of partner and domestic violence in the failure to control anger. She examines the cases of two men prone to relational aggression toward their partners and considers the value and virtue of alternative ways to express anger. Hanson reconsiders research on aggression and its treatment and offers a more elaborated set of considerations for dealing with hostility and aggression in the context of counseling itself, in other words with clients who may become openly hostile with therapists. And Ford and Ocampo review the research on the relationship between social rejection and school violence, a contemporary problem that has teacher, parents and community residents vexed, distressed and desperate for answers. The authors' consideration of hostile attribution bias is particularly promising in that regard.

Counseling psychologists and other mental health workers also commonly encounter clients who have been victimized by prejudice and discrimination. Estevez provides a comprehensive view of the dynamics of prejudice and introduces such topics as stereotype threat and microaggression that are experienced by minority communities that have been marginalized and alienated as a result. With considerable clinical experience, the authors of this volume are generally adept at applying basic social psychological principles as registered in most social psychological textbooks to the practice of counseling, but some offer a revisionist challenge to mainstream thinking. For example, Moxley's personal narrative approach to understanding stereotype threat and the impostor syndrome faced by minority graduate students and especially African American females, utilizes the controversial construct of *microaggression* (Sue, 2009; 2010) that has earned some disfavor among mainstream social psychologists (e.g., Haidt, 2017; Lilienfeld, 2017), who question the construct validity of the term. But Moxley's personal history shows that there may be no better word to talk about the experience of prejudice reflected in the insults and invalidations implied in comments and decisions made by others. Evidence of intent is critical to definitions of aggression in mainstream social psychological interpretations (e.g., Aronson, 2012; Fiske, 2008); but statements and positions suggesting stereotyping and prejudice, however naïve and unintentional, may have the effect of diminishing a person's status and aspirations and thus are hardly innocuous. Moxley effectively demonstrates the serious effects of "microaggression" in disempowering women and people of color in academic settings and offers constructive solutions for reducing and surviving their impact. Joseph and Atilano provide additional information on stereotype threat related more specifically to college undergraduates and to Latinx as well as African American college students in particular, recognizing that the threat is real for them and must be handled with due respect to the dynamics at play.

Turning in a more positive direction, a unit on 'Liking, Loving and Interpersonal Sensitivity' would seem to offer insight into the kinder and gentler aspects of human behavior and how to promote them in practice. But clearly, interpersonal relations that may seek the best are often fraught with conflict and disappointment in ways that may become pathological. Thus, Crosby Gross treats the subject of romantic attachments in the most general way albeit with respect to the minefield that romantic pairing seems to be. Clarke and Harper then consider the dynamics as particularly problematic within the intersectionality of race and gender and with respect to the external threats that may undermine intimacy in African American couples in particular.

The final section of the book addresses cultural, environmental and developmental perspectives. The importance of culture is infused throughout many of the early chapters of the book, but the chapter by Zhu deals with it specifically in setting out its now recognized importance for understanding social psychology in a more general, comprehensive way and working with diverse clients in a variety of settings. In this case, Zhu speaks specifically to different patterns of acculturation of immigrants and the consequences for mental health. And while this book is inherently applied in drawing implications of the dynamics of social psychology – from both research and theory – for practice in clinical settings, environmental and developmental perspectives reveal important intersecting influences with relevance to the issues introduced in earlier chapters. A. Stewart demonstrates that environmental factors interact with other social influences to determine behavior and that the negative impacts of climate and weather disasters do not occur evenly across populations and disadvantage some more than others. E. Stewart and Kleiber then consider how the primary dynamics of social psychology – mostly studied with younger populations – may in fact change with age. The chapter reviews how aging itself is changing but also how challenges of aging are unique to some extent, requiring different considerations of clinicians, while demonstrating patterns of adaptability and resiliency that may offer ideas for mental health practice across the lifespan.

Douglas A. Kleiber
Edward Delgado-Romero

REFERENCES

American Psychological Association (2017). *Multicultural guidelines: An ecological approach to context, identity, and intersectionality*. Retrieved from: http://www.apa.org/about/policy/multicultural-guidelines.pdf

Aronson, E. (2012). *The social animal* (11th ed.) New York City: Worth.

Baumeister, R. (1991). *Escaping the self*. NYC: Basic Books.

Fiske, S.T. (2004). *Social beings: A core motives approach to social psychology*. NYC: Wiley.

Gergen, K. (2001). Psychological science in a postmodern context. *American Psychologist*, *56*, 803-813.

Haidt, J. (2017). The Unwisest idea on campus: Commentary on Lilienfeld (2017). *Perspectives on Psychological Science, 12*, 176-177.

Lilienfeld, S.O. (2017). Microaggressions: Strong claims; inadequate evidence. *Perspectives on Psychological Science, 12*, 138-169.

Maslow, A. H. (1943). A theory of human motivation. *Psychological Review, 50*, 370-396.

Ryan, R.M., & Deci, E.L. (2000). Self-determination theory and the facilitation of intrinsic motivation, social development, and well-being. *American Psychologist*, *55*, 68-78.

Seligman, M., & Csikszentmihalyi, M. (2000). Positive psychology. *American Psychologist*, *55*, 5-14.

Sue, D. W. (2009). Racial microaggressions and worldviews. *American Psychologist*, *64*, 220–221.

Sue, D. W. (2010). *Microaggressions in everyday life: Race, gender, and sexual orientation*. Hoboken, NJ: John Wiley & Sons.

SECTION I.
SOCIAL MOTIVATION AND MENTAL HEALTH

In: Social Psychology and Counseling
Editors: D. A. Kleiber and E. Delgado-Romero
ISBN: 978-1-53616-548-7

Chapter 1

SELF-DETERMINATION THEORY AND MOTIVATIONAL INTERVIEWING IN PSYCHOTHERAPY

Matthew S. Varley and Ashlee E. Zito

THE ROLE OF MOTIVATION IN PSYCHOTHERAPY

Unless mandated for treatment, people typically engage voluntarily in therapy for the purpose of changing one or more problematic thoughts, feelings, behaviors or interpersonal relationships (Prochaska & Norcross, 2010). Therefore, different theories of psychotherapy (e.g., psychoanalytic, interpersonal, cognitive-behavioral, etc.) tend to share the assumption that clients are typically *motivated* to change at the start of treatment. Research on psychotherapy suggests motivation is a key factor in treatment outcomes (Huppert et al., 2006; Orlinsky, Rønnestad & Willutzki, 2004; Stobbe et al., 2013). As Ryan and Deci (2008) argue, "…psychotherapy depends upon the ongoing willingness of clients to recognize and work on specific, and often multiple, problem areas in their lives" (p. 186). In other words, if clients are not interested in - or actively engaged in - psychotherapy, the results will not likely be efficacious, regardless of which form of psychotherapy is used. But what factors influence a client's motivation in the first place, and how is motivation best cultivated in a therapy relationship?

The word "motivation" – from the Latin *motivus*, meaning "moved" or "stirred" – refers both to the internal "condition of being motivated" and to any external "motivating force, stimulus, or influence" (Motivation, 2019). In terms of psychotherapy, both meanings of motivation are relevant to case conceptualization, course of treatment, and outcomes. Motivation's first meaning, the internal "condition of being motivated" has been typically understood psychologically in terms of energy and direction towards goals (Oettingen & Gollwitzer, 2015, p. 3). For the new psychotherapy client, initial goals might include resolving a personal problem, relieving distress, or establishing a relationship with the clinician. Although theories of psychotherapy differ in their concept and approach to internal motivation, most address it in some fashion. For one form of psychotherapy, *Motivational Interviewing* (Miller & Rollnick, 2002), the client's internal motivation for change is the explicit focus of treatment. In other models, such as *Dialectical Behavior Therapy* (Cameron et al., 2014) and substance abuse counseling (U.S. Center for Substance Abuse Treatment, 2012), initial assessment of a client's internal level of motivation informs treatment planning. Cognitive therapies also aim to stir client motivation, though the process may be more implicit (Ryan & Deci, 2017, p. 13).

The second meaning of motivation, as a "force, stimulus, or influence" that moves people, often appears in psychological terms as expectations and incentives (Oettingen & Gollwitzer, 2015, p. 3). Differing ideas about what forces most motivate people helps distinguish schools of psychology: for example, consider the emphasis on basic drives in psychoanalysis versus rewards and punishments in behaviorism. Formal psychological theories of motivation emerged in the 1940's. Hull's Drive Reduction Theory, for example, conceptualized motivation as the arousal of a physiological need and resulting expenditure of psychological energy to satisfy the need. According to Hull, a human was "a machine-like reactive organism compelled to act by internal and/or external forces" (Oettingen & Gollwitzer, 2015, p. 937). Later theorists accounted more for individual difference and choice in motivation. For example, in the 1960's, Atkinson's Expectancy-Value Theory considered how variables such as the personal value of a goal and the relative likelihood of achieving may influence motivation to act. In the 1970's, Bandura's Self-Efficacy Theory identified self-perceptions of personal competence and the social pressure of others' evaluations as factors mediating people's decisions to pursue goals (Oettingen & Gollwitzer, 2015, p. 937).

Although different schools of psychology and psychotherapy conceptualize motivation differently, Ryan and Deci (2017) argue most theories share the assumption that motivation is a "unitary concept," relatively "undifferentiated" and simply contrasted with "the lack of motivation" (p. 13). In contrast, Self-Determination Theory (SDT) takes "a more differentiated approach to motivation," inquiring not simply how much but "what kind of motivation is being exhibited" (Ryan & Deci 2000, p. 69) and investigating how "different types and sources of motivation" intrinsic and extrinsic to the person may "impact the quality and dynamics of behavior" (Ryan & Deci 2017, p. 14). Motivational Interviewing (MI; Miller & Rollnick, 2002), mentioned above, guides the psychotherapy process in identifying and cultivating motivation in a client's experience. Like SDT, MI represents motivation not as a personal and individual process, but as largely shaped by interpersonal and social contexts, including the psychotherapy relationship. If SDT provides a unique comprehensive theory of motivation, then MI guides clinical interventions consistent with SDT's core premises, and its techniques have demonstrated clinical effectiveness.

SELF-DETERMINATION THEORY

Over the past thirty years, Ryan and Deci (1985, 2002, 2008, 2017) have developed Self-Determination Theory (SDT) towards a unitary theory of motivation. Although SDT had no original relationship to psychotherapy, its premises have been increasingly incorporated into therapeutic settings in recent years (Markland et al., 2005; Ryan & Deci, 2008; Sheldon & Williams, 2013). In the humanistic tradition of Erikson, Maslow and others, SDT assumes humans are motivated by innate tendencies to grow. The construct of *organismic integration* recognizes a process common to all living things towards synthesis and harmony within the self and in the environment (Ryan & Deci, 2008, p. 188). Among humans, this drive may manifest as self-actualizing tendencies: the urges, for example, to learn new things, achieve goals, connect with others, and grow in multidimensional ways. At the same time, SDT recognizes that people may stagnate, become discouraged, and reject opportunities for growth and change (Ryan & Deci, 2000). These outcomes may be determined in part by the extent to which people's basic physiological and psychological needs are satisfied (Ryan & Deci, 2000).

Basic Needs in Self Determination Theory

Ryan and Deci (2000) define a basic need as "an energizing state that, if satisfied, conduces towards health and well being but, if not satisfied, contributes to pathology and ill-being" (p. 74). Self-Determination Theory holds that humans share three basic psychological needs – for *autonomy*, *competence* and *relatedness* – while acknowledging the nature of these needs varies somewhat across cultures as a function of different social norms and values (Ryan & Deci, 2000). The first basic need, *autonomy*, refers to the need for people to feel agency in personal experiences and actions and behave in a manner congruent with personally held interests and values (Ryan & Deci, 2017). Importantly, autonomy is not analogous to independence, as people could autonomously choose in different contexts to be dependent, independent, or interdependent in relation to others.

Ryan and Deci (2000) note the concept of a basic need for autonomy is controversial because it has "often been portrayed as being antagonistic to relatedness or community" (p. 74). As such, autonomy may be misunderstood as the type of "WEIRD" value, i.e., associated with Western, educated, industrialized, rich, and democratic societies, as described by Henrich and colleagues (2010). However, in Self Determination Theory, "autonomy refers not to being independent, detached or selfish but rather to the feeling of volition that can accompany any act, whether dependent or independent, collectivist or individualist" (Ryan & Deci, 2000, p. 74). This view differs from Smith (2006), who distinguished "individualistic" from "collectivist" cultures and claimed autonomy is "a highly valued personal strength" in the former while "social competence and connectedness skills" are favored in the latter (p. 25). At the same time, Smith's (2006) strength-based counseling model acknowledges clients develop autonomy alongside competence in problem solving (p. 44). Further, as will be shown, SDT considers the need to develop connection with others both basic and cross-cultural.

The second basic need in SDT, *competence*, refers to feelings of acting effectively or demonstrating mastery in various arenas of life (Ryan & Deci, 2017). Similar constructs with different names proliferate in psychology. For example, Bandura (1982) described the construct of self-efficacy in terms of an individual's tendency to evaluate his or her capabilities for a given task, which in turn influences decisions about what actions to take and how much effort to invest; he also linked self-efficacy to how people respond to challenge and adversity and ultimately to the quality of performance. Consistent with the traditional unitary view of motivation, Bandura described a direct relationship between self-efficacy and motivation (Ryan & Deci, 2017). According to Bandura, increased self-efficacy was, above all else, determined by achieving a personal "mastery experience," or demonstrated competence in a given domain (Pajares, 2003, p. 140). Competence is also key to Smith's (2006) strength-based counseling model, which he calls a "competence development" approach to psychological treatment in contrast to the more deficit-based "medical model" (p. 68).

The third basic need in SDT in particular speaks to the importance of social factors for human motivation. According to Ryan and Deci (2017), *relatedness* means feeling a sense of social belonging and engaging in meaningful relationships with others (p. 11). Echoing Bowlby's attachment theory, SDT proposes that the more related a person feels interpersonally connected, the more he or she may be available for taking risks and growing psychologically. According to Ryan and Deci (2008) the sense that one is cared for and valued by others – including friends and family, a partner, or a therapist – may influence motivation to pursue a goal. In the counseling context, voluminous research shows "therapy is an interpersonal process in which a main curative competent is the nature of the therapeutic relationship" (Lambert & Barley, 2001, p. 357). As such, creating a therapeutic alliance is an important first step in Smith's (2006) strength-based counseling approach. Furthermore, the importance of relatedness in SDT extends to social contexts, as the degree to which needs are satisfied is assumed to depend, at least in part, on the quality and regularity of immediate and extended relationships among family, friends and lovers (Ryan & Deci, 2000).

Taken together, the basic needs of autonomy, competence and relatedness inform motivation in SDT because they underlie all human behavior (Ryan & Deci 2017). As noted, however, different social contexts shape the nature of basic needs and influence the extent to which they are met. Ryan and Deci (2017) hold that some environments accommodate basic psychological needs and in turn facilitate more effective behaviors, while others impede psychological needs and thereby inhibiting integration. This is consistent with the core premise of Bronfenbrenner's 1979 ecological systems theory, which assumes the "environment has an impact on an individual's development," and, therefore, environmental enhancements lead to improved developmental outcomes (Ecological systems theory, 2018). Similarly, strength-based counseling approaches (Smith, 2006) consider client actions in social context in order to better understand how problems emerge and how they are best resolved. Strength-based counseling also recognizes that individual competencies are not fixed, but rather "develop from a dynamic, contextual process rooted deeply in one's culture" (Smith 2016, p. 25) and which serve clients differently depending on specific time, location and social milieu.

SDT assumes all social contexts may be understood as more or less supportive of each of the three basic needs for autonomy, competence and relatedness (Ryan & Deci, 2017, p. 12).

SDT Views on Motivation

As noted, Ryan and Deci (2017) observe a tendency among many cognitive theories to view motivation as a unitary and undifferentiated construct. In contrast, Self-Determination Theory (SDT) takes a more nuanced approach, inquiring as to the type and quantity of motivation in a given context (Ryan & Deci, 2000). When considering how "different types and sources of motivation impact the quality and dynamics of behavior" (Ryan & Deci, 2017, p. 14), SDT distinguishes *intrinsic* from *extrinsic* sources of motivation, and describes a process by which extrinsic sources of motivation may become relatively internalized. According to Ryan and Deci (2017), intrinsic motivation is rooted in a person's interest and engagement and drives behaviors undertaken for their own inherent rewards. By definition, all intrinsically motivated behaviors are by definition autonomous, as they are undertaken with agency and not due to external control (Ryan & Deci, 2017, p. 14). Acting from intrinsic motivation is epitomized in the psychological state of "flow" state described by Csikszentmihalyi (1990), when a person's sense of competence encounters an appropriate challenge, and senses of time and self dissolve into meaningful activity. Intrinsic motivation is essentially interest-driven in that sense.

In contrast to intrinsic motivation, extrinsic motivation emerges from some entity outside the individual, such as the prospect of a reward or threat of some punishment. Furthermore, externally motivated behaviors may be external and may "vary widely in the degree to which they are controlled versus autonomous" (Ryan & Deci, 2017, p. 14).

Indeed, Ryan and Deci (2017) describe an *autonomy-control continuum* along which extrinsically motivated behaviors may be plotted. This reflects an observation that some behaviors are partially internally endorsed while still, to some extent, driven by outside pressures (Ryan & Deci, 2017). For example, a person acting from a sense of guilt or obligation may not be overtly controlled by an external force, but he or she is nonetheless motivated by an outside pressure that has become internalized. On one end of the autonomy-control continuum are *externally regulated* behaviors, which are essentially controlled by outside forces under circumstances of high pressure or coercion.

Farther along the spectrum of control and autonomy fall extrinsic motivations that have become partially internalized – and hence more autonomous – through processes of *introjection*, *identification* and *integration* (p. 14). *Introjection* refers to a process by which "a person has taken in but not fully accepted external controls" over behavior; this is evident when "guilt, shame, contingent self-esteem, and fear of disapproval" are primary motivating forces, and a person's internal feelings of pressure or tension influence behaviors (pp. 14 –15). *Identification* and *integration*, on the other hand, refer to processes through which extrinsic motivations become synchronized with a person's own beliefs and sense of agency, and are hence more personally accepted and internalized. If extrinsic forms of motivation are brought entirely into congruence with an individual's own values, they become essentially intrinsic.

SDT's Relevance for Psychotherapy

Ryan and Deci (2008) argued that SDT principles may promote and facilitate motivation in human beings, including motivation in psychotherapy. According to them, SDT can be used in conjunction with various forms of psychotherapies (i.e., interpersonal, cognitive-behavioral, psychodynamic, etc.), or as an independent set of guiding principles to conceptualize and facilitate client motivation to change. This process occurs by fostering motivation in clients to recognize and satisfy their basic psychological needs in the context of the psychotherapy relationship (Legault & Inzlicht, 2013). Additional research by Ryan and Deci (2017) shows that supporting a person's autonomy and competence needs leads to enhanced intrinsic motivation, and relational support contributes to internalization of extrinsic motivation. Therefore, a therapeutic relationship that attends to basic psychological needs may help a client develop competence and motivation towards goals. Further, SDT holds that "people 'naturally' tend to internalize the values and goals of those with whom they are or wish to be connected or affiliated" (p. 17). This speaks to the importance of the therapist modeling need satisfaction for clients.

According to Ryan and Deci (2008), any psychotherapy grounded in SDT will be more concerned with a client's basic psychological need satisfaction and development of internal motivation than with behavioral change. The theory also assumes that pursuing intrinsic goals such as growing personally, deepening relationships with others, and becoming involved in community leads to better psychological health than pursuing extrinsic goals such as growing in wealth or social status. Ideally, a therapy relationship may be a so-called facilitative environment in the life of the client, promoting reflection on basic needs as they emerge in a client's lived experience, and empowering clients to pursue basic need fulfillment (Ryan & Deci, 2017). This may occur both through the process of therapy and in the content of sessions, for example when a clinician prompts a client to consider how well his or her basic psychological needs are being met. No matter their style or specific theoretical orientation, all SDT-informed therapists aim to increase client intrinsic motivation by creating a relationship supportive of autonomy, competence and relatedness needs.

SDT-informed therapy is rooted in understanding and raising awareness of basic needs for autonomy, competence and relatedness, which clients may have denied or minimized prior to engaging in treatment. To some extent, the need for relatedness may itself be met in the context of an effective therapeutic relationship. Indeed, Ryan and Deci (2008) emphasized that SDT-informed therapists conveying interpersonal warmth remain truly invested in the process of therapy. As a result, patients ideally develop attachment to the therapist, which research shows is associated with improved therapy outcomes (Ryan & Deci, 2008). Somewhat paradoxically, attachment in therapy also helps meet a client's psychological need for autonomy, which according to SDT can be fostered through interpersonal factors. As Ryan and Deci (2017) write, "the more therapists support their clients' autonomy and relatedness need satisfaction, the more the clients' engagement in therapy is likely to be autonomous, the more the therapeutic process is likely to proceed effectively, and the more the internalization of positive changes is likely to occur and maintain" (p. 438). A strong therapeutic alliance may therefore help clients both understand and meet their basic psychological needs as described in SDT.

Promoting client autonomy in SDT-informed therapy means clinicians attempt to understand clients' worldviews. When a client faces internal conflict, rather than advocate for a particular course of action, an SDT-informed clinician helps the person explore the conflict in terms of personal values and goals (Ryan & Deci, 2008). Valuing a client's internal frame of reference is being "truly noninvested in a specified outcome… [and trusting] in the client's capacity to take interest in and integrate information" (Ryan & Deci, 2008, p. 188). It also implies providing a rationale for clinical interventions, acknowledging feelings of resistance as they arise, promoting choice, avoiding control and pressure, and setting appropriate therapeutic boundaries. SDT holds that clinicians who support autonomy help clients develop self-regulation, or the ability to themselves inhibit behaviors they find unhelpful or out of synch with their internalized values. As a part of this process, SDT-informed clinicians help clients identify and confront *introjects*

– the internalized pressures and rewards inconsistent with personal values that rob clients of autonomous choice.

Finally, SDT-informed clinicians may foster clients' needs for competence by promoting mindful awareness of emotions, feelings, experiences, and introjects (Ryan & Deci, 2008, p. 189 - 190). Competence support involves helping the client identify barriers and focusing attention on optimal challenges that are neither too easy nor too difficult for the individual. Assuming that "structure can be implemented in either controlling or autonomy-supportive ways" (p. 189), SDT-informed clinicians strive to promote autonomy as they work to nurture a client's' sense of competence. Client competence is enhanced when clinicians provide appropriate feedback and structure in therapy (Ryan & Deci, 2008). As clients develop competence over the course of treatment, they ideally are better equipped to internally evaluate need satisfaction, as clinicians continue to offer helpful feedback and encourage reflection on outcomes or consequences of behaviors (see also Ryan & Deci, 2017 p. 448-449). Taken together, SDT's assumptions about effective psychotherapy amount to general principles, deduced from the theory's claims about basic psychological needs and the power of internalized motivation. Motivational interviewing, a specific program of psychotherapy, provides more developed clinical interventions consistent with SDT.

Motivational Interviewing

Drawing on social psychology principles of self-efficacy, cognitive dissonance, and self-justification theory, Miller (1983) developed Motivational Interviewing (MI) as a technique to increase motivation in substance abuse treatment. MI has since evolved in application to a wide range of clinical settings and issues (Ryan & Deci, 2008). Using person-centered techniques (cf. Rogers, 1951) MI explores client ambivalence about change and seeks to develop internal motivation (Miller & Rollnick, 2013). A core principle of MI is that attempting to persuade a client to change – introducing, in SDT terms, an extrinsic source of motivation – may lead the client to adopt an oppositional stance (i.e., taking the postion that change is not necessary or desirable). This phenomenon, which Brehm (1966) termed *reactance,* in turn contributes to therapeutic impasse. Instead, the role of the therapist in MI is to nurture clients' intrinsic motivations for change (Markland et al., 2005). Clinicians practicing MI assume ambivalence is a natural feature of the change process, and they attend to both *change talk* – that is, a client's own arguments in favor of changing behavior – and *sustain talk*, or statements a client makes in favor of their status quo (Miller & Rollnick, 2013). Rather than attempt to persuade or argue with a client to change, the clinician takes a person-centered approach inclusive of ambivalence in MI.

MI employs four fundamental techniques to enhance client motivation for change: *expression of empathy*, *development of discrepancy*, *rolling with resistance*, and *support for self-efficacy* (Markland et al., 2005; Resnicow & McMaster, 2012). According to Miller and Rollnick (2013), therapist *empathy* is the primary principle of MI. Research shows therapist empathy builds rapport and predicts successful therapeutic outcomes (see, for example, Elliott et al., 2018). The second principle, *development of discrepancy*, occurs as therapists help clients explore the advantages and disadvantages of changing a behavior. As cognitive dissonance theory (cf. Aronson, 2012) demonstrates, raising awareness of the discrepancy between a client's core values on one hand and his or her current behaviors on the other may motivate positive behavioral change. The third MI principle holds that directly confronting perceived client resistance may only increase the resistance and reluctance to change. By *rolling with resistance*, a therapist may instead join the client in acknowledging the normal urge to maintain equilibrium. Simultaneously, a therapist may introduce other perspectives on presenting problems in non-confrontational ways. The final principle of MI, *self-efficacy*, posits that lasting change is ultimately predicated on a client's internal acceptance of the need for change and the belief that he or she has the resources or capabilities to enact change. Raising client awareness in treatment of the resources available for making and maintaining change increases client self-efficacy (Miller & Rollnick, 2013).

Integrating Self-Determination Theory and Motivational Interviewing

Although some have argued that MI is atheoretical, or derived in a "bottom-up" fashion, SDT may in fact offer an adequate theoretical underpinning for MI (Markland et al., 2005; Resnicow & McMaster, 2012; Ryan & Deci, 2008, 2017). As Ryan and Deci (2017) argue, "SDT can be viewed as a theory that gives a meaningful account of why MI works" (p. 436). Rooted in the humanistic psychotherapy tradition, MI shares SDT's core assumption of organismic integration, or the belief that "people are inherently inclined to engage in life" (Ryan & Deci, 2017 p. 436). Moreover, unlike therapies that seek to change behavior through external rewards, punishments, controls, or influences, MI seeks to identify and nurture change impulses already within the individual. In this way, the practice of MI aligns closely with SDT's theoretical emphasis on the value of intrinsic motivation over extrinsic motivation. Finally, Markland et al., (2005) argue MI provides support for the three basic needs – autonomy, competence, and relatedness – associated in SDT with enhanced internal motivation and behavior change.

As noted, clinicians practicing MI utilize client-centered, Rogerian principles of genuineness, empathy, and unconditional positive regard. These core stances are "highly congruent with the concept of autonomy support" in SDT (Ryan & Deci, 2017, p. 435). For example, a clinician using MI may support a client's autonomy by seeking to understand his or her worldview and perspectives. Entering into a client's internal frame of reference implies the clinician is "truly noninvested in a specified outcome" and trusts "the client's capacity to take interest in and integrate information" (Ryan & Deci, 2008, p. 188). Rather than attempting to exert control or pressure, MI clinicians support autonomy needs by being transparent, providing rationales for clinician interventions, and giving clients opportunities to make choices in treatment (Ryan & Deci, 2017). This is consistent with the SDT concept of therapy as a facilitative environment promoting "authentic reflection, integration, empowerment, competence, and choice" (p. 442).

An autonomy-supportive, facilitative environment in therapy supports a client's awareness of emotions, experiences, and introjects – the "intrapersonal pressures and rewards" that rob people of "real choice about how they live their lives" (Ryan & Deci, 2008, p. 189 - 190). Consistent with SDT, MI helps clients identify introjects as such and choose to integrate those that resonate authentically while discarding those deemed incongruent. This process occurs in therapy as the client increasingly recognizes how emotions may inform rather than control behavior, identifies gaps between values and behaviors, and integrates core values with behaviors (Ryan & Deci, 2008). In both SDT and MI, the ultimate clinical goal is client autonomy rather than particular behavioral outcomes (Ryan & Deci, 2017). Nevertheless, as clients make values-informed choices about reducing unhelpful or unwanted behaviors, develop desired courses of action, and prepare for future challenges, they nurture the basic SDT need for competence.

As Ryan and Deci (2008) note, clinicians may promote client competence and autonomy by providing structure in therapy - for example, by setting clear boundaries and providing feedback or information when needed. In MI, competence support may include clinicians focusing on optimal challenges (neither too easy nor too difficult); promoting internal evaluation; and encouraging reflection on values, behaviors, outcomes and consequences (Ryan & Deci, 2017). As clients develop regulatory processes in MI to control behaviors through internalization and integration of values, they increasingly satisfy the SDT need for competence. Competence, therefore, grows from both the content and the process of MI: content in the clinician's attention to need satisfaction in the everyday life of the client, and process in the clinician's support for client's "engagement and volition" in treatment itself (Ryan & Deci, 2017, p. 442).

MI's roots in client-centered practice supports a client's basic need for relatedness in the treatment process. Relatedness in therapy may be conveyed through a clinician's warm or invitational interpersonal style, as well as his or her commitment to therapy work (Ryan & Deci, 2008). It may also emerge as a clinician holds the client in unconditional positive regard, acknowledges and addresses conflict as it emerges, and is authentic and transparent during treatment (Ryan & Deci, 2017). Research in SDT shows "people 'naturally' tend to internalize the values and goals of those with whom they are or wish to be connected or affiliated;" however, autonomy and competence supports must be in place for the internalization to occur (Ryan & Deci, 2017, p. 17). As a result, the more a client feels attached to a clinician, the more likely he or she is to make progress in therapy (Ryan & Deci, 2008). From this foundation, clinicians practicing MI may help clients develop awareness of their relatedness needs and values and to evaluate their own interpersonal behaviors. And clearly, relatedness needs and relationship problems often drive the need for therapy in the first place.

CONCLUSION

Across different psychotherapeutic theories, client motivation is recognized as a significant factor in treatment outcomes (Cooper 2008; Orlinksy, Ronnestad, & Willutzki, 2004). Specifically, client motivation is effective when it is grounded internally and contributes to self-regulation (Legault & Inzlicht, 2013; Ryan & Deci, 2008). In Self Determination Theory, internal motivation is predicated upon clients adequately meeting basic psychological needs for autonomy, competence, and relatedness (Ryan & Deci, 2008). MI provides client-centered stances such as empathy and positive regard, and specific interventions like reflective listening and rolling with resistance, that help meet these basic needs in the context of the therapeutic relationship (Markland et al., 2005). Moreover, by helping clients identify their own needs and values, and determining courses of action that bring in values and behaviors together, MI promotes self-regulation skills development in clients. SDT was developed as a theory for understanding human motivation in general (Miller & Rollnick, 2002; Ryan & Deci, 2000). However, it is useful in explaining how and why MI works in psychotherapy, and it provides rationale for implementing and grounds for improving specific MI techniques (Markland et al., 2005; Resnicow & McMaster, 2005). Together, SDT and MI provide a model for understanding and enhancing client motivation with diverse clients in a variety of treatment contexts and without compromising other models of psychotherapy (Markland et al., 2005; Resnicow & McMaster, 2005; Ryan & Deci, 2008).

REFERENCES

Aronson, E. (2012). *The social animal.* (11th ed.) New York: Worth.

Aronson, E., Wilson, T., & Akert, R. (2013). *Social psychology* (8th ed.). Boston: Pearson.

Bandura, A. (1982). Self-efficacy mechanism in human agency. *American Psychologist* 37(2), 122–147.

Brehm, J. (1966). *A theory of psychological reactance.* New York: Academic Press.

Cameron, A. Y., Palm Reed, K., & Gaudiano, B. A. (2014). Addressing treatment motivation in borderline personality disorder: Rationale for incorporating values based exercises into dialectical behavior therapy. *Journal of Contemporary Psychotherapy: On the Cutting Edge of Modern Developments in Psychotherapy* 44(2), 109–116.

Center for Substance Abuse Treatment (2012). *Enhancing motivation for change in substance abuse treatment*. Rockville, MD: U.S. Department of Health and Human Services, Substance Abuse and Mental Health Services Administration.

Cooper, M. (2008). *Essential research findings in counselling and psychotherapy: The facts are friendly*. London: Sage.

Csikszentmihalyi, M. (1990). *Flow: The psychology of optimal experience*. New York: Harper & Row.

Deci, E. L., & Ryan, R. M. (1985). *Intrinsic motivation and self-determination in human behavior*. New York, NY: Plenum Press.

Ecological systems theory (2018) *Salem Press Encyclopedia of Science*.

Elliott, R., Bohart, A. C., Watson, J. C., & Murphy, D. (2018). Therapist empathy and client outcome: An updated meta-analysis. *Psychotherapy* 55(4), 399-410.

Henrich, J., Heine, S., & Norenzayan, A. (2010). The weirdest people in the world? *Behavioral and Brain Sciences* 33(2-3), 61-83.

Huppert, J. D, Barlow, D. H., Gorman, J. M., M., Shear, K., & Woods, S. W. (2006). The interaction of motivation and therapist adherence predicts outcome in Cognitive Behavioral Therapy for Panic Disorder: Preliminary findings. *Cognitive and Behavioral Practice* 13(3), 198-204.

Lambert, M. J. and Barley, D. E. (2001). Research summary on the therapeutic relationship and psychotherapy outcome. *Psychotherapy* 38(4), 357-361.

Legault, L., & Inzlicht, M. (2013). Self-determination, self-regulation, and the brain: Autonomy improves performance by enhancing neuroaffective responsiveness to self-regulation failure. *Journal of Personality and Social Psychology* 105(1), 123-138.

Markland, D., Ryan, R. M., Tobin, V. J., & Rollnick, S. (2005). Motivational interviewing and self-determination theory. *Journal of Social and Clinical Psychology* 24, 811-831.

Miller, W. R. (1983). Motivational interviewing with problem drinkers. *Behavioral Psychotherapy* 11, 147–172.

Miller, W. R., & Rollnick, S. (2013). *Motivational interviewing*. New York, NY: Guilford Press.

Miller, W., & Rollnick, S. (2012). Meeting in the middle: Motivational interviewing in self-determination theory. *International Journal of Behavioral Nutrition and Physical Activity* 9(25), 9-25.

Motivation (2019). In Merriam Webster online. Retrieved from https://www.merriam webster.com/dictionary/motivation.

Oettingen, G., & Gollwitzer, P. (2015). Self-regulation: Principles and tools. In Oettingen & Gollwitzer (Eds.), *Self-regulation in adolescence* (pp. 3-29). Cambridge: Cambridge University Press.

Orlinsky, D. E., Rønnestad, M. H., & Willutzki, U. (2004). Fifty years of psychotherapy process-outcome research: Continuity and change. In M. J. Lambert (Ed.), *Bergin & Garfield's handbook of psychotherapy and behavior change* (5th ed.) (pp. 307-389). Chicago, IL: John Wiley and Sons.

Pajares, F. (2003). Self-efficacy beliefs, motivation, and achievement in writing: A review of the literature. *Reading & Writing Quarterly* 19: 139 – 158.

Prochaska, J. O., & Norcross, J. C. (2010). *Systems of psychotherapy: A transtheoretical analysis*. Belmont, CA: Brooks-Cole.

Resnicow, K., & McMaster, F. (2012). Motivational interviewing: moving from why to how with autonomy support. *International Journal of Behavioral Nutrition and Physical Activity* 9(19), 1-9.

Rogers, C. (1951). *Client-centered therapy: Its current practice, implications and theory*.London: Constable.

Ryan, R. M., & Deci, E. L. (2000). Self-determination theory and the facilitation of intrinsic motivation, social development, and well-being. *American Psychologist* 55(1), 68-78.

Ryan, R. M., & Deci, E. L. (2008). A self-determination theory approach to psychotherapy: The motivational basis for effective change. *Canadian Psychology* 49(3), 186-193.

Ryan, R. M., & Deci, E. L. (2017). *Self-determination theory: Basic psychological needs in motivation, development and wellness*. New York: The Guilford Press.

Stobbe, J., Wierdsma, A. I., Kok, R. M., Kroon, H., Depla, M., Roosenschoon, B.-J., & Mulder, C. L. (2013). Lack of motivation for treatment associated with greater care needs and psychosocial problems. *Aging and Mental Health* 17(8), 1052–1058.

Sheldon, K. M. & Williams, G. (2013) *Self-Determination Theory in the clinic: Motivating physical and mental health*. New Haven, CT; Yale University Press.

Smith, E. J. (2006). The strength-based counseling model. *The Counseling Psychologist* 34 (1), 13 – 79.

SECTION II.
SOCIAL INFLUENCE I: CONFORMITY, OBEDIENCE, AND RESISTANCE

In: Social Psychology and Counseling
Editors: D. A. Kleiber and E. Delgado-Romero
ISBN: 978-1-53616-548-7

Chapter 2

CONFORMITY AND ADOLESCENT RISK-TAKING

Catherine Stamateris Flaherty and Amy Perkins

In most Western societies' conformity is considered somewhat of a personal failing. Particularly in the United States, society tends to prize the value of individualism and independent thought. As such, conformity has acquired a connotation of limitation and unnecessary compliance. Non-conformity is idealized by Western values in all forms of entertainment as well. Non-conformists are hailed as heroes and heroines who go against the grain of society to inspire change or good in some way. But the construct of conformity is much more complex, and it clearly has some adaptive, positive value in all cultures. Aronson (2012) defined conformity as "a change in a person's behavior or opinions as a result of real or imagined pressure from a person or group of people" (p. 19), but that also describes socialization and accommodation to others with whom we live. Social conformity and nonconformity impact individuals' relationships to others in nearly every stage of life's development.

One might imagine that an individual may be more susceptible to conform to a group during certain periods of life, however, when the perceived benefits outweigh the perceived risks of conforming. Given the unique period of development that is adolescence, teens between the ages of 12 and 17 are especially susceptible to conforming to the norms, ideas, and behaviors of their peers. Partly as a result of an improved capacity for perspective taking, adolescents look to peers to a greater extent than ever before (cf. Harter, 2012). A peer group has the potential to influence the thoughts, emotions, and behaviors of an individual adolescent in both positive and negative ways. In particular, researchers have long documented the part that peers of adolescents play in impacting high-risk or risk-taking behavior such as substance use and other illegal activities. The purpose of this chapter is to review the literature on conformity and its impacts on adolescent development and peer group affiliation among adolescents while drawing implications for clinical practice.

Conformity

The motivation to conform varies by individual and groups. Decades ago Deutsch and colleages (1955) distinguished between *informational* and *normative* conformity motives. Researchers describe informational conformity as the desire to form an accurate interpretation of reality and behave correctly, "being right," as Aronson (2012) and others have referred to it. In contrast, normative conformity is said to be motivated by the goal of obtaining social approval from others, i.e., "being liked." In essence, individuals fall prey to conformity based on one's desire to belong or to be appropriately accurate.

With respect to informational conformity one is likely to be influenced by the expertise of the individual or individuals with whom one would conform, while with normative conformity, the popularity and group status of the influencers is likely to prevail (cf. Aronson, 2012). Other factors may also apply. Castelli and colleagues (2001) suggested that there is a certain type of person to whom a collective group looks for valid information in a time of uncertainty. Interestingly, the researchers in the study were able to show that participants were more likely to conform to the "objective" estimates of an individual who used stereotype-consistent traits to describe out-group members. In one sense this may reveal that in times of uncertainty individuals are inclined to draw upon stereotypes or biases to feel safety in their attempt to conform. It has the effect of reducing some uncertainty for those who do, however inaccurate they may ultimately be.

Other researchers found that the goal of accuracy – to be right - could counteract the normative pressures individuals face when making a decision that will need to be explained to a group of people whose views and opinions are unknown (Quinn & Schlenker, 2002). In the normative situation, on the other hand, the researchers hypothesized that individuals tend to conform to the audience's position in an attempt to gain the approval of the group of people rather than risk their disapproval (Pennington & Schlenker, 1999).

Conformity can also lead to *groupthink*. Janis (1973) defined groupthink as "the mode of thinking that persons engage in when concurrence seeking becomes so dominant in a cohesive in-group that it tends to override realistic appraisal of alternative courses of action." Groups that fall victim to groupthink often see themselves as invulnerable. That is, groups of individuals who adopt a groupthink mentality are often blinded by a collective optimism. The outcome of groupthink can be seen in numerous historic events, the Holocaust, the Watergate cover-up, among others (Aronson, 2012). These historical incidences of conformity leading to groupthink indicate the complexity as well as the dangers of social conformity.

When the tendency to conform to the social group is motivationally related to the desire to be liked and accepted or show loyalty, individuals may engage in deliberate and conscious, or sometimes unconscious, attempts to gain social approval and standing with group members. Gaining the approval of others or feeling likeable contributes to a higher level of self-esteem (Bond & Smith, 1996). Conforming in such situations aids in feeling good about oneself where social approval is concerned, which turns out to be an especially compelling aspect of adolescence.

ADOLESCENCE

Adolescence is a unique era in human development. It's a time when one is: (a) learning to individuate and separate from parents while still relatively protected from the need to be self-sufficient, (b) seeking a sense of self – an identity - among peers, and (c) honing and developing values that may or may not be consistent with the values instilled by one's parents. Among the risks that follow is a susceptibility to the influence of peers and groups outside of the family (Arnett, 2001; Harter, 2012) which also makes adolescent vulnerable to patterns of behavior that are compromising to health, both physical and mental.

Adolescent Peer Groups

Among the many transformations in family relationships expected to occur as a child enters adolescence, one of the most worrisome for adults is the shift in reference group orientation from parents to the peer group (Gecas & Seff, 1990). Adolescence is the first time that friends and relationships outside of their family of origin deeply impact their self-concept, self-esteem, and behavior. One of the developmental tasks of adolescence is integrating with a reference group of peers. Peer influence rises dramatically during middle school, although adolescents generally still maintain strong emotional ties to parents (Harter, 2012; Steinberg, 1990).

Adolescents often characterize their peers through the use of social labels that apply to groups of peers affiliated by common interests (Kinney, 1993). The labels used to describe peer groups often reflect the groups' characteristics in some form. Researchers have found that peer crowd categories are often remarkably consistent across gender, regions of the country, and racial and ethnic groups (Brown, 1989; Phillips, Hughes, & Wilkes, 1998). Contrary to popular belief, children and adolescents do not fall haphazardly into one crowd or another, but rather self-select into a certain crowd or crowds based on the reputation they establish for themselves (Brown, 1990). In essence, peer group affiliation reinforces the individual's own self-concept but also has the effect of increasing conformity to the whims and wishes of members of that reference group.

Crowd Affiliation and Risk-Taking Behavior

Throughout the literature there is ample evidence that peers are influential in shaping adolescent behavior (Barnes, 1990; Jessor & Jessor, 1977). Numerous studies indicate that peer crowd affiliation has been linked with adolescents' reports of cigarette smoking and alcohol use (Brown, 1989; Brown, Mounts, Lamborn, & Steinberg, 1993; Urberg, 1992). Pegg, O'Donnell, Lala, and Barber (2018) demonstrated that adolescent alcohol use and friends' alcohol use are often parallel, meaning that groups of friends are often participating in the same high-risk behaviors either together or separately. These data offer insight into the role of peer support in adolescent decision-making. In other words, if adolescents believe that their friends will support their choices, they are more likely to engage in a given risk-taking behavior (Hawkins, Catalano, & Miller, 1992; Johnston, O'Malley, Bachman, & Schulenberg, 2003). To that end, La Greca, Prinstein, and Fetter (2001) found that in a cohort of 250 adolescents from a High School in Miami-Dade County, Florida, peer group affiliation greatly influenced health-risk behaviors such as engaging in casual sex, drinking alcohol, and smoking cigarettes and using other drugs. In the study the adolescents were asked to complete several questionnaires related to their health behavior and the health behavior of their primary friends. The students were designated by certain social groups: Burnouts, Nonconformists, Brains, Jocks, and Popular Kids. Overall, the researchers found that the adolescents in the "Burnouts" and "Nonconformist" groups had the highest health-risk behavior among all students included in the study. Moreover, the Burnouts and Nonconformists reported that high proportions of their friends engaged in similar health-risk behaviors, and both groups had close friends who affiliated with the same peer crowd. In these groups alone, adolescents likely have substantial support from their friends for their health-risk behaviors. In contrast, students in the "Brains" peer group, meaning those students who prioritized studying and doing well in their educational pursuits, reported the lowest level of casual sexual activity and substance use. Students in that category also reported that their friends similarly do not engage in health-risk behavior. Finally, students in the "Jocks" category reported low levels of substance use but higher levels of risk-taking behaviors (such as driving cars above the speed limit) and casual sexual engagement. Researchers found that the adolescents in the "Popular Kids" peer group engaged in similar health-risk behaviors to the "Jocks." All together, the data suggest that conformity among adolescents, particularly as it relates to health-risk behavior, is certainly influenced by the norms of particular reference groups.

Mediators of Adolescent Conformity

There are variables that serve to support adolescents through their development and that act as mediators to peer group influence. These include self-esteem, parenting orientation, mentoring, and prosocial activities.

Self-Esteem

Individuals are often motivated to conform to the beliefs and behaviors of others in order to enhance, protect, or repair their self-esteem (Harter, 2012). One study revealed that people who had a core sense of self-acceptance and positive self-regard were less likely to conform to others than those who focused primarily on an external source of self-esteem, such as achievement or physical attractiveness (Arndt et al., 2002). These findings indicate that one of the best ways to combat overly conforming behavior may be to affirm individuals' self-concepts. Other researchers have argued that individuals *maintain* positive self-assessment by identifying with, and in some ways conforming to, valued groups (Brew & Roccas, 2001). Nevertheless, Blanton and Christie (2003) indicate that individuals who deviate from the behaviors and attitudes of others may actually enhance their individual self-concept by providing the self a sense of uniqueness and individuality.

Parenting

Parents strongly influence teens throughout childhood and into adolescent years. Parents often shape the values and beliefs that children hold (Fox & Calkins, 2003), setting limits and imposing consequences when limits are not respected (Kerr & Stattin, 2000). As children become adolescents, parents play a redefined and somewhat more circumscribed role in their child's life. During the adolescent years, teens often develop an increased understanding of their "multiple selves," that is, the difference in the self across different settings at home, school, and with friends (Harter, 2012). When relationships with parents are strong, adolescents are more open to parental influence with respect to adolescents' friendships and other relationships and activities outside of the home (Harris et al., 2015). Parents who respect adolescent autonomy tend to have a more impactful and sustainable relationship with their adolescent children than those parents who still relegate the adolescents to their control. Parental over-control may interfere with completion of developmental tasks and the acquisition of problem-solving skills and strategies for negotiation of stressful experiences (Fox & Calkins, 2003; Lippold, Glatz, Fosco, & Feinberg, 2018). Parental over-control also detracts from overall adolescent well-being (Caldwell & Witt, 2011; Kerr & Stattin, 2000) and may make resistance to deviant peer activities less rather than more likely.

Parents may of course serve as a strong deterrent to such as risk-taking behaviors like substance use and abuse (Andrews, Hops, Ary, Tildesley, & Harris, 1993). The presence and quality of parental relationships strongly predict adolescent substance use patterns. Researchers have found that whereas conflict-ridden relationships with parents appear to heighten the risk for adolescent alcohol and drug use, close relationships with parents seem to protect adolescents from substance use (Bell, Forthun, & Sun, 2000). Researchers have found that parental closeness discouraged drug use directly and indirectly impacted their child's choice of non-drug-using friends (Kandel & Andrews, 1987). Kandel and colleagues (Kandel, Bogenschneider, Wu, Raffaelli, & Tsay, 1998) provided additional support for this indirect effect, suggesting it is through the quality of parental relationships, rather than direct parental monitoring, that parents influence peer relationships. Taken together, this body of research implies that improvements in parent-adolescent relationships may lead to positive peer-group affiliation for the teen and resistance to conformity pressures in risk-taking situations.

Mentoring

Researchers have found that mentor relationships can positively influence adolescents in their development as they begin to become more independent of parents and build skills for better relationships with agemates (Rhodes, Haight, & Briggs, 1998) and those of different ages. To that end, mentors' positive influence may help adolescents' maximize the benefit of peer friendships and navigate potential problems that may arise with adolescent peers. Close mentor relationships give the adolescent a place to not only receive guidance from an authority figure who is not a parent – a teacher or a coach for example - but also offers a safe space to talk about opportunities and challenges, such as conformity pressures, in peer relationships (Rhodes, Haight, & Briggs, 1998). The emotional support and positive feedback of a mentor may serve to enhance adolescents' sense of self-worth, which has been associated with resistance to risk-taking peer influence and reduced levels of both drug and alcohol use (Sharp et al., 2011).

Prosocial Activities

Another protective factor for adolescents is affiliation with peers in more pro-social ways. While conformity among adolescents is commonly based on the nature of adolescent relationships and adolescent development, conforming to others' more positive, pro-social behavior may offer associations that pre-empt more negative activities. Bogenschneider and colleagues (1998) found that stronger connections with pro-social peers lead to a reduction in substance use by a cohort of adolescents who had previously used substances. These data suggest that while conformity may be inevitable in a cohort of adolescents, conformity with pro-social peers may enhance wellness and positive behavior in adolescents.

Structured activities that rely on cooperation and perspective taking and benefit others may be particularly effective in diverting conformity in more positive directions.

Positive leisure and recreation activity serve as another protective factor against risk-taking behavior among cohorts of adolescents. Research on recreation and free time activity indicates that when adolescents are engaged in structured leisure activities, positive health behaviors are generally enhanced (Caldwell & Witt, 2011; Donovan, Jessor, & Costa, 1991). This suggests that when pro-social and healthy behaviors are the norm, adolescents conform in more positive ways (Donovan et al, 1991).

Implications for Individual Psychotherapy: The Case of James

> A sixteen-year-old male client named James was referred for counseling from the Department of Juvenile Justice. He became involved with the juvenile justice system after being charged with truancy. While he was originally charged in 2011, James stayed on probation for many years because he struggled to discontinue his recreational marijuana use. A condition of James' probation was that he pass a monthly drug screen, and over the past two years he continuously failed all of his drug screens. Therapy is now an additional condition of James' probation, as he is seen through the eyes of the court as having a substance abuse problem.

But what are the potentially more manageable factors contributing to his tendency toward substance abuse? To what extent is he simply conforming to his esteemed reference group? The first issue that James faced when dealing with conformity was his lack of outside protective factors. Mouttapa, Huang, Shakib, Sussman, & Unger (2003) examined whether *conformity* to three different types of authority (parents, teachers, and religion) was protective against susceptibility towards several risk-taking behaviors, such as alcohol consumption, marijuana use, physical fighting, and risky sexual behaviors, etc. They found that authority-related conformity, specifically toward parents, teachers, and religion, was a protective factor against susceptibility toward various health risk behaviors among their adolescent sample. Unfortunately for James, he did not have a strong authority figure in his life. Per his own report, James' mother was the most influential person in his life, but his parents were divorced, his mother moved out of town, and he did not get to see her regularly. Additionally, James changed schools and developed few close relationships with his new teachers. And because James' family was not religious, there was no religious leader present in his life. Therefore, he was more susceptible to peer conformity than adolescents who have strong authority figures in their lives. James and his friends often discussed their use of marijuana, and, because they all accepted its use, they did not discuss differing opinions. James did not seek outside information regarding the harm the prolonged use of marijuana can cause, nor did he discuss the negative effects that his current marijuana use had on his life with his peer group

Another factor that made James more susceptible to conformity was the fact that he and his friends were very similar. James identified very strongly as a “skater.” He enjoyed skateboarding and going to the skate park with his friends. He hung out with the same group for years and accepted the norms and characteristics of this group. Mok and Morris (2010) found that individuals who are less integrated into cultural groups are able to defy salient cultural norms that they do not agree with compared to those who are more integrated into that cultural group. The authors suggested that individuals who are less culturally integrated into a specific cultural group are better able to facilitate constructive conflict and resist the groupthink that often results from group homogeneity. Again, this was not the case with James. He was very similar to others in his peer group and, it seemed, accepted their collective identity as his own. The members of his peer group believed that they were being “nonconformists.” Regarding the legality of marijuana use and the reasons that it is still an illegal substance in this country, James believed that he and his friends were fighting against the system by continuing to use marijuana. However, when viewing his marijuana use in light of the fact that all of his friends were using, it was arguably more of a matter of conformity than an act of defiance against the government. While James continued to stay on probation due to his marijuana use, he did not attempt to justify his defiance to the judge or to his probation officer on political grounds. It seemed that his smoking was simply a part of his identifying with and conforming to his peer group. They saw themselves as the “skater group” and smoking marijuana as part of the culture of that group.

Previous research suggests that James would not change his behavior based on the ruling of the judge or the punishment from his probation officer, as he was more influenced by his peer group than authority figures. Further, James was not likely to change a behavior or opinion that accorded with others in his peer group, as ‘being liked’ continued to be his motivation.

IMPLICATIONS FOR PRACTICE AND RESEARCH

Clearly, James’ issue with marijuana should not be viewed simply, or perhaps at all, as a substance abuse issue. James could likely have quit smoking if he had chosen. Continuing to drug test James might have changed his behavior but likely for the worse. Obviously, the punishment of continued probation was not enough to curb the behavior. James was struggling with the challenge of peer influence and group identification. He was conforming to the cultural norms of his peer group and had few outside sources of support to act as protective factors against this conformity. Therapy might have better focused on James’s sources of support outside of his peer group, exposing him to differing positions without the threat of being ostracized from his group. This would have meant bringing the information to session or challenging James to explore dissenting information on his own time. Because James' is not struggling with substance abuse but with an issue of conformity, a different approach may be needed. A more thoughtful approach may have allowed James to be more introspective and gain an understanding of the dynamics involved in directing his maladaptive behavior.

CONCLUSION

The data on the mediators between adolescents and risk-taking behaviors among peer groups call into question whether or not conformity among adolescents is to a great extent inevitable. In some ways, looking to peers for information on how to behave and think is in many circumstances pro-social. Adolescents are navigating new and varied social and cultural situations and often need their peers to learn the best ways to get through such experiences, i.e., to be "right." Where conformity in adolescence becomes problematic is when adolescents engage in and influence others to engage in risky behaviors such as drinking alcohol, smoking cigarettes and using other drugs, engaging in casual and unprotected sexual relationships, and driving too fast. But it would seem that the tendency to conform – whether to be liked or to be right – can be promoted with more constructive and prosocial behavior as well.

REFERENCES

Andrews, J. A., Hops, H., Ary, D., Tildesley, E., & Harris, J. (1993). Parental influence on early adolescent substance use specific and nonspecific effects. *The Journal of Early Adolescence*, *13*(3), 285-310.

Arndt, J., Greenberg, J., Schimel, J., Pyszczynski, T., & Solomon, S. (2002). To belong or not to belong, that is the question: terror management and identification with gender and ethnicity. *Journal of Personality and Social Psychology*, *83*, 26.

Aronson, E. (2012). *The social animal*. New York City: Worth.

Barnes, G. M. (1990). Impact of the family on adolescent drinking patterns. *Alcohol and the Family: Research and Clinical Perspectives*, 137-161.

Bell, N. J., Forthun, L. F., & Sun, S. W. (2000). Attachment, adolescent competencies, and substance use: Developmental considerations in the study of risk behaviors. *Substance use & misuse*, *35*, 1177-1206.

Blanton, H., & Christie, C. (2003). Deviance regulation: A theory of action and identity. *Review of General Psychology*, *7*, 115.

Bogenschneider, K., Wu, M. Y., Raffaelli, M., & Tsay, J. C. (1998). Parent influences on adolescent peer orientation and substance use: The interface of parenting practices and values. *Child Development*, *69*, 1672-1688.

Bond, R., & Smith, P. B. (1996). Culture and conformity: A meta-analysis of studies using Asch's (1952b, 1956) line judgment task. *Psychological Bulletin*, *119*, 111.

Brody, G. H., & Forehand, R. (1993). Prospective associations among family form, family processes, and adolescents' alcohol and drug use. *Behaviour Research and Therapy*, *31*, 587-593.

Brown, B. B., Mounts, N., Lamborn, S. D., & Steinberg, L. (1993). Parenting practices and peer group affiliation in adolescence. *Child Development*, *64*, 467-482.

Caldwell, L. L., & Witt, P. A. (2011). Leisure, recreation, and play from a developmental context. *New directions for youth development*, *2011*(130), 13-27.

Castelli, L., Pavan, G., Ferrari, E., & Kashima, Y. (2009). The stereotyper and the chameleon: The effects of stereotype use on perceivers' mimicry. *Journal of Experimental Social Psychology*, *45*, 835-839.

Cialdini, R. B., & Goldstein, N. J. (2004). Social influence: Compliance and conformity. *Annual Review of Psychology*, *55*, 591-621.

Deutsch, M., & Gerard, H. B. (1955). A study of normative and informational social influences upon individual judgment. *The Journal of Abnormal and Social Psychology*, *51*, 629-.

Donovan, J. E., Jessor, R., & Costa, F. M. (1991). Adolescent health behavior and conventionality-unconventionality: An extension of problem-behavior therapy. *Health Psychology*, *10*, 52.

Endler, N. S., & Marino, C. J. (1972). The effects of source and type of prior experience on subsequent conforming behavior. *The Journal of Social Psychology, 88*, 21-29.

Fox, N. A., & Calkins, S. D. (2003). The development of self-control of emotion: Intrinsic and extrinsic influences. *Motivation and Emotion*, *27*, 7-26.

Gecas, V., & Seff, M. A. (1990). Families and adolescents: A review of the 19805. *Journal of Marriage and the Family*, *52*(94), 58.

Harter, S. (2012). *The construction of the self*. New York City, Guilford Press.

Harris, M. A., Gruenenfelder-Steiger, A. E., Ferrer, E., Donnellan, M. B., Allemand, M., Fend, H., & Trzesniewski, K. H. (2015). Do parents foster self-esteem? Testing the prospective impact of parent closeness on adolescent self-esteem. *Child Development*, *86*, 995-1013.

Hawkins, J. D., Catalano, R. F., & Miller, J. Y. (1992). Risk and protective factors for alcohol and other drug problems in adolescence and early adulthood: implications for substance abuse prevention. *Psychological Bulletin*, *112*, 64.

Janis, I. L. (1973). Groupthink and group dynamics; A social psychological analysis of defective policy decisions. *Policy Studies Journal*, *2*, 19-25.

Johnston, L. D., O'Malley, P. M., Bachman, J. G., & Schulenberg, J. E. (2003). Teen smoking continues to decline in 2003, but declines are slowing. *Ann Arbor, MI: University of Michigan News and Information Services*.

Kandel, D. B., & Andrews, K. (1987). Processes of adolescent socialization by parents and peers. *International Journal of the Addictions*, *22*, 319-342.

Kandel, D.B., Bogenschneider, K., Wu, M. Y., Raffaelli, M., & Tsay, J. C. (1998). Parent influences on adolescent peer orientation and substance use: The interface of parenting practices and values. *Child Development*, *69*, 1672-1688.

Kerr, M., & Stattin, H. (2000). What parents know, how they know it, and several forms of adolescent adjustment: further support for a reinterpretation of monitoring. *Developmental Psychology*, *36*, 366.

Kim, H., & Markus, H. R. (1999). Deviance or uniqueness, harmony or conformity? A cultural analysis. *Journal of Personality and Social Psychology*, *77*, 785.

Kinney, D. A. (1993). From nerds to normals: The recovery of identity among adolescents from middle school to high school. *Sociology of Education*, 21-40.

La Greca, A. M., Prinstein, M. J., & Fetter, M. D. (2001). Adolescent peer crowd affiliation: Linkages with health-risk behaviors and close friendships. *Journal of Pediatric Psychology*, *26*, 131-143.

Lippold, M. A., Glatz, T., Fosco, G. M., & Feinberg, M. E. (2018). Parental perceived control and social support: Linkages to change in parenting behaviors during early adolescence. *Family Process*, *57*, 432-447.

Mackie, D. M. (1987). Systematic and nonsystematic processing of majority and minority persuasive communications. *Journal of Personality and Social Psychology*, *53*, 41-.

Mok, A., & Morris, M. W. (2010). An upside to bicultural identity conflict: Resisting groupthink in cultural ingroups. *Journal of Experimental Social Psychology*, *46*, 1114-1117.

Moscovici, S. (1980). Toward a theory of conversion behavior. *Advances in Experimental Social Psychology*, *13*, 209-239.

Mouttapa, M., Huang, T. K., Shakib, S., Sussman, S., & Unger, J. B. (2003). Authority-related conformity as a protective factor against adolescent health risk behaviors. *Journal of Adolescent Health, 33*, 320-321.

Pegg, K. J., O'Donnell, A. W., Lala, G., & Barber, B. L. (2018). The role of online social identity in the relationship between alcohol-related content on social networking sites and adolescent alcohol use. *Cyberpsychology, Behavior, and Social Networking*, *21*, 50-55.

Pennington, J., & Schlenker, B. R. (1999). Accountability for consequential decisions: Justifying ethical judgments to audiences. *Personality and Social Psychology Bulletin*, *25*, 1067-1081.

Quinn, A., & Schlenker, B. R. (2002). Can accountability produce independence? Goals as determinants of the impact of accountability on conformity. *Personality and Social Psychology Bulletin*, *28*, 472-483.

Rhodes, J. E., Haight, W. L., & Briggs, E. C. (1999). The influence of mentoring on the peer relationships of foster youth in relative and nonrelative care. *Journal of Research on Adolescence*, *9*, 185-201.

Sharp, C., Pane, H., Ha, C., Venta, A., Patel, A. B., Sturek, J., & Fonagy, P. (2011). Theory of mind and emotion regulation difficulties in adolescents with borderline traits. *Journal of the American Academy of Child & Adolescent Psychiatry*, *50*, 563-573.

Steinberg, L. (1990). *Authoritative parenting and adolescent adjustment across varied ecological niches*.

Triandis, H. C., McCusker, C., & Hui, C. H. (1990). Multimethod probes of individualism and collectivism. *Journal of Personality and Social Psychology*, *59*, 1006.

Urberg, K. A. (1992). Locus of peer influence: Social crowd and best friend. *Journal of Youth and Adolescence*, *21*, 439-450.

In: Social Psychology and Counseling
Editors: D. A. Kleiber and E. Delgado-Romero
ISBN: 978-1-53616-548-7

Chapter 3

SOCIAL MEDIA AND CONFORMITY

Bailey J. Nevels and Marjory Vazquez

Conformity-the natural instinct to passively yield to that vague something recognized as authority. -Mark Twain

INTRODUCTION

Conformity is instinctual yet generally held in some contempt. Engagement with social media has become almost instinctual as well. For example, the investigation into how hackers used social media to influence the results of the 2016 U.S. Presidential elections suggests that social media could use the tendency to conform to influence human behavior.

The alleged hacking was done with the assumption people would change their behavior based on the information presented in the social media posts. Anecdotally people perceive social media as influential, with the term "influencer" being used to describe people who market products to their followers.

To understand how social media influences our likelihood to conform, this chapter seeks to present research related to conformity and social media and identify areas for future research.

Additionally, social media often comes up in the therapy room due to its effects on self-concept and behavior, so this chapter will present a case integrating findings from the available research.

Conformity: A Primer

Researching conformity has historically been both informative and controversial. Solomon Asch (1956) demonstrated people's tendency to conform to the majority, even when they disagreed with the majority. For example, participants in his study acquiesced to the majority opinion to preserve group cohesion by knowingly providing inaccurate responses when asked about the length of line segments. Interestingly, he discovered participants were less likely to conform when they were "relieved of the necessity of announcing [their] dissent openly" (p. 70). He observed fears of being exposed as different, judged and isolated by the group. In summary, people conformed to a group even when the group was inaccurate due to losing confidence in their own accuracy and fearing judgement. This study seems particularly relevant to social media, given its nature as a platform to express and receive opinions publicly. Asch (1956) showed how people are willing to conform even when they disagree, perhaps under the influence of wanting to please people they perceive to be authoritative and reputable.

Aronson (2012) defined conformity as "a change in a person's behavior or opinions as a result of real or imagined pressure from a person or group of people" (p. 19). For example, adolescents often change their appearance and wardrobe to be accepted by the most popular social group. Aronson describes two types of conformity: *informational* and *normative*. Informational conformity stems from the *desire to be right* and normative conformity stems from the *desire to be liked*. Informational social influence (conforming to be accurate) occurs explicitly or subtly. For example, political candidates engage in explicit informational social influence when they try to convince audiences that they are better candidates based on the information they provide. A subtler example of informational social influence is conforming to the beliefs of people who appear more knowledgeable and trustworthy, as when people change their opinion of a candidate based on what an established journalist says about that person. Compared to informational social influence, *normative social influence* is conforming with the goal of being liked. For example, adolescents changing the type of music they listen to in order to understand their friend group's conversations demonstrates normative social influence. Normative social influence underscores how powerful a sense of belonging is as a social motive (cf. Fiske, 2004) and will be the primary focus of this chapter.

While researchers began studying conformity more than sixty years ago (e.g., Asch, 1956), social media is a recent phenomenon that has changed the way people interact with the world. Literally, at the click of a button, people broadcast what they eat, wear, believe, and support to their social networks worldwide. Similarly, people in those same social networks cast their votes about what they want to see by liking or commenting on those posts. For example, in 2018, Pew Research discovered that more Americans receive their news from social media than newspapers (Pew, 2018). Recent statistics estimate that 68% of people use *Facebook*, and 88% of people aged 18 to 29 use some form of social media. Additionally, the majority of those people visit their preferred social media sites daily, and many people use multiple social media platforms. They cannot get enough. This technological revolution has changed the way people interact with the world, and there is real or perceived pressure to conform to the preferences of one's social network. So how do conformity and social media intersect?

SOCIAL MEDIA, CONFORMITY AND INDIVIDUAL DIFFERENCES

Facebook remains the most popular social media platform (Pew, 2018); therefore, a substantial portion of social media research examines *Facebook* exclusively. Nadkarni and Hofmann (2012) completed a thorough analysis of available social media research articles to examine underlying motives for engaging with *Facebook*. Their results indicated that people use *Facebook* to meet two needs: to belong and to present oneself. Researchers also noted that cultural orientations toward collectivism or individualism and personality characteristics like self-esteem, extraversion and self-worth affected trends in *Facebook* participation. They suggested future research should examine how different cultural groups use social media for different reasons. For example, for European Americans, "having a more homogeneous friendship network was associated with a higher life satisfaction" (p. 244), whereas homogeneity of the network was less important to other cultural groups. Overall, Nadkarni and Hoffman suggest people use *Facebook* to belong and to be known, with clear tendencies to conform with others of their culture of origin.

Vogel, Rose, Roberts, and Eckles (2014) studied the use of *Facebook* and its relationship to self-evaluation and social comparison. They suggested that people compare "their realistic *offline* selves to the idealized *online* selves of others," resulting in negative self-evaluation (p. 207). Through both correlational and experimental studies, they demonstrated that social comparison on social media can detrimentally affect self-evaluation. For example, in the correlational study by Vogel and colleagues, researchers found that participants who used social media more often were more likely to have poorer self-esteem, and results indicated that social comparison mediated that relationship. That is, upward social comparison explained why people who used *Facebook* more frequently showed lower self-esteem.

Similar results were found in the *experimental* study by Vogel and associates. When participants viewed a fictitious social media profile of someone engaging in healthy behavior, like eating a healthy meal, they scored lower on a measure of self-esteem than those who viewed a profile of someone who posted their video game scores. In this second study, researchers also discovered that perceiving a profile to have higher social networking potential, like having a larger social network or receiving many "likes" and comments on a post, affected self-esteem to a greater degree than the content (healthy vs.

unhealthy) of their posts. Social comparison on social media can negatively affect people's self-perceptions, particularly when people perceive those in their social networks to be more engaged with their shared networks.

How do these findings connect with conformity? Intuitively, if someone engages in upward social comparison with their social media networks, they would be likely to conform to the behaviors and opinions of those people in order to improve their social position to be admired by others. For example, if adolescents view their more popular peers posting pictures of using e-cigarettes, they may start engaging in that behavior to increase felt belonging to that group. Upward social comparison explains why people feel annoyed while looking at people's vacation photos on Instagram in the middle of a tough work week, feeling their experiences may pale by comparison. It might also explain why a person would be reluctant to post a photo, fearing that someone perceived as higher status in their social network might judge it.

Another study completed by Zywica and Danowski (2008) explored self-esteem and its relationship to popularity on social media online and offline. Results indicated that those who were more extroverted with higher self-esteem were popular both online and offline. In contrast, those who were more introverted and had lower self-esteem were less popular online and more likely to strive to appear popular on *Facebook.* These findings suggest that social media could provide a platform for those with lower self-esteem to gain a sense of popularity and self-esteem. Given that those with lower self-esteem are also more likely to conform, perhaps conformity via social media is how those people attempt to improve their self-perceptions, which could be clinically relevant for a client suffering from low self-confidence. When low self-confidence is a clinical concern, a therapist might want to examine a client's social media activity in order to understand and help modify cognitions diminishing self-confidence.

The research results are mixed regarding whether to recommend more or less social media activity if the goal is to improve self-esteem. In a review of research on social media involvement and social connection, Twenge (2013) discussed social media involvement as having the potential to improve self-perception; but she noted it may also increase *self-focus* which is problematic in its own right. For example, Twenge highlighted research suggesting that although people might sign an online petition, they may not actually give to charity or engage with political candidates directly to express their views. Perhaps this "slacktivisim" relates to conformity, because conforming to a popular social movement via an online petition might boost someone's self-perception or sense of being altruistic while engaging in behavior offline to support the cause carries with it less notoriety or approval. This research also indicated that social media activity does not necessarily translate to values-driven behavior (Hayes, 2004).

It is also generally recognized that social media involvement is associated with narcissism, given its focus on self-promotion (e.g., Buffardi & Campbell 2011; McCain &Campbell 2018; Twenge 2013). A meta-analysis by McCain and Campbell (2018) demonstrated a connection between *grandiose narcissism*, defined as more extraverted and callous, and increased social media use. Findings suggested that those with narcissistic traits used social media for self-enhancement (p. 309), which is consistent with previous research identifying enhancing self-esteem as a *motive* for social media use if not a predictable *effect* (Buffardi & Campbell, 2011).

In general, research on social media and self-esteem is limited by its tendency to focus on number of posts or number of friends, making it difficult to determine the extent to which people are conforming on these platforms. There has been little research on the actual content of the posts. Understandably, frequency and duration of social media use are much more objective variables than the actual content posted. To enhance the research on how people interact with and are influenced by social media, future research should focus on the qualitative content in posts and whether people's behavior is shaped by those posts. For example, a study investigating the decision-making process when posting, such as whether people consider how their posts will be received, would be informative for understanding the relationship between conformity and social media. Furthermore, another study testing how people shape their behavior based on the content of social media posts would clarify whether people conform their behavior based on the posts of their friends on social media. Both approaches would better illuminate the nature of the relationship between social media use and negative mental health outcomes such as anxiety and depression.

In one attempt to go a bit deeper, Goel, Mason and Watts (2010) studied the actual content of social media posts in order to understand the level of agreement between friends connected through *Facebook*. Expressed agreement is generally another way to gain popularity and a sense of belonging. The goal of this study was to determine whether people were accurate in their perceptions of the level of agreement between themselves and their social networks on *Facebook*. The researchers surveyed 2,504 participants about their attitudes and their friends' attitudes. Topics ranged from politics to what superpower the participants believed their friends would prefer. Researchers found that friends agreed more frequently than strangers would agree, suggesting that people are attracted to others who are similar to them. However, results demonstrated perceived agreement between friends was greater than actual agreement and friends were unaware of their disagreements, suggesting that ignorance is bliss in this area. Therefore, conforming to the more popular opinion of the social network may be preferable to preserve a sense of belonging.

SOCIAL MEDIA USE AND MENTAL HEALTH

Most of the research reviewed thus far seeks to document how people look to social media to learn what to believe. Less research is available about how conformity to a specific set of beliefs affects the type of social media consumed or its effect on mental health. Parent and colleagues (2018) examined the relationship between social media behavior, toxic masculinity and depression and discovered that men who conformed to toxic masculinity norms and who defaulted to negative social media interactions (e.g., heated arguments) experienced an increase in symptoms of depression. Participants who chose more positive social interactions, in contrast, experienced fewer depression symptoms. This study demonstrated that conformity to a certain belief system can affect the type of social media we engage with, which can negatively affect mental health. Type of social media interaction, not just frequency, can impact mental health. This research sheds light on potential interventions in the therapy room to improve mental health via social media use. That is, if a client presents with significant interpersonal stress and acknowledges frequent, contentious social media encounters, a therapist may recommend intentionally engaging in positive social media interactions as a corrective emotional experience for the client or reducing the frequency of social media use (see Teyber * Teyber, 2017).

How people respond to posts is a unique feature with the potential to influence likelihood of conforming to be liked or to experience a sense of belonging. As of 2015, *Facebook* users generated 4.1 million "likes" per minute, and Instagram users liked 1.7 million pictures per minute (DOMO, 2015). The opportunity to interact with one's social network instantaneously is a unique draw to social media, yet there is a concern about developing dependence on social media "likes" for a sense of approval or self-worth. People may choose to take their pictures from a certain angle, or post material at a certain time, or draft a comment that increases the likelihood of people seeing and liking their posts, which all illustrate the power of normative social influence to foster a sense of belonging.

Similarly, the *absence* of response can also be impactful. Researchers demonstrated having unresponsive *Facebook* friends correlated with "a decreased sense of control, self-esteem, and meaningful existence," and an "increased experience of loneliness" (Greitemeyer, Mügge, Bollermann, 2014, p. 256). The effect of "interpersonal neglect" (p. 256) remained even when participants had a large social network, suggesting that the number of friends matters less for meeting those psychological needs compared to the types of interactions received from friends. Greitemeyer and colleagues suggest that bolstering someone's in-person social network might buffer against the effects of experiencing interpersonal neglect online.

The link between social media involvement and self-concept has become a fertile subject of research and is somewhat controversial (see Twenge 2013 for a review), with the dynamics that particularly impact mental health not yet fully understood. So how do mental health providers help their clients navigate a world in which self-concept can be affected by someone they have never met in person? Burrow and Rainone (2017) suggest examining participants' feelings when they are on social media and how engaging with social media relates to their other priorities. They suggest that developing a clearer *sense of purpose* may moderate the effects of social media feedback and self-esteem. Researchers found more likes on social media correlated with higher self-esteem for participants with little sense of purpose, indicating perhaps a lack of direction. The self-esteem of those who indicate a greater sense of purpose in life was unrelated to the number of likes received on social media. These results indicate that interactions on social media affect self-esteem, but they also suggest working with people to develop a sense of their purpose and value could decrease dependence of their self-esteem on the types of interactions experienced on social media.

Research results are mixed regarding social media use and depression symptoms. Baker and Algorta (2016) demonstrated that only 16% of research studies found a positive correlation between social media use and depression. However, they discovered the relationship between social media use and depression symptoms is often mediated or moderated by individual differences in the research findings. One such finding was how social comparison mediates the relationship, which connects to conformity. For example, when someone views another perceived to be superior on social media, that comparison is based on some internally held standards to which they both conform. If that person sees a friend post about a certain parenting technique, the standard to which to conform might be, "One must parent children in this way to be considered an acceptable, adequate parent." Perhaps people who are more likely to conform to certain societal norms are also those who are more likely to engage in social media comparison. This potential relationship is another important area to study to better understand how social media, conformity, and mental health converge.

Regarding specific interventions targeting social media use to affect mental health, Tromholt (2016), found that participants who stopped using *Facebook* for 1 week reported improved life satisfaction and emotional well-being. Additionally, the effect of quitting *Facebook* was more pronounced for those who experience envy when browsing *Facebook* compared to those who reported little "*Facebook* envy" (p. 663). Tromholt noted that intentional efforts to educate people about mental health and the potential dangers of social media use can make that use more positive. Therefore, the suggestion may be to consider moderating use rather than completely quitting *Facebook* and other social media use all together.

CASE ILLUSTRATION: MIA

Mia is a 19-year old, African-American female student-athlete who presents to her first appointment reporting symptoms consistent with Generalized Anxiety Disorder. She is an accomplished soccer player at a prestigious Division 1 school, on full scholarship due to her talent. She complains of consistent worry, difficulty concentrating, sleep disturbance and irritability, all of which are impacting her ability to be successful athletically and academically. Mia explains how she was referred for therapy by her athletic trainer who noticed her lack of focus, frequent crying and reports from her academic advisor that Mia has struggled more this semester compared to last year.

After a few sessions, Mia starts to open up about her internal experience. She is naturally driven and high achieving. She emphasizes that she chose her school due to the academic rigor and athletic opportunity. However, last spring she began to be consistently worried she was not doing enough. She explained a tendency to compare herself to her friends on campus who seemed more socially active and smarter. She described jealousy towards her friends from home who always seemed to be having more fun. Mia eventually described how her thoughts and tendency to engage in self-comparison are based primarily on what she views on social media. Her teammates get more likes on their posts, her old friends are always spending time together without her, her other friends posted their grades on their Snapchat stories like badges of honor. She expresses guilt when she describes putting off homework to go out with her friends, because she did not want to miss out or not understand her teammates' inside jokes in the locker room.

Therapy, primarily from an Acceptance and Commitment Therapy (ACT) orientation (Hayes, 2004), focuses on defusing unhelpful cognitions and identifying Mia's values in hopes of encouraging values-driven, committed action. Mia begins to look at her thoughts about her friends objectively and starts to understand that social media provides a glimpse, not the whole picture, of someone's life (Steers, Wickham & Atelli 2014). Additionally, based on research examining the improvement in well-being after reducing Facebook use (Tromholt, 2016), Mia was asked to try limiting her social media use for one week to test for any effects on her mood.

Eventually, Mia presents excitedly to therapy discussing how she successfully let an unhelpful thought go when she saw a picture of her friends out at a party one night when she took a study break. Mia gains insight into how she values academics, athletics, and her family and friends, and she takes the suggestion to limit social media use to 15 minutes per day. She begins to study with her phone in her backpack, and she makes pick-up soccer on Sundays a priority. She sets goals for her academic work each week, and she starts to reward herself with a fun night out with her friends when she takes steps towards achieving those goals. Over time, her self-reported anxiety reduces and she terminates treatment hopeful for continued success in the future.

CONCLUSION

Because social media is such a prevalent part of our culture, it is necessary to determine how social media platforms affect conformity and how both impact mental health. From the studies reviewed here, it seems that users with lower self-esteem are more likely to not only use social media but also to perceive it as a way to gain popularity, which is an indicator of *normative social influence* (Aronson, 2012). Additionally, social media is used to connect people who already agree with one another, or at least are perceived to agree with one another. It can be inferred that those with lower self-esteem would be more likely to conform to friends' opinions on social media to reduce the likelihood of conflict and rejection. Furthermore, the majority of social media research involves frequency of social media engagement rather than the type or valence of social media posts. Therefore, future research should focus on the content of the social media posts rather than how often people use it or check their phones.

Diversity factors are also underrepresented in the available research on social media. For example, as previously noted, most research focuses on *Facebook*, because it is the most popular. However, younger people engage with different types of social media. For example, 78% of 18 to 24 year-olds use *Snapchat* and 71% of them use it daily (Pew, 2018), so future research could focus on how other social media platforms besides *Facebook* influence behavior. Given the increased divisiveness in culture, to understand how people of different ethnicities, sexual orientations and gender identities engage in social media could increase relating to diverse groups on social media effectively and respectfully (Pew, 2016). In general, though, there is more to be done to increase insight into how people engage with social media and change their behavior as a result.

Clients bring up social media interactions frequently in the counseling room. So what implications does the intersection of conformity and social media have for counseling psychology? The available research suggests that social media involvement may have the effect of either enhancing self-esteem or diminishing it. Further, social media may impact the opinions, thoughts, and political preferences of counselor's clients. Social media is another outlet for people to compare themselves and conform both implicitly and explicitly. Mia's case demonstrates how self-comparison on social media can increase anxiety via negative assumptions about the people in one's social network. The relationship between depression and social media is particularly nuanced. Research indicates that mediating factors, especially social comparison, can determine the relationship between social media use and depressive symptoms (Baker & Algorta 2016). When appropriate, it would be important for mental health clinicians to examine clients' use of social media to understand contributing factors to their pathology. Parent et al. (2018) suggest examining reactions to social media posts in session to help regulate emotions, modify maladaptive cognitions, and thus manage symptoms of anxiety and depression. For example, a therapist using ACT could ask a client like Mia to reflect on her perceptions about an Instagram photo in session, then teach her to examine those perceptions objectively rather than accept them as automatic truth (Hayes, 1994). From an *Interpersonal Process* approach, a therapist could help Mia increase insight into how social media posts contribute to unhealthy interpersonal relationship patterns (Teyber & Teyber, 2017). Together, Mia and her therapist could create a corrective emotional experience in session, such as increasing her awareness of the inherent value of personal expressiveness regardless of how many "likes" her posts receive. Tromholt (2016) found that asking people to reduce *Facebook* use improved their life satisfaction and emotional well-being. Therefore, instructing a client like Mia to reduce social media activity could be a viable option for reducing mental health distress. Such interventions could help clients gain insight into how social media influences their mood and behavior and practice healthy ways of responding to posts that can be generalized to life outside of therapy.

REFERENCES

Aronson, E. (2012). *The Social Animal.* 11th ed. New York, NY: Worth Publishers.

Asch, S. E. (1956). Studies of independence and conformity: I. A minority of one against a unanimous majority. *Psychological Monographs: General and Applied, 70*, 1 - 70. doi:10.1037/h0093718.

Baker, D. A., & Algorta, G. P. (2016). The Relationship between online social networking and depression: A systematic review of quantitative studies. *Cyberpsychology, Behavior, and Social Networking, 19*. 638 - 648. doi: 10.1089/ cyber.2016.0206.

Buffardi, L. E., & Campbell, W. K. (2011). Narcissism and social networking websites. *Personality and Social Psychology Bulletin, 34*. 1303 - 1314. doi: 10.1177/ 0146167208320061.

Burrow, A. L., & Rainone, N. (2017). How many likes did I get?: Purpose moderates links between positive social media feedback and self-esteem., *Journal of Experimental Social Psychology*, *69*. 232 - 236. doi: 10.1016/j.jesp.2016.09.005.

Campbell, W. K. (1999). Narcissism and romantic attraction. *Journal of Personality and Social Psychology*, *77*, 1254 - 1270. doi:10.1037/0022-3514.77.6.1254.

DOMO (2015). Data never sleeps 3.0: How much data is generated every minute? Retrieved from: https://wersm.com/how-much-data-is-generated-every-minute-on-social-media/.

Fiske, S. T. (2004). *Social beings: A core motives approach to social psychology*. NYC: Wiley.

Goel, S., Mason, W., & Watts, D. J. (2010). Real and perceived attitude agreement in social networks. *Journal of Personality and Social Psychology, 99*. 611 - 621. doi: 10.1037/ a0020697.

Greitemeyer, T., Mügge, D. O., & Bollerman, I. (2014). Having responsive *Facebook* friends affects the satisfaction of psychological needs more than having many *Facebook* friends. *Basic and Applied Social Psychology, 36*. 252 - 258. doi: 10.1080/ 01973533.2014.900619.

Hayes, S. C. (2004). Acceptance and Commitment Therapy, Relational Frame Theory, and the third wave of behavioral and cognitive therapies. *Behavior Therapy,* 35, 639 - 665. doi: 10.1016/S0005-7894(04)80013-3.

McCain, J. L., & Campbell, W. K. (2018). Narcissism and social media use: A Meta-analytic review. *Psychology of Popular Media Culture, 7*. 308 - 327. doi: 10.1037/ppm0000137.

Milgram, S. (1963). Behavioral study of obedience. *Journal of Abnormal and Social Psychology,* 67. 371 - 378.

Nadkani, A. & Hofman, S. G. (2012). Why do people use *Facebook*? *Personality and Individual Differences, 52*. 243 - 249. doi: 10.1016/j.paid.2011.11.007.

Parent, M. C., Gobble, T. D. & Rochien, A. (2018). Social media behavior, toxic masculinity, and depression. *Psychology of Men and Masculinity*, doi: 10.1037/men0000156.

Pew (2018). *Social Media Use in 2018*. Retrieved from: http://www.pewinternet.org/2018/03/01/social-media-use-in-2018/.

Pew Research Center (2014). *What people like and dislike about Facebook*. Retrieved from: https://www.pewresearch.org/fact-tank/2014/02/03/what-people-like-dislike-about-*Facebook*/.

Pew Research Center (2016). Partisanship and political animosity in 2016. Retrieved from: https://www.people-press.org/2016/06/22/partisanship-and-political-animosity-in-2016/.

Steers, M. N., Wickham, R. E. & Acitelli, L. K. (2014). Seeing everyone else's highlight reels: How *Facebook* use is linked to depressive symptoms. *Journal of Social and Clinical Psychology*, *33*. 701 - 731. doi: 10.1521/jscp.2014.33.8.701.

Teyber, E., & Teyber, F. H. (2017). *Interpersonal Process in Therapy: An Integrative Model*. 7th Ed. Boston: Cengage.

Tromholt, M. (2016). The *Facebook* experiment: Quitting *Facebook* leads to higher levels of well-being. *Cyberpsychology, Behavior, and Social Networking, 19*. 661 - 666. doi: 10.1089/cyber.2016.0259.

Twenge, J. M. (2013). Does online social media lead to social connection or social disconnection? *Journal of College and Character, 14*. 11 - 20. doi: 10.1515/jcc-2013-0003.

Vogel, E. A., Rose, J. P., Roberts, L. R. & Eckles, K. (2014). Social comparison, social media, and self-esteem. *Psychology of Popular Media Culture*, *3*. 206 - 222. doi: 10.1037/ppm0000047.

Zywica, J., & Danowski, J. (2008). The faces of *Facebook*ers: Investigating social enhancement and social compensation hypotheses; predicting *Facebook*™ and offline popularity from sociability and self-esteem and mapping the meanings of popularity with semantic networks. *Journal of Computer-Mediated Communication*, *14*, 1 - 34. doi: 10.1111/j.1083-6101.2008.01429.x.

SECTION III.
SOCIAL INFLUENCE II: MASS COMMUNICATION, PROPAGANDA AND PERSUASION

In: Social Psychology and Counseling
Editors: D. A. Kleiber and E. Delgado-Romero ISBN: 978-1-53616-548-7

Chapter 4

PERSUASION IN THE CONTEXT OF THERAPY

Amelia Hoyle and Anthony Hansen

THE CASE OF ALEX

Alex self-identifies as an 18-year-old, White, queer, gender non-binary student (pronouns they/them/theirs) in their senior year of high school. Alex has been competing in gymnastics since childhood and presents to therapy at the encouragement of their gymnastics coach, pointing out Alex's significant weight loss in the previous year. When assessing Alex's current experience, the clinician learns that Alex has been engaging in restrictive behavior for approximately a year. Alex reports that they initially experienced weight loss from a decreased appetite after their closest friend moved to a different state but reported experiencing positive reinforcement from others in their gym and school regarding this change. Additionally, they point out that the recent weight loss has made them look more masculine of center, an appreciated change in their body image. They further disclose perusing a Pro-Anorexia website, specifically for gymnasts. They report that they feel supported through this online community, stating that they believe others on the site truly understand what it has been like to grow up as a gymnast. While Alex acknowledges that they do not feel as energetic when competing, they describe feeling supported both by their classmates and through their online community. They note the joy that they are experiencing in not feeling as alone.

PERSUASION

Persuasion is a common social exchange where one voice (either of a person or a group) attempts to convince another of its beliefs, desires or behavioral intentions (Falk et al., 2010). As Aronson (2012) states, attempts at persuasion are prevalent in all aspects of society, in radio and television, books and newspapers, as well as through the internet. The Greek philosopher, Aristotle, devoted considerable attention to the art of persuasion in his writing and, in the past century, thousands of books and research articles have been published regarding the general subject of persuasion (Aristotle, trans. 1926; O'Keefe, 1990). It could be argued that an entire industry has been crafted around the ideas generated by the study of persuasion, from sales to advertising and marketing to political "education" and public service announcements. Furthermore, the thriving development of television, and especially internet outlets, has helped advertising and "infotainment" penetrate our lives on a daily basis. The following chapter will outline two significant challenges for therapists regarding persuasion. Firstly, how does a therapist empower and support clients to counter their own maladaptive thought patterns and beliefs when considering the significant forces of persuasion? And secondly, how is persuasion used, effectively and ethically, in the therapeutic process itself?

Aristotle claimed that an individual could be subjected to persuasion in one of three ways: by the logic of argument (*logos*), the emotional appeal of an argument (*pathos*), or by factors related to the source of the persuasive message (*ethos*) (Aristotle, 1926; Falk et al., 2010). Attempts at persuasion can appeal to a person's reasoning skills and/or emotions. Similarly, Petty and Cacioppo (1986) identified the two essential routes to persuasion that are most common. In their *Elaboration Likelihood Model* (ELM), the central route to persuasion involves systematic thinking, logic, and careful consideration of the weight of the evidence and the arguments presented. The peripheral route, on the other hand, involves more simple cues that might invoke emotion or fear rather than appealing to logic or evidence. Persuasive appeals often utilize both routes to persuasion; however, one or the other can be more effective with certain audiences.

Therapists may not be able to assist clients in discerning each misleading message they receive from various media. However, by addressing the impact of persuasion as it impacts people generally, therapists may be able to assist clients in developing barriers to persuasion by, first, recognizing dynamics of persuasion and, second, cultivating self-compassion. While the impact of persuasion comes in many forms that may present in therapy, this chapter will focus on one particularly salient message source, that is *Pro-Anorexia* (*Pro-Ana*) websites. These sites will be explored in order to address the central and peripheral routes of persuasion that may influence the development and course of eating disorders, particularly Anorexia Nervosa. Subsequently, the role of *Cognitive-Behavioral Therapy* (CBT) will be examined as a powerful tool that must be cautiously used by clinicians when enacting significant change in the lives of clients. Examining persuasion in the context of therapy for the treatment of Anorexia Nervosa may advance the connections between social psychology and applications for practice more generally.

THE MEDIA AND PERSUASION

The act of persuasion is commonly observed and documented (and most easily delivered) through mass media outlets such as cable news, commercials, online news sites, blogs and periodicals. Through propaganda and persuasion, various media cause a set of beliefs to become established or cause an existing set of beliefs to be either reinforced or challenged (Aronson, 2012). The effects of persuasion on the consumer side are evidenced by a documented increase of sales in advertised products or, in politics, by an increase in approval ratings when a candidate's agenda is pushed constantly until election time. Skilled advertising and marketing executives know the susceptibility of the human mind to emotion and reason, utilizing purposeful and strategic placement of their messages to gather optimal support from the consumer. Indeed, some studies have suggested that a provocative television program may affect a viewer's emotions to the extent that they are especially susceptible to targeted ads that appeal to those emotions (Khouaja & Bouslama, 2011). On the other hand, there is comparatively little research on enabling individuals to *resist* persuasion or on using persuasion effectively and ethically in the course of therapy.

SUSCEPTIBILITY TO PERSUASION

Generally, people have only a moderate awareness of the persuasive techniques that bombard them on a daily basis. Advertisements are everywhere in U. S. media, either in the form of actual commercial ads or in subtler product placement in ones' favorite shows and games. The unsolicited bombardment of ads has been found to have an effective influence on purchasing habits of consumers. Children are targeted at an early age; indeed, studies have shown that advertising has a clear effect on children's expressed desires (Khouaja & Bouslama, 2011). The main purpose of advertising is to get the consumer to purchase the product, maximizing the persuasive effect of the ad on the person's emotions, feelings and values (Dastjerdi, Davoudi-Mobarakeh, & Zare, 2012).

The source of the communication appears to directly affect the persuasive appeal of the message (Aronson, 2012). Specifically, the credibility of the person doing the persuading means a great deal to the person subjected to the persuasive attempt. Someone perceived as an *expert* or as *trustworthy* appears to carry more weight in shifting an individual's beliefs and decisions. The prevalence of this tactic is apparent in paid spokespeople for products, as well as special guests on news programs. These individuals tend to add credibility to the narrative and their selection is purposeful. But what makes a person credible? It appears that trustworthiness and attractiveness impact credibility, but neither is absolutely essential for a persuasive message to be successful.

Trustworthiness, within the broader concept of credibility, appears to mean a great deal to people exposed to persuasive communication. Trust can be greatly increased when an individual takes a position in which nothing can be gained and perhaps even something could be lost as a result. On the other hand, Aronson argues that attractiveness, or likability, is a factor in persuasion, even when it is clear that the attractive person is actively *trying* to be persuasive and may not be entirely trustworthy.

The psychological research abounds describing the importance of trustworthiness in the therapeutic relationship. Gaining momentum in the 1960s, Strong (1968) and others began to conceptualize psychotherapy as an interpersonal influence process. Examining counselor characteristics of attractiveness, trustworthiness and expertise, it appeared that the initial display of certain counselor characteristics allowed the clinician more leverage in subsequent client-counselor interactions (Strong, 1968). A subsequent study by Strong (1970) explored this concept further, concluding that trustworthiness of a therapist does not influence a client's perceptions upon an initial interaction (although attractiveness or reputation of the therapist might, but wasn't examined in this study); however, if the client believes in the trustworthiness of the counselor, agreement with the counselor increases over time under confidential conditions (Strong, 1970). This research describes the magnitude of clinician influence over clients' cognitions, suggesting the power of persuasion a perceived "trustworthy" clinician may hold over a clients' beliefs (Strong, 1970).

Barriers to Susceptibility

Johansen and Joslyn (2008) found that a person's education level can reduce susceptibility to misinformation and persuasion. Specifically, their research findings suggested that education can be an important cognitive resource that can undermine political propaganda. According to Johansen and Joslyn, more educated individuals tend to call upon many sources of information, in addition to stored knowledge, in order to counter new and opposing information. Despite the myriad of misinformation in U. S. society, a higher level of education appears to contribute to an individual's level of resistance, diminishing one's propensity to succumb to persuasive misinformation attempts. Of course, a therapist has little recourse to utilize this defense against persuasion as education is what it is for a client; but psychoeducation, providing information to raise a client's awareness of the nature of the seductive nature of persuasion would be possible for all levels of education.

In addition to education, Aronson (2012) pointed out that self-esteem has a strong impact on the tendency to be persuaded as well. He argued that people with low self-esteem who harbor feelings of inadequacy are more easily influenced by persuasive communication than those who value themselves highly. However, therapists are currently moving away from the historical emphasis on self-esteem (Neff, 2009). Instead, current research appears to be shifting towards the concept of *self-compassion* and ways to empower clients to be kind to themselves (2009). Breines and Chen (2012), for example, found that experimentally induced self-compassion increased participants' beliefs that perceived shortcomings could be changed and increased motivation to improve weaknesses.

THERAPEUTIC APPLICATION: PERSUASION AND EATING DISORDER TREATMENT

An extensive amount of research literature has exposed the ubiquitous prevalence of body dissatisfaction of women, particularly concerning women's views of their weight and body shape (Tiggemann & Zaccardo, 2015; see also, Williams, this volume). Sociocultural pressures, including the pervasive impact of mass media, have been frequently studied in terms of their link to body dissatisfaction, low self-esteem, and eating pathology (Bissell & Rask, 2010; López-Guimerá, Levin, Sánchez-Carracedo, & Fauquet, 2010). Theories of sociocultural influence have proposed that "media portrayals of ideal body figures are among the most antecedent constructs in the causal paths towards body image dissatisfaction and eating disorder symptomology among girls and women" (Benton & Karazsia, 2015, p. 22). Across studies, a consistent small-to-moderate negative effect has been demonstrated of the thin-ideal body image on body satisfaction, particularly for women who have denoted body image concerns (Tiggemann & Zaccardo, 2015). The importance of studying body dissatisfaction is paramount, given that body dissatisfaction is one of the most robust risk and maintenance factors of eating disorders (Stice, 2002; see also Williams, this volume).

Social comparison theory (Festinger, 1954) would suggest that women compare themselves to an unattainable cultural ideal of beauty and thinness that is presented in U. S. society. Women can rarely attain this ideal and engage in *upward comparison*, comparing their appearance to those they believe are more attractive than themselves. Inevitably, women feel that they fall short and become dissatisfied with their bodies (Myers, Ridolfi, Crowther, & Ciesla, 2012). The consensus has been that these upward appearance comparisons occur mainly as a result of exposure to the "ideal" body image of celebrities and fashion models (Fardouly & Vartanian, 2015). However, recent studies have explored the potential relationship between social media use, such as *Facebook*, and these upward comparisons, suggesting that appearance comparisons may be responsible for the relationship between social media use and body image concerns (Tiggemann & Slater, 2013).

As the trend continues for individuals to present an "idealized version" of themselves on social media, models for upward social comparisons on sites such as *Facebook*, *Instagram*, or *Pro-Anorexia* (*Pro-Ana*) websites have also become more widespread. While social media broadly claims to be a platform for which people can connect and share content, *Pro-Ana* websites exist for those with Anorexia to exchange disorder and health-related ideas and tips (Teufel et al., 2013). Social media sites provide a platform in which speed and ease are no obstacles for connecting to peers and allowing multiple comparisons. Furthermore, not only are the opportunities to engage in comparisons almost unfathomable, but these comparisons are likely made with at least somewhat idealized images that can be digitally altered. *Instagram*, for example, offers a feature in which users can "filter" their photograph in order to make their appearance more appealing.

Thinspiration, a term combining "thin" with "inspiration," has been found on pro-eating disorder websites that encourage disordered eating for weight loss. *Pro-Ana* sites display content that showcases idealized images of thin women, negative portrayals of overweight women, and motivational quotes meant to inspire weight loss (Boepple & Thompson, 2014). Research suggests that typical images of *thinspiration* on social media and *Pro-Ana* sites are likely to increase self-objectification, promote unhealthy standards of beauty, and encourage over-sexualization of women (Bardone-Cone & Cass, 2007). The results of viewing images of emaciated women that promote an eating disorder lifestyle have demonstrated damaging effects on body image for women (see also Williams, this volume).

Importantly, people who frequent *Pro-Ana* sites appear to have higher levels of body dissatisfaction and eating disorders. A 2006 survey of eating disorder patients at Stanford Medical School found that 35.5% had visited *Pro-Ana* websites, with 96% discovering new weight loss or purging methods from such sites (Wilson, Peebles, Hardy, & Litt, 2006). According to Wilson et al. (2006), these sites appear to increase one's perception of being overweight and increase negative body image.

Brotsky and Giles (2007) delved into the world of *Pro-Ana* internet sites by entering 20 discussion forums. These sites claim to exist as non-judgmental environments for individuals with Anorexia. According to Brotsky and Giles, those who viewed themselves as members of the "intragroup" in *Pro-Ana* sites tended to feel strongly as to who could have membership in the group, as if members had to earn this privilege.

Pro-Ana sites are particularly persuasive to persons with eating disorders due to their ability to tap into both central and peripheral routes of persuasion. Indeed, these sites often provide messages regarding the rights individuals have to engage in such behaviors and hail the ability to have freedom of personal choice. These messages are often attributed to "professionals," which makes the information appear credible, trustworthy, and attractive (Brotsky & Giles, 2007). A more peripheral route includes the numerous testimonies that support the individual's maladaptive mindset. Persons with eating disorders may be more attracted to these sites, and messages, due to lower self-esteem. To reemphasize Aronson's (2012) point, lower self-esteem may foster feelings of inadequacy, increasing the influence of communications intended to be persuasive.

While some individuals seek therapy, actively wanting help, others may be obligated or mandated by important others. Clinicians run the risk of invalidating their clients' perspectives and alienating them if they automatically assume clients want to change in a certain direction because clinicians regard their clients' behaviors as maladaptive or dangerous. As strongly as a clinician believes that *Pro-Ana* behavior is harmful, clients may be equally as committed to the belief that their disordered eating behavior is desirable and acceptable. This discrepancy can be exacerbated when a client is actively involved in a *Pro-Ana* internet community that promotes continued engagement in food restricting.

COGNITIVE-BEHAVIORAL THERAPY AND PERSUASION

Clinicians often utilize a *Cognitive-Behavioral Therapy* (CBT) framework when working with clients; this paradigm emphasizes challenging and changing existing beliefs that interfere with the client's best interests (see also Edner & Cassiello-Robbins, this volume). This can be accomplished by gaining awareness of distorted beliefs and maladaptive behaviors and refuting them through various techniques and activities, i.e., using more central-route approaches to persuasion. Indeed, the refuting of these beliefs from the CBT framework may be viewed as the conscious application of persuasive messages as well, the second major focus of this chapter. A client's change process occurs when they begin to adopt healthier ways of thinking and behaving, within a specific context, ultimately changing initial attitudes. When people perceive persuasive messages as strong, and must work harder to counter-argue, they are more likely to change their initial attitudes (Aronson, 2012). Clients must engage in challenging work in combatting distorted beliefs that have plagued them well before coming to therapy. With this in mind, clinicians must be mindful of the messages they present when working with clients, understanding the power in persuasive messages and the potential for significant change.

In order to ethically approach persuasion in therapy, the work must be completed with the client as the expert of their own experience, being cognizant of the power differential between the therapist and the client. While clinicians may assist clients in challenging persuasive messages, they must also honor that these strategies have worked for the client to help them survive. As a helping professional bound by ethical guidelines, clinicians offer alternative solutions to clients while respecting the autonomy of the client to make their own decisions. In the case of Alex, the client from the beginning of the chapter, the strategies they used had helped them to overcome the loss of a close friend and assisted them in feeling connected. Ultimately, the clinician's work is to focus on the goals of the client from a *strengths-based* perspective, figuratively walking alongside of them as they consider new thoughts and behaviors that they may not have had the resources to explore before.

Returning to the Case of Alex

The influence of negative persuasion on Alex's symptomology is clear. However, positive persuasion could be beneficial for Alex in the therapeutic work. Through CBT and an emphasis on fostering self-compassion, the clinician and Alex may be able to counter the forces of persuasion that are prevalent for this client. Specifically, by focusing on one key component of Alex's presenting concern, the lack of energy they feel when competing, the clinician and Alex may collaborate to drive a wedge between their unhelpful thought patterns and their goals for the future. As described in a case example by Karbasi (2010), Alex could be encouraged to track their emotions, thoughts and behaviors when eating. They could also monitor their feelings and thoughts when engaging with *Pro-Anorexia* websites. Importantly, there may be a benefit to openly discussing these online communities in therapy. The clinician may explore what Alex believes that they receive by being a part of these communities and connect with Alex by acknowledging the benefit of these communities in providing support, connection, and combatting isolation. Eventually, Alex and their clinician may explore what could be possible healthy alternative sources of support for them. Modifying maladaptive cognitions and behaviors and devising other possible responses are key tenets of Cognitive Behavioral Therapy.

Moreover, Alex may benefit from self-compassion work in order to build resilience against persuasive messages. Research by Adams and Leary (2007) suggests the benefit of increasing self-compassionate eating attitudes among participants with restrictive symptomology. Self-compassion may be fostered through three main components: self-kindness, mindfulness, and common humanity (Adams & Leary, 2007; Neff, 2009). Indeed, promoting self-compassion may be more effective than attempting to increase self-esteem for Alex, given their emphasis on social comparison evidenced by their use of *Pro-Ana* sites. With a foundation of trust built in the therapeutic alliance, the clinician may be able to provide psychoeducation regarding *Pro-Ana* websites, challenge maladaptive thoughts, and empower Alex to foster their own self-compassion.

This work must all be completed in a respectful and collaborative context, incorporating Alex's intersecting identities throughout the entire therapeutic process. As Alex's case suggested, restriction can lead clients who identify as nonbinary and transgender to appear more masculine of center by inducing amenorrhea and minimizing breast and hip growth (Strandjord, Ng, & Rome, 2015). The goals of weight loss for nonbinary and transgender clients may differ from those of cisgender clients with eating disorders. Without an understanding of the impact of intersecting identities on clinical presentation, the therapist may miss the opportunity to establish trust and credibility with the client.

Conclusion

When reflecting on the magnitude of advertising and other persuasive attempts of American mainstream media, the impact on the individual consumer becomes irrefutable. The tactics are unique and successful and, due to human tendencies to be susceptible to both logical and emotional appeals, nothing short of constant awareness will counteract the carefully calculated messages of news reporters, politicians, and advertisers. Ultimately, access to higher education, ability to develop high self-regard, and a quest for heightened awareness can assist people to overcome the onslaught of persuasive messages that perpetuate maladaptive thinking and behavior. While counseling psychologists may not be able to sit with clients in their living rooms, pointing out the dysfunctional messages they could be susceptible to, client-centered therapeutic work can increase the client's aptitude for discernment. By addressing the impact of persuasion in therapy or assisting the client in fostering self-compassion, awareness of attempts at persuasion is increased as is the capacity for resistance. A *strengths-based* therapeutic approach also has enhanced potential to counteract the impact of low self-esteem on susceptibility to media influence. And by using direct, logical appeals to alternative viewpoints, whether through CBT or other methods, clients can be empowered to choose behaviors that are more congruent with their values.

References

Adams, C., & Leary. M. (2007). Promoting self-compassionate attitudes toward eating among restrictive and guilty eaters. *Journal of Social and Clinical Psychology*, 26(10), 1120-1144.

Aristotle, & Freese, J. H. (1926). *The art of rhetoric/Aristotle; with an English translation by J. H. Freese*. London: Loeb Classical Library/Harvard University Press.

Aronson, E., (2012). *The social animal*. New York, New York: Worth Publishers.

Bardone-Cone, A. M. & Cass, K. M. (2007). What does viewing a pro-anorexia website do? An experimental examination of website exposure and moderating effects. *International Journal of Eating Disorders*, 40(6), 537-548.

Benton, C. & Karazsia, B.T. (2015). The effect of thin and muscular images on women's body satisfaction. *Body Image*, 13, 22-27.

Bissell, K. & Rask, A. (2010). Real women on real beauty: Self-discrepancy, internalisation of the thin ideal, the perceptions of attractiveness and thinness in Dove's campaign for real beauty. *International Journal of Advertising: The Quarterly Review of Marking Communications*, 29(4), 643-668.

Boepple, L., & Thompson, J. K. (2014). A content analysis of healthy living blogs: Evidence of content thematically consistent with dysfunctional eating attitudes and behaviors. *International Journal of Eating Disorders*, 47(4), 362-367.

Breines, J. G., & Chen, S. (2012). Self-compassion increases self-improvement motivation. *Personality and Social Psychology Bulletin*, 38(9), 1133-1143.

Brotsky, S. R., & Giles, D. (2007). Inside the 'pro-ana' community: A covert online participant observation. *Eating Disorders: The Journal of Treatment & Prevention*, 15(2), 93-109.

Dastjerdi, H., Davoudi-Mobarakeh, S., & Zare, M. (2012). A multimodal analysis of differences between TV commercials and press advertisements: A discoursal study of persuasion-seeking strategies in the mass media. *Studies in Literature & Language*, 4(2), 115-121.

Falk, E., Rameson, L., Berkman, E., Liao, B., Kang, Y., Inagaki, T., & Lieberman, M. (2010). The neural correlates of persuasion: A common network across cultures and media. *Journal of Cognitive Neuroscience*, 22(11), 2447-2459. doi:10.1162/jocn. 2009.21363.

Fardouly, J., & Vartanian, L. R. (2015). Negative comparisons about one's appearance mediate the relationship between Facebook usage and body image concerns. *Body Image*, 12, 82-88.

Festinger, L. (1954). A theory of social comparison processes. *Human Relations*, 7, 117-140.

Karbasi, A. L. (2010). Enhanced cognitive-behavioral therapy (CBT-E) for eating disorders: Case study of a client with anorexia nervosa. *Clinical Case Studies*, 9(3), 225-240.

Khouaja, F. B., Bouslama, N. (2011). The role of media context in the advertising persuasion process: A modeling attempt among children. *Journal of Knowledge Management, Economics, and Information Technology*, 1(6), 453-468.

Johansen, M. S., & Joslyn, M. R. (2008). Political persuasion during times of crisis: The effects of education and news media on citizens' factual information about Iraq. *Journalism & Mass Communication Quarterly*, 85(3), 591-608.

López-Guimerá, G., Levine, M. P., Sánchez-Carracedo, D., & Fauquet, J. (2010). Influence of mass media on body image and eating disordered attitudes and behaviors in females: A review of effects and processes. *Media Psychology*, 13(4), 387-416.

Myers, T., Ridolfi, D., Crowther, J., & Ciesla, J. (2012). The impact of appearance-focused social comparisons on body image disturbance in the naturalistic environment: The roles of thin-ideal internalization and feminist beliefs. *Body Image*, 9(3), 342-351.

Neff, K. (2009). The role of self-compassion in development: A healthier way to relate to oneself. *Human Development*, 52(4), 211-214.

O'Keefe, D. (1990). *Persuasion: Theory and Research*. Newbury Park, CA: Sage Publications.

Petty, R. E., & Cacioppo, J. T. (1986). The elaboration likelihood model of persuasion. *Advances in Experimental Social Psychology*, 19, 123-205.

Stice, E. (2002). Risk and maintenance factors for eating pathology: A meta-analytic review. *Psychological Bulletin*, 128(5), 825-848.

Strandjord, S. E., Ng, H., & Rome, E. S. (2015). Effects of treating gender dysphoria and anorexia nervosa in a transgender adolescent: Lessons learned. *International Journal of Eating Disorders*, 48(7), 942-945.

Strong, S. R. (1968). Counseling: An interpersonal influence process. *Journal of Counseling Psychology*, 15(3), 215-224.

Strong, S. R., & Schmidt, L. D. (1970). Trustworthiness and influence in counseling. *Journal of Counseling Psychology*, 17(3), 197-204.

Teufel, M., Hofer, E., Junne, F., Sauer, H., Zipfel, S., & Giel, K. (2013). A comparative analysis of anorexia nervosa groups on Facebook. *Eating and Weight Disorders*, 18(4), 413-420.

Tiggemann, M., & Slater, A. (2013). NetGirls: The Internet, Facebook, and body image concern in adolescent girls. *International Journal of Eating Disorders*, 46(6), 630-633.

Tiggemann, M., & Zaccardo, M. (2015). "Exercise to be fit, not skinny": The effect of fitspiration imagery on women's body image. *Body Image*, 15, 61-67.

Wilson, J., Peebles, R., Hardy, K., & Litt, I. (2006). Surfing for thinness: A pilot study of pro-eating disorder website usage in adolescents with eating disorders. *Pediatrics*, 118(6), 1635-1643.

Section IV. Social Cognition, Attribution and Self-Justification

In: Social Psychology and Counseling
Editors: D. A. Kleiber and E. Delgado-Romero
ISBN: 978-1-53616-548-7

Chapter 5

IMPACTS OF MEDIA DEPICTIONS ON UNDOCUMENTED IMMIGRANTS' SUBJECTIVE WELL-BEING

Beth L. Perlman and Edward A. Delgado-Romero

Immigration in the United States is a highly charged and politically divisive topic that has been debated within the political arena as well as in the media and popular press. Comprehensive immigration reform has been impossible since the Immigration Reform and Control Act of 1986. Frustration over political inaction on immigration became a central domestic policy issue in the 2016 US presidential election with stated positions ranging from a clear path to citizenship for immigrants with undocumented status to mass deportation (Nowicki, 2015), and the rhetoric and policy has continued to intensify with talk of construction of a border wall, ending programs such as Temporary Protective Status and Deferred Action for Childhood Arrivals and controversy over family separation at the southern border. The area of immigration policy is multifaceted and often contentious, blending issues surrounding race, economics, national security, nativism, and xenophobia (Hird, Reese, & Shilvock, 2004). Historically, immigration laws and ideologies have revealed contradictory intentions, which are frequently aimed at either restricting or affording access to employment, education, and public services (Hilfinger Messias, Morris McEwen, & Boyle, 2015). Various federal, state, and local immigration laws have led to insidious policing, mass detention of immigrants, and heightened racial anxieties about Latinx immigrants, who tend to be the majority of undocumented immigrants (Rosas, 2015).

Punitive legislation is often masked under the guise of "colorblind" language to falsely legitimize the policy as a response to economic and security issues (Vargas,

Sanchez, & Valdez Jr, 2017). However, upon further investigation, racial motivations become evident, and these policies are often traced to "negative stereotypical accounts of undocumented communities" as well as "anti-Latino sentiment" (Vargas et al., 2017, p. 2). By way of example, following the terrorist attacks on September 11, 2001, there was an intensification of general anxiety about the criminal behaviors of immigrants, especially non-White immigrants, with a corresponding increase in militarized law enforcement (Rosas, 2015). Subsequent to the attack, the USA-PATRIOT Act was enacted in 2001 under the Bush Administration (Chomsky, 2014; Hilfinger Messias, Morris McEwen, & Boyle, 2015). This law notably increased the offenses by which an individual can be deported.

While the US immigration laws are often a basis for national conversation and debate, it is important to note that immigration policies and restrictions are not only determined on a federal level, but on a state and local level as well. According to the National Conference of State Legislatures (NCLS), there were 206 immigration state laws enacted in the US in 2017 and 175 laws in 2018 (NCSL, 2019). Due to the relative absence of comprehensive federal laws, states often enact their own immigration policies, particularly surrounding immigrants' day-to-day activities and access to state public resources. In Indiana, for instance, a law was enacted in 2017 that prohibits public and private universities funded by the state or federal government to impede the enforcement of federal immigration laws. This law also mandates university employees disclose information about a person's immigration status to law enforcement officials (NCSL, 2018). The increasing national and state rancor about immigration reform has continued to fuel debate about the role of immigrants in the US. However, prior to any changes in state, local, or federal laws, immigration-related topics are typically explored and debated through media, news agencies, and a wide range of social channels.

Media sources and social channels are often influenced by complex, recursive dynamics that involve power, dominance, stereotypes, and inequality. The resulting coverage of immigration is complicated by sociocultural beliefs, personal values, and economic anxieties. Research repeatedly shows that the language employed in the media demonstrates an insidious function in forming differential and imbalanced perceptions of power (Kinefuchi & Cruz, 2015) where style, rhetoric, and tone tend to legitimize prejudices and "privileged access to socially valued resources, such as wealth, income, position, status, force, group membership, education, or knowledge" (van Dijk, 1993, p. 254). Further, because White Americans often have reduced contact and understanding of people of color, their beliefs about race, ethnicity, and citizenship are often developed and bolstered by media characterizations (Cornell & Hartmann, 2007), which can be shaped or determined by cultural biases and misinformation. Media is a potentially potent influence, and, consequently, it is critically important to explore the wide-ranging impact of the media system on social values, individual beliefs as well as collective psychological well-being.

The primary purpose of this chapter will be to highlight how media systems, by distorting the story of unauthorized immigrant communities, foster an atmosphere of oppression. The chapter will also explore the negative emotional health implications of media bias on individuals and communities and the dangers of having a monolithic understanding of people, places, and situations. The role of these negative mental health implications in the prevision of psychotherapeutic services will also be examined. Even though the number of psychologists of color nearly doubled from 2007-2016 (APA's Center for Workforce Studies, 2018), the active psychological workforce continues to be predominantly White and needs to be aware of ethnic, racial, and citizenship injustice faced by different marginalized communities. Consequently, recommendations for psychologists and other mental health providers will also be reviewed.

Latinx is a general term used to designate individuals with Spanish-speaking country ancestry (Balderas, 2016; Comas-Díaz, 2001). However, it is important to be cognizant of the fact that this is not a homogenous group. The term Latinx functions "as a superset of many nationalities" (Comas-Díaz, 2001, p. 116) and is composed of individuals from a number of countries with a wide range of cultural values, beliefs, and experiences with the US. An *undocumented immigrant* is defined as a citizen from another country residing in the US without authorization or residence papers (Hipolito-Delgado & Mann, 2012). The terms *illegal immigrant* and *illegal alien* are purposely avoided since the terms carry inaccurate, dehumanizing, and negative sociopolitical connotations (Hipolito-Delgado & Mann, 2012; Vargas, Sanchez, & Valdez Jr., 2017). It is also worth highlighting that, although the term undocumented immigrant is utilized in this paper, some social justice activists have advocated for the use of term *unauthorized immigrant* instead (Arredondo, Gallardo-Cooper, Delgado-Romero, & Zapata, 2014)

Media Depictions

The use of storytelling through the media is particularly evident as issues surrounding immigration law and policy are discussed and, at times, debated in a range of settings in the US. The intricacies of the immigration debate that are evident in public dialogue and media depictions offer a small-scale view of how media can contribute to and shift beliefs in societal discourse (Grimm, 2015). By way of example, characterizations of immigrants across media sources are frequently created through negative metaphors and framing (Kinefuchi & Cruz, 2015). Mainstream media often depict immigration as a danger to US culture with coverage "linking" immigrants to crime, substance use, and economic issues (Tukachinsky, Mastro, & King, 2011). The dominant verbal and visual depictions of immigrants convey that these individuals, particularly Latinx immigrants, overuse state and federal social services and can be seen as uneducated, criminal, lazy, contaminated, victims, and involved in drug sales (Kim & Diaz, 2013; Kinefuchi & Cruz, 2015;

Tukachinsky, Mastro, & King, 2011). The media's framing of Cuban refugees leaving Mariel Harbor on a massive flotilla of boats between April and October 1980 to come to the US highlights this media trend. While the media's initial coverage of the flotilla was positive, the coverage later shifted to depict Cuban dictator Fidel Castro as using the flotilla to empty his jails and mental health facilities of undesirable people. This coverage resulted in the new Cuban immigrants, who were mostly Afro-Cuban people fleeing communist rule being labeled as criminal. Although immortalized in films such as *Scarface* (1983), the reality was that the Cuban immigrants were as law-abiding and hard-working as the Cuban immigrants before them (Delgado-Romero, Rojas-Vilches & Shelton, 2008).

These widespread anti-immigrant sentiments are also exemplified in the political focus on the perceived permeability of the US-Mexico border during the 2019 federal government shut down. President Donald Trump initiated what became the longest government shutdown in the nation's history over an impasse to fund the $5.7 billion he wanted for a border wall. The shutdown lasted a total of 34 full days, surpassing the previous record of 21 days under President Bill Clinton in 1995. During his televised 2019 State of the Union Address, President Trump, responding to Washington gridlock over his Wall, declared "an urgent national crisis" due to the "lawless state" of the southern border ("President Donald J. Trump's State of the Union Address", n.d.). Trump expressed to four supreme court justices, various lawmakers, and House chamber members that the government had a "moral duty" to "show the world that America is committed to ending illegal immigration and putting the ruthless coyotes, cartels, drug dealers, and human traffickers out of business" ("President Donald J. Trump's State of the Union Address", n.d.). In remarks that further inflamed views about immigration, Trump added that working-class Americans are left to "pay the price" for unauthorized immigration including "reduced jobs, lower wages, overburdened schools, hospitals that are so crowded you can't get in in, increased crime and a depleted social safety net" ("President Donald J. Trump's State of the Union Address", n.d.). Trump's judgmental and emotionally charged depiction of immigration has been linked to White nationalism and allegedly emboldened perpetrators of hate crimes.

Research often indicates that views of immigrants as criminal, unhealthy, and a drain on the US economy are often unfounded in fact. As a specific example, less than 1 percent of immigrants come to the US for social services. Individuals with undocumented status are, in fact, less likely to utilize public services when compared to US citizens because of their acute fear of heightened visibility (Kim & Diaz, 2013) and a risk for deportation. Ultimately, the promulgation of these inaccuracies through the media serves to heighten negative views of immigrants and cultivates an atmosphere of hostility toward immigrants.

In a quantitative study examining the role of media in shaping views of immigration, Esses, Medianu, and Lawson (2013) explored the belief that immigrants often carry infectious diseases that threaten the health of the host country. The researchers predicted that this association might lead to the dehumanization of immigrants because "vermin are typically associated with the spreading of disease" (p. 525). The researchers explored the issue through an experiment utilizing editorial cartoons. Participants perused an online article about the actor Steve Martin and were told that they would be subsequently answering questions regarding what they had just learned. The bottom right-hand side of the article contained a small editorial cartoon, which was designed specifically for the study. The cartoon depicted an immigrant checking in at an Immigration Canada booth, hoisting several suitcases and a number of documents. In one condition, the largest suitcase displayed labels for various diseases such as AIDS and SARS. In the second condition, there were no labels present on the luggage. Although the participants were told that they would be asked questions about the article, they were instead administered a series of items assessing their memory of the editorial cartoon, their perceptions of immigrants as sources and spreaders of disease, as well as their emotions and attitudes toward immigrants. The findings of the study suggest that many of the participants' memories of the editorial cartoons were poor, with a number of participants reporting no memory of the cartoon at all. Notwithstanding this lack of specific memory of the cartoon and its' contents, participants who observed the cartoon with the disease labels were significantly more likely to endorse notions of immigrants as sources and spreaders of disease. In addition, they were more apt to report feelings of contempt and lack of admiration toward immigrants on the dehumanization measure. Furthermore, individuals who were exposed to the editorial cartoon with the disease-labels exhibited increased antipathy towards immigrants and the immigration process. The obtained results demonstrate that even seemingly minor expressions of media bias may shape attitudes and beliefs about cultural groups.

Although 17.6% of the US population identifies as Latinx (PEW, 2015), Santa Ana (2013), in an analysis of over 12,000 news stories from ABC, CBS, NBC, and CNN, found that Latinx matters were represented in only 1% of the news coverage. However, when Latinx communities *were* specifically covered in stories, there was an overrepresentation of the community in the areas of crime and immigration. Conversely, the positive contributions and strengths of Latinx people and communities to the US economy and society were rarely highlighted or discussed. By merging Latinx and immigrant groups while overstating their criminality the media propagates an image of all Latinx people as being foreigners and criminals. In a myriad of mainstream news stories about immigration reform, the voices of immigrants themselves are also conspicuously absent (Kinefuchi & Cruz 2015).

In a qualitative study about geo-ethnic storytelling in local media, Grimm (2015) conducted semi-structured interviews of 11 journalists and editors in California. Grimm highlighted an incongruence where the participants acknowledged that race and nativism factored into the immigration debate while concurrently contending that race did not significantly influence news stories due to perceived adherence to the journalistic principles of uniformity and objectivity. When discussing the newspaper coverage of immigration protests in 2006, one editor, with over two decades of experience as a journalist, stated that when determining what to cover, he will "evaluate events on newsworthiness" where editors "monitor and report about protests from either side of the debate based on a protocol that applies to protests on any issue" (p. 10). The media focus on criminality, at the expense of more balanced reporting, creates and supports concerns that immigrants are a danger to the U.S.

Ultimately, the disproportionate reporting of immigrant criminal behavior in the media serves to normalize practices such as immigration raids, indefinite detention, and deportations. While there is no clear evidence that the detention of immigrants achieves immigration policy goals, detention has clear negative effects including being costly to enact as well as harmful to detainees, their families and wider communities. Nevertheless, there has been a dramatic rise in detention and a considerable broadening of deportable offenses (Chomsky, 2014). During the Obama administration, a record 2.5 million undocumented individuals and families were deported, which greatly surpasses the number of deportations carried out by any previous administration. According to Pew Research Center (2014), the surge in deportation numbers can be primarily attributed to an increased number of individuals who were removed for reasons other than a criminal conviction. During the 2013 fiscal year, 438,421 undocumented immigrants were deported (Pew Research Center, 2014) of which 240,000 (55%) individuals did not have a previous criminal conviction (Pew Research Center, 2014). Moreover, immigrants who had criminal records were typically guilty of minor, non-violent offenses. In illustration of this point, more than half of the 391,953 immigrants deported by ICE (Immigration Control and Enforcement) in 2011 did not have a previous criminal history (Chomsky, 2014) and of the 188,380 individuals who had been charged with a criminal violation, 60% were guilty of non-violent offenses such as minor drug crimes, immigration violations, or driving infractions. As a point of information, having undocumented status in the US is a civil violation, not a crime, although some states have been successful in criminalizing immigration through legislation. For example, in Georgia driving without a license was made into a felony offense, a change that disproportionately impacted immigrants.

The skewed reporting in the media about immigrants and the ways in which the reporting informs the beliefs and values of individuals can be understood within the context of social psychology. The concept of *cognitive dissonance* (Aronson, 2012) for example, applies to how the linking of immigrants with crime and disease can promote inaccurate and racist beliefs. A key feature of cognitive dissonance is that individuals who simultaneously hold two or more incongruent beliefs and/or behaviors will feel stress (dissonance). The psychological discomfort caused by the dissonance between the viewpoints forces individuals to re-think their thoughts and actions to create a new congruent mindset which reduces psychological distress but may also result in a distortion of understanding in the process, a kind of false consonance.

A number of researchers have suggested that the negative connotations of race and ethnicity has diminished in the United States (Feagin, 2010; Grimm, 2015; Hutchings, 2009). In a society or community that does not support overt racism, the direct expression of dislike, distrust or hatred for immigrants might not be tolerated. As a consequence, the appearance of being prejudiced or racist towards immigrants is incongruent with a societal value of racial colorblindness. By the media redefining immigrants as criminals, however, individuals can acceptably hate criminals without experiencing cognitive dissonance (Chomsky, 2014). Kim and colleagues (2011) conducted a content analysis of television transcripts of ABC, NBC, and CBS as well as six regional and national newspapers, found that coverage related to immigration reform largely concentrated on crimes committed by undocumented immigrants. Moreover, a study by Chavez, Whiteford, and Hoewe (2010) also supported the increased incidence of media reports about immigrants as criminals. The researchers found that over 50% of the stories examined from *New York Times*, *Washington Post*, *USA Today*, and *Wall Street Journal* were about crimes committed by immigrants. By contrast, education policy and accessibility was the least covered immigration topic. The linkage of an entire group of undocumented immigrants to destructive criminal behavior allows privileged individuals to diminish another ethnic group without appearing obviously racist.

In addition to influence of cognitive dissonance, social psychological concepts of identity and intergroup relations depict the impact of media on attitudes toward immigrants. Social identity theory (Tajfel & Turner, 1986) posits that individuals strive to preserve a positive social identity with the groups in which they affiliate. This goal may be accomplished by comparing the standing of groups of which they are members to the status of other social groups. Peoples' perceptions of undocumented individuals and immigration policy are guided by social as well as environmental desires (Diaz, Saenz, & Kwan, 2011) to elevate their perceived social standing. Further, the concept of ingroup-outgroup bias suggests that hostile attitudes and restrictive policies are driven, at least to some degree, by intergroup competition (Brewer, 1979; Diaz, Saenz, & Kwan, 2011). Essentially, this phenomenon refers to individuals' subconscious tendency to divide themselves and others into similarity-based groups, or ingroups and outgroups (Brewer, 1979). This cognitive pattern can foster an *us-and-them mentality* in which cultural differences are exaggerated or perceived as negative (Comas-Díaz, 2000). As a consequence, when people experience group threat, or perceive that their group's status, influence, or hierarchical position in society is unstable, they commonly express prejudice or practice discrimination toward the threatening group. The frequent media reporting which equates immigrants with criminals can be an effective way of defining immigrants as a dangerous outgroup.

During the 2016 election, presidential candidate Donald Trump appeared to successfully utilize the "us-and-them" mentality by portraying immigrants as criminals who steal jobs and jeopardize American well-being. By way of example, now-President Donald Trump infamously stated during his successful 2016 campaign that "when Mexico sends its people, they're not sending their best. They're sending people that have lots of problems, and they're bringing those problems with them. They're bringing drugs. They're bringing crime. They're rapists" (Phillips, 2017, para. 13). This type of ethnocentric thinking often becomes more pervasive during periods of national insecurity and economic recession, with a cultural tendency to scapegoat people of color (Comas-Díaz, 2000). As a point of information, *ethnocentrism* refers to individuals' partiality for and positive appraisals of their own ethnic or racial group (ingroup) relative to all other groups (outgroups) (Valentino, Brader, & Jardina, 2012). During times where there is a perceived threat such as a scarcity of resources or threat to social status, this process may prompt or exacerbate conflict between groups (Diaz, Saenz, & Kwan, 2011).

The US Census Bureau has predicted that racial minority groups will comprise the majority of the US national population by 2042 (Craig & Richeson, 2014). This majority-minority racial demographic transition may prompt endorsements of conservative political ideology among White Americans. In particular, the researchers postulated that White Americans would view this change as a threat to their racial group's social status. In a series of four experiments, Craig and Richeson (2014) examined how the salience of racial demographic changes influenced White Americans' political ideology and policy positions. Findings from the study indicate that the participants who were informed of the national racial demographic shifts were more likely to strongly support conservative policy positions, irrespective of their own political party affiliation. The results from this study suggest that, despite the widespread belief that shifting racial demographics are a growing problem for the Republican Party, White Americans might be more likely to endorse conservative candidates and agendas in connection with changing demographics (Craig & Richeson, 2014). Furthermore, the findings provide preliminary support that changing racial demographics could cause an increasingly divided political environment.

Clinical Implications for Mental Health Providers

The hostile tenor of current attitudes toward immigrants and the ways in which the media is implicitly and explicitly promoting these views has fostered an adverse atmosphere for immigrant and non-citizen individuals, families, and communities. These communities contend with suspicion, discrimination, and hostility partially due to the stereotypes reinforced and promulgated by the American media. Mental health providers have a responsibility to employ culturally-sensitive practices where the unique needs, values, and intersecting identities as well as cultural experiences of clients are recognized. Given the inherent power differential in the therapeutic space, it is counselor's responsibility to initiate and manage difficult dialogues with clients surrounding power, privilege, and oppression. With the pervasive, inaccurate portrayals of the immigrant community in various forms of media, it is essential that therapists resist the dehumanization of their clients by identifying and acknowledging media systems that promote inequalities and validating for clients that the media can trigger feelings of fear and unpredictability.

Notwithstanding evidence of the resilience of undocumented immigrants (Arredondo, Gallardo-Cooper, Delgado-Romero & Zapata, 2014), this group is more prone to experience depression, anxiety, substance abuse, post-traumatic stress, and decreased self-efficacy due to these aforementioned barriers. Additionally, undocumented immigrants typically underuse health services, including counseling services, due to lack of health insurance, systemic injustice, fear of deportation, cultural stigma, and uncertainty surrounding confidentiality practices (Kantamneni et al., 2016). The impact of marginalization and negative stereotyping coupled with the underuse of health as well as mental health resources can lead to negative health outcomes.

Research suggests that social and economic immigration policies influence health-seeking behaviors as well as various facets of physical and psychological well-being. Local, state, and federal-level policies create broader systems which undeniably mold the conditions of day-to-day life. Vargas, Sanchez, and Juárez (2017), for instance, investigated how anti-immigrant policies influence the physical health outcomes of Latinxs in the US. The researchers examined two data sets: the sum anti-immigrant policies by state from 2005 to 2011 and a 2011 Robert Wood Johnson Center for Health Policy nationally representative sample of Latinxs (n = 51,200.) The findings show that anti-immigrant laws implemented by states reduce the likelihood of respondents' describing ideal health. Notably, this trend occurred even when controlling for other variables including the language of interview, interethnic variation, and citizenship status. While punitive social and economic policies further marginalize immigrant communities, particularly Latinx immigrants, the study also provides evidence that anti-immigrant policies at the state level are detrimental to the health status of the broader Latinx population.

Similarly, there are adverse health outcomes for Latinx US citizen children as a result of punitive immigration policies. A study conducted by Vargas and Benitez (2019) used the 2015 Latino National Health and Immigration Survey (n = 584) to assess how Latinx parent's association to immigrants is connected to their child's risk of being referred or diagnosed with a developmental disorder. The results demonstrate that participants who were personally familiar with another person who had been detained or deported are 2.4 times more likely to report that their child has been referred or diagnosed with a developmental disorder. Further, the results indicate that knowing more deportees, if the deportee was a familial member, and if the deportee was a family member as well as primary wage earner, positively influenced the likelihood of a referral or diagnosis of a developmental disorder in their child. Ultimately, this study provides support that deportations are damaging for Latinx children's (many of whom are US citizens by birth) developmental health.

In response to the growing awareness of the impact of oppression, there has been a push in the mental health field for therapists to incorporate sociopolitical commitments to justice across race, ethnicity, citizenship status, gender, class, and nationality in their psychotherapeutic work. For instance, when working with Latinx clients, it necessary to acknowledge intersectionality and complexity within Latinx populations (Delgado-Romero, Singh, De Los Santos, 2018). The Latinx population is an amalgam of more than 20 distinct countries all of which represent unique histories, traditions, and political practices, as well as distinctive histories with the U.S (Mohamed, 2017). To adequately address the mental health needs of Latinx clients, therapists must develop a base of knowledge across the cultural groups within the Latinx community.

In 2017, the American Psychological Association released a revised version of multicultural guidance for practice, *The Multicultural Guidelines: An Ecological Approach to Context, Identity, and Intersectionality*, which discusses diversity and multicultural practice within an intersectional framework. Using a layered ecological model, APA provides 10 key guidelines which are designed to assist clinicians in understanding the parameters of culturally-competent services. APA encourages psychologists, through these guidelines, to consider client social locations within the context of domestic and international realities and human rights. Since it is not the job of clients to inform and teach mental health providers, it is also imperative for psychologists to understand and challenge their own citizenship privilege and become agents of change. To interrupt therapist privilege, psychologists will need to stay educated about the unique barriers encountered by the immigrant community, particularly for those individuals with undocumented status, and monitor potential blind spots through introspection, supervision, and training, as well as by being cognizant of the circumstances in which they maintain (knowingly or not) the status quo. For instance, only individuals with documentation or citizenship privilege have the ability to travel internationally without the fear that they will not be admitted back into the country. In a similar vein, since the enactment of the Personal Responsibility and Work Opportunity Reconciliation Act by President Bill Clinton in 1996, undocumented immigrants and non-citizens have been barred access to federal public benefits such as healthcare services, food assistance, public housing and unemployment insurance. Undocumented immigrants who have a paycheck do not see any financial benefits for paying into Social Security and Medicare, while citizens know that these taxes will ultimately benefit them or their dependents. Another way to challenge internalized biases is by pursuing narratives that counter the hegemonic immigrant discourse and center voices of the undocumented communities. Clinicians, for instance, can broaden their awareness by accessing a diversity of sources such as local media, books, podcasts, and social media advocacy pages, which can present a more accurate and nuanced picture.

The *Ethical Guidelines of the National Latinx Psychological Association* (2018) provide Latinx-grounded advice to psychologists in their professional endeavors in psychotherapy, advocacy, assessment, research and consultation. NLPA is an independent, non-profit professional association that promotes the training, practice, and organizational change necessary to improve the physical and psychological health of Latinx communities. A core foundation to providing culturally competent services when working with Latinxs clients, as outlined in the ethical guidelines, is the recognition that the dominant power structure in society, and in psychology, perpetrates an environment in which a Latinx communities are frequently misdiagnosed and pathologized (NLPA, 2018). Because psychologists are culturally embedded, they are inevitably susceptible to prejudices and blind spots. The guidelines also highlight how traditional Eurocentric views are infused in mainstream psychology, which have contributed to culturally bound perspectives on worldviews, developments, as well as evidenced-based practice. Due to this bias, the guidelines outline an epistemological approach for psychologists to broaden their awareness of Latinx beliefs, world views, and practices. These approaches include a knowledge of cultural values, structural inequalities, language diversity, and beliefs in collective consciousness. Similarly, Arrendondo, Gallardo-Cooper, Delgado-Romero, and Zapata (2014), offer a number of counseling competencies for clinicians which include, but are not limited to, familiarizing themselves with legislation that may affect clients, understanding the impact of colorism and racism in interpersonal interactions, increasing awareness of personal biases and prejudices, attending to potential internal and external stressors for clients, and not buying into the myths surrounding Latinx communities.

The existing literature underscores the importance of considering the ways to intentionally confront the status quo in mental health settings and navigate conversations about connections between anti-immigrant stances, racist nativism, classism, and sexism. Counseling psychologists are unified by a core value in psychological research, training, and supervision that explores broad social environments as well as the ways in which cultural structures enhance and impede optimal development (Delgado-Romero, Lau, & Shulman, 2012). Therefore, it is important for psychologists to consider, practice, research, and train future psychologists on how macro-level factors such as media impact on the emotional health of immigrants, their families, and broader communities. Theoretical models, assessment strategies, and interventions that explore inequitable social conditions can serve as tools for psychologists to increase awareness of cultural similarities and differences, as well as improve intercultural responsiveness and humility.

Overall, psychologists' capacity to address and advocate against vestiges of power, xenophobia, and racist nativism are important in responding to the emotional health needs of clients. Thus, psychotherapists' sociopolitical commitments to justice across race, ethnicity, gender, and nationality differences are integral to their practice. In order to alleviate stress caused by inequitable systems, mental health providers and educators must work collaboratively, considering the social psychological factors underlying media influence, and engage in consciousness-raising efforts by confronting xenophobia, power, racist nativism, and patriarchy in the media as well as the culture at large.

REFERENCES

American Psychological Association. (2017). *Multicultural guidelines: An ecological approach to context, identity, and intersectionality*. Retrieved from: http://www.apa.org/about/policy/multicultural-guidelines.pdf.

American Psychological Association, Presidential Task Force on Immigration. (2012). *Crossroads: The psychology of immigration in the new century*. Retrieved from http://www.apa.org/topics/immigration/report.aspx.

American Psychological Association. (2018). *Demographics of the U.S. psychology workforce: Findings from the 2007-16 American Community Survey*. Washington, DC: Author.

Aronson, E. (2012). *The social animal.* New York City, NY: Worth Publishers.

Arredondo, P., Gallardo-Cooper, M., Delgado-Romero, E. & Zapata, A. (2014). *Culturally responsive counseling with latinas/os*. Alexandria, VA: American Counseling Association.

Brewer, M. B. (1979). In-group bias in the minimal intergroup situation: A cognitive motivational analysis. *Psychological Bulletin*, *86*(2), 307-324. http://dx.doi.org/10.1037/0033-2909.86.2.307.

Chavez, M., Whiteford, S. & Hoewe, J. (2010). Reporting on immigration: Content analysis of major U.S. newspapers' coverage of Mexican immigration. *Norteamérica*, *5*(2), 111-125. doi: 10.22201/cisan.24487228e.2010.02.4.

Chomsky, A. (2014). *How immigration became illegal.* Boston, Massachusetts: Beacon Press books.

Comas-Díaz, L. (2000). An ethnopolitical approach to working with people of color. *American Psychologist*, *55*, 1319-1325.

Comas-Díaz, L. (2001). Hispanics, Latinxs, or Americanos: The evolution of identity. *Cultural Diversity and Ethnic Minority Psychology*, *7*(2), 115-120, doi: 10.1037//1099-9809.7.2.115.

Cornell, S. & Hartmann, D. (2007). *Ethnicity and race: Making identities in a changing world*. Thousand Oaks, CA, USA: Pine Forge Press.

Craig, M. A. & Richeson, J. A. (2014). On the precipice of a "majority-minority" America: Perceived status threat from the racial demographic shift affects White

Americans' political ideology. *Psychological Science*, *25*, 1189–1197. doi: 10.1177/0956797614527113.

Delgado-Romero, E. A., Galván, N., Hunter, M. R. & Torres, V. (2008). Latino/Latina Americans. In G. McAuliffe (Ed.), *Culturally alert counseling: A comprehensive introduction*, (pp. 323-352). Thousand Oaks, CA: Sage.

Delgado-Romero, E. A., Lau, M. Y. & Shulman, S. L. (2012). The Society of Counseling Psychology: Historical values, themes, and patterns viewed from the American Psychological Association presidential podium. In N. A. Fouad, J. A. Carter, L. M. Subich (Eds.), *APA handbook of counseling psychology*, *Vol. 1: Theories*, *research*, *and methods*, (pp. 3-29). Washington, DC, US: American Psychological Association. doi:10.1037/13754-001.

Delgado-Romero, E. A., Rojas-Vilches, A. & Shelton, K. L. (2008). Immigration history and therapy considerations with Hispanics from Cuba, Central and South America. In C. Negy (Ed.), *Cross-cultural psychotherapy: Toward a critical understanding of diverse clients (2nd ed.)*, (pp. 133-160). Reno, NV: Bent Tree Press.

Delgado-Romero, E. A., Singh, A. A. & De Los Santos, J. (2018). Cuéntame: The promise of qualitative research with Latinx populations. *Journal of Latina/Latino Psychology*, *6*, 318-328. 10.1037/lat0000123.

Diaz, P., Saenz, D. & Kwan, V. (2011). Economic dynamics and changes in attitudes toward undocumented Mexican immigrants in Arizona. *Analyses of Social Issues and Public Policy*, *11*, 300-313, doi: 10.1111/j.1530-2415.2011.01255.x.

Esses, V., Medianu, S. & Lawson, A. (2013). Uncertainty, threat, and the role of the media in promoting the dehumanization of immigrants and refugees. *Journal of Social Issues*, *69*, 518-536.

Feagin, J. R. (2010). The white racial frame: Centuries of racial framing and counter framing. New York, NY: Routledge.

Grimm, J. (2015). Tenacity of routine: The absence of geo-ethnic storytelling in constructing immigration news coverage. *Howard Journal of Communications*, *26*, 1, 120, doi: 10.1080/10646175.2014.971983.

Hilfinger Messias, D., Morris McEwen, M. & Boyle, J. (2014). Undocumented migration in the United States: An overview of historical and current policy contexts. *Nursing Outlook*, *63*(1), 60-67. http://dx.doi.org/10.1016/j.outlook.2014.10.006.

Hipolito-Delgado, C. P. & Mann, J. (2012). Illuminating the Shadows: Sociopolitical and counseling needs of undocumented Mexican immigrants. *Interamerican Journal of Psychology*, *46*(3), 395-402.

Hird, J., Reese, M. & Shilvock, M. (2004). *Controversies in American public policy*, New York: Wadsworth Publishing Company.

Hutchings, V. L. (2009). Change or more of the same? Evaluating racial attitudes in the Obama era. *Public Opinion Quarterly*, *73*, 917–942.

Kim, S. h., Carvalho, J. P., Davis, A. G. & Mullins, A. M. (2011). The view of the border: News framing of the definition, causes, and solutions to illegal immigration. *Mass Communication & Society*, *14*(3), 292-314 http://dx.doi.org/10.1080/15205431003743679.

Kim, E. & Diaz, J. *Immigrant students and higher education: ASHE higher education.* Hoboken, NJ: Wiley. doi: 10.1002/aehe.20006.

Kantamneni, N., Dharmalingam, K., Tate, J., Perlman, B., Majmudar, C. & Shada, N. (2016). Dreaming big: Understanding the current context of academic and career decision-making for undocumented students. *Journal of Career Development*, *43*, 483-497, doi: 10.1177/0894845316633527.

Kinefuchi, E. & Cruz, G. (2015). The Mexicans in the news: Representation of Mexican immigrants in the Internet news media. *The Howard Journal of Communications*, *26*(4), 333-351. doi:10.1080/10646175.2015.1049759.

McKeever, B. W., Riffe, D. & Carpentier, F. D. (2012). *Southern Communication Journal*, *77*, 420-437.

Mohamed, H. (2017). *The new Americans?: Immigration, protest, and politics of Latino identity.* Lawrence, Kansas: University Press of Kansas.

National Latinx Psychological Association. (2018). NLPA ethical guidelines. Retrieved from https://www.nlpa.ws/assets/docs/ ethical%20guidelines%20nlpa_ adopted%20jan%201st.pdf.

National Conference of State Legislatures (2018). *2017 immigration report.* Retrieved from http://www.ncsl.org/research/immigration/2017-immigration-report.aspx.

National Conference of State Legislatures (2019) *Report on state immigration laws 2018.* Retrieved from http://www.ncsl.org/research/immigration/report-on-state-immigration-laws.aspx.

Nowicki, D. (2015). Immigration at front of 2016 presidential race. *USA Today.* Retrieved from http:www.usatoday.com/story/news/politics/elections/2015/05/15/immigration-2016-presidential-race/27360717/.

Pew Hispanic Center (2006). *Modes of entry for the unauthorized migrant population.* Retrieved from http://www.pewhispanic.org/2006/05/22/modes-of-entry-for-the unauthorized-migrant-population/.

Pew Hispanic Center. (2014). *U.S. deportations of immigrants reach record high in 2013.* Retrieved from http://www.pewresearch.org/fact-tank/2014/10/02/u-s-deportations-of immigrants-reach-record-high-in-2013/.

Pew Hispanic Center. (2016). *Americans' views of immigration marked by widening partisan, generational divides.* Retrieved from http://www.pewresearch.org/ facttank/ 2016/04/15/americans-views-of-immigrants-marked-by-widening-partisan generational-divides/.

Phillips, A. (2017). The Washington Post. Retrieved from: https://www.washingtonpost.com/news/the-fix/wp/2017/06/16/theyre-rapists-presidentstrump-campaign-launch-speech-two-years-later-annotated/ ?utm_term=.141f9737b528.

President Donald J. Trump's State of the Union Address. (n.d.). Retrieved from https://www.whitehouse.gov/briefings-statements/president-donald-j-trumps-state-unionaddress/.

Rosas, G. (2015). The border thickens: In-securing communities after IRCA. *International Migration*, *54*, 119-130, doi: 10:1111/imig/12198.

Santa Ana, O. (2013). *Juan in a hundred: The representation of Latinos on network news*. University of Texas Press.

Tukachinsky, R., Mastro, D. & King, A. (2011). Is a picture worth a thousand words? The effect of race-related visual and verbal exemplars on attitudes and support for social policies. *Mass Communication and Society*, *14*, 720–742, doi 10.1080/15205436.2010.530385.

Tajfel, H. & Turner, J. C. (1986). The social identity theory of intergroup behavior. In: Worchel, S. and Austin, W. G., Eds., *Psychology of Intergroup Relation*, Hall Publishers, Chicago, 7-24.

Valentino, N. A., Brader, T. & Jardina, A. E. (2012). Immigration opposition among Whites: General ethnocentrism or media priming of attitudes about latinos?. *Political Psychology*, *34*, 149-166, doi: 10.1111/j.1467-9221.2012.00928.

van Dijk, T. A. (1993). *Sage series on race and ethnic relations*, *Vol. 6. Elite discourse andracism.* Thousand Oaks, CA, US: Sage Publications, Inc. http://dx.doi.org/10.4135/9781483326184.

Vargas, E. D. & Benitez, V. L. (2019). Latino parents' links to deportees are associated with developmental disorders in their children. *Journal of Community Psychology*, 1-18, doi: 10.1002/jcop.22178.

Vargas, E. D., Sanchez, G. R. & Juárez, M. (2017). Fear by association: Perceptions of anti-immigrant policy and health outcomes. *Journal of Health Politics Policy and Law*, 45, 312-337. Retrieved at http://jhppl.dukejournals.org/content/early/2017/02/17/03616878 3802940.abstract.

In: Social Psychology and Counseling
Editors: D. A. Kleiber and E. Delgado-Romero ISBN: 978-1-53616-548-7

Chapter 6

PRINCIPLES OF SOCIAL COGNITION AND COGNITIVE BEHAVIOR THERAPY

Benjamin J. Edner and Clair Cassiello-Robbins

The foundation of social cognition lies in examining the role of cognitive processes in how people process, store, interpret, and use information about socially relevant events and situations (Aronson, 2012; Fiske & Taylor, 2013). Humans contain a myriad of biases, adaptive strategies, and cognitive shortcuts to help navigate the social spheres in which they are embedded. While social cognitive processes are typically adaptive because they facilitate social interaction and support, they can also become ineffective and lead to the development and maintenance of many forms of psychopathology.

Throughout the next sections, social cognitive processes will be described along with how errors in these processes might present in anxiety and depressive disorders, the most common forms of psychopathology (Kessler, Chiu, Demler, & Waleters, 2005). Finally, this chapter will discuss how such psychopathologies develop within a cognitive-behavioral framework and how Cognitive Behavioral Therapy (CBT) can be effectively employed in such situations.

THE SELF AND OTHER

Social cognition first requires the process of perceiving and encoding complex sensory information in the environment, which allows for the extraction, analysis, and synthesis of social context. During this process, individuals naturally appraise the intentions of others to procure the fulfillment of social needs, resources, and survival

(Beck & Haigh, 2014; Klumpp, Fitzgerald, & Phan, 2013; Schaafsma, Pfaff, Spunt, & Adolphs, 2015; Waytz, & Mitchell, 2011). This process necessitates the ability to successfully evaluate or infer the representational mental state, intentions, and/or motivations of others (Schaafsma et al., 2015; Waytz & Mitchell, 2011).

To evaluate the representative mental state of others, *behavioral simulation* is used to approximate intent and predict others' behaviors (Waytz & Mitchell, 2011). Behavioral simulation is made up of mirroring and self-projection. The process of mirroring involves vicariously experiencing the perceived mental state of another person. Self-projection on the other hand involves mentally projecting oneself to the scenario wherein the other person is responding, allowing the observing individual to approximate the thoughts and emotions of the person being observed. This process occurs however, under the assumption that the other individual would perceive and respond in the same fashion as the observer. Nevertheless, the perceptible cues of another individual's experiences induce neural responses that help approximate the mental state of the individual being observed (Schaafsma et al., 2015; Waytz & Mitchell, 2011).

These neural responses implicate several specific brain regions that facilitate the processes of mirroring and self-projection (Waytz & Mitchell, 2011). For example, Waytz and Mitchell's (2011) review of the literature highlight activation of the parieto-frontal circuit, anterior cingulate cortex, temporo-parietal junction, and paralimbic and amygdalar regions of individuals in response to observing others whose behavior(s) activate these same regions. Some of the cognitive processes corresponding to these brain regions include, but are not limited to, disgust, fear, goal-directed orientation, reward-learning, and subjective pain (Mobbs et al., 2009; Singer et al., 2004; Waytz & Mitchell, 2011; Whalen et al., 2001; Wicker et al., 2003). Broadly speaking, the syncopated activation of these brain regions between individuals during social interactions highlights the neurobiological foundations of social connection and formation of social bonds. Taken together, development within the social world is predicated on ability to 1) encode and integrate information from others and the environment (Beck & Haigh, 2014; Pinker, 1997), 2) learn and adopt sets of behaviors from others through observation and systems of reinforcement (Bandura, 1986; Prochaska & Norcross, 2014), and 3) experience the subjective psychological states of others (Waytz & Mitchell, 2011). Thus, individuals are inextricably linked to, and defined by, social groups and inevitable engagement with social infrastructure (Aronson, 2012; Bussey & Bandura, 1999). One of the primary cognitive mechanisms that facilitate how individuals learn and thrive within the social environment is pattern recognition.

PATTERN RECOGNITION AND JUDGMENT HEURISTICS

"The idea of cause and effect is deriv'd (sic) from experience, which presenting us with certain objects constantly conjoin'd (sic) with each other, produces such a habit of surveying them in that relation, that we cannot without a sensible violence survey them in any other" (Hume, 1738/2000, p. 86). The quote by the 18th century British philosopher David Hume addresses the innate human ability to recognize patterns and infer causal relationships in the external world. This observation, in many ways, forms the bedrock for philosophical principles underpinning social cognition and cognitive neuroscience (Swearer, Wang, Berry, & Myers, 2014).

Within the scope of social cognition and neuroscience, the previous sections broadly discuss the development of social- and self-concept formation through engagement with the external world as well as mechanisms corresponding to the mental state representations of both self and others. Both of these areas require pattern recognition and association between cause and effect. Such association is needed to 1) stimulate and optimize neural network connections that allow for navigation of the physical world (Hartley & Lee, 2015; Hostinar, Sullivan, & Gunnar, 2014) and 2) allow one to predict and anticipate the response of others through simulation/mental representation of their experiences (Waytz & Mitchell, 2011). These causal inferences occur in order to anticipate/predict the future behavior of self and others to avoid aversive stimuli and/or obtain reward (Cusi et al., 2012). To make sense of all the perceptual data competing for attention at any given moment, shortcuts are developed that allow for quick judgments based on previous interactions within one's social spheres. These shortcuts, rules, or strategies used to approximate answers when solving problems or making predictions are referred to as *judgment heuristics* (Tversky & Kahneman, 1974).

Humans are programmed to conserve cognitive energy by adopting shortcuts that simplify complex problems by extracting pertinent information and ignoring irrelevant information (Aronson, 2012; Fiske & Taylor, 1991). Fiske and Taylor (1991) refer to this phenomenon as operating as a "cognitive miser." Neural circuitry is organized and optimized to infer relations between perceptual representations and then assign these representations to categories (Harnad, 2005). This process is done is several ways. One way heuristics are created is by focusing on the similarity of objects, allowing inference that one object operates like the second object, a phenomenon known as *representative heuristics* (Kahneman & Tversky, 1973). For instance, imagine you are driving through an unfamiliar area. For some reason, instead of traffic lights there are machines on the side of the road that pop out different colored signs like a toaster. How would you know when to stop or go? The first thing that probably comes to mind is green equals go, red equals stop, and yellow equals slow down. Why is this the first thing that comes to mind? This is an example of a representative heuristic. The colors of traffic lights are so ubiquitous, and people's interactions with them so frequent, that these colors have come to be reflexively associated with particular concepts.

A similar pattern can be observed in how much an individual is exposed to different objects or situations. As an exercise, take a minute to think about or write down the names of as many animals as you can in 10 seconds. What were the first couple of animals that came to mind? Cat? Dog? If these were in your top 5, then you are using *availability heuristics*. This heuristic can be described as the ease at which one can retrieve associations that influence behavior (Aronson, 2012). Due to limited capacity for processing information, heuristics serve as an essential filtering mechanism necessary for adaptive survival; cognitive misers preserve mental energy in all ways possible.

While judgment heuristics optimize survival, research has demonstrated inaccurate heuristics can also generate and perpetuate *cognitive distortions* that can lead to symptoms of depression and anxiety. For example, patients with anxiety disorders consistently overestimate subjective personal risk (Butler & Mathews, 1983). These estimations may increase their likelihood to engage in avoidance of feared stimuli, which in turn reinforces the original anxious beliefs (e.g., "I must have avoided X because it is dangerous").

On a larger scale, these observations can be generalized, in which case the attributions may become *stereotypes*. Stereotyping occurs when assumptions, predictions, or attributions extend from the generalizing of ideas or observations that are reinforced by the environment or through greater cultural transmission (Aronson, 2012). While there are well known stereotypes transmitted through previous generations, people tend to assign stereotypes – more accurately negative stereotypes – to people perceived to fall outside of their social group or milieu. Such groups can function as one's political party, religious affiliation, SES, or a diehard fan of the Los Angeles Chargers silently muttering, "that's about what I would expect from a typical Raiders fan." This division of the world into differing realities facilitates a tendency to view members of other groups (outgroups) as more similar to each other than to members of the in-group; this is referred to as the *homogeneity effect* and impacts the attributions individuals make about others (Aronson, 2012). Unsurprisingly, how one attributes positive and negative characteristics to others is strongly predicted by perceived membership or adherence to values upheld by certain groups; for example, political party, SES, religious affiliation, etc. (Haidt, 2012). These mechanisms can be statistically predicted by reported and unreported prejudices, further highlighting how social experiences define us, define others, and shape the rules, values, and prejudices that govern the social world (Bussey & Bandura, 1999; Fiske & Taylor, 2013). Next, authors discuss how this process manifests in the individual.

Beginning in infancy, individuals categorize perceptual stimuli within their environment based on similarity and function, respectively (Mandler, 2000). The process of categorization is interwoven with the development of early schemas; this in turn provides reference points for how individuals assign meaning to, and predict the outcome of interactions with, the future, objects, ideas, other individual agents, and/or groups with whom they socially interact. Put another way, the implicit predictions people make about the consequences of their behaviors or the behaviors of others are based upon preexisting expectations that guide interpretation of social information (Fiske & Taylor, 2013). For example, being taught relative inferiority or superiority – or simply difference – exists between certain groups based on race, ethnicity, religion and/or social class. This provides reference for how individuals interpret, categorize, and integrate such new information. Part of the way people maintain consistency with what they experience/interact with in their environment and the schemas upon which perceptual semantic categorization is organized, is to naturally make attributions to help make sense of what and why something happened as it did.

Humans demonstrate the proclivity to attribute the result of events to the dispositional characteristics of individuals rather than the role of situational factors (Fiske & Taylor, 2013). This phenomenon is known as the *fundamental attribution error.* Research indicates the neural regions activated when inferring the mental states of others strongly predict whether another person's behavior is attributed to situational factors or the individual's dispositional characteristics (Moran, Jolly, & Mitchell, 2014). This relationship illustrates people's hard-wired neural mechanisms for assigning types of attributions to perceived events. Again, these cognitive errors are commonly observed in psychopathology, especially when patients misattribute an unwanted outcome to their disposition as opposed to the situation (e.g., assuming a friend who has declined an invitation is fundamentally unfriendly, rather than recognizing the friend has competing demands and is too busy). Another example might be overgeneralizing the characteristics of a perpetrator, as is sometimes seen in posttraumatic stress disorder (PTSD). For example, a patient assaulted by a man with brown hair might develop a belief that men with brown hair are dangerous. While this belief is understandable given the traumatic experience, it ignores other dispositional characteristics and circumstances of the man who committed the assault.

Humans also have tendencies to attribute their own successes to their own capacities and their failures to situational factors – a concept known as *self-serving bias* (Aronson, 2012). However, research suggests patients with depression and low self-esteem show a reversal of this pattern (Tennen & Herzberger, 1987), as do patients with social anxiety disorder (SAD) (Arkin, Appelman, & Burger, 1980); in other words, they assume responsibility for failure and attribute success to good luck and circumstantial factors. It is important to note that the degree to which this reversal is related to psychopathology is by and large culturally dependent (Markus & Kitayama, 1991). The example above is rooted in the independent self-construal typical of Western culture; this is discrepant with more Eastern cultures that base their self-construal within an interdependence framework (Markus & Kitayama, 1991). This difference highlights the impact of cultural transmission on social cognitive processes and has important implications for evidence-based treatment, best practices, and the necessity for ensuring multicultural competence in the provision of treatment services.

The previously described cognitive errors are likely further reinforced by a phenomenon known as the *confirmation bias* – the tendency to seek out information that confirms or supports preexisting beliefs and/or cognitive distortions. For instance, the patient in the previous example expresses an unhelpful interpretation of why a friend declined her invitation. Let's assume that the same friend had come over several times in the past month, each time indicating she had fun and was grateful for the social opportunity. Despite data suggesting that the patient's friend enjoys her company, this instance is highlighted to confirm the patient's belief that she is unappealing as a friend.

Etiological models of psychopathology often acknowledge the role of the described social cognitive processes in the development of psychological disorders. For example, the triple-vulnerability model of etiology for emotional (e.g., anxiety, mood, and related) disorders describes an interacting set of vulnerabilities for developing one of these conditions: a generalized biological vulnerability (i.e., genetic), a generalized psychological vulnerability (i.e., early life experiences that lead to a diminished sense of control over one's emotions), and specific psychological vulnerabilities (i.e., factors contributing to the development of a specific disorder; these are often thought to be related to early learning experiences as well; Barlow, 2000; Suarez, Bennet, Goldstein, & Barlow, 2009). The latter two vulnerabilities highlight the importance of early learning, much of which occurs in a social context (i.e., observing parents and peers). For example, a child who observes his parents avoiding situations in which they feel uncomfortable may do the same. Further, from observing how others manage their emotions, an individual may develop the perception that some emotions are intolerable or unacceptable, leading them to engage in efforts to *avoid* experiencing these emotions. A substantial literature highlights the prominent role of avoidance in the development and maintenance of psychopathology (e.g., Hayes, Wilson, Gifford, Follette, & Strosahl, 1996; Sauer-Zavala & Barlow, 2014) and the triple vulnerability model may provide some insight as to how a social context can contribute to the development of avoidance-based emotion regulation strategies.

Beliefs, Thoughts, and Treatment

As discussed previously, the process of encoding, interpreting, and integrating early perceptual and sensory experiences within established social and culture contexts coalesce to form the schemas that underlie how people understand their world and their place within that world. Such understandings subsume the rules, assumptions, fears, and expectancies that inform self-concept. These understandings manifest as *core beliefs*.

Core beliefs stem from the schemas that are cultivated through adapted behavioral responses that allow one to thrive in their environment at an early age (Beck & Haigh, 2014). Examples of adaptive core beliefs include, "I'm capable," "I'm worthy," "I'm a strong person," etc. These ideas are the integration of social information through the mechanisms of social cognition as previously discussed. The development of maladaptive core beliefs may be viewed as a distortion of the normative development of the social cognitive processes that facilitate adaptive self-representation. Examples of maladaptive core beliefs include, "I'm incompetent," "I'm unworthy," "I'm a weak person," etc. Through the framework of CBT, core beliefs manifest in various ways. More specifically, core beliefs are exercised through *automatic thoughts* and *intermediate beliefs* (Beck, 2011).

Automatic thoughts can be understood as thoughts that occur reflexively in response to stimuli. By their nature, automatic thoughts serve an adaptive purpose. For example, if you're walking through the woods and you see a poisonous snake slithering your way, you'll likely have the automatic thought "time to get out of here!" This process is instinctual and rooted in human neurology, reflected in such autonomic responses as hair standing up on the back of the neck. The immediacy of the automatic thought in this example is necessary in order to react quickly and move towards safety. However, imagine you've been standing in line for 40 minutes waiting for tickets to see your favorite sports team play. Now imagine that right as you get up to the window to buy your tickets, the cashier says, "We just sold out." If your automatic thought is "It's just my luck that they sold out; I'm such a loser!" chances are that unhelpful beliefs are driving how you are seeing the world.

The automatic thought "It's my typical bad luck" is drawing causal inference from the proximity to two events occurring successively in time and space. However, if thought about only momentarily, one can easily see the flaw in drawing these causal relations. The question then becomes, out of all the possible conclusions drawn from this event, why was such an improbable one reached automatically? It is likely because this automatic thought is congruent with an existing assumption or intermediate belief.

Intermediate beliefs are the underlying sets of assumptions, rules, or guidelines that impact how information about the social world is processed and synthesized. In the example, the intermediate belief of the person not able to buy tickets is "I do not deserve things that make me happy." If this is the person's underlying assumption, guideline, or rule of thumb, then the automatic thought (or cognitive distortion) of "I'm such a loser" doesn't seem as outlandish. So where does this intermediate belief and its corresponding set of automatic thoughts originate? This is where core beliefs come into play. Core beliefs are the architects that construct and organize the rules, guidelines, and assumptions that dictate how social information is processed as well as how individuals navigate their worlds. In this case, the core belief "I'm worthless" is driving how this individual is engaging with the world, resulting in the aforementioned cognitive distortion.

Cognitive distortions have two features in common: 1) they operate to reinforce an understanding of the world that, at one point, was needed for survival (Beck & Haigh, 2014); and 2) they serve as heuristics that reduce cognitive load by activating default or automatic cognitive processes (Beck, 2011). Thus, such cognitive distortions are the manifestations of common automatic and social cognitive processes that – by way of experience, maladaptive predispositions, and/or a combination of some kind – no longer serve to be advantageous and, in fact, incur deleterious social consequences (Beck & Haigh, 2014).

Cognitive Behavior Therapy

Cognitive behavioral therapy (CBT) is the most researched form of psychotherapy to date (David, Cristea, & Hofmann, 2018) and has been shown to be effective in managing the previously-discussed social cognitive processes as well as beliefs at all levels (i.e., automatic, intermediate, core) if they are unhelpful to the patient (Beck, 2011; Craske, 2010). This therapy is predicated on the idea that human experiences consist of an interplay between one's thoughts, emotions, and behaviors. Further, CBT theorists recognize how interactions among these components influence one another (Beck & Haigh, 2014). That is, thoughts can affect emotions, which in turn impact behavior and vice versa. For example, thinking "No one likes me" might lead to feelings of sadness that cause an individual to withdraw from their friends. CBT targets this process by teaching strategies designed to remediate ineffective emotion regulation strategies that perpetuate symptoms of psychopathology.

Skills taught include those designed to facilitate accurate cognitive appraisal of situations (i.e., beliefs). Exploration of the automatic thoughts in relation to particular events can help one identify the cognitive distortions that activate the self-concept and elicits the affective responses (Beck, 2011; Golden et al., 2013). By recognizing automatic thoughts and drawing awareness to the intermediate beliefs that trigger them, patients can work to challenge and restructure these beliefs. Thus, CBT treatments endeavor to help patients develop more helpful and realistic beliefs about themselves, others, and the world. Consistent treatment using CBT techniques has been shown to help patients restructure their beliefs, which in turn is associated with symptom reduction in patients with SAD, depression, and obsessive compulsive disorder (OCD) (e.g., Adler, Strunk, & Fazio, 2015; Gregory, Wong, Marker, & Peters, 2018; Jonsson, Hougaard, & Bennedsen, 2011; Koerner, Antony, Young, & McCabe, 2013) as well as other skills focused on decreasing behavioral avoidance of feared stimuli. Taken together, these skills are used to target many forms of psychopathology as they facilitate behavior in line with patients' long-term goals. For example, patients with anxiety disorders are taught to engage in situations they might typically avoid, patients with depression are encouraged to challenge negative beliefs about themselves, and patients with psychotic disorders learn to challenge the reality of their hallucinations and delusions before accepting them as fact.

The efficacy of CBT has been rigorously examined with differing populations across treatment settings, and CBT has been consistently shown to be an effective form of treatment (Craske, 2010; Epp, & Dobson, 2010; Watts, Turnell, Kladnitski, Newby, & Andrews, 2015). After well over 200 meta-analytical studies (Hofmann et al., 2012), CBT has been empirically shown to be an effective treatment for adult patients with unipolar depression, generalized anxiety disorder (GAD), panic disorder (PD) with or without agoraphobia, SAD, OCD, PTSD, specific phobias, marital distress, anger, psychosis, insomnia, and chronic pain (Butler, Chapman, Forman, & Beck, 2006; Okajima, Komada, & Inoue, 2011; Ruhmland & Margraf, 2001). Further, research suggests CBT is more effective than a placebo in treating GAD, PD, PTSD, OCD, and SAD (Carpenter et al., 2018) and is also superior to 'treatment-as-usual' (i.e., the treatment typically provided in a given setting) for anxiety and depressive disorders (Watts et al., 2015) – some of which are associated with the misattribution problems referred to earlier, such as the fundamental attribution error, self-serving bias, and its antithesis (Craske, 2010). A well-discussed advantage of CBT is its theoretical and empirical grounding with other social and biological sciences (Goldin et al., 2014; Ingram & Siegle, 2010; Klumpp, Fitzgerald, & Phan, 2013).

Recent developments in the understanding of psychopathology have brought about changes in CBT. Notably, research has begun to highlight the commonalities across psychological disorders. Indeed, the social cognitive processes discussed in this chapter appear to transcend diagnostic boundaries. For example, unhelpful automatic thoughts and core beliefs are observed across anxiety, depressive, and related (i.e., emotional) disorders. Given the shared psychopathological processes observed across diagnoses, transdiagnostic treatments targeting the core mechanisms believed to underlie various disorders have been developed. One such treatment is the Unified Protocol for Transdiagnostic Treatment of Emotional Disorders (UP; Barlow et al., 2018). This treatment purports to intervene on aversive, avoidant reactions to the experience of strong emotions. Using traditional CBT skills, the UP aims to facilitate a willing and accepting attitude toward the experience of strong emotions by teaching patients skills to modify faulty emotion regulation strategies. For example, cognitive restructuring, termed cognitive flexibility in the UP, teaches patients to observe, challenge, and restructure their beliefs about emotions as well as about themselves, others, and the world. As with more traditional CBTs, transdiagnostic CBTs such as the UP are well poised to intervene on the social cognitive processes discussed earlier in this chapter. Patients with panic disorders, for example, who are told throughout their lives that being anxious is a bad thing might do whatever they can to avoid getting anxious. Their efforts to avoid getting anxious reinforce the idea anxiety is a dangerous or "bad" emotion. Further, their interpretations of anxiety are judgmental; they are likely to fall prey to a fundamental attribution error if they become anxious, blaming themselves for experiencing the emotion rather than noting aspects of the situation that contributed to them feeling anxious. Through treatment with the UP, this patient would be provided with psychoeducation regarding the purpose of anxiety to help address the belief this emotion is "bad."

Treatment, then, would focus on facilitating a non-judgmental and accepting attitude toward the experience of anxiety in order to help patients reduce their efforts to avoid this emotion. Cognitive restructuring could be used to help them consider other interpretations of the emotion (e.g., "It makes sense I feel anxious because I need to prepare for the presentation"). Finally, behavior change skills could help the patient identify effective ways to express anxiety (when appropriate) and cope with the experience of this emotion.

As previously reviewed, CBT has been shown to successfully intervene on a wide variety of psychopathologies. Not only does research support the efficacy of CBT in changing maladaptive emotional regulation strategies, neuroimaging data have revealed CBT impacts areas of the brain implicated in social cognitive processes (Cusi et al., 2012; Goldin et al., 2013; Goldin et al., 2014). CBT has been found to reduce over activity of orbitofrontal cortex, a relation that corresponds to reductions in emotional reasoning automaticity. Research demonstrates use of CBT can alter patterns of fear learning as indicated by alterations of amygdalar and paralimbic functioning (Goldin et al., 2014). Further, CBT has been shown to activate areas of higher-order cognitive processes (e.g., prefrontal cortex, anterior cingulate, superior temporal sulcus, and temporoparietal junction) when engaging in social tasks (Cusi et al., 2012; Goldin et al., 2013; Goldin et al., 2014) – areas implicated in social cognitive processes.

Taken together, the practice of CBT targets automatic thought processes through established neural networks adapted for previous or current environments. By activating and altering these neural traces through identifying distorted heuristics, introducing alternative interpretations, and activating altering behavioral patterns, mental health practitioners may help patients make lasting changes – not just to their behavior and thought patterns, but to their neural circuitry. Although approached as separate areas, the research foci of cognitive neuroscience and social cognition may compliment research seeking to understand the effects of CBT and, more importantly, how traditional and transdiagnostic CBT treatment efficacy may be improved in the future.

REFERENCES

Adler, A. D., Strunk, D. R. & Fazio, R. H. (2015). What changes in cognitive therapy for depression? An examination of cognitive therapy skills and maladaptive beliefs. *Behavior Therapy*, *46*, 96-109.

Arkin, R. M., Appelman, A. J. & Burger, J. M. (1980). Social anxiety, self-presentation, and the self-serving bias in causal attribution. *Journal of Personality and Social Psychology*, *38*, 23-35.

Aronson, E. (2012). Social cognition. In E. Aronson & J. Aronson (Eds.), *The social animal*, 11th Edition, (pp. 117-132). New York, NY: Worth Publishers.

Bandura, A. (1986). *Social foundations of thought and action: A social cognitive theory*. Englewood Cliffs, NJ: Prentice-Hall.

Barlow, D. H. (2000). Unraveling the mysteries of anxiety and its disorders from the perspective of emotion theory. *American Psychologist*, *55*, 1247-1263. doi:10.1037/0003- 066X.55.11.1247.

Barlow, D. H., Farchione, T. J., Sauer-Zavala, S., Latin, H., Ellard, K. K. & Cassiello-Robbins, C. (2018). *Unified Protocol for the Transdiagnostic Treatment of Emotional Disorders: Therapist Guide*, 2nd Edition. New York, NY: Oxford University Press.

Beck, A. T. & Haigh, E. A. (2014). Advances in cognitive theory and therapy: The generic cognitive model. *Annual Review of Clinical Psychology*, *10*, 1-24.

Beck, J. S. (2011). *Cognitive behavior therapy: Basics and beyond*, 2nd Edition. New York, NY: Guilford Press.

Bussey, K. & Bandura, A. (1999). Social cognitive theory of gender development and differentiation. *Psychological Review*, *106*, 676-713.

Butler, A. C., Chapman, J. E., Forman, E. M. & Beck, A. T. (2006). The empirical status of cognitive-behavioral therapy: A review of meta-analyses. *Clinical Psychology Review*, *26*, 17-31.

Butler, G. & Mathews, A. (1983). Cognitive processes in anxiety. *Advances in Behaviour Research and Therapy*, *5*, 51-62.

Carpenter, J. K., Andrews, L. A., Witcraft, S. M., Powers, M. B., Smits, J. A. & Hofmann, S. G. (2018). Cognitive behavioral therapy for anxiety and related disorders: A meta-analysis of randomized placebo-controlled trials. *Depression and Anxiety*, *35*, 502-514.

Craske, M. G. (2010). *Cognitive-behavioral therapy*. Washington, DC: American Psychological Association (APA).

Cusi, A. M., Nazarov, A., Holshausen, K., MacQueen, G. M. & McKinnon, M. C. (2012). Systematic review of the neural basis of social cognition in patients with mood disorders. *Journal of Psychiatry and Neuroscience*, *37*, 154-169.

David, D., Cristea, I. & Hofmann, S. G. (2018). Why cognitive behavioral therapy is the current gold standard of psychotherapy. *Frontiers in Psychiatry*, *9*, 4. doi.org/10.3389/fpsyt.2018.00004.

Epp, A. M. & Dobson, K. S. (2010). Evidence base for cognitive-behavioral therapy. In K. S. Dobson (Eds.), *Handbook of cognitive-behavioral therapies*, 3rd Edition, (pp. 39-73). New York, NY: Guilford Press.

Fiske, S. T. & Taylor, S. E. (2013). *Social cognition: From brains to culture*, 2nd Edition. Los Angeles, CA: Sage Publications.

Fiske, S. T. & Taylor, S. E. (1991). *Social cognition.* New York, NY: McGraw-Hill.

Goldin, P. R., Ziv, M., Jazaieri, H., Hahn, K., Heimberg, R. & Gross, J. J. (2013). Impact of cognitive behavioral therapy for social anxiety disorder on the neural dynamics of cognitive reappraisal of negative self-beliefs: Randomized clinical trial. *Journal of American Medical Association Psychiatry*, *70*, 1048-1056.

Goldin, P. R., Ziv, M., Jazaieri, H., Weeks, J., Heimberg, R. G. & Gross, J. J. (2014). Impact of cognitive-behavioral therapy for social anxiety disorder on the neural bases of emotional reactivity to and regulation of social evaluation. *Behaviour Research and Therapy*, *62*, 97-106.

Gregory, B., Wong, Q. J., Marker, C. D. & Peters, L. (2018). Maladaptive self-beliefs during cognitive behavioural therapy for social anxiety disorder: A test of temporal precedence. *Cognitive Therapy and Research*, *42*, 261-272.

Haidt, J. (2012). *The righteous mind: Why good people are divided by politics and religion.* New York, NY: Pantheon Books.

Harnad, S. (2005). To cognize is to categorize: Cognition is categorization. In H. Cohen & C. Lefebvre (Eds.), *Handbook of categorization in cognitive science*. Elsevier.

Hartley, C. A. & Lee, F. S. (2015). Sensitive periods in affective development: Nonlinear maturation of fear learning. *Neuropsychopharmacology*, *40*, 50-60.

Hayes, S. C., Wilson, K. G., Gifford, E. V., Follette, V. M. & Strosahl, K. (1996). Experiential avoidance and behavioral disorders: A functional dimensional approach to diagnosis and treatment. *Journal of Consulting and Clinical Psychology*, *64*, 1152-1168.

Hofmann, S. G., Asnaani, A., Vonk, I. J. J., Sawyer, A. T. & Fang, A. (2012). The efficacy of cognitive behavioral therapy: A review of meta-analyses. *Cognitive Therapy and Research*, *36*, 427-440. doi:10.1007/s10608-012-9476-1.

Hostinar, C. E., Sullivan, R. M. & Gunnar, M. R. (2014). Psychobiological mechanisms underlying the social buffering of the hypothalamic–pituitary–adrenocortical axis: A review of animal models and human studies across development. *Psychological Bulletin*, *140*, 256-303.

Hume, D. (1738/2000). *A treatise of human nature: Being an attempt to introduce the experimental method of reasoning in moral subjects.* North Chelmsford, MA: Courier Corporation.

Ingram, R. E. & Siegle, G. J. (2010). Cognitive science and the conceptual foundations of cognitive-behavioral therapy: Viva la evolution! In K. S. Dobson (Eds.), *Handbook of cognitive-behavioral therapies*, 3rd Edition, (pp. 74-93). New York, NY: Guilford Press.

Jónsson, H., Hougaard, E. & Bennedsen, B. E. (2011). Dysfunctional beliefs in group and individual cognitive behavioral therapy for obsessive compulsive disorder. *Journal of Anxiety Disorders*, *25*, 483-489.

Kahneman, D. & Tversky, A. (1973). On the psychology of prediction. *Psychological Review*, *80*, 237-251.

Kessler, R. C., Chiu, W. T., Demler, O. & Walters, E. E. (2005). Prevalence, severity, and comorbidity of 12-month DSM-IV disorders in the National Comorbidity Survey Replication. *Archives of General Psychiatry*, *62*, 617-627.

Klumpp, H., Fitzgerald, D. A. & Phan, K. L. (2013). Neural predictors and mechanisms of cognitive behavioral therapy on threat processing in social anxiety disorder. *Progress in Neuro-Psychopharmacology and Biological Psychiatry*, *45*, 83-91.

Koerner, N., Antony, M. M., Young, L. & McCabe, R. E. (2013). Changes in beliefs about the social competence of self and others following group cognitive-behavioral treatment. *Cognitive Therapy and Research*, *37*, 256-265.

Mandler, J. M. (2000). Perceptual and conceptual processes in infancy. *Journal of Cognition and Development*, *1*, 3-36.

Markus, H. R. & Kitayama, S. (1991). Culture and the self: Implications for cognition, emotion, and motivation. *Psychological Review*, *98*, 224-253.

Mobbs, D., Yu, R., Meyer, M., Passamonti, L., Seymour, B., Calder, A. J., et al. (2009). A key role for similarity in vicarious reward. *Science*, *324*, 900. doi:10.1126/science.1170539.

Moran, J. M., Jolly, E. & Mitchell, J. P. (2014). Spontaneous mentalizing predicts the fundamental attribution error. *Journal of Cognitive Neuroscience*, *26*, 569-576.

Okajima, I., Komada, Y. & Inoue, Y. (2011). A meta-analysis on the treatment effectiveness of cognitive behavioral therapy for primary insomnia. *Sleep and Biological Rhythms*, *9*, 24-34.

Pinker, S. (1997). *How the mind works.* New York, NY: W. W. Norton.

Prochaska, J. O. & Norcross, J. C. (2014). Behavioral therapies. *Systems of psychotherapy: A transtheoretical analysis*, 8th Edition, (pp. 217-260). Stamford, CT: Cengage Learning.

Ruhmland, M. & Margraf, J. (2001). Efficacy of psychological treatments for specific phobia and obsessive compulsive disorder. *Verhaltenstherapie*, *11*, 14-26.

Schaafsma, S. M., Pfaff, D. W., Spunt, R. P. & Adolphs, R. (2015). Deconstructing and reconstructing theory of mind. *Trends in Cognitive Sciences*, *19*, 65-72.

Singer, T., Seymour, B., O'Doherty, J., Kaube, H., Dolan, R. J. & Frith, C. D. (2004). Empathy for pain involves the affective but not sensory components of pain. *Science*, *303*, 1157-1162.

Suarez, L., Bennett, S., Goldstein, C. & Barlow, D. H. (2009). Understanding anxiety disorders from a "triple vulnerability" framework. In M. M. Anthony & M. B. Stein (Eds.), *Oxford Handbook of anxiety and related disorders*, (pp. 153-172). New York, NY: Oxford University Press.

Tennen, H. & Herzberger, S. (1987). Depression, self-esteem, and the absence of self-protective attributional biases. *Journal of Personality and Social Psychology*, *52*, 72-80.

Tversky, A. & Kahneman, D. (1974). Judgment under uncertainty: Heuristics and biases. *Science*, *185*, 1124-1131.

Watts, S. E., Turnell, A., Kladnitski, N., Newby, J. M. & Andrews, G. (2015). Treatment-as-usual (TAU) is anything but usual: A meta-analysis of CBT versus TAU for anxiety and depression. *Journal of Affective Disorders*, *175*, 152-167.

Waytz, A. & Mitchell, J. P. (2011). Two mechanisms for simulating other minds: dissociations between mirroring and self-projection. *Current Directions in Psychological Science*, *20*, 197-200.

Whalen, P. J., Shin, L. M., McInerney, S. C., Fischer, H., Wright, C. I. & Rauch, S. L. (2001). A functional MRI study of human amygdala responses to facial expressions of fear versus anger. *Emotion*, *1*, 70-83.

Wicker, B., Keysers, C., Plailly, J., Royet, J. P., Gallese, V. & Rizzolatti, G. (2003). Both of us disgusted in my insula: The common neural basis of seeing and feeling disgust. *Neuron*, *40*, 655-664.

In: Social Psychology and Counseling
Editors: D. A. Kleiber and E. Delgado-Romero
ISBN: 978-1-53616-548-7

Chapter 7

MANAGING COGNITIVE DISSONANCE AND SELF-JUSTIFICATION IN COUNSELING SETTINGS

Ashley J. Britton

Social psychologists have long believed that people are motivated to justify their own actions, beliefs, and feelings if only for purposes of self-consistency (e.g., Lecky, 1945). The mechanism of self-justification can be useful and adaptive, contributing to people's motivation to do good, but it can also perpetuate self-destructive and irrational actions (Aronson, Wilson, & Akert, 2013). The aims of this chapter are four-fold. First, we will examine the nature of cognitive dissonance and processes by which reasonable, intelligent people succumb to these maladaptive self-justifications (rationalizations). Second, we will explore the ways in which such maladaptive justifications may be treated through therapy. Third, we will consider practical ways to utilize cognitive dissonance to create positive attitude and behavior changes. And finally, we will consider the virtue and value of therapists managing their own tendencies toward self-justification.

COGNITIVE DISSONANCE: A BRIEF OVERVIEW

One of the most powerful determinants of human behavior stems from our need to preserve a stable, positive, consistent self-image (Aronson, Wilson & Akert, 2013; Baumeister & Bushman, 2013). Midway through the last century psychologist Leon Festinger (1957) introduced a seminal theory of human motivation, the *Theory of Cognitive Dissonance*, with the ideas that tension occurs whenever an individual simultaneously holds two cognitions (ideas, attitudes, beliefs, opinions) that are psychologically inconsistent and that the tension can only be resolved through change in one of the two inconsistent cognitions, attitudes or behaviors. Cognitive dissonance is a phenomenon that is well-substantiated and deeply rooted in the evolution of social psychology (Aronson, 2012; Tryon & Misurell, 2008).

Others have emphasized the role that emotions play in dissonance theory by empirically supporting the proposition that emotion distorts cognition. Kunda (1990) demonstrated that the rationale people provide for their behaviors are recurrently influenced by their emotional state. More specifically, "[t]here is considerable evidence that people are more likely to arrive at conclusions that they want to arrive at, but their ability to do so is constrained by their ability to construct seemingly reasonable justifications for these conclusions" (Kunda, 1990, p. 480). When people consider alternative possibilities, they often creatively maintain an "illusion of objectivity" (Kunda, 1990, p. 483) by selectively combining beliefs and supporting evidence for the preferred conclusion (Tryon & Misurell, 2008).

Dissonance Reduction

Eliot Aronson (2012), a student of Festinger, noted that dissonance effects are greatest when two conditions are present: (1) when people feel personally responsible for their actions and (2) their actions have serious consequences. This is because dissonance reduction is an ego-defensive process that allows people to maintain positive images of themselves that is consonant with their morals and values (Aronson et al., 2013; McLeod, 2018).

Dissonance reduction is achieved in one of the following three ways. The first is by changing the behavior to bring it in line with the dissonant cognition. For example, for a smoker, the most direct means of reducing dissonance between the act of smoking and the awareness of its health risks is to change the behavior by quitting or reducing smoking. The smoker's behavior would then become more consonant with the knowledge of the health problems smoking causes. However, smoking cessation is difficult to achieve, and many have relapsed. The second means of dissonance reduction is attempting to justify our behavior through changing one of the dissonant cognitions. Heavy smokers, who relapse after a smoking cessation attempt, manage to lower their perceptions of the dangers of smoking and construct creative justifications that allow them to continue smoking without feeling guilt (e.g., convincing themselves that smoking improves their health by reducing stress or that the data linking cigarette smoking to cancer is inconclusive) (Aronson et al., 2013; Baumeister & Bushman, 2013; McLeod, 2018).

A third means of dissonance reduction is by attempting to justify the behavior by adding new cognitions. For instance, a smoker will add a cognition that allows him to focus on a vivid exception, such as an elderly grandparent who has smoked her entire life without significant health problems. An individual may also add a new cognition of self-affirmation that will allow him or her to focus on one or more positive qualities or traits (i.e., "I have no other vices and I take good care of the people around me.") to lessen the dissonance of continuing to engage in an obviously unhealthy behavior (smoking) (Aronson et al., 2013; Baumeister & Bushman, 2013; McLeod, 2018).

SELF-JUSTIFICATION IN DAILY LIFE AND (SOMETIMES MALADAPTIVE) DECISION-MAKING

Self-justification is characterized by Aronson (2012) as: "When they do something, they will try, if at all possible, to convince themselves (and others) that it was a logical, reasonable thing to do" (p. 182). Essentially, wherever people find themselves with some question as to why they did what they did, they are inclined to look for cues, internally and externally, to justify their actions and consequently adjust discrepant cognitions and emotions accordingly. Life is full of decisions that, generally, produce dissonance. When people hold conflicting beliefs or attitudes during the decision-making process, particularly in difficult or ambiguous situations, they often set out to justify why they have chosen a particular course of action over another. Even though the aforementioned smoking justifications seem non-sensical to non-smokers, it illustrates how people experiencing dissonance will distort or deny reality to reduce their discomfort. The most common situations associated with self-justification include effort justification, misattribution, rationalization, inadequate justification, hypocrisy and justification of cruelty, all of which can be personally maladaptive and destructive to human relations.

Justification of Effort

According to social psychologists, our activities and behaviors "are open to a variety of interpretations; if we are motivated to see the best in people and things, we will tend to interpret these ambiguities in a positive way" (Aronson et al., 2013, pp. 146). The tendency for individuals to increase their attraction to or interest in something they have worked hard to attain is called the "justification of effort." Aronson and colleagues asserted that if a person agrees to go through a demanding or an unpleasant experience in order to attain some goal or object (e.g., membership in a fraternity/sorority), that goal or object becomes more attractive (see also Bigham, this volume). This explains how the harsh methods and training of specialized military groups (e.g., Marines, Navy SEALs) can enhance and intensify the feelings of commitment and cohesion among the recruits, as well as pride in their group. In other words, the more effort we put into a particular goal or becoming members of a group, and the tougher the initiation, the more attraction we hold towards the group we have just joined – regardless of whether or not the goal was worth the effort in some "objective" analysis.

Rational vs. Rationalizing Behavior

In *The Social Animal* (Aronson, 2012), the author's "First law" asserts that "people who do crazy things are not necessarily crazy" (pp. 9). Aronson explained that humans have a tendency to explain undesirable and strange actions of others by attaching negative labels (sadistic, crazy, etc.); The rationale for this tendency is to exclude those persons from the rest of 'us nice, rational people,' which allows these maladaptive behaviors to be attributed to inherent characteristics rather than to situational influences. Aronson asserted that these situational influences can move many "normal" people to behave in very unpalatable ways, and it is imperative that these situational factors are considered and understood along with the processes that produce such unpleasant or destructive behaviors. Jarcho and colleagues (2011) similarly stated, "People rationalize the choices they make when confronted with difficult decisions by claiming they never wanted the option they did not choose" (pp. 460). According to Aronson et al., (2013), the rationale for this is that humans will attempt to avoid or reduce dissonance, even at the expense of honest reasoning (Aronson et al., 2013; Jarcho et al., 2011; Lawler, 2018).

External, Internal and Insufficient Justification

In dissonance reduction, two routes of justification can be adopted: internal justification or external justification. External justification is providing an explanation for behaviors that are outside of a person's cognitions, for example, "I was under the influence of drugs/alcohol; that's why I did what I did." With this route, there are typically sufficient and consonant beliefs about the action taken to limit the amount of dissonance an individual may feel after a particular action. But what happens when a person acts or makes a statement that is not consonant with their beliefs and there is insufficient external justification for it? When there is insufficient external justification for an action the individual will attempt to change their attitudes and cognitions to match their behavior – this is called internal justification (Aronson et al., 2013; Baumeister & Bushman, 2013; Sanderson, 2010).

The Hypocrisy Paradigm and Hypocrisy Induction

Self-justification not only minimizes our bad decisions and mistakes, but it also explains why people are less likely to see themselves as hypocritical as they do others. Self-justification allows us "to create a distinction between our moral lapses and someone else's and blur the discrepancy between our actions and our moral convictions" (Tavris & Aronson, 2015, pp. 5). *Inducing* hypocrisy – the act of making people face the discrepancies in their speech and actions – is a way of actually using the human tendency to reduce dissonance through self-justification to foster socially beneficial behaviors (Aronson et al., 2013; McConnell & Brown, 2010), a process that has implications for use in therapy. While research on the benefits of hypocrisy induction interventions has emerged in recent decades, there is a breadth of literature illustrating both psychological and physiological effects on the hypocrisy induction/ prosocial behavior relationship (Southard, 2016). A recent meta-analysis of dissonance-based interventions for health behavior change identified the *hypocrisy paradigm* process as one of the most effective means of inducing change across a range of health behaviors (Freijy & Kothe, 2013).

Justifying Good Deeds and Harmful Acts

When people have positive attitudes toward others, it is often apparent in their treatment of them which may be overly kind. Similarly, when people do not like others, they may make a point of indicating this through their behaviors as well. Interestingly, according to Aronson and colleagues (2013), the reverse can also be true: our behaviors towards others can affect our feelings towards them. According to the "justification of kindness" paradigm, humans are likely to feel more positively towards someone they have done a personal favor for as opposed to if they had not done the favor or did an impersonal favor.

And of course, the reverse is true; the *justification-of-cruelty effect* is the inclination to dehumanize those viewed as enemies or even "other" and is considered a universal phenomenon across all cultures (Aronson et al., 2013; Tavris & Aronson, 2015). Aronson et al., (2013) referenced a dramatic experiment on the justification-of-cruelty effect that examined the relationship between torture and blame with hypotheses based upon dissonance theory. As predicted, the closer people were to committing acts of cruelty (observing torture vs. listening to a description of it on the radio), the greater their need to reduce the dissonance between "I am causing another human to suffer" and "I am a good person." Unfortunately, the easiest route of dissonance reduction is through victim-blaming with statements or beliefs such as: "he is guilty anyway," "it is his own fault" or "he is the enemy" (Aronson et al., 2013).

The research findings on cruelty justification have very unsettling implications, in that successful dehumanization effectively guarantees continued and even escalation in cruelty; This can subsequently create a seemingly endless cycle of violence, where self-justification (with victim dehumanizing and victim-blaming) escalates acts of human cruelty. Consider past atrocities such as the Nazi's "Final Solution" that began with propaganda and resulted in genocide, a not-so-distant scandal of American guards at Iraq's Abu Ghraib prison who dehumanized their prisoners with casual brutality (Aronson et al., 2013), and patterns of racism where the simple assertion that "Black lives matter" is necessary to resist the tendency to justify acts of police misconduct toward African Americans by blaming the victims.

While dissonance is an unavoidable consequence of decision-making, embracing the dissonance allows for the possibility of making better choices. However, it is also possible that dissonance can be reduced in counterproductive ways (Tryon & Misurell, 2008). Returning to old habits, for example, is an unproductive means of dissonance reduction (Tryon & Misurell, 2008). Motivational Interviewing (Miller & Rollnick, 2002) literature in particular cautions therapists that intentionally-induced dissonance could be reduced through several forms of rationalizations. For instance, if people spend all their time and energy defending their egos they would never learn from past mistakes, incorrect beliefs or poor decisions. Rather, people would continue to ignore their mistakes, justify them or, in worse case scenarios, try to turn them into virtues. Consequently, people would fail to grow or change and become stuck within the confines of their own narrow minds; And in extreme cases, people end up justifying larger mistakes that can harm themselves or others (Aronson et al., 2013).

Managing Cognitive Dissonance and Self-justification in Psychotherapy

Most clients in psychotherapy seek to grow and learn from past mistakes that resulted in their current situation. Aronson (2012) emphasized that to understand and learn from past mistakes, an individual must examine those past mistakes from a non-defensive perspective. Aronson outlined the following procedures to facilitate this process: individuals must (1) obtain a greater understanding of his or her own defensiveness and dissonance-reducing tendencies; (2) realize that behaving in an immoral or foolish manner does not mean that the he or she is immoral or stupid (i.e., do not make dispositional attributions for situational influences); (3) develop enough ego-strength to tolerate own errors; and (4) increase the ability to recognize the benefits of admitting one's errors in terms of self-growth and learning, in addition to one's own ability to form meaningful relationships with others (Aronson, 2012, pp. 247).

Dissonance induction, also known as the hypocrisy induction paradigm, occurs in two stages. To increase engagement in a prosocial behavior – whether it be in therapy, medical or educational settings – participants must first advocate publicly for the importance and utility of engaging in the behavior. Participants are then asked to reflect on past failures when previously engaging in said prosocial behaviors. Interestingly, within this paradigm, it is not necessary for the client to fabricate an inconsistency because this paradigm asks participants to confront an already-established inconsistency. Research studies suggest that individuals increase their intention to engage in prosocial behaviors more frequently when these conditions are met. The mechanism of this paradigm is that making pro-attitudinal speeches will rally individuals, thereby reminding them why they believe the target behavior is important. The hypocrisy-confrontation component is when the client relives past failures of a target behavior, which reminds him that although he promotes that behavior verbally, he does not always adhere to his own promotions. The dissonance induction is intended to create a stronger desire from those in the hypocrisy condition to reduce it, theoretically causing them to engage in it more frequently (Aronson et al., 2013; McConnell & Brown, 2010; Southard, 2016).

Tryon and Misurell (2008) examined dissonance induction/reduction principles as a possible explanatory basis for how and why anxiety and depression are treated effectively in psychotherapy. They determined that cognitive dissonance theory could also help explain numerous empirical findings related to information processing patterns among depressed individuals such as depressive realism, variants of learned helplessness theory, and the rumination process involved in maintaining depressive symptoms (Tryon & Misurell, 2008). Information processing biases observed among depressed individuals include tendencies to not only seek out information that supports a consonant negative view of self, others, and the world but also to disregard dissonant contradictory information. It is in these two ways that depressed individuals distort information to manage dissonance between incongruent thoughts, feelings and behaviors (Tryon & Misurell, 2008).

Tryon and Misurell (2008) argued that regardless of the therapist's theoretical orientation, effective clinicians probably implement the dissonance induction/ reduction principle, to some degree, to promote change. Their takeaway is that effective clinicians use this principle because it changes the way clients think, feel, and behave – the aim of many health behavior change approaches – by causing the client's brain network to process information differently (Tryon & Misurell, 2008). Furthermore, Tryon and Misurell (2008) identified the following positive expectations: First, they anticipated that clinicians could become more effective by consciously implementing the dissonance induction/reduction principle in therapy. Second, more clinicians may be motivated to implement this principle when they possess a true understanding of the fact that dissonance induction/reduction is a common factor responsible for the effectiveness of therapy. Lastly, they anticipated that their transtheoretical perspective would foster theoretical unification within psychology and neuroscience, thus making clinical psychology more scientifically convergent (Tryon & Misurell, 2008).

There is a wealth of literature about evidence-based treatments (EBTs) for the treatment of depression, namely *Cognitive and Behavior Therapy* (CBT; e.g Cujipers et al., 2013) as well as *Interpersonal Therapy* (IPT; e.g., Tryon & Misurell, 2008). Dissonance theory functions at a fundamental level of mental processing that can be incorporated in varying models of psychotherapy; it is more than simply introducing alternative terminology (de Vries, 2012). The dissonance induction/reduction principle is commonly shared with regard to both. Although each therapeutic modality differs in emphasis as well as the underlying assumptions about the etiology and maintenance of psychological disorders, Tryon and Misurell (2008) argue that the dissonance induction/reduction principle is a commonly shared principle with respect symptom identification and alleviation. Below, we will briefly identify how each theoretical orientation applies dissonance theory, via dissonance induction and/or reduction, to address presenting problems as well as initiating change behaviors.

Cognitive Behavior Therapy

Cognitive Behavior Therapy (CBT) is the most well-researched and empirically supported psycho-social approach used in psychotherapy today (see also Edner & Casiello-Robbins, this volume, for a review). Both the cognitive and behavioral components of CBT are designed to restructure the patient's cognitive schemas or patterns that are believed to be directly causing the presenting symptoms. CBT treatment approaches involve a dual approach whereby behavior techniques are employed to increase the frequency of positive activities while the therapist concurrently engages the client in the cognitive restructuring of dysfunctional thoughts. Both the cognitive and behavioral components serve as dissonance induction procedures that affect change upon the affective mood state. Additional dissonance induction techniques include *Socratic Questioning* and *Collaborative Empiricism* (Beck & Weishaar, 2014; Tryon & Misurell, 2008).

Interpersonal Psychotherapy

Interpersonal psychotherapy for depression (IPT) rests on the theory that depression typically takes place within social contexts (Klerman, Weissman, Rounsaville & Chevron, 1984; Tyron & Misurell, 2008). Interpersonal therapists focus on the client's current interpersonal problems that are contributing to the presenting symptoms. In IPT, the client's problems are formulated in the context of four categories (grief, role disputes, role transitions, and interpersonal deficits). Interpersonal therapists engage in a variety of techniques designed to help move the patient through the therapeutic process (i.e., to acquire new beliefs, experiences and behaviors) that are dissonant with symptoms of depression. By assisting the client with adopting new social roles, the client can develop a new social identity that is dissonant with depressive emotions. IPT also improves self-efficacy through behavioral techniques such as role play, modeling and interpersonal skill building (Klerman, Weissman, Rounsaville & Chevron, 1984; Tyron & Misurell, 2008).

Motivational Interviewing

Motivational interviewing (Miller & Rollnick, 2002) incorporates concepts of self-efficacy and cognitive dissonance as well as principles of person-centered therapy and the transtheoretical model (see also Varley & Zito, this volume). MI assumes that interventions are most effective when they correspond to the client's current stage of change and is particularly useful for clients in the precontemplation or contemplation stages of change. The following are the predominant MI techniques: expressing empathy, supporting self-efficacy, *developing a discrepancy*, and rolling with resistance. A distinctive characteristic of motivational interviewing is the use of questions, reflections, affirmations, and other strategies to elicit and reinforce a client's "change talk" – statements that move the client toward making positive changes in behavior (Miller & Rollnick, 2002).

Enabling Clients to Understand Dissonance Effects

Cognitive dissonance theory has "a sound theoretical basis, well defined properties, and its predictions are supported by rigorous research" (de Vries, 2012). Furthermore, this theory can potentially be utilized as a means of communicating with clients to provide a basis for understanding their own cognitive functioning. De Vries (2012) posits that the process whereby an individual's problematic cognitions, emotions and behaviors become generally resolved could be perceived as dissonance reduction. Specifically, experiencing depression, anxiety or another psychological disorder clashes with the perception of the self as competent. As the problem persists, the evidence for the competent self no longer holds. In other words, this means accepting a self that is no longer competent. Reduction in self-esteem will go hand in hand with this (de Vries, 2012).

Interestingly, for many clients, simply receiving a psychiatric diagnosis serves as a defining moment towards attaining a new status quo. CBT aims to challenge and change the thoughts, emotions, and behaviors that maintain the negative psychological state. Aiding clients to initiate behaviors that are considered inconsistent with his/her mental health problems may offer powerful evidence against the negative mental state and thus motivate change. For instance, doing something brave is inconsistent with an anxious state whereas engaging in a fun activity challenges a depressed state (de Vries, 20102).

Managing One's Own Self-Justification in Healthcare Provision

What is important to remember is that everyone experiences dissonance in daily life related to decision-making and conflict. Healthcare providers are no exception to this phenomenon and awareness of this fact is imperative to provision of safe, effective treatment. In the revised edition of *Mistakes Were Made (But Not by Me): Why We Justify Foolish Beliefs, Bad Decisions, and Hurtful Acts,* Tavris and Aronson (2015) provide a comprehensive assessment of the mechanisms of self-justification and the resulting damage as well as the means of overcoming it. They reviewed the processes of cognitive dissonance that alter one's feelings of self-worth consequent to mistreating others, making mistakes and clinging to outdated beliefs/attitudes. Interestingly, Tavris and Aronson (2015) provided many examples of how leaders, professionals, policy makers, couples and healthcare providers also fall subject to the pitfalls of self-justification as well as the significant consequences this has posed for others.

> "We look at the behavior of politicians with amusement or alarm or horror, but what they do is no different in kind, though certainly in consequence, from what most of us have done at one time or another in our private lives. We stay in an unhappy relationship or one that is merely going nowhere because, after all, we invested so much time in making it work. We stay in a deadening job way too long because we look for all the reasons to justify staying and are unable to clearly assess the benefits of leaving. We buy a lemon of a car because it looks gorgeous, spend thousands of dollars to keep the damn thing running, and then spend even more to justify that investment. We self-righteously create a rift with a friend or relative over some real or imagined slight yet see ourselves as the pursuers of peace—if only the other side would apologize and make amends." (Tavris & Aronson, 2015, pp. 4-5)

A particularly salient perspective that Tavris and Aronson (2015) provided was related to people in the healing professions, as the stakes are especially high in this context. When providers learn that some of their beliefs that guide their practices are incorrect, they can either admit the error and change the approach or reject the new evidence. They determined that providers are likely willing to change their approach if two conditions are met: when the mistakes do not greatly threaten their self-perceived competence and if the provider has not publicly defended these beliefs/approaches. As mentioned earlier, if the severity of the consequences of misdiagnosis are high (i.e., exacerbated client problems, ruined clients' families, or worse) then the provider will likely experience a significant amount of dissonance. And this must be resolved in some way.

An issue specifically among mental health providers is that the various professionals in these fields have a combination of credentials and training that often share few commonalities. Additionally, over the past two decades, the majority of psychotherapy training programs have eradicated research training requirements altogether. The inherent problem is that therapists who lack both skepticism and training in science have no internal corrections to the cognitive biases everyone falls prey to. Instead, what therapists observe in their work subsequently confirms what they believe and thus shapes future observations – this is a closed loop (Tavris & Aronson, 2015). However, Tavris and Aronson (2015) hold that even when the scientist-practitioner is not initially self-correcting, eventually science is. Through scientific research, therapists are provided with means of both avoiding mistakes and improving clinical practices (Tavris & Aronson, 2015).

From an individual perspective, cognitive dissonance can be effectively managed when practitioners who experience dissonance accept the resulting discomfort as opposed to trying to quickly alleviate the feeling and justify what is happening. Additionally, Aronson's four procedures, mentioned previously, are a good starting point for therapists to become more aware of their own dissonance reduction and self-justification tendencies and become better decision-makers. To achieve resolution, when therapists feel anxiety from decisions they are facing, they should first *embrace* the anxiety, then give themselves adequate time to work through their feelings related to a decision. Indeed, by writing down thoughts about a decision, therapists can reflect on the challenge most effectively. Some examples include making a pro-con list, recording corresponding emotions, exercising, and meditating. By thinking through the decision clearly, the need to later rationalize a poor decision is eliminated or greatly reduced at the very least. Lastly, a well-considered, if difficult, decision likely produces feelings of pride to stand by (Lawler, 2018), though this feeling should be treated cautiously as having a potential for 'hardening of the categories,' i.e., being overly committed to a position as a result.

IMPLICATIONS FOR FURTHER RESEARCH

Intentional dissonance induction may prove difficult for therapists because dissonance is not easily assessed in others no less oneself (McLeod, 2018). From a scientific perspective, physical observation and measurement of dissonance induction requires real-time assessment of physiological arousal (i.e., heart rate, skin temperature) during individual therapy sessions or for each participant in group sessions that is both too disruptive and potentially expensive (McLeod, 2018; Rohde et al., 2016).

Nevertheless, future research should more objectively examine the mechanisms that may explain positive therapeutic outcomes and changes in psychiatric symptoms (Rohde et al., 2016).

CONCLUSION

Humans frequently process information in a biased way to fit preconceived notions and avoid dissonance. But dissonance is an unavoidable consequence of decision-making that everyone, including healthcare providers and national leaders, is susceptible to. Although dissonance reduction is a largely unconscious process, dissonance reduction can also be counterproductive because it solidifies negative values and behaviors. Understanding that humans are dissonance-reducing beings can also make us more aware of the process. Moreover, by embracing the dissonance it is possible to intervene in the self-justification process to make better choices. Whenever we or our clients feel the discomfort from acting counter to our morals or values, a pathway for reflection emerges that can be exploited to reduce maladaptive self-justification and enhance more effective decision making.

REFERENCES

Aronson, E. (2012). *The social animal* (11th Ed.) New York City: Worth Publishers.

Aronson, E., Wilson, T., & Akert, R. (2013). *Social psychology* (8th Ed.). New Jersey: Pearson Education.

Baumeister, R., & Bushman, B. (2013). *Social psychology and human nature: Brief version* (3rd ed.). Belmont, CA: Wadsworth.

Beck, A., & Weishaar, M. (2014). Cognitive therapy. In D. Wedding, & R. J. Corsini (Eds.), *Current psychotherapies* (10th ed., pp. 231-264). Belmont, CA: Brooks/Cole.

Coopersmith, S. (1967). *The antecedents of self-esteem*. San Francisco: Freeman.

Cujipers, P., Berking, M., Andersson, G., Quigley, L., Kleiboer, A., & Dobson, K. (2013). A meta-analysis of cognitive-behavioural therapy for adult depression, alone and in comparison with other treatments. *The Canadian Journal of Psychiatry, 58*(7), 376-385.

De Vries, J. (2012, May 09). The 'Cognitive Dissonance Meme' and Psychotherapy. Retrieved from https://iahip.org/inside-out/issue-57-winter-2008/the-cognitive-dissonance-meme-and-psychotherapy.

Festinger, L. (1957). *A theory of cognitive dissonance*. Stanford, CA: Stanford University Press.

Fiske, S. (2004). *Social beings: A core motives approach to social psychology*. NYC: Wiley.

Freijy, T., & Kothe, E. (2013). Dissonance-based interventions for health behaviour change: A systematic review. *British Journal of Health Psychology, 18*(2), 310-337. https://doi.org/10.1111/bjhp.12035.

Jarcho, J., Berkman, E., & Lieberman, M. (2011). The neural basis of rationalization: Cognitive dissonance reduction during decision-making. *Social Cognitive and Affective Neuroscience, 6*(4), 460-467. Doi: 10.1093/scan/nsq054.

Klerman, G., Weissman, M., Rounsaville, B., & Chevron, E. (1984). *Interpersonal psychotherapy of depression.* Basic Books: New York.

Kunda, Z. (1990). The case for motivated reasoning. *Psychological Bulletin*, 108, 480–498.

Lawler, M. (2018, February 28). Cognitive dissonance is part of every decision we make everyday. *Health* (S. Mackenzie, Ed.). Retrieved from https://www.everydayhealth.com/neurology/cognitive-dissonance/every-decision-we-make/.

Lecky, P. (1945). *Self-consistency; a theory of personality*. Washington, DC, US: Island Press.

McConnell, A. & Brown, C. (2010). Dissonance adverted: Self-concept organization moderates the effect of hypocrisy on attitude change. *Journal of Experimental Social Psychology, 46*(2), 361-366.

McLeod, S. (2018, February 05). *Cognitive dissonance*. Retrieved from https://www.simplypsychology.org/cognitive-dissonance.html.

Miller, W., & Rollnick, S. (2002). *Motivational interviewing: Preparing people for change*. New York: Guilford Publications.

Rohde, P., Stice, E., Shaw, H. & Gau, J. (2016). Pilot trial of a dissonance-based cognitive-behavioral group depression prevention with college students. *Behaviour Research and Therapy*, 82, 21-27.

Sanderson, C. (2010). *Social psychology*. Hoboken, NJ: John Wiley & Sons.

Southard, H. (2016). *The Advantage of Hypocrisy: Using Dissonance to Improve Exercise Habits and Reduce Stress* (Master's thesis, Southern Illinois University Edwardsville, 2016) (pp. 1-76). Ann Arbor: ProQuest LLC. Retrieved from https://media.proquest.com/media/pq/classic/doc/4135209501/fmt/ai/rep/NPDF?_s=paJB7Phj2fUWA83M4viwnv1nc74=.

Tavris, C., & Aronson, E. (2015). *Mistakes were made (but not by me): Why we justify foolish beliefs, bad decisions and hurtful acts*. HMH Books. Kindle Edition.

Thinking Ourselves Right - The Good and Bad Sides of Self-Justification. (2016, January 07). Retrieved from http://www.freetopursue.com/blog/2016/1/7/good-and-bad-of-self-justification.

Tryon, W. & Misurell, J. (2008). Dissonance induction and reduction: A possible principle and connectionist mechanism for why therapies are effective. *Clinical Psychology Review, 28*(8), 1297-1309. https://doi.org/10.1016/j.cpr.2008.06.003.

In: Social Psychology and Counseling
Editors: D. A. Kleiber and E. Delgado-Romero
ISBN: 978-1-53616-548-7

Chapter 8

THE PSYCHOLOGY OF HAZING

Lauren Bigham

> Colgate University Men's Sports Team Suspended for Hazing, 'High-risk Alcohol Consumption'
>
> HAMILTON, NY - Colgate University has suspended its men's swimming and diving team for the fall season due to "hazing and high-risk alcohol consumption," officials announced. The team is suspended from all fall competition and its winter training trip, according to a statement by the university. After an investigation by the university's athletics department and dean's office, the university found the team engaged in hazing that included high-risk alcohol consumption. "We regret the need to make this decision but also want to communicate clearly and unequivocally that hazing and high-risk drinking have no place in Colgate's Division I athletics program or at Colgate University," said Colgate Vice President and Director of Athletics. Hazing is prohibited by Colgate University policy and state law. Members of the team also must undergo mandatory education regarding hazing. In September 2017, Colgate's men's rowing team also was suspended for a season due to hazing. (Doran, 2018)

This news story is just one example of hazing in U.S. colleges as reported by the media within the last several years. Generally considered to be 'horseplay,' 'harmless pranks,' or even 'rites of passage,' experts in the field of higher education describe hazing with significantly different terminology. Allan and Madden (2008) describe hazing as secretive, unacceptable, high-risk, abusive, dangerous, and illegal. Hazing has also been described as "maladaptive, destructive, and dehumanizing" (Kirby & Wintrup, 2002, p. 82) since the behaviors can have severe physical, psychological, and social implications (Chin & Johnson, 2011). Consisting of physical, psychological, and/or alcohol-related experiences (Diamond, Callahan, Chain, & Solomon, 2016; Waldron & Kowaiski, 2009), hazing is not limited to the world of sport. Research indicates the presence of hazing across various organizations and groups, including military groups, club sports, intramural teams, recreational clubs, collegiate fraternities and sororities, marching bands, theater groups, honor societies, and academic clubs (Allan, Kerschner, & Payne, 2019; Allan & Madden, 2008, 2012; Campo, Poulos, & Sipple, 2005; Hoover & Pollard, 1999, 2000).

Allan and Madden (2008, 2012) conducted the first nationwide research study examining the nature and extent of hazing in a sample of 11,482 undergraduate students from 53 US college campuses. Behavior that met criteria for hazing was identified across student groups, with the highest percentages observed in varsity athletics (74%), social fraternities/sororities (73%), club sports (64%), performing arts organizations (56%), service fraternities/sororities (50%), intramural teams (49%), recreation clubs (42%), academic clubs (28%), and honor societies (20%). Whereas 69% of respondents reported awareness of hazing in other student organizations, 55% reported personally experiencing at least one behavior that met criteria for hazing. Respondents affiliated with varsity athletics and Greek-letter organizations were found to be most likely to experience hazing with seven out of ten reporting at least one hazing behavior when attempting to join or maintain membership.

Besides the high reported frequency of hazing behavior across student groups and the elevated awareness of hazing occurring elsewhere on campus, what is most curious about this nationwide research study is the statistical gap observed between respondents' experiences of hazing behavior and the limited frequency in which the experiences were then labeled as hazing by those same respondents. Of the 55% who endorsed experiencing at least one hazing behavior, nine out of ten did not consider themselves to be hazed when provided with a definition for comparison. Of the respondents who did identify their experiences as hazing, 95% denied reporting the events to officials. Rather, these respondents often endorsed favorable or positive outcomes stemming from hazing (Allan & Madden, 2008, 2012).

Interestingly, Allan and Madden (2008, 2012) were not the first to observe the disconnect between self-report and the high frequency in which hazing behaviors are actually endorsed. In cooperation with the National Collegiate Athletic Association (NCAA) and Alfred University, Hoover and Pollard (1999) conducted the first and most comprehensive national study examining the scope of initiation rites in collegiate athletics. Of the 2,027 student-athletes sampled from around the US, approximately 80% reported experiencing at least one behavior that met criteria for hazing. Comparable to the results of Allan and Madden (2008, 2012), only 12% reported personal involvement in hazing when directly asked.

Campo and colleagues (2005) examined hazing prevalence, attitudes, beliefs, and behaviors in a sample of 736 undergraduate students from a mid-sized northeastern university. As found in previous research (Allan & Madden, 2008; 2012; Hoover & Pollard, 1999) participants who identified as varsity student-athletes, Greek-letter members, male, leaders on campus, and upperclassmen were more likely to engage in hazing. Though 36% of the sample endorsed engagement in hazing-type behaviors, only 6.7% reported being a 'hazer' and 12.4% a 'hazee.' This finding is consistent with the underreporting found in prior research.

More recently, Allan and colleagues (2019) examined the nature and extent of hazing in college students enrolled in universities committed to comprehensive hazing prevention. Elevations in hazing behaviors were detected across student groups in spite of data being collected from universities committed to hazing prevention. The two groups that endorsed hazing behaviors most frequently continued to be varsity athletics and fraternities/sororities. It is also notable that only 4.4% of participants reported being hazed despite nearly 70% reporting awareness of hazing elsewhere on campus. Similar trends have also been observed in high school students in terms of underreporting and failing to identify personal behaviors as hazing. With prevalence rates ranging from 42% to 50% among high school students (Allan & Madden, 2008, 2009; Hoover & Pollard, 1999, 2000), it appears that youth are exposed to and experience hazing at relatively high rates. And similar to college students, they often times do not identify these personal experiences as hazing, indicating considerable accommodation to the various practices. And, although research has made substantial discoveries regarding hazing, there are several perplexing discrepancies in the research that warrant further consideration and examination for potential improvements in prevention and intervention efforts.

For example, in addition to the notable disconnection between low self-report and the high frequencies in which hazing-type behaviors are actually endorsed (Allan & Madden, 2008, 2009, 2012; Campo et al., 2005; Hoover & Pollard, 1999, 2000), it is remarkable that approximately 70% of participants in earlier research studies reported an awareness of hazing in other groups (Allan et al., 2019; Allan & Madden, 2008, 2012). Considered to be a complex, multifaceted problem with the potential for humiliation, embarrassment, degradation, social deviance, abuse, and even death (Finkel, 2002; Jeckell et al., 2018; Keating et al., 2005; Srabstein, 2008), the question remains, what is prompting these discrepancies throughout the hazing literature?

Researchers have offered several possible hypotheses. Owen and colleagues (2008) proposed the potential impact of embarrassment and social desirability bias, defined as the tendency to project a favorable image of oneself (Crowne & Marlowe, 1960). Reports of involvement may also be low and misleading since people could be cautious to avoid self-incrimination or to associate themselves with illegal hazing behaviors (Waldron & Kowalski, 2009). Other potential hypotheses include the culture of secrecy and silence that surrounds hazing, an allegiance to the team or group, or the fear of retribution and other negative consequences (Allan & Madden, 2008; Hoover & Pollard, 1999; Waldron, 2008).

Diamond and colleagues (2016) attributed the discrepancy in reporting to poor or limited understanding of hazing. Campo and colleagues (2005) offered a comparable hypothesis, proposing that respondents utilized too narrow a definition of hazing by only focusing on the extreme or severe hazing behaviors. Both hypotheses are supported by research performed by Crow and MacIntosh (2009) in which administrators, coaches, and student-athletes were found to lack a clear understanding of what is considered hazing practices versus acceptable initiation behaviors. However, significant efforts have been made within the past 20 years by key stakeholders to prevent the occurrence of hazing behaviors through legislation, anti-hazing policies, and educational awareness programming (Crow & Rosner, 2002; Fields, Collins, & Comstock, 2010; Wilfert, 2007). And yet current research continues to affirm the persistence of hazing and the under-reporting of personal involvement (Allan et al., 2019).

Campo and colleagues (2005) offered a second hypothesis for the observed under-reporting of hazing. According to Campo and colleagues, the discrepancy may be due to "psychological barriers in students recognizing their own involvement, such as dissonance caused by feelings of guilt or hypocrisy" (p. 146). This is an interesting hypothesis since it suggests respondents were unable to recognize or perceive their own behaviors as hazing. Although the previously described hypotheses of embarrassment, social desirability bias, lack of knowledge, and cultural secrecy provide as reasonable explanations for the different reactions to hazing, cognitive dissonance and other social psychology constructs may offer a more comprehensive conceptualization of the underlying psychological and motivational processes responsible for hazing.

Therefore, this chapter will seek to use research in social psychology to provide a more complete explanation or framework of hazing that can account for the consistent discrepancies found throughout the literature. The proposed framework will rely on the constructs of cognitive dissonance, self-justification, and conformity to explore *how* and *why* hazing continues to persist despite the potential for significant physical, emotional, social, financial, and legal consequences (Crow, 2008; Crow & Rosner, 2002; Finkel, 2002; Srabstein, 2008). To facilitate an in-depth exploration of hazing and how it may be better conceptualized in relation to the aforementioned social psychological constructs, a brief overview of hazing will be provided with emphasis on working definitions, related constructs, and the specific behaviors that comprise hazing. This chapter will then explore the social psychology underpinnings of hazing. Recommended interventions and future directions will be outlined at the conclusion of the chapter.

THE PHENOMENON OF HAZING

Hazing Defined

Prior to unpacking the nuances of hazing as explained through social psychology, it is important to distinguish the behavior from what is frequently discussed, scrutinized, and sometimes even glorified in the media and pop culture (Crow, 2008; Diamond et al., 2016; Nuwer, 2004). Frequently defined as "any activity expected of someone joining a group that humiliates, degrades, abuses, or endangers, regardless of a person's willingness to participate" (Hoover & Pollard, 1999, p.8), hazing is considered to be a form of interpersonal violence that is not impacted by perceived willingness or consent of the newcomer (Allan & Madden, 2012; Diamond et al., 2016; Hollmann, 2002; Wilfert, 2007). Illegal in 44 states (Hazing Law, 2018), experts question the ability to truly provide consent given the inherently secretive and coercive nature of hazing (Allan & Madden, 2012; Crow, 2008).

Also commonly acknowledged throughout the literature is the lack of a clear, precise, and universally agreed upon definition of hazing that can be used across contexts and with varying populations (Crow & MacIntosh, 2009; Diamond et al., 2016; Kirby & Wintrup, 2002). As such, another notable definition of hazing, focused on sport but applicable to other settings, was offered by Fields, Collins, and Comstock, (2010):

> Hazing among youth is sports-related violence perpetrated by member(s) of a sports-related group against individual(s) seeking inclusion within, admittance to, and/or acceptance by that group. Hazing may be perpetrated by and/or endorsed by parents, coaches, or other non-athlete members of the sports-related group as well as by adolescent athletes. (p. 32)

Focused on youth in sport and describing hazing as "sport-related violence," this particular definition merits inclusion as it highlights the motivation of newcomers and the potential role that parents, coaches, and other persons of influence may have on hazing. In order to gain acceptance and admission into a group, students participate in unacceptable, high-risk, and potentially illegal behaviors (Allan & Madden, 2012). Other reported benefits of undergoing hazing include feeling more like a part of the group, a sense of accomplishment, and feeling stronger (Allan & Madden, 2008, 2019).

Previously asserted by Bronfenbrenner's Ecological Systems Theory (1979), research studies suggest a student's hazing-related attitudes and behaviors are likely impacted by persons of influence within the immediate environment. Allan and colleagues (2019) reported that among students who endorsed experiencing hazing behaviors previously, 42.5% noted that a coach or advisor was aware of the hazing activity. Moreover, 27.9% of those same students also reported that a coach or advisor was present when hazing occurred. Kowalski and Waldron (2010) indicated that a majority of sampled student-athletes believed their coaches to be knowledgeable and tolerant of hazing. In addition, high school students who knew an adult who had been hazed were found to be more likely to experience hazing themselves (Hoover & Pollard, 2000). In total, the research indicates that the experiences and attitudes of adults likely influence students' normalization of and involvement in hazing.

Hazing versus Bullying

Hazing is considered to be a different form of interpersonal violence from that of bullying (Diamond et al., 2016). According to the United States Centers for Disease Control and Prevention (2019), bullying is:

> Any unwanted aggressive behavior(s) by another youth or group of youths, who are not siblings or current dating partners, that involves an observed or perceived power imbalance and is repeated multiple times or is highly likely to be repeated. Bullying may inflict harm or distress on the targeted youth, including physical, psychological, social or educational harm.

Although hazing and bullying both stem from an observed or perceived power differential and can result in physical, psychological, and social harm, the two forms of interpersonal violence differ from one another in intention and duration (Diamond et al., 2016). The intention of hazing differs from that of bullying since hazing is purported to initiate newcomers into the group, whereas bullying is used for exclusion and alienation purposes (Hazing and Bullying, 2018). Furthermore, the definition of hazing does not include the expectation of repetition (Diamond et al., 2016) and may be done for more instrumental and even prosocial intents (e.g., to gain allegiance and commitment) while hostile aggression is characteristic of bullying. Hazing behaviors may be limited to a single incident (e.g., a rookie initiation night) or they may occur over a period of days to weeks (Allan & Madden, 2012). Nonetheless, both hazing and bullying are considered to be forms of maltreatment (Stirling, 2009).

Hazing Taxonomy and Associated Behaviors

For classification purposes, hazing can be broken down into physical, psychological, and alcohol-related behaviors (Diamond et al., 2016; Waldron & Kowalski, 2009). Physical forms of hazing include: forced consumption of inappropriate/unsafe foods, enduring harsh weather without appropriate clothing, beatings, paddling, tattooing, piercing, branding, calisthenics, head shaving, kidnapping, abandonment, destruction or theft of property, simulation of sexual acts, and sexual assault. Psychological methods of hazing include: public humiliation (e.g., singing/chanting, wearing embarrassing clothing in public, or forced public nudity), being yelled/cursed at, personal servitude, isolation, sleep deprivation, and confinement. And finally, alcohol-related hazing consists of drinking games and/or forced consumption of alcohol (Allan et al., 2019; Allan & Madden, 2008, 2012; Hoover & Pollard, 1999, 2000).

Originally specific to sport but used throughout the hazing literature, Hoover and Pollard (1999) organized hazing behaviors into sub-categories based on intensity or severity. Unacceptable or illegal hazing initiation activities are defined as those activities with a high probability of danger or injury, including being kidnapped, beaten, tied up, or abandoned. Alcohol-related hazing activities, not otherwise considered unacceptable, involve drinking contests and/or alcohol-related games that often include people who are under the legal drinking age. Questionable hazing behaviors include humiliating or degrading activities, such as being yelled at, sworn at, and forced to wear embarrassing clothing. Hoover and Pollard (1999) further distinguished hazing from other common practices in sport. According to Hoover and Pollard, hazing does not include activities such as new members carrying equipment, team parties with community games, or going out with teammates "unless an atmosphere of humiliation, degradation, abuse or danger arises" (p. 8).

Research indicates that the most common hazing practices across student groups involve behaviors that require high-risk alcohol consumption, sleep deprivation, social isolation, personal servitude, and humiliation (Allan et al., 2019; Allan & Madden, 2008, 2012; Campo et al., 2005; Owen et al., 2008). Hoover and Pollard (1999) discovered that two thirds of sampled student-athletes were subjected to humiliating hazing, 19% reported experiencing questionable initiation rites, and 21% reported experiencing non-alcohol related unacceptable hazing behaviors. And more than half were required to participate in drinking contests or alcohol-related initiation activities.

COGNITIVE DISSONANCE THEORY AND HAZING

In order to develop a comprehensive understanding of *how* hazing continues to persist despite awareness of hazing laws, education aimed at reducing hazing, and highly publicized formidable legal and financial consequences, an introduction to cognitive dissonance theory is warranted. Proposed by Festinger in 1957 and considered to be a theory of human motivation, cognitive dissonance is based on the assumption that people are motivated to be consistent, logical, and reasonable across thoughts, beliefs, and behaviors. When a person experiences incongruent thoughts, beliefs, and/or actions, an unpleasant state of tension or dissonance typically occurs. Efforts may then be taken to reduce this dissonance by specifically changing one or more cognitions or by acquiring new cognitions to create adequate justification (Aronson, 2012; see also Britton and Wu & Bathje, this volume).

Engagement in initiation practices can increase dissonance as hazing-related behaviors may be incongruent with the individual's self-concept (Aronson & Mills, 1959; Hinkle Smith & Stellino, 2007). To mitigate the dissonance, research indicates that persons involved in hazing may alter their cognitions to be more positive or accepting of that experience. As an example, individuals who self-labeled prior experiences as hazing not only endorsed a more favorable perception of hazing, but they also described those same experiences as productive (Allan et al., 2019; Allan & Madden, 2008, 2012; Owen et al., 2008). Moreover, a positive linear relationship has been identified between hazing behaviors and attitudes. As the number of hazing experiences increased, so did positive or accepting attitudes towards hazing (Owen et al., 2008). By emphasizing the positive and productive aspects of hazing, there is a de-emphasis of the negative aspects. And it is this distortion that assists in alleviating incongruency while promoting continued engagement in hazing.

To maintain one's self-concept and reduce dissonance, Aronson (2012) proposed the utilization of various ego-defense mechanisms, such as excuse making and self-justifications. Regarding cognitive dissonance and hazing specifically, a review of the literature indicates that persons involved in hazing use relatively predictable thought patterns or self-justifications. In addition to the tendency to dismiss or question institutional and legal definitions of hazing, experts have observed the minimization of hazing's potential harm (Allan & Madden, 2012). Hinkle Smith and Stellino (2007) also observed that student-athletes commonly downplayed, rationalized, and justified their hazing experiences. As such, it is through the use of various self-justifications that persons involved in hazing reduce dissonance. The proceeding sections are dedicated to some of the most commonly reported hazing justifications and their corresponding arguments.

Moral Justification

Commonly observed in the hazing literature is the use of moral justifications, where the importance or value of a behavior is cognitively emphasized as justification for personal involvement. Bandura (1990) noted that people do not usually engage in reprehensible conduct until they have justified the morality of the action. And it is during the justification process that "What is culpable can be made righteous through cognitive reconstrual" and "…detrimental conduct is made personally and socially acceptable by portraying it as in the service of moral purposes" (p. 29).

Described as an important 'rite of passage' or 'tradition' (Allan & Madden, 2008, 2012; Crow & MacIntosh, 2009; Hoover & Pollard, 1999; Waldron & Kowalski, 2009), hazing is often justified as a method to promote group unity, chemistry, or cohesion (Allan & Madden, 2008, 2012; Campo et al., 2005; Hoover & Pollard, 1999; Johnson, 2011; Van Raalte et al., 2007; Winslow, 1999). For example, and as reported by Hoover and Pollard (1999), one student-athlete wrote:

> "Don't prevent it. Hazing does and should happen as a part of team chemistry. It makes you stronger...builds mental toughness. It is a valuable and important part of both growing up as a person and as a team..." (p. 23).

Further suggestive of the connection between hazing behavior and the use of moral justifications, a positive relationship has been detected between hazing participation and the belief that it contributes to group cohesion (Campo et al., 2005).

Though there is research to support the argument that group cohesion leads to enhanced performance (Carran et al., 1998), the research has not demonstrated a positive relationship between hazing and cohesion. Instead, Johnson (2011) argues that hazing fractures relationships, erodes trust and respect, as well as creates division among group members. Van Raalte and colleagues (2007) reported a negative association between hazing behaviors and team cohesion with athletes reporting significant decreases in perceived team cohesion as the number of hazing activities increased. Notably, Van Raalte and colleagues (2007) reported a positive association between adaptive or appropriate team building activities and enhanced team cohesion. With the research lacking in support of hazing behaviors for improvements in group cohesion, prevention and intervention efforts should emphasize alternative orientation and team building activities to promote trust, respect, and cohesion among group members (Johnson, 2009, 2011; Van Raalte et al., 2007; Waldron & Kowalski, 2009).

Attribution of Blame

Another common justification found throughout the hazing literature is the attribution of blame. This justification embraces the redirection of responsibility and blame back onto the newcomer by emphasizing their perceived willingness or consent. According to Bandura (1999), "By blaming others… not only are one's own actions made excusable, but one can even feel self-righteous in the process" (p. 41). Students who have been subjected to hazing also appear to adopt the justification of consent in order to rationalize engagement and lack of reporting. For example, among the participants in the Allan and Madden (2008) study who self-labeled prior experiences as hazing, many attributed their lack of reporting to personal consent or choice. Students' qualitative responses included

"I had a choice to participate or not" and "I was happy and willing to do all of the things I did; I have no desire to report them" (p. 29). This internalization of responsibility was once again demonstrated by Allan and colleagues in 2019. When asked why students did not report prior hazing experiences, the most common response with 75% was "I chose to participate."

Reflecting back on the hazing definitions discussed earlier in this chapter, it is important to recall that the act of hazing still occurs regardless of the perceived willingness or consent of newcomers (Diamond et al., 2016; Hollmann, 2002; Wilfert, 2007). And there are serious legal implications that need to be underscored for those involved since hazing is illegal in 44 states (Hazing Law, 2018). Hazing perpetrators can be held legally and civilly liable for maladaptive initiation practices and any co-occurring crimes, such as the provision of alcohol to minors, underage drinking, kidnapping, forcible confinement, sexual assault, and manslaughter (Crow, 2008; Crow & MacIntosh, 2009). It is also possible to bring civil suits against coaches and university administration for lack of oversight and supervision (Crow & Rosner, 2002). With more colleges adopting anti-hazing policies and educational awareness programming (Fields et al., 2010), possible institutional implications entail team seasons being cancelled, fines, suspensions, expulsions, and the withholding of diplomas (Crow & Rosner, 2002; Diamond et al., 2016; Gervais, 2006). In total, the justification of consent does not prove advantageous when compared to the actual legal and institutional implications of hazing.

Minimization of Dangers

By using expressions such as 'horseplay' and 'harmless pranks' to describe hazing, there is the tendency to trivialize involvement by minimizing or downplaying the seriousness of the behaviors (Aronson, 2012). When asking why students did not report prior experiences of hazing, Allan and Madden (2008) observed minimization with responses like "it was no big deal" and "no one got hurt." Describing hazing as a "non-issue" and requesting that researchers "…just leave it alone" (Hoover & Pollard, 1999), student-athletes often do not consider hazing to be harmful (Waldron, 2008; Waldron & Kowalski, 2009). And as Bandura (1990) indicated, "As long as the detrimental results of one's conduct are ignored, minimized, distorted, or disbelieved, there is little reason for self-censure to be activated" (p. 37). And without self-censure, or the judgment of personal wrongdoing, perpetrators will not likely deviate from their actions, and hazing will continue.

Despite the tendency to minimize or downplay the seriousness of hazing (Allan et al., 2019; Allan & Madden, 2008; Hoover & Pollard, 1999, 2000), maladaptive initiation behaviors continue to result in significant physical and psychological harm, and even death (Srabstein, 2008). Among high school students who reported being subjected to hazing, Hoover and Pollard (2000) noted that 71% endorsed negative emotional and physical consequences stemming from the experience. These consequences included: fighting, injury, poor academic performance, anger, difficulty with eating, sleeping, and concentrating; and feeling confused, embarrassed, or guilty.

Other potential injuries from hazing can include: intra-cranial, thoracic, abdominal, and chest trauma; organ damage; hypoxic brain damage; burns; cold exposure; heat stroke; suffocation; aspiration; and sexual assault (Crow, 2008; Finkel, 2002; Johnson & Holman, 2004). Regarding possible emotional or psychological harm, hazing has also been associated with feelings of regret, shame, apathy, mistrust, anxiety, isolation, and stress (Caudill, 2014; Finkel, 2002; Gervais, 2006; Hollmann, 2002; Hoover & Pollard, 1999, 2000). The minimization of hazing and its potential implications can be disastrous and even cruel to all of those involved. And yet, hazing persists.

OTHER PREDICTABLE EFFECTS OF DISSONANCE AND SELF-JUSTIFICATION

Denial

It is likely that cognitive dissonance and self-justifications contributed to the denial and under-reporting of hazing explored throughout the introduction of this chapter. According to prior research, students often concluded that behaviors could not be qualified as hazing if there was a purpose, consent was obtained, and positive benefits accrued (Allan & Madden, 2008, 2012; Waldron, 2008). Thus, by relying on the psychological processes of moral justification and the misattribution of responsibility, students' own degree of involvement and understanding of hazing is likely distorted. And by minimizing or downplaying the seriousness of hazing, individuals further trivialize and distort their experiences as something different and less offensive to self-concept. Cognitive dissonance and self-justifications may be adaptive in certain situations to reduce psychological distress, but in relation to hazing, these psychological mechanisms limit self-awareness and potentially allow continued engagement in maladaptive behaviors.

Escalation

Though the dangers associated with hazing are often minimized (Allan et al., 2019; Allan & Madden, 2008; Hoover & Pollard, 1999, 2000), there is risk for escalation into egregious acts of physical, psychological, and sexual abuse. Hoover and Pollard (1999) reported that of the student-athletes who endorsed participating in questionable hazing behaviors, over 80% endorsed experiencing unacceptable or illegal hazing initiation activities. And since there is the tendency to justify earlier actions with more extreme behaviors (Aronson, 2012), the research performed by Hoover and Pollard (1999) underscores the importance of reconceptualizing harmless or questionable hazing behaviors as "a warning sign of more dangerous and destructive behavior" (p. 9). Zero-tolerance anti-hazing policies are strongly encouraged to limit the risk of escalation (Diamond et al., 2016; Fields et al., 2014; Hollmann, 2002; Wilfert, 2007).

A Cycle of Hazing

It is through the experience of cognitive dissonance and the use of self-justifications that the maladaptive and harmful practice of hazing not only continues to persist in the short-term but also in the long-term. Indicative of the cyclical nature of hazing, research has detected a high positive correlation between the number of hazing incidents experienced and then committed against another person (Owen et al., 2008). Hamilton, Scott, LaChapelle, and O'Sullivan (2016) also identified personal rookie hazing experiences to be the strongest predictor of hazing perpetration. By justifying hazing as a 'rite of passage' or 'tradition' (Allan & Madden, 2008, 2012; Crow & MacIntosh, 2009; Hoover & Pollard, 1999; Waldron & Kowalski, 2009), and by perceiving the experience in a favorable and productive manner (Allan et al., 2019; Allan & Madden, 2008, 2012; Owen et al., 2008), hazing may then be internalized, normalized, and passed down to the next group of newcomers.

Conformity

Why does hazing persist? Why do senior group members feel the need to haze? And why do newcomers undergo humiliation, degradation, and potential abuse to be a part of a group or team? The answers to these questions are complicated. In this section, the perspectives of the hazing senior member and the hazed newcomer will be examined. And though the nuances of each perspective may be somewhat different, the overarching motivation for hazing can best be described as the desire to belong, which is well-recognized as one of the basic motives behind any conformity (see Aronson, 2012; see also Varley & Zito, this volume), including that which characterizes hazing. And to be clear, conformity is defined as the "change in a person's behavior or opinions as a result of real or imagined pressure from a person or group or people" (Aronson, 2012, p. 19).

Broadly described as a process of socialization (Waldron & Kowalski, 2009), it is through the mechanism of hazing that senior group members encourage newcomers' conformity to group values and norms. Prior research suggests that hazing is used to elicit group allegiance, reinforce status hierarchies, and promote group-relevant skills and attitudes (Keating, et al, 2005). Following data collection from 269 undergraduate students, Keating and colleagues concluded that initiations "function as a training ground" (p.122) for group-relevant skills and attitudes as student-athletes reported engaging in more physically demanding and painful initiation activities as compared to Greek-letter members. They also concluded that initiations are used to facilitate group allegiance, with group importance being predicted by initiation severity (see also Aronson, 2012) and the amount of fun experienced during the initiations.

Also reported by Keating and colleagues (2005), the belief that hazing indoctrinates newcomers to the hierarchy or power structure of a group is frequently cited in the literature. Johnson (2011) suggested that despite creating division and a lack of trust among group members, hazing is used to educate "newcomers as to their place in the hierarchical structure of the group" (p. 203). While researching hazing in student-athletes, Waldron and Kowalski (2009) noted that participants often identified hazing as being necessary to "keep the pecking order" of the team. Relatedly, Cimino (2011) asserted that hazing is a process through which senior group members confirm their power and dominance over newcomers.

Regarding the newcomers' thinking, it is through deviant over-conformity, or the uncritical and unquestioning acceptance of group norms to include that of hazing (Coakley, 2007), that newcomers seek to: (a) demonstrate their dedication and commitment to the group (Alan & Madden, 2008; Johnson, 2011; Kirby & Wintrup, 2002; Waldron & Kowalski, 2009); (b) earn the respect and acceptance of senior group members (Allan & Madden, 2008; Crow, 2008; Waldron & Kowalski, 2009); (c) acquire 'in-group' status and distinction (Kirby & Wintrup, 2002; Waldron & Kowalski, 2009); and (d) gain access to all privileges and benefits associated with group membership (Diamond et al., 2016; Hollmann, 2002). Nevertheless, despite these perceived benefits of hazing, the fact remains that there is no added benefit to hazing that couldn't be obtained in another manner.

INTERVENTION

A comprehensive multifaceted approach that includes policy, education, and intervention is required to effectively address the complex issue of hazing (Stirling, 2009). On an institutional level, it is necessary to develop clearly defined anti-hazing policies, procedures, and penalties that will then serve as the backbone for all prevention and intervention efforts (Crow, 2008; Fields et al., 2010; Waldron, 2009). Clear, consistent, and regular articulation of these policies and procedures is necessary to combat the potential lack of knowledge, understanding, and awareness among group members (Crow, 2008; Crow & MacIntosh, 2009; Diamond, et al., 2016). In addition to using printed anti-hazing documents (Crow, 2008), alternative communication strategies, such as email, *Facebook*, *Instagram*, and other social media platforms, may be helpful in increasing the breadth and depth of messaging (see also Nevels & Vasquez, this volume). It is also critical to provide a clear definition of hazing as well as information on confidential reporting in all messaging (Crow, 2008; Waldron, 2009).

To break the cycle of hazing (Diamond et al., 2016; Frangione et al., 2017; Kirby & Wintrup, 2002), there must be a balance between reactive and proactive anti-hazing efforts. This balance assists in preventing future instances of hazing from occurring while also intervening on current maladaptive initiation behaviors. Regarding reactive intervention efforts, a zero-tolerance policy emphasizing prompt investigation is strongly recommended (Diamond et al., 2016; Fields et al., 2014; Hollmann, 2002; Wilfert, 2007). This approach eliminates current hazing practices, prevents the risk for future escalation, and limits the harmful implications of hazing.

Prevention efforts in the form of educational presentations and workshops are encouraged to support students' knowledge of hazing and associated policies (Crow, 2008; Crow & Macintosh, 2009; Waldron, 2009). Educational programming may also help in clarifying and addressing the diverse nuances of hazing, including the common myths and justifications that appear to perpetuate hazing (Diamond et al., 2016; Fields, et al., 2014). In addition to student leadership development, prevention efforts targeting alcohol abuse are recommended since hazing and alcohol consumption frequently occur at the same time (Hollmann, 2002).

With research highlighting the potential influence that adults' attitudes and behaviors have on students' involvement in hazing (Hoover & Pollard, 2000), prevention and intervention efforts are warranted to support parents, teachers, advisors, coaches, and other persons of authority. Through psychoeducational programming, definitions of hazing can be provided, an explanation of how and why hazing continues can be offered, and the perceived benefits versus actual consequences can be processed (Wilfert, 2007). This open and honest dialogue with authority figures may further support awareness and implementation of anti-hazing policies and procedures. Interactive skill-based instruction on how to recognize and respond to hazing may help prepare authority figures in the implementation of policies and procedures.

Additional intervention opportunities with authority figures can focus on supporting the development of alternative entry rituals and team-building traditions (Diamond et al., 2016; Hoover & Pollard, 1999; Johnson, 2009, 2011; Van Raalte et al., 2007; Waldron, 2008; Waldron & Kowalski, 2009). As Johnson (2011) noted, it is still important that positive and alternative entry rituals are used to commemorate group membership and identity. And authority figures, such as coaches, have been identified as one of the most influential factors in the elimination of abusive initiation practices and the creation of a "more welcoming, democratized, inclusive, and rewarding orientation experience"

(Johnson, 2009, p. 3). As a result, administration, teachers, coaches, advisors, parents, and team leaders should be supported in the development of trust and respect through new orientation and team-building traditions, such as co-operative games, ropes courses, and team-building exercises.

Given the pervasive and harmful nature of hazing, Diamond and colleagues. (2016) advocate an interdisciplinary approach to prevention and intervention. It will ultimately be through the combined efforts of administration, teachers, advisors, coaches, parents, and students that real change will occur regarding the reduction and prevention of hazing. However, given the deep-rooted culture of hazing, the inclusion of mental health providers in comprehensive anti-hazing efforts is also warranted (Diamond et al., 2016). Trained and licensed to provide individual and group interventions for behavioral health concerns that often stem from or are worsened by hazing, mental health providers can also provide valuable insight in the psychological and motivational processes that contribute to hazing. As such, the expertise of mental health professionals may be helpful in administrative and institutional efforts that attempt to address the underlying causes of these harmful initiation behaviors.

With differences in training, scope of competency, and licensure, not all mental health professionals may be a good fit for hazing prevention and intervention efforts. Trained in the provision of strength-based and culturally sensitive practices for common developmental concerns to more severe mental health disorders (Horne, 2014; Munley et al., 2004), counseling psychologists are uniquely qualified to provide services targeting hazing prevention, intervention, and treatment in all contexts.

Equipped to provide individual therapy to hazing perpetrators, victims, and bystanders for depression, anxiety, aggression, substance abuse, trauma symptoms, and crisis resolution, licensed counseling psychologists can assist in the development of mutual trust, respect, unity, communication, and cohesion through group intervention. Relatedly, with the support of a licensed counseling psychologist, groups can also be guided in the development of alternative initiation and teambuilding traditions that promote the well-being of individual members while encouraging elevations in the group's overall performance. Trained to provide consultation services addressing systemic, institutional, and interpersonal functioning, a counseling psychologist's expertise would lend itself well to the development of anti-hazing policies and procedures.

FUTURE DIRECTIONS

To limit possible confusion and ambiguity surrounding hazing, the adoption of a clear and consistent definition of hazing that can be used across contexts and populations is necessary (Crow & MacIntosh, 2009; Diamond et al., 2016). This clarification would allow for consistency in measurement and comparison across research studies. And most relevant to his chapter, a universally adopted definition may limit the power that self-justification has in the reduction of cognitive dissonance and the persistence of the maladaptive initiation practices. And of course, continued adoption of anti-hazing policies, procedures, and programming is strongly recommended (Crow, 2008; Fields et al., 2014).

To support continued prevention and intervention efforts across contexts and populations, additional research on the various nuances of hazing is needed. In addition to the identification and clarification of risk and protective factors (Fields et al., 2014; Stirling, 2009), research on the justifications and motivations for hazing would assist in the tailoring of programming and intervention efforts. And as the current research is lacking in empirically informed and tested approaches to hazing, now is an ideal time to focus on the development and empirical evaluation of prevention programing and treatment interventions (Fields et al., 2014; Stirling, 2009).

As high school students experience hazing behaviors at alarmingly high rates (Allan & Madden, 2008, 2009; Hoover & Pollard, 1999, 2000), and given the research suggesting likely hazing perpetration following rookie initiation experiences (Hamilton et al., 2016; Owen et al., 2008), prevention and intervention efforts must begin before high school to protect members of groups from normalizing hazing. It will be important to work towards empirically-informed prevention and intervention efforts for both middle school and high school as well as college students. Other populations that may benefit from additional research and intervention include authority figures given their influence on students' attitudes and behaviors.

REFERENCES

Allan, E., Kerschner, D., & Payne, J. M. (2019). College student hazing experiences, attitudes, and perceptions: Implications for prevention. *Journal of Student Affairs Research and Practice*, *56*, 32-48.

Allan, E., & Madden, M. (2008). *Hazing in view: College students at risk. Initial findings from the National Study of Student Hazing*. Retrieved from http://www.stophazing.org/wp-content/uploads/2014/06/hazing_in_view_web1.pdf.

Allan, E., & Madden, M. (2009, April). *Hazing in view: High school students at risk.* Paper presented at the meeting for the American Educational Research Association, San Diego, CA.

Allan, E., & Madden, M. (2012). The nature and extent of college student hazing. *International Journal of Adolescent Medicine and Health, 24*, 83-90.

Aronson, E. (2012). *The social animal* (11th ed.). New York: Worth Publishers.

Aronson, E., & Mills, J. (1959). The effect of severity on initiation on liking for the group. *Journal of Abnormal and Social Psychology*, *59*, 177-181.

Bandura, A. (1990). Selective activation and disengagement of moral control. *Journal of Social Issues*, *46*, 27-46.

Bronfenbrenner, U. (1979). *The ecology of human development: Experiments by nature and design*. Cambridge, Massachusetts: Harvard University Press.

Campo, S., Poulos, G., & Sipple, J. W. (2005). Prevalence and profiling: Hazing among college students and points of intervention. *American Journal of Health Behavior*, *29*, 137-149.

Carran, A. V., Brawley, L. R., & Widmeyer, W. N. (1998). The measurement of cohesiveness in sport groups. In J. L. Duda (ed.), *Advances in sport and exercise psychology measurement* (pp. 213-226). Morgantown, West Virginia: Fitness Information Technology.

Caudill, K. (2014, July 24). *What is hazing?*. Retrieved from http://www.nfhs.org/hazing.aspx.

Centers for Disease Control and Prevention. (2019). *Preventing bullying*. Retrieved from https://www.cdc.gov/violenceprevention/pdf/bullying-factsheet508.pdf.

Chin, J. W., & Johnson, J. (2011). Making the team: Threats to health and wellness within sport hazing cultures. *International Journal of Health, Wellness, and Society*, *1*, 29-38.

Cimino, A. (2011). The evolution of hazing: Motivational mechanisms and the abuse of newcomers. *Journal of Cognition and Culture*, *11*, 241-267.

Coakley, J. (2007). *Sports in society: Issues and controversies* (9th ed.). Boston, MA: McGraw-Hill.

Crow, R. B. (2008). The prevalence and prevention of hazing in sport. *Pennsylvania Journal of Health, Physical Education, Recreation, and Dance*, *78*, 33-36.

Crow, R. B., & MacIntosh, E. W. (2009). Conceptualizing a meaningful definition of hazing in sport. *European Sport Management Quarterly*, *9*, 433-451.

Crow, R. B., & Rosner, S. R. (2002). Institutional and organizational liability for hazing in intercollegiate and professional team sports. *St. John's Law Review*, *76*, 87-114.

Crowne, D. P., & Marlowe, D. (1960). A new scale of social desirability independent of psychopathology. *Journal of Consulting Psychology*, *24*, 349-354.

Diamond, A. B., Callahan, S. T., Chain, K. F., & Solomon, G. S. (2016). Qualitative review of hazing in collegiate and school sports: Consequences from a lack of culture, knowledge, and responsiveness. *British Journal of Sports Medicine*, *50*, 149-153.

Doran, E. (2008, October 19). Colgate University men's sports team suspended for hazing, 'high-risk alcohol consumption.' Retrieved from https://www.syracuse.com/schools/2018/10/colgate_university_mens_team_swimming_diving_team_suspended_for_hazing.html.

Festinger, L. (1957). *A theory of cognitive dissonance*. Evanston, IL: Row, Peterson and Company.

Fields, S. K., Collins, C. L., & Comstock, R. D. (2010). Violence in youth sports: Hazing, brawling, and foul play. *British Journal of Sports Medicine*, *44*, 32-37.

Finkel, M. A. (2002). Traumatic injuries caused by hazing practices. *American Journal of Emergency Medicine*, *20*, 228-233.

Frangione, M., Mayfield, C., Walsh, A., Bonura, K. B., & Galli, N. (2017, June). Hazing in sport, *SportPsych Works*, *5*(2). Retrieved from https://www.apadivisions.org/division-47/publications/sportpsych-works/hazing-sport.pdf.

Hamilton, R., Scott, D., LaChapelle, D., & O'Sullivan, L. (2016). Applying social cognitive theory to predict hazing perpetration in university athletics. *Journal of Sport Behavior*, *39*, 255-277.

Hazing and bullying. (2018). *HAZINGPREVENTION.ORG*. Retrieved from https://hazingprevention.org/home/hazing/hazing-and-bullying/.

Hazing Law. (2018). *HAZINGPREVENTION.ORG*. Retrieved from https://hazingprevention.org/home/hazing/statelaws/.

Hinkle Smith, S. L., & Stellino, M. B. (2007) Cognitive dissonance in athletic hazing: The roles of commitment and athletic identity. *Journal of Sport & Exercise Psychology, 29,* S169-S170.

Hollmann, B. B. (2002). Hazing: Hidden campus crime. *New Directions for Student Services*, *99*, 11-23.

Hoover, N. C., & Pollard, N. J. (1999). *National survey: Initiation rites and athletics for NCAA sports teams*. Retrieved from https://www.alfred.edu/about/news/studies/docs/hazing.pdf.

Hoover, N. C., & Pollard, N. J. (2000). *Initiation rites in American high schools: A national survey. Final report*. Retrieved from https://files.eric.ed.gov/fulltext/ED445809.pdf.

Horne, A. (2014). We've been great places, We will go to even greater places: 2013 presidential address. *The Counseling Psychologist*, *42*, 124-138.

Jeckell, A. S., Copenhaver, E. A., Diamond, A. B. (2018). The spectrum of hazing and peer sexual abuse in sports: A current perspective. *Sports Health*, *10*, 558-564.

Johnson, J. (2009). From the sidelines: The role of the coach in affecting team unity and cohesion in place of hazing traditions. *Journal of Coaching Education*, *2*(1), 1-28.

Johnson, J. (2011). Through the liminal: A comparative analysis of communitas and rituals of passage in sport hazing initiations. *Canadian Journal of Sociology, 36*, 199-227.

Keating, C. F., Pomerantz, J., Pommer, S. D., Ritt, S. J., Miller, L. M., & McCormick, J. (2005). Going to college and unpacking hazing: A fundamental approach to decrypting initiation practices among undergraduates. *Group Dynamics: Theory, Research and Practice, 9*, 104-126.

Kirby, S. L., & Wintrup, G. (2002). Running the gauntlet: An examination of initiation/hazing and sexual abuse in sport. In C. Brackenridge & K. Fasting (Eds.), *Sexual harassment and abuse in sport: International research and policy perspectives* (pp.65-90). London, England: Whiting & Birch.

Kowalski, C., & Waldron, J. (2010). Looking the other way: Athletes' perceptions of coaches' responses to hazing. *International Journal of Sports Science and Coaching*, *5*, 87-100.

Munley, P. H., Duncan, L E., McDonnell, K. A., & Sauer, E. M. (2004). Counseling psychology in the United States of America. *Counseling Psychology Quarterly, 17*, 247-271.

Nuwer, H. (2004). How sportswriters contribute to a hazing culture in athletics. In J. Johnson, & M. Holman (Eds.), *Making the team: Inside the world of sport initiations and hazing* (pp. 118-131). Toronto: Canadian Scholar's Press.

Owen, S. S., Burke, T. W., & Vichesky, D. (2008). Hazing in student organizations: Prevalence, attitudes, and solutions. *Oracle: The Research Journal of the Association of Fraternity Advisors*, *3*(1), 40-58.

Srabstein, J. (2008). Deaths linked to bullying and hazing. *International Journal of Adolescent Medicine and Health*, *20*, 235-239.

Stirling, A. E. (2009). Definition and constituents of maltreatment in sport: Establishing a conceptual framework for research practitioners. *British Journal of Sports Medicine*, *43*, 1091-1099.

Van Raalte, J. L., Cornelius, A. E., Linder, D. E., & Brewer, B. W. (2007). The relationship between hazing and team cohesion. *The Journal of Sport Behavior, 30*, 491-507.

Waldron, J. J. (2008). I have to do what to be a teammate?. *Journal of Physical Education*, *79*(5), 4-5.

Waldron, J. J., & Kowalski, C. L. (2009). Crossing the line: Rites of passage, team aspects, and ambiguity of hazing. *Research Quarterly for Exercise & Sport*, *80*, 291-302.

Wilfert, M. (2007). *Building new traditions: Hazing prevention in college athletics.* Indianapolis, IN: National Collegiate Athletic Association.

Winslow, D. (1999). Rites of passage and group bonding in the Canadian airborne. *Armed Forces and Society*, *25*, 429-457.

In: Social Psychology and Counseling
Editors: D. A. Kleiber and E. Delgado-Romero
ISBN: 978-1-53616-548-7

Chapter 9

COGNITIVE DISSONANCE AND EAST-WEST CULTURAL DIFFERENCES

Yi-Chen (Jenny) Wu and Geoff J. Bathje

Misgivings and 'second guessing' about one's decisions and actions taken are relatively common in everyday life. Daily choices ranging from simple to difficult reflect such decisional conflicts. Thus, it is not unusual to hear people complain or express guilt over relatively common decisions in everyday life. This chapter will review the typical patterns of pre- and post-decision dissonance that occur in more or less serious situations and the patterns of self-justification that are used to resolve such dissonance (see also chapters by Britton and Bigham, this volume). But it will also show variations in such patterns that occur along cultural lines, some with distinct implications for mental health and for counseling practice.

COGNITIVE DISSONANCE THEORY

Cognitive dissonance theory was first proposed by Festinger in 1957 to describe the discomfort and anxious feelings one experiences when faced with a situation wherein two psychologically inconsistent cognitions are simultaneously held (Aronson, 2012). Here cognitions can stand for thoughts, beliefs, attitudes, and behaviors. In Festinger and Carlsmith's study in 1959, participants were asked to perform a rather boring task. After finishing the task, participants in experimental group received either $1 or $20 to tell the next participants that the task was fun. Participants in the control group did not receive any money and could speak the truth about the task to the next participants. Before leaving the experiment, participants were asked to share their real thoughts about the task. The result showed that those received $20 tended to be more negative about the tasks while those who received only $1 tended to have more positive attitudes towards it. This confirmed the hypothesis proposed by the cognitive dissonance theory: people who received more money could use the reward to justify their misleading suggestions to others. However, people not receiving sufficient reward to justify their doing the boring task wound up changing their attitude toward the task – to 'not really boring' - so that they could lessen their dissonance.

The core notion of cognitive dissonance theory derived from cognitive consistency theory, which refers to a person's strong motivation for being consistent with respect to beliefs, attitudes, and behaviors (Abelson et al., 1968). According to Festinger (1957), "there is pressure to produce consonant relations among cognitions and to avoid and reduce dissonance" (p. 9). Adverse feelings arise from cognitive dissonance. To avoid adverse feelings, one is motivated to reduce the cognitive inconsistency by changing an attitude or belief to be consistent with one's behavior. Or one may also change behavior or add a new belief to reduce dissonance. In the experiment mentioned before, participants who received only $1 experienced what was called *insufficient justification*, so they were more likely to talk themselves into a different attitude to match their recent behavior.

The same assumption was applied to research on matters of education, law, and economics. Aronson and Carlsmith (1963) designed an experiment to test the long-term behavioral effect on children who received mild or severe threat to avoid giving into temptation when instructed not to play with certain appealing toys. The results confirmed that children who were given *less* of a threat of punishment experienced greater dissonance when resisting the temptation to play with an appealing toy than did those who received a higher threat. Due to insufficient external justification (inadequate threat), these children felt greater dissonance about resisting temptation to play with the appealing toy and avoided playing with the toy for 45 days after the initial manipulation took place, apparently 'deciding' it was of less interest.

Summarized by Greenberg (2015), past experiments have supported the finding that four factors that may intensify one's experience of dissonance: degree of external justification, choice, commitment, and foreseeable adverse consequences. If someone has adequate justification or lack of choice for carrying out a behavior, he or she is less likely to experience discomfort and the need to change. Also, if someone is committed to a dissonant cognition or can foresee an adverse consequence for engaging in an act, a greater degree of stress is predictable and thus brings greater motivation to change either actions or cognitions to restore consonance.

For decades subsequent to those early investigations, researchers have continued to challenge the theoretical propositions to better understand the cognitive dissonance experience and self-justifying reactions. Two theories that have been hypothesized rejected the idea of motivation for consistency. Bem's *Self-perception theory* (Bem, 1965) proposed that people often observe themselves to understand their own attitudes. Instead of experiencing contradictory feelings that motivate attitude change, people explained their attitudes based on making an inference from their behaviors. *Impression Management Theory* (Tedeschi, Schlenker, & Bonoma, 1971) also offered another explanation that opposed the motivation for cognitive consistency. Rather than seeking cognitive consistency, people tend to correct their attitudes or behavior according to what was expected of them.

Following the same track of thought, Steele's *Self-affirmation Theory* (1988) posited that people are motivated to maintain integrity of the self. When participants in this experiment were given a chance to affirm an important value, they didn't show the same motivation to reconcile inconsistent cognitions. On the other hand, Harmon-Jones (1999) proposed an action-based model of dissonance by stating that a person with inconsistent cognitions would feel uncomfortable because the inconsistency might interfere with effective action. These alternative theories of dissonance phenomena and self-justification patterns lead one to further consider the circumstances that might make for differences.

CULTURAL FACTORS

Some researchers have questioned whether cognitive dissonance is a trans-cultural phenomenon that applies to all human beings (Choi & Choi, 2002; Heine & Lehman, 1997; Markus & Kitayama, 1991; Peng & Nisbett, 1999). Most dissonance studies have been done in North America and have generally supported original cognitive dissonance theory, including findings from brain imaging studies. To this date, data collected from fMRI studies have indicated that the activation of two brain regions (dorsal anterior cingulate cortex and left anterior insula) were correlated with the degree of cognitive dissonance experienced by participants (Izuma, Matsumoto, Murayama, Samejima, Norihiro, & Matsumoto, 2013; Kitayama, Chua, Tompson, & Han, 2013; Vries, Byrne, & Kehoe, 2015). These studies suggested a biological basis for cognitive dissonance experiences as a common human behavior. However, there is some research indicating cultural differences in the cognitive contents that induce dissonant discomfort and dissonance-reducing behavior (see also Zhu, this volume).

Setting out to test cognitive dissonance theory with Japanese participants, Sakai (1981) conducted an induced compliance paradigm study with Japanese high school sophomores in Japan. Surprisingly, the result showed that Japanese students only made significant change in their private opinions when making a counter-attitudinal speech in public; they did not change their private opinions when making an anonymous speech. At the time, the different results were explained by impression management theory and self-perception theory rather than looking for a cultural explanation. Different from Sakai's interpersonal procedure, Heine and Lehman (1997) conducted a free-choice paradigm experiment which was designed with an intrapersonal procedure. The results suggested that Canadians tended to convince themselves that they made the best choice of CDs for themselves while Japanese participants displayed no justification behaviors for the choices they made and viewed both chosen and unchosen CDs as equally attractive and desirable. Heine and Lehman attempted to explain the differences found in both populations by using self-affirmation theory and argued that East Asians showed no dissonance reduction because it did not threaten their interdependent self. Although neither study discussed culture differences further, they provided a challenge to cognitive dissonance theory and implied that cognitive dissonance may be a phenomenon that is limited to Western cultures.

Two more recent studies attempted to further examine the cultural differences in cognitive dissonance experience and confirmed that cultural influences can impact the magnitude of dissonance (Greenberg, 2015). Kitayama, Snibbe, Markus, and Suzuki (2004) conducted four experiments based on a free-choice dissonance paradigm. The results showed that Japanese students experienced a greater dissonance towards displays of inconsistency in public, while European American students showed a stronger dissonance effect when a choice is perceived as private and personal. Similarly, in a cross-cultural cognitive study conducted by Hoshino-Browne, Zanna, Spencer, Kitayama, and Lackenbauer (2005), East Asian Canadian participants tended to justify their behavior when making a choice for a friend, whereas European Canadians exhibited their dissonance reduction when making a decision for themselves. Based on interdependent self-construal in comparison with independent self-construal (cf. Markus & Kitayama, 1991), these studies suggested that dissonance may be experienced in a different way in Eastern and Western cultures.

In the following sections, we attempt to explain the cultural differences in cognitive dissonance by various aspects that were commonly discussed when exploring cross-cultural research between Western and Eastern cultures. First, we looked at differences in self-concept and self-esteem due to dichotomous and dialectical cognition. Second, we examined the influence of individualism and collectivism on one's self-concept and self-esteem. Third, we considered the notion of looseness and tightness which may affect one's experience with cognitive dissonance.

Dichotomous and Dialectical Thinking

To explain how culture affects one's experience and response to cognitive dissonance, we should revisit the core notion of cognitive dissonance theory, which is that "dissonance could arise from logical inconsistency" (Festinger, 1957, p. 14) and that people are motivated to maintain a consistent self. The assumption that cognitive incongruity causes individuals to feel uncomfortable and forces individuals to integrate contradictory cognitions may be embedded in Aristotelian philosophy (Peng & Nisbett, 1999).

Aristotelian philosophy emphasized three principles: the law of identity, the law of non-contradiction, and the law of the excluded middle, all of which are more consistent with Western than Eastern philosophy (Spencer-Rodgers, Peng, Wang, & Hou, 2004). This means Westerners tend to be synthetic in their cognitive orientation and view an object or event as either positive or negative. Based on these three principles, Westerners may be inclined to believe that attitude is dichotomous or bipolar in nature; thus, they are less likely to tolerate attitudinal ambivalence and more likely to seek resolution of incongruity (Lewin, 1951; Peng & Nisbett, 1999). Therefore, it is easy to understand that cognitive dissonance theory would apply especially to individuals in Western culture.

On the other hand, Eastern cultures were influenced by Confucianism and Buddhism, that promotes tolerance for contradiction, constant change, and holism (Peng & Nisbett, 1999). Other ways to describe the features of dialectical thinking are moderation, balance, and staying neutral (Kitayama & Markus, 1999; Peng & Nisbett, 1999). Influenced by these tenets, Easterners tend to present dialectical thoughts which allow them to accept psychological contradiction (Peng, Ames, & Knowles, 2001). Individuals in dialectical cultures can accept negative emotions more than those in dichotomous cultures, whereas individuals in dichotomous cultures may express a greater intolerance of negative emotions (Schimmack, Oishi, & Diener, 2002). Also, Japanese individuals appear to accept their failures as easily as their successes and experience less cognitive dissonance when presented with negative personality feedback (Heine et al., 1999; Kitayama et al., 1997). Thus, since Easterners may tend to seek a balance of positive and negative emotions, they may experience lower levels of aversive feelings when encountering contradictory cognitions.

Furthermore, different cognitive orientations affect how individuals evaluate the self and form self-concepts and self-worth. According to Aronson's self-consistency theory, cognitive dissonance relies heavily on an individual's need to maintain a self-concept that is competent and morally good, which is highly valued in Western more dichotomous culture (Heine, Lehman, Markus, & Kitayama, 1999). However, influenced by dialectical thinking, Asians seemed to identify both positive and negative traits with self in an implicit association test (Boucher et al., 2009). A more recent study also confirmed that individuals in dialectical-thinking cultures are inclined to acknowledge and accept greater ambivalence in appraisal of self than those in synthesis-oriented cultures (Spencer-Rodgers et al., 2016). Thus, these studies suggest that the need to see oneself as a coherent whole and positive self may cause more dissonance in Westerners than in Easterners since Easterners are expected to be flexible and alter the self to situate appropriately across different interpersonal situations.

From another perspective, compared to individuals in Western culture, Easterners with dialectical thinking are discouraged from the adoption of extreme positions so that they are more willing to acknowledge their negative traits, hence they tend to report lower self-esteem more often than those in Western cultures (Heine et al., 1999; Oishi, Diener, Lucas, & Suh, 1999, Spencer-Rodgers et al., 2009). According to Steele's (1988) self-affirmation theory, those with higher self-esteem would be more likely to experience greater dissonance when losing self-consistency. Therefore, when acting in a counter-attitudinal way, Easterners will likely experience less dissonance than Westerners do.

Individualism and Collectivism

An abundance of research has shown that constructs like individualism and collectivism are defining cultural factors when examining psychological and behavioral differences between European American and East Asian cultural frames (Chan, 1994; Hofsted, 1980; Kitayama, Markus, Matsumoto, & Norasakkunkit, 1997; Oyserman, et al, 2002; Yamaguchi, 1994). Individualism and collectivism are not opposite ends of a continuum but should be viewed as separate constructs, with more or less of each coexisting within any particular cultural group (Harter, 2015). Although individualism is more likely to be found in Western countries (e.g., the United States, France, and Germany) and collectivism is more likely to be found in Eastern countries (e.g., China, Japan, and Korea), most countries contain both collectivistic and individualistic attributes within its culture.

The distinctions between individualism and collectivism can be traced back to Hofstede (1980) and Triandis (1989). Individualist culture puts emphasis on one's uniqueness so that it is critical to be distinct and to stand out in a group. A person is encouraged to pursue personal goals and tends to attribute success to personal ability. In contrast, collectivistic culture values one's loyalty to family, team, company, or nation and one's duty to in-group unity. Instead of pursuing personal accomplishment, one puts group goals prior to one's personal need and views one's status in the group as an indicator of success which can be attributed to help from others. In terms of different communication styles, individualistic culture promotes open and direct communication and expression of emotions while people from collectivist cultures are used to indirect communication and the suppression of emotion.

Sense of self also differs between collectivistic and individualistic societies. These two cultural orientations impact *self-construal* which can be largely independent or interdependent (Markus & Kitayama, 1991). The goal of those from collectivist cultures with interdependent self-construal is to achieve harmony within supportive social relationships, while Westerners, those with more independent self-construal, seek to be particularly talented, unique, and distinct from others (Harter, 2015). In more collectivistic cultures, additional motivators of behavior become more relevant, such as the motivation to maintain relationships, belongingness, or group harmony.

In the interdependent collectivist context, social identity is at least as important as individual identity, and so behavior is more likely to be interpreted through a social lens. For example, children as young as four years old in Singapore were more likely to consider interdependent causes and consequences than American children when asked their thoughts about going against social, moral, and interpersonal norms (Chernyak, Kang, & Kushnir, 2019). By using this understanding to interpret results of dissonance experiments that showed cultural differences (Hoshino-Browne et al., 2005; Kitayama et al., 2004), it seems that participants from the East Asian culture demonstrated little dissonance when a decision was made on behalf of important others rather than in one's own interests.

Cultural differences exist in the perception of self as well as in relation to self-esteem (Nesbitt, 2003). For example, when asked, "Tell me about yourself," North Americans will tend to describe their personality traits and attributes (e.g., extraverted and industrious), favorite activities (e.g., camping), or social roles they occupy (e.g., their professions), without providing much information about context. However, when the same question is asked in Japan, China, or Korea, context is typically part of the description of self (e.g., one might describe oneself as both "very serious at work" and "fun-loving with friends").

Nesbitt (2003) also compared the concept of self-esteem in Eastern and Western culture by noting that there is no indigenous concept in Japan for feeling good about oneself. Unlike Westerners who tend to use self-enhancement to increase positive feelings of self-esteem and accept pride as an appropriate emotional reaction to personal accomplishment, self-criticism is a strategy in Eastern Asian cultures for both improving social relationships and obtaining favorable social responses from the others (Wang & Ollendick, 2001).

Triandis (1989) argued that the concept of self-esteem is too limited as conventionally understood, suggesting three dimensions of self that can be meaningfully differentiated: private, public, and collective. In his view, the private sense is an assessment of the self by the self, the public self is an assessment of self by a generalized other, and the collective self is an assessment of self in relation to one's reference group(s). Western psychology clearly places more focus on the private self than on the public and collective self, which produces a bias in both published research and theory (Luhtanen & Crocker, 1992).

Tightness and Looseness

Another construct that reflects variations in the sense of self and behavior across cultures is *tightness versus looseness*. Both collectivism and individualism, can be defined in terms of cultural flexibility as "tight" or "loose" with respect to demand for conformity, compliance, and obedience (Bond & Smith, 1996). In cultures where there is either greater identification with the group or more conformity to group norms, this provides a potential source of justification that can mitigate dissonance.

Tightness and looseness are terms used to define how strong the cultural norms are within a culture and how much the culture either tolerates or disciplines behavior that deviates from the norms (Gelfand et al., 2011). Tightness does *not* correlate strongly with collectivism and looseness with individualism, as might be assumed. These constructs independently impact which dimensions of self are most relevant to a given situation. For example, while collectivist contexts tend to activate the collective self and concern with harmony in one's in-group, tightness is associated with activation of the public self and compliance with generalized societal expectations (Triandis, 1989). This may seem particularly relevant to dissonance theory, as strong external pressures more easily lend themselves to justification and therefore produce less dissonance. Tightness in a society may provide easier opportunities for external justification, while looseness may lead to more dissonance due to fewer sources of external justification and less activation of public and collective dimensions of self. This also corresponds to the 'New Look' model (Cooper & Fazio, 1984), according to which people in cultures where tightness prevails would experience less cognitive dissonance when their counter-attitudinal behavior actually follows the norms of the society and are likely to be considered appropriate under the circumstances. Thus, people in Eastern cultures who also experience the social construct of tightness would be expected to experience less cognitive dissonance.

However, the more important cultural difference in one's experience of cognitive dissonance may exist in justification, which in this context would be the complaint behavior. Take the Chinese for example, Chinese culture values compliance to authority more than Western culture does and is taught to children from a very early age (Chao, 1995; Luo, 1996). In recent cross-cultural research conducted by Chen, and associates (2010) on compliance behaviors, the results showed that 2-year-old Chinese toddlers demonstrated more voluntary committed compliance than Canadian toddlers. This means that Chinese toddlers presented more mature self-control and self-discipline than Canadian toddlers. Self-control refers to a process that requires one to recognize a conflict between two goals, concentrate on the more desired goal, and control one's behavior to meet the standards (Grass et al., 2019). Therefore, regardless of the intensity of dissonance experience, we can expect that people from tightness culture would choose to behave accordance to social norms or standards set by authority figures.

IMPLICATIONS FOR CLINICAL PRACTICE

To understand the impact of dissonance on clients in counseling from different cultural backgrounds, there are several variables that must be considered, including degree of individualism and collectivism, degree of tightness and looseness of their cultural reference group, and the aspects of self that are most likely to be activated by these factors. In response, clinicians may promote dialecticism as a means of helping clients to manage dissonance, as mindfulness-based therapies like *Dialectical Behavior Therapy* (DBT; Dimeff & Koermer, 2007) and *Acceptance and Commitment Therapy* (ACT; Hayes, Strosahl, & Wilson, 2009) tend to do. Approaches like *Motivational Interviewing* (Miller and Rollnick, 2012) also promote tolerance for ambivalence (i.e., dissonance in decision making), while challenging black-and-white thinking about behavior and change. To more clearly illustrate such interventions, two problem areas for counseling - the issues of substance abuse and medication adherence - can be considered.

Substance Use Treatment and Prevention

Standard practices for approaching stigmatized and difficult-to-change clinical issues, such as substance use, seem almost designed to produce significant cognitive dissonance among people who are in violation of the norms and rules through their substance use. There are strong (tight) cultural norms against addiction, and the illegal use of substances in the United States has been countervailed by a harsh and punitive war on drugs. When people who use drugs internalize these punitive messages yet continue to use drugs, there is a dissonance because they are engaging in a behavior that they believe to be wrong. This may at times encourage them to attempt to abstain from using drugs, but such attempts fail far more often than they succeed (Ferri, Amoto, & Davoli, 2006). When change fails, particularly in Western contexts that so often activate the private sense of self, self-justification becomes necessary to preserve a consistent self or self-esteem. In this case, justification may include taking on a totalizing label (e.g., "I'm an addict"), seeing behavior as outside one's control (e.g., "this is what addicts do"), devaluing one's desire for change ("I must not want change badly enough," or "I guess I haven't hit rock bottom yet.") or minimizing the significance of the drug use ("At least I'm not injecting.").

Treatment approaches like Motivational Interviewing (Miller and Rollnick, 2012) recognize that people are more likely to change when they are helped to tolerate inconsistencies and work through their ambivalence and dissonance while addressing basic needs (see also Varley & Zito, this volume). MI seeks to create a tolerance for dissonance in part by promoting dialectical thinking, such as acknowledging that people have reasons for and against change at the same time, or that change occurs gradually.

Counselors may promote the idea that relapse and recovery are not opposites but rather that slips and relapses are part of the recovery process. Similarly, *Harm Reduction Psychotherapy* (Denning and Little, 2011) attempts to address this dissonance by promoting "any positive change," as opposed to all-or-nothing abstinence goals, where failure leads to dissonance. In this approach, there is a focus on the client's self-chosen goals with a recognition that any progress toward that goal is a success. Thus, goals are often easily achievable or incremental, such as using new syringes rather than sharing syringes or reflecting on one's relationship to drug use without the short-term intent of changing one's drug use. Because of the strong focus on autonomy and choice, the harm reduction approach may be particularly well suited for cultures that are high in looseness and individualism, while the approach may be adapted in cultural contexts higher in tightness or collectivism by adding a focus on social motives and consideration of the perspective of others.

In Eastern cultures that have more of a dialectic tradition, where sense of self is more dependent on context, these may be treated as resources to protect self-concept and promote reflection in the face of substance use disorders. Rather than taking on a label like "addict," which is overdetermining to some and stigmatizing to others, clients may be able to reflect more easily on the contexts in which their substance use is problematic while also maintaining a more holistic view of themselves. For example, a client may more easily recognize that he drinks too much when working long hours or is unable to sleep, but that he doesn't feel as much of a need to drink when spending time with family.

On the other hand, substance use may be particularly stigmatizing, and people who use drugs or experience addictions may be particularly marginalized in societies that have strong norms against drug use and higher degrees of tightness and collectivism. This threat to the public and collective self may lead to great dissonance at the social level, rather than the individual level, and can pose significant barriers to seeking help while forcing users to go to great lengths to conceal their substance use.

Strong cultural messages against drug use may not even be effective as a prevention strategy, particularly in cultures with higher degrees of looseness. For example, where there are strong outside norms against substance use but the culture is generally tolerant of deviance from cultural norms (looseness), substance use can simultaneously be considered a means of individuating and an unacceptable deviance from norms. Strong prohibitions can also make the prohibited object more desirable because strong external justification leads people to attribute their decisions to external threats rather than to their personal choice. In other words, if a teenager greatly fears harsh punishment for smoking cannabis, then cannabis will tend to be more appealing if she believes that the only reason she hasn't tried it is due to the strong threat of punishment. Strong threats of punishment only work well in the short-term, when there is a sense that one is being observed or is likely to be caught. Weaker threats of consequences are actually more effective at leading someone to internalize a belief about a behavior, as per cognitive dissonance theory.

So, for example, a more mild consequence such as a parent telling their teen, "I'd be worried if you tried marijuana in high school because it's not good for your brain development at this age" might be more effective in preventing early drug use than a threat of harsh consequences. Because if the teen is not smoking marijuana, she is more likely to attribute the choice to her own preference rather than to an outside force that is constraining her. In the study referred to earlier, where children were threatened with either a strong consequence for touching a toy ("I would be angry and take the toy away") or a mild consequence ("I'd be a little disappointed"), researchers found the toy became much more desirable when there was a harsher threat (Aronson & Carlsmith, 1968, as cited in Greenberg, 2015).

However, strong messages may be relatively more effective for prevention in cultures that have high degrees of tightness and collectivism as this will tend to activate the collective and public self. For example, if adolescents believe that substance use is not acceptable for someone of their age and they are oriented toward conforming to the opinions of others and connection to their group, they would be more likely to see substance use as unattractive (see also Flaherty & Perkins, this volume). This may in part explain significantly lower rates of substance use among Asian Americans as compared to other American racial and ethnic groups, though there may be other factors, like "model minority" pressures (Chou & Feagin, 2016), that are also likely part of the picture.

Medication Adherence and Behavioral Health

Dissonance and self-justification patterns may have similar effects on medication adherence and health promoting behaviors (such as dietary changes) as with substance use. Though substance use is far more stigmatized and punished than lack of compliance with medication or diabetes prevention, there are parallels. With any behavior there is the potential for dissonance, as there are usually reasons for and against the behavior or change. For example, a young man may want the therapeutic effects of taking a psychiatric medication but dislike the side effects. If he believes he has to be on the medication but doesn't want to be, he may rely on external rather than internal justification to understand why he is taking the medication.

As notes previously, external justifications can be helpful or unhelpful, but they are less motivating than internal justifications in contexts where the private self is activated and also less likely to ensure adherence when external sanctions are no longer in force. For example, contrast the impact of co-existing supportive and unsupportive internal and external reasons for taking psychiatric medication for different levels of self. There is an interaction between internal and external pressures that has a different effect on dissonance and justification based on the level of self (private, public, or collective) that is activated by the person's cultural context. By taking these factors into consideration, the counselor can identify the client's barriers and the best course of action. For the client who is oriented toward collectivism, it may be particularly important to inquire about the degree of support from family and the social sources of dissonance. For the client who is relatively individualistic, it may be particularly important to understand intrinsic motivation and internal sources of cognitive dissonance. Of course, it is important to remember that individualism and collectivism are not opposite ends of a continuum and that all people have a personal, public, and collective self, though they may be activated to different degrees in different contexts.

The Course and Outcomes of Therapy More Generally

Dissonance may also impact the outcome of therapy in general. In a pioneering study, Joel Cooper (1980) examined the impact of choice on the outcome of therapy for a challenging issue. He studied participants with severe snake phobias, and he divided them into an exposure therapy group and a non-therapy control group that involved exercising. Within each group, he created a high choice and low choice condition, where participants could choose the therapy. He found that participants who felt more choice in picking the more challenging therapy (exposure therapy) reduced their phobia more than those with low choice. This finding may be most relevant to therapies that require more client effort and discomfort, as having a sense of choice allows clients to justify putting in the effort. If choice has a strong impact on outcome, it would also provide some explanation of why mandated treatments are less effective and provides a rationale for promoting choice and autonomy within mandated treatments (the so-called "menu of options" in treatment).

Finally, dissonance may come into play in different ways for different clinical issues (see also Britton, this volume). Clients' behaviors may conflict with their values; their cognitions may conflict with emotions, etc. Thinking through the role of dissonance in relation to a client's presenting concerns can help counselors to anticipate important barriers to success in counseling. For example, clients experiencing low energy and anhedonia associated with depression may come to explain their lack of desire to go to work in terms of dissatisfaction with their job or their lack of enthusiasm for life in general as evidence that they want to die. Here, there may be dissonance between "I want to be alive." and "I don't enjoy anything about living," particularly for clients who are not accustomed to tolerating dialectical thoughts. The counselor may help the client resolve this conflict by focusing on any of the three options for reducing dissonance: change one's cognitions (e.g., "I do still enjoy life sometimes"), add a third cognition that makes the first two less inconsistent (e.g., "I have been through this before, so I know my unhappiness is temporary"), or trivialize the cognitions that are inconsistent (e.g., "I know my life has meaning even if I'm not always happy."). Note that the statements above are more individualistic and relevant to the private self, but they can easily be adapted to focus on the public or collective self. For example, changing one's cognitions (e.g., "I want to be alive to take care of my family"), adding a third cognition (e.g., "I've heard that children are more likely to commit suicide if a parent has committed suicide, and I could never put them at risk of that."), or trivializing the inconsistent thoughts (e.g., "Life isn't just about happiness; I have a responsibility to other people.") are all ways out of the cognitive dissonance conundrum. Counselors can increase their effectiveness by recognizing points of dissonance for clients, while identifying the parts of the self that are most relevant to the individual client in a particular social and cultural context.

REFERENCES

Abelson, R. P., et al., 1968. (Eds.). *Theories of cognitive consistency: A source book.* Chicago, IL: Rand McNally.

Aronson, E. (2012). *The social animal.* (11th ed). New York: Worth.

Aronson, E. & Carlsmith, J. M. (1963). The effect of the severity of threat on the de-valuation of forbidden behavior. *Journal of Abnormal Social Psychology, 66*, 584-588.

Bem, D. J. (1965). An experimental analysis of self-persuasion. *Journal of Experimental Social Psychology, 1*, 199-218.

Bond, R., & Smith, P. B. (1996). Culture and conformity: A meta-analysis of studies using Asch's (1952b, 1956) line judgment task. Psychological Bulletin, 119(1), 111-137.http://dx.doi.org/10.1037/0033-2909.119.1.111

Boucher, H. C., Peng, K., Shi, J., & Wang L. (2009). Culture and implicit self-esteem: Chinese are "good" and "bad" at the same time. *Journal of Cross-cultural Psychology, 40*(1), 24-45. doi: 10.1177/0022022108326195.

Chan, D. K. (1994). COLINDEX: A refinement of three collectivism measures. In U. Kim, H. C. Triandis, C. Kagitcibasi, S. Choi, & G. Yoon (Eds.), *Individualism and collectivism: Theory, method, and applications* (pp. 200–210). Thousand Oaks, CA: Sage.

Chao, R.K. (1995). Chinese and European American cultural models of the self reflected in mothers' childrearing beliefs. *Ethos*, 23, 328–354.

Chen, X., Rubin, K. H., Liu, M., Chen, H., Wang, L., Li, D., … Li, B. (2003). Compliance in Chinese and Canadian toddlers: A cross-cultural study. *International Journal of Behavioral Development*, *27*(5), 428–436. https://doi-org.nthulib-oc.nthu.edu.tw/10.1080/01650250344000046

Chernyak, N., Kang, C., & Kushnir, T. (2019). The cultural roots of free will beliefs: How Singaporean and US Children judge and explain possibilities for action in interpersonal contexts. *Developmental Psychology, 55*, 866-876. Retrieved from http://search.ebscohost.com/login.aspx?direct=true&db=pdh&AN=2019-01675-001&lang=zh-tw&site=ehost-live. doi:10.1037/dev0000670.

Choi, I., & Choi, Y. (2002). Culture and self-concept flexibility. *Personality and Social Psychology Bulletin, 28*, 1508-1517.

Chou, R. S. & Feagin, F. R. (2016). *The myth of the Model Minority: Asian Americans facing racism* (2nd ed.). New York, NY: Routledge.

Cooper, J. (1980). Reducing fears and increasing assertiveness: The role of dissonance reduction. *Journal of Experimental Social Psychology,16*(3),199-213.

Cooper, J., & Fazio, R. H. (1984). A new look at dissonance theory. In L. Berkowitz (Ed.), *Advances in Experimental Social Psychology*, 17, 229–264. Orlando, FL: Academic Press.

Denning, P. & Little, J. (2011). *Practicing harm reduction psychotherapy: An alternative approach to addictions*, (2nd ed.). New York, NY: Guilford Press.

Dimeff, L. A., & Koerner, K. (Eds.). (2007). *Dialectical behavior therapy in clinical practice.* New York, NY: Guilford Press.

Ferri, M., Amato, L., & Davoli, M. (2006). Alcoholics Anonymous and other 12-step programmes for alcohol dependence. The Cochrane Library, 3, 1-22.

Festinger, L. (1957). *A theory of cognitive dissonance*. Stanford, CA: Stanford University Press.

Festinger, L., & Carlsmith, J. M. (1959). Cognitive consequences of forced compliance. *Journal of Abnormal and Social Psychology, 58*, 203–210.

Gelfand, Michele J.; Raver, Jana L.; Nishii, Lisa; Leslie, Lisa M.; Lun, Janetta; Lim, Beng Chong; et al. (2011-05-27). "Differences between Tight and Loose Cultures: A 33-Nation Study." *Science*. 332 (6033): 1100–1104. doi:10.1126/science.1197754.

Grass, J., Krieger, F., Paulus, P., Greiff, S., Strobel, A., & Strobel, A. (2019). Thinking in action: Need for cognition predicts self-control together with action orientation. *PLoS ONE, 14*(8), 1–20. https://doi-org.nthulib-c.nthu.edu.tw/10.1371/journal.pone.0220282

Greenberg, J., Schmader, T., Arndt, J., & Landau, M. J. (2015). *Social psychology: The science of everyday life*. New York, NY: Worth Publishers.

Harmon-Jones, E. (1999). Toward an understanding of the motivation under lying dissonance effects: Is the production of aversive consequences necessary to cause dissonance? In E. Harmon-Jones & J. Mills (Eds.), *Cognitive dissonance: Progress on a pivotal theory in social psychology* (pp. 71–99). Washington, DC: American Psychological Association.

Harter, S. (2015). *The construction of the self: Developmental and sociocultural foundations* (2nd Ed). New York, NY: The Guilford Press.

Hayes SC, Strosahl K, & Wilson KG. (2009). *Acceptance and commitment therapy: An experiential approach to behavior change.* New York, NY: Guilford Press.

Heine, S., & Lehman, D. (1997). Culture, dissonance, and self-affirmation. *Personality and Social Psychology Bulletin, 23*, 389-400.

Heine, S., Lehman, D., Markus, H., & Kitayama, S. (1999). Is there a universal need for positive self-regard? *Psychological Review, 106*, 766-794.

Hofstede, G. (1980). Culture's consequences. Beverly Hills, CA: Sage.

Hoshino-Browne, E., Zanna, A. S., Spencer, S. J., Zanna, M. P., Kitayama, S., & Lackenbauer, S. (2005). On the cultural guises of cognitive dissonance: The case of Easterners and Westerners. *Journal of Personality and Social Psychology, 89*, 294-310.

Izuma, K., Matsumoto, M., Murayama, K., Samejima, K., Norihiro, S., & Matsumoto, K. (2013). Neural correlates of cognitive dissonance and decision conflict. *Advances in Cognitive Neurodynamics*, 623-628.

Kitayama, S., Chua H. F., Tompson, S., & Han, S. (2013). Neural mechanisms of dissonance: an fMRI investigation of choice justification. *NeuroImage, 69*, 206-2012. doi: 10.1016/j.neuroimage.2012.11.034.

Kitayama, S., & Markus, H. (1999). The yin and yang of the Japanese self: The cultural psychology of personality coherence. In D. Cervone & Y. Shoda (Eds.), *The coherence of personality: Social cognitive bases of personality consistency, variability, and organization* (pp. 242-302). New York: Guilford.

Kitayama, S., Markus, H., R., Matsumoto, H., & Norasakkunkit, V. (1997). Individual and collective processes in the construction of the self: Self-enhancement in the United States and self-criticism in Japan. *Journal of Personality and Social Psychology, 72*, 1245-1267.

Kitayama, S., Snibbe, C. A., Markus, H. R., & Suzuki, T. (2004). Is there any free choice? Self and dissonance in two cultures. *Psychological Science, 15*, 527–533.

Lewin, K. (1951). *Field theory in social science*. New York: Harper.

Luhtanen, R., & Crocker, J. (1992). A collective self-esteem scale: Selfevaluation of one's social identity. *Personality and Social Psychology Bulletin, 18*, 302–318.

Luo, G. (1996). Chinese traditional social and moral ideas and rules. Beijing, China: The University of Chinese People Press.

Markus, H. & Kitayama, S. (1991). Culture and the self: Implications for cognition, emotion, and motivation. *Psychological Review, 98*, 224-253.

Miller, W. R., & Rollnick, S. (2012). *Motivational interviewing: Preparing people to change* (3rd ed.). New York, NY: Guildford Press.

Nisbett, R. E. (2003). *The geography of thought: How Asians and Westerners think differently and why.* New York: Free Press.

Oishi, S., Diener, E. F., Lucas, R. E., & Suh, E. M. (1999). Cross-cultural variations in predictors of life satisfaction: Perspectives from needs and values. *Personality and Social Psychology Bulletin, 25,* 980–990.

Oyserman, D., Coon, H. M., & Kemmelmeier, M. (2002). Rethinking individualism and collectivism: Evaluation of theoretical assumptions and meta-analysis. *Psychological Bulletin, 128*, 3–72.

Peng, K., Ames, D., & Knowles, E. (2001). Culture, theory and human inference: Perspectives from three traditions. In D. Matsumoto (Ed.), *The handbook of culture and psychology*. Oxford, UK: Oxford University Press.

Peng, K., & Nisbett, R. (1999). Culture, dialectics, and reasoning about contradiction. *American Psychologist, 54,* 741-754.

Sakai, H. (1981). Induced compliance and opinion change. *Japanese Psychological Research, 23,* 1-8.

Schimmack, U., Oishi, S., & Diener, E. (2002). Cultural influences on the relation between pleasant emotions and unpleasant emotions: Asian and dialectic philosophies or individualism-collectivism? *Cognition & Emotion, 16,* 705-719.

Spencer-Rodgers, J., Boucher, H. C., Mori, S. C., Wang, L., & Peng, K. (2009). The dialectical self-concept: Contradiction, change, and holism in East Asian cultures. *Personality and Social Psychology Bulletin, 35*, 29-44.

Spencer-Rodgers, J., Major, B., Forster, D. E., and Peng, K. (2016). The power of affirming group values: group affirmation buffers the self-esteem of women exposed to blatant sexism. *Self Identity*, *15*, 413–431. doi: 10.1080/15298868.2016.1145593

Spencer-Rodgers, J., Peng, K., Wang, L., & Hou, Y. (2004). Dialectical self-esteem and East-West differences in psychological well-being. Personality and Social Psychology Bulletin, 30, 1416-1432.

Steele, C. M. (1988). The psychology of self-affirmation: Sustaining the integrity of the self. In L. Berkowitz (Ed.), *Advances in experimental social psychology* (Vol. 21, pp. 261–302). San Diego, CA: Academic Press.

Triandis, H. C. (1989). The self and social behavior in differing cultural contexts. *Psychological Review, 96,* 506–520.

Tedeschi, J. T., Schlenker, B. R., & Bonoma, T. V. (1971). Cognitive dissonance: Private ratiocination or public spectacle? *American Psychologist, 26*, 685-695.

Vries, J. de, Byrne, M., & Kehoe, E. (2015). Cognitive dissonance induction in everyday life: An fMRI study. *Social Neuroscience, 10* (3), 268-281.

Wang, Y. & Ollendick, T. H. (2001). A cross-cultural and developmental analysis of self-esteem in Chinese and Western children. *Clinical Child and Family Psychology Review, 4*, 253-271. https://doi.org/10.1023/A:1017551215413.

Yamaguchi, S. (1994). Collectivism among the Japanese: A perspective from the self. In U. Kim, H. C. Triandis, C. Kagitcibasi, S. Choi, & G. Yoon (Eds.), *Individualism and collectivism: Theory, method, and applications* (pp. 175–188). Thousand Oaks, CA: Sage

Section V.
Self and Identity

In: Social Psychology and Counseling
Editors: D. A. Kleiber and E. Delgado-Romero
ISBN: 978-1-53616-548-7

Chapter 10

Self-Discrepancy and Mental Health

JungSu Oh

Finding a person who is completely satisfied with herself or himself is almost impossible. It is a part of our human nature to experience a gap between our current and ideal selves. Without this tendency, it would be much harder to reflect on our mistakes and motivate ourselves to remedy them. This sense of discrepancy is like a warning sound like an alarm that is intentionally designed to be unpleasant, so that it can draw users' attention and allow them to take relevant actions. Discomfort coming from recognizing the discrepancy between our actual and ideal self gives us an opportunity to better regulate and change ourselves. Indeed, several psychological theories on the self, such as self-awareness theory (Duval & Wicklund, 1972) and regulatory focus theory (Higgins, 1997), point out the essential role of self-discrepancy in our motivational system.

Despite these intended positive functions, self-discrepancy seems to be one of the major concerns in psychotherapy. It is not uncommon to meet clients who complain about how badly they feel about themselves and how desperate they are to get rid of this discomfort. For those clients who feel trapped in the middle of their self-discrepancy, warning signals from their self-regulatory systems seem to keep them distressed rather than helping them take action to resolve the issue. Stretching the warning signal metaphor, these clients seem to be like a person who is preoccupied with turning off the fire alarm rather than leaving a burning house or seeking to put out the fire.

The negative impact of self-discrepancy illustrates a paradoxical nature of human suffering – such thoughts are an essential part of our functioning rather than an external threat to it. In other words, contrary to the *healthy normality* assumption which claims that psychological health is the default condition, the human mind often operates in a "destructive" way by its very nature (Hayes, 2005). Considering the implications for mental health, it is worthwhile to examine why self-discrepancy often creates suffering and how we can better manage this problem.

THE NEGATIVE IMPACT OF SELF-DISCREPANCIES ON MENTAL HEALTH

Carl Rogers, arguably one of the most influential figures in the history of psychotherapy, shed light on the importance of self-discrepancy in psychological adjustment. Rogers (1959) claimed that incongruence between one's actual experience and ideal self is at the center of our internal struggle and psychopathology. According to Rogers, the degree of incongruence is dependent upon the amount of conditional love from parents (or any agent of socialization). As children seek positive regard from their parents, they often internalize their parents' value and may conceal or even suppress who they really are in the process. This need for positive regard may come with the ultimate cost of alienation from their authentic self. As it is painful to be aware of this estrangement, people often develop defensive strategies to prevent realizing their true experiences which are in conflict with their working self-concepts. For example, if a child was raised in an environment that emphasizes sexual restraint, as an adult she might find sexual impulses troubling enough to completely deny her sexual drive, so that she can cover up the discrepancy between her actual, sexualized self and the internalized ideals of her family upbringing. However, although this solution might work temporarily, we cannot escape from the negative influences of chronic and significant incongruence. The fundamental solution to this problem lies in achieving congruence between our actual experience and ideal self, by attending to authentic parts of ourselves. According to Rogers, this goal can be achieved in therapy through the provision of empathy, unconditional positive regard, and genuineness, all of which are necessary for helping clients.

In this sense, incongruence (or self-discrepancy) can be understood as a challenge to mental health rather than simply an important part of our motivational system as it was discussed earlier. This is because, in Roger's view, incongruence is commonly experienced as a conflict between our inner/authentic-selves and outer/imposed/internalized values rather than the mere discrepancy between who we are and who we hope to be. Despite this different understanding of the nature of self-discrepancy, Roger's theory provides an important perspective on how self-discrepancy can have a harmful impact on our mental health, showing how it creates discomfort and how our natural tendency to suppress it can lead to greater harm.

Meanwhile, in social psychology, self-discrepancy theory (Higgins, 1987) provides a compelling framework on how self-conception can impact emotion. Self-discrepancy theory asserts that there are three domains of the self: the actual self (the attributes that the individuals believe they actually possess), the ideal self (the attributes that they hope to possess), and the ought self (the attributes they feel obliged to possess), the latter two of which are called *self-guides*. According to the theory, inconsistency between the actual self and self-guides creates emotional vulnerability. In other words, when people perceive that they do not meet the standards set by their self-guides, this discrepancy will likely leave them vulnerable to emotional distress. In addition, the theory further claims that the type of emotional distress differs by the source of discrepancy. While the discrepancy between the actual self and ideal self is likely to result in dejection-related emotions (e.g., sadness, dissatisfaction, disappointment), discrepancy between the actual self and ought self is presumably related to agitation-related emotions (e.g., restlessness, anxiety, alienation).

Self-discrepancy theory has been supported by a number of studies that have provided empirical evidence on the relationships between the type of self-discrepancies and distinct emotional distress (Higgins, Bond, Klein, & Strauman, 1986; Scott & O'Hara, 1993). In addition, self-discrepancy is also believed to have a negative impact on self-esteem. Theoretically, self-esteem is closely associated with the idea of self-discrepancy; self-esteem does not merely reflect how good we feel about ourselves, but it also involves a comparison between their perceived current state and the ideal standard to be achieved (Rosenberg, 1979). Therefore, it is reasonable to assume that greater perceived self-discrepancy leads to a decreased level of self-esteem, which is consistent with some of the research findings (e.g., Moretti & Higgins, 1990; Renaud & McConnell, 2007).

Moderating the Negative Effects of Self-Consciousness and Self-Discrepancy

While the relationship between self-discrepancy and emotional distress is supported by theories and research, an important question still remains. At the beginning of this chapter, it was pointed out that self-discrepancy is a vital part of our functioning. Indeed, it would be unrealistic, and to some extent maladaptive, to completely eliminate self-discrepancy from our experience despite its negative impacts on well-being. But it is noteworthy that not every person experiencing self-discrepancy is likely to become vulnerable to negative emotions. Some people are more resilient to the risk of emotional vulnerability caused by self-discrepancy than others, and some are better able to manage the negative impacts than others through effective coping mechanisms. If this is the case, what are these differences, and how subject are they to the influence of psychoeducation and therapy? To address these questions, we need to identify what *moderates* the negative relationship between self-discrepancy and mental health.

To provide more detailed explanation on the relationships between self-discrepancies and corresponding emotional vulnerabilities, Higgins (1999) proposed four variables that are likely to moderate this relationship - the magnitude of self-discrepancy, accessibility, applicability, and relevance of discrepancy to the current context. Among these variables, the relevance to the current context is especially important in shedding light on our question. This variable implies that the more relevant and important the self-discrepancy is to a person, the more likely a negative emotional outcome will result. According to this explanation, it is notthe self-discrepancy itself that results in emotional struggle, it is how we process and react to the displeasure of it.

Then, what might be people's visceral reaction when facing discomfort caused by self-discrepancy? The most common and natural response would be to escape from self-awareness (Baumeister, 1991); when people find their self-image is not consistent with who they want to be, they often face considerable discomfort. In some cases, people may take productive actions to reduce the gap between the actual self and ideal self, but others may be overwhelmed by this discomfort and use maladaptive strategies to avoid it by suppressing self-awareness.

Avoidance of self-awareness is not necessarily detrimental (Baumeister, 1995). For example, by giving up the control and ownership about oneself and narrowing focus on here-and-now sensations, sexual intercourse may serve effectively to reduce the burden of self-awareness. It is a relatively harmless way to escape from oneself and is not associated to negative mental health consequences. Nevertheless, escaping from self-awareness is also a common source of risky and unhealthy behaviors, especially in the absence of healthier alternatives. For instance, Heatherton and Baumeister (1991) claimed that binge eaters tend to have high standards for themselves and high sensitivity toward criticism from others, which exacerbates the negative impact of self-discrepancy. When they find themselves unable to meet their own appearance ideals, they are likely to suppress their self-awareness by focusing on the food and binge eating. Specifically, for binge eaters, binge eating is used as a strategy to narrow down their attention to immediate stimuli and bodily sensations, which allows them to escape from negative emotions and painful self-discrepancy. This inhibits their attention and healthy thought processes, which leads them to uncritically accept their irrational behavior. Similar arguments were proposed regarding how suicide and alcohol consumption can function as a strategy to escape self-awareness (Baumeister, 1990; Hull, 1981).

But again, escaping from self-awareness does not always manifest itself in distinctly unhealthy behaviors. Rather, it often serves as a source of motivation behind our everyday activities. For example, various self enhancement strategies are used to reduce awareness of painful discrepancies between the real and ideal self (cf. Fiske, 2004).

Downward social comparison is one of the most common strategies people use for this purpose (e.g., Harter, 2012). People often compare themselves with someone who they think is inferior to them in some respects, which temporarily protects their self-concept and elevates their self-esteem.

Another cognitive strategy people often use is a *self-serving attributional bias* (cf. Aronson, 2012). This concept illustrates how people's reasoning on their performance may serve as a mechanism to maintain their self-esteem. For instance, when people perform well in a certain task, they are more likely to attribute it to their skill and knowledge, which is based on their abilities. In contrast, when they do poorly on it, they are likely to attribute the failure to bad luck or other situational factors that are out of their control. Through use of this attributional style, they can take less responsibility for their failure, which serves the purpose of protecting their self-esteem and suppressing the discomfort coming from self-discrepancy.

Excessive reliance on downward social comparison and self-serving attributional biases can be problematic when they lower the motivation to change. Such tendencies can provide a temporary safeguard against attacks on one's self-concept; however, without attempting to change one's behavior, one's self-concept would remain vulnerable to risks that were originally threatening. Mahler, Kulik, Gerrard and Gibbons (2010) addressed the problem by showing experimentally how downward social comparison may prevent positive behavioral changes. Using a potentially health- and appearance-threatening manipulation, the investigators showed that an appearance-based sun protection intervention (attempt to highlight the relationship between sun exposure and its negative impact on appearance, such as wrinkles, age spots) could impact sun protection behavior. In this experiment, 126 college students were randomly assigned into four different groups - control, intervention, intervention with upward social comparison, intervention with downward social comparison. Upward and downward social comparison were each manipulated by an exposure to three UV facial photos of students who either have less (upward) or more (downward) severe skin damages. The result indicated that all interventions, regardless of the existence of upward or downward social comparison, led participants to be more aware of sun protection behavior. However, this positive gain was offset after 5 weeks in the downward comparison group, whereas it was maintained in the upward comparison group. This result illustrates a side-effect of downward social comparison; it brings us relief that we are not as bad as some of the other people out there. But at the same time, it also decreases our motivation to change our behavior, as we know that we would remain still better than others even without making changes. In this case, comfort in the short-run comes with the cost of impeded growth in the long-run, which might partially explain why avoiding awareness on self-discrepancies can eventually cause detrimental results.

It is also important to note that the urge to rely on these strategies to escape from self-awareness can be exacerbated by the level of self-focus. In other words, the more we are preoccupied with the gap between our current and ideal state, the more likely we are motivated to escape from self-awareness. This may paradoxically produce harm to our mental health. Research evidence shows an association between self-focus and negative affect (Mor & Winquist, 2002). For example, self-focus plays an important role in provoking and maintaining anxiety (Sarason, 1988). Performance anxiety is often exacerbated by one's heightened attention on the possible failure to achieve a goal. This leads to elevated level of anxiety and physiological arousal, which actually increases the possibility of making mistakes. Self-focus is also associated with depression. Pyszczynski and Greenberg (1987) argued that depressive individuals are often trapped in fruitless efforts to reduce the irreducible self-discrepancies. This is in line with a number of research findings that rumination triggers and sustains depressogenic mindsets (Just & Alloy, 1997; Kuehner & Weber, 1999). Evidence from these studies illustrate the important role of self-focus in dealing with self-discrepancy, which will be further discussed in the following section.

LIVING WITH SELF-DISCREPANCY

Decentering

Escaping from self-awareness (at least when using maladaptive strategies to suppress awareness) can exacerbate negative impacts of self-discrepancies on our emotional and behavioral struggles. This raises an important question for therapists who want to facilitate change for clients: how can they mitigate the cost of self-discrepancy awarenesswhen it is an essential human condition from which there is no complete escape?

The answer lies in relating to self-discrepancy in a healthier way. As we have seen earlier, a large portion of emotional vulnerability we experience from self-discrepancy comes from the fact that we are too immersed in ourselves. Considering the critical role of self-focus in amplifying the discomfort coming from self-discrepancy, being able to distance oneself from them – by *decentering* - is important. Decentering can be defined as an ability to step outside of one's inner experiences which leads to dis-identification with them (Safran & Segal, 1990). In relation to self-discrepancy, it can be also understood as "the ability to objectively observe negative self-discrepancy and not to judge whether the discrepancy is good or bad" (Mori & Tanno, 2015, p.618). By raising meta-cognitive awareness of negative thoughts and emotions coming from self-discrepancies, decentering brings about different cognitive, behavioral, and emotional outcomes (Teasdale et al., 2002). Decentering is becoming more popular in the field of psychology and psychotherapy research and empirical studies have provided supports for the positive impact of decentering on mental health issues, such as depression, anxiety, and treatment gain from mindfulness-based interventions (Bernstein et al., 2015).

Self-Compassion

Self-compassion is another concept that may reduce the detrimental impact of self-discrepancy. According to Neff (2003) self-compassion consists of three elements: self-kindness (being kind to oneself rather than being critical), common humanity (understanding one's experience within the larger context of human experience rather than interpreting it as an individual, isolated experience), and mindfulness (maintaining balanced awareness of one's pain rather than identifying with it). Neff (2003) argued that, by maintaining this non-evaluative attitude and recognizing interconnectedness of beings, we can protect ourselves from the negative impact of self-judgment and rumination. Considering that self-judgment and rumination often exacerbate the discomfort of self-discrepancy, self-compassion can be a healthier way to avoid those feelings. Among a number of studies demonstrating this, MacBeth and Gumley (2012) conducted a meta-analysis on the relationship between self-compassion and various psychopathologies and concluded that self-compassion is an important variable to explain mental health and resilience. In addition, in a longitudinal study, Marshall and colleagues (2015) found that self-compassion played a protective role in mitigating the negative consequences of low self-esteem.

Regarding the relationship between self-discrepancy and self-compassion, it is worth noting how self-compassion is different from self-esteem. In the earlier section, the close relationship between self-discrepancy and self-esteem was pointed out. When maintaining self-esteem is based on the comparison between a current state and an ideal one, greater self-discrepancy is likely to generate diminished self-esteem. But might reversing the process by enhancing self-esteem first reduce the amount of self-discrepancy and its corresponding negative impacts? This argument provided a theoretical foundation on several educational initiatives and programs that emphasize promoting self-esteem in schools, such as the California Task Force to Promote Self-Esteem and Personal and Social Responsibility (Mecca, 1990). But this approach has drawn considerable criticism. Although self-esteem is highly correlated with positive academic outcome, researchers view self-esteem as the result of doing well, rather than the cause of it (Baumeister, Campbell, Krueger, & Vohs, 2003). Efforts to artificially raise self-esteem often make people pursue self-validation goals while adopting self-serving biases and self-enhancement strategies that may provide short-term relief but are costly in the long term (Croker & Park, 2004). Responding to this pitfall of pursuing high self-esteem, Neff (2011) proposed self-compassion as a better alternative. Similar to self-esteem, self-compassion also provides a source of positive self-regard. However, unlike self-esteem, self-compassion does not involve self-judgment. Even with the existence of significant self-discrepancy, self-compassion can minimize embarrassment from the perceived failure. By being kind to oneself and accepting the discrepancies between one'sactual and ideal/ought self, the need to artificially inflate self-esteem is diminished (Neff, 2011).

Mindfulness

The two concepts discussed previously in this section (e.g., decentering and self-compassion) are components of *third-wave therapies* (Prochaska & Norcross, 2013. Third-wave therapies refer to a set of different approaches, such as Acceptance and Commitment Therapy (ACT), Dialectical Behavioral Therapy (DBT), and Mindfulness-Based Cognitive Therapy(MBCT); but all of these approaches share the practice of *mindfulness*. Mindfulness can be defined as non-evaluative attention to one's experience. It not only facilitates distancing oneself from self-focused thoughts and feelings (as emphasized in decentering), it also emphasizes the importance of being comfortable with oneself (as in self-compassion; Carlson, 2013). Research indicates that decentering and self-compassion either incorporate mindfulness or mediate the relationship between mindfulness and mental health (Carmody, Baer, Lykins, & Olendzki, 2009; Svendsen, Kvernenes, Wiker, & Dundas, 2017).

Interventions addressing mindfulness can be an effective way to control natural yet maladaptive responses to reduce self-discrepancy. According to Carlson (2013), mindfulness can enhance self-knowledge by reducing two major barriers: informational barriers and motivational barriers. By lowering informational barriers, individuals more easily access information about themselves; by lowering motivational barriers, people reduce ego-protective motives which hinder processing information relevant to self-knowledge. The fact that mindfulness is useful in addressing motivational barriers is especially relevant to this discussion. In the previous section, it was pointed out that self-enhancement strategies and self-serving biases are used to avoid painful self-discrepancy awareness. Carlson's (2013) argument on mindfulness suggests that mindfulness may be useful in reducing risks attached to these self-protective strategies.

Evans, Baer, and Segerstrom (2009) provided preliminary evidence on the relationship between mindfulness and self-discrepancy and its impact on well-being. In this study, participants were asked to do a difficult lab task (i.e., solving anagrams). Persistence was measure by total time participants spent working in this task. The result indicated the positive correlation between persistence and two aspects of mindfulness (nonjudging and nonreactivity). Based on this result, Evans et al., (2009) conjectured that being nonjudgmental and nonreactive might lead to acknowledging self-discrepancy in performing difficult tasks without being self-critical thus leading participants to be more persistent. This study demonstrated that mindfulness is an important skill for living with self-discrepancy without needing to escape from it.

CONCLUSION

Self-discrepancy is a natural condition of our motivational system from childhood into adulthood. However, it is also a source of discontent in our lives and can lead to negative mental health outcomes such as depression, anxiety, and low self-esteem. Among the more common reactions to managing this displeasure is to avoid self-awareness by engaging in escapist behavior patterns such as heavy alcohol use or using self-serving and self-deceptive cognitive strategies that become maladaptive in the long run. Regardless of their short-term benefits, excessive reliance on these strategies can cause long-term damage to psychological and behavioral health. To better handle self-discrepancy, this chapter introduced two important concepts that might serve as healthier alternatives – decentering and self-compassion. These constructs are closely related to the concept of mindfulness, which is gaining increasing popularity in the field of psychotherapy. Compared to more traditional approaches like self-esteem enhancement, this alternative approach provides a way to manage self-discrepancy without escaping from it.

Although it has been constantly reiterated throughout this writing, it is worth emphasizing that self-discrepancy is not only a source of suffering, it is an indispensable part of human functioning. However irritating a warning signal may be, it should not be extinguished. Instead, it would be important to interpret the message behind the signal and take appropriate action. Similarly, as discussed earlier, while it is tempting to find a quick way to escape self-awareness when facing self-discrepancy once this natural tendency to react to self-discrepancy can be attenuated to allow for more constructive self-awareness including mindfulness, decentering and self-compassion, more positive adjustments are likely. This idea may still seem counterintuitive to some. If suffering is like a harmful virus that causes illness, it would be logical to find a way to completely eliminate it from one's experience. However, as discomfort is an inevitable part of human functioning and growth, it needs to be recognized for its value. This idea has became a central tenet of third-wave psychotherapies (mindfulness-based therapies). Jon Kabat-Zinn, the founder of Mindfulness-Based Stress Reduction (MBSR), entiteld his first book *"Full Catastrophe Living"* (Kabat-Zinn, 1990), not because he held the pessimistic view that all human life should be catastrophic but because he believed that it is important to accept and embracethe negative experiences of life to become fully human. Of course, this is not a completely new idea in the history of psychotherapy; Carl Jung, a pioneer in psychotherapy, clearly articulated this point as follows:

> Therefore, the principal aim of psychotherapy is not to transport the patient to an impossible state of happiness, but to help him acquire steadfastness and philosophic patience in face of suffering. (...) Behind a neurosis there is so often concealed all the natural and necessary suffering the patient has been unwilling to bear (p. 81).

This perspective should be carefully considered by both research and practitioner. As a researcher, it is not only important to investigate the cause of human suffering (uncomfortable self-discrepancy, in the context of this writing), but also what moderates this relationship (maladaptive ways of escaping from self-awareness, in this writing) which can be a focus of intervention. And a practitioner needs to be aware that completely avoiding the cause of suffering is both unrealistic and harmful, as it is based on the faulty understanding of human nature (as demonstrated in some of the miscalculations of the self-esteem movement).

REFERENCES

Aronson, E. (2012). *The social animal (11th ed.)*. New York, NY: Worth.

Baumeister, R. F., Campbell, J. D., Krueger, J. I., & Vohs, K. D. (2003). Does high self-esteem cause better performance, interpersonal success, happiness, or healthier lifestyles? *Psychological Science in the Public Interest, 4*, 1-44.

Baumeister, R. F. (1991). *Escaping the self: Alcoholism, spirituality, masochism, and other flights from the burden of selfhood.* New York, NY: Basic Books.

Baumeister, R. F. (1995). Self and identity: An introduction. In (ed.) A. Tesser, *Advanced social psychology*. New York, NY: McGraw Hill.

Baumeister, R. F. (1990). Suicide as escape from self. *Psychological Review*, *97*, 90-113.

Bernstein, A., Hadash, Y., Lichtash, Y., Tanay, G., Shepherd, K., & Fresco, D. M. (2015). Decentering and related constructs: A critical review and metacognitive processes model. *Perspectives on Psychological Science, 10*, 599-617.

Carlson, E. N. (2013). Overcoming the barriers to self-knowledge mindfulness as a path to seeing yourself as you really are. *Perspectives on Psychological Science, 8*, 173-186.

Carmody, J., Baer, R. A., LB Lykins, E., & Olendzki, N. (2009). An empirical study of the mechanisms of mindfulness in a mindfulness-based stress reduction program. *Journal of Clinical Psychology, 65*, 613-626.

Crocker, J., & Park, L. E. (2004). The costly pursuit of self-esteem. *Psychological Bulletin, 130*, 392-414.

Duval, S., & Wicklund, R. A. (1972). *A theory of objective self-awareness*. Oxford, England: Academy Press.

Evans, D. R., Baer, R. A., & Segerstrom, S. C. (2009). The effects of mindfulness and self-consciousness on persistence. *Personality and Individual Differences, 47*, 379-382.

Fiske, S. T. (2004). *Social beings: Core motives in social psychology*. New York, NY: Wiley.

Harter, S. (2012). *The construction of the self: Developmental and sociocultural foundations*. New York, NY: Guilford Publications.

Hayes, S. C. (2005). *Get out of your mind and into your life: The new acceptance and commitment therapy*. Oakland, CA: New Harbinger Publications.

Heatherton, T. F., & Baumeister, R. F. (1991). Binge eating as escape from self-awareness. *Psychological Bulletin, 110*, 86-108.

Higgins, E. T. (1997). Beyond pleasure and pain. *American Psychologist, 52*, 1280-1300.

Higgins, E. T. (1987). Self-discrepancy: A theory relating self and affect. *Psychological Review, 94*, 319-340.

Higgins, E. T. (1999). When do self-discrepancies have specific relations to emotions? The second-generation question of Tangney, Niedenthal, Covert, and Barlow (1998). *Journal of Personality and Social Psychology, 77*, 1313-1317.

Higgins, E. T., Bond, R. N., Klein, R., & Strauman, T. (1986). Self-discrepancies and emotional vulnerability: How magnitude, accessibility, and type of discrepancy influence affect. *Journal of Personality and Social Psychology, 51*, 5-15.

Hull, J. G. (1981). A self-awareness model of the causes and effects of alcohol consumption. *Journal of Abnormal Psychology, 90*, 586-600.

Jung, C. G. (1966). The practice of psychotherapy (R. F. C. Hull, Trans.). In H. Read et al., (Series Eds.), *The collected works of C. G. Jung* (vol. 16 pt. 1, 2nd. ed., pp. 1-125). Princeton, NJ: Princeton University Press. (Original work published 1958).

Just, N., & Alloy, L. B. (1997). The response styles theory of depression: Tests and an extension of the theory. *Journal of Abnormal Psychology, 106*, 221–229.

Kabat-Zinn, J. (1990). *Full catastrophe living: Using the wisdom of your body and mind to face stress, pain, and illness*. New York: Delacorte.

Kuehner, C., & Weber, I. (1999). Responses to depression in unipolar depressed patients: An investigation of Nolen-Hoeksema's response styles theory. *Psychological Medicine, 29*, 1323–1333.

MacBeth, A., & Gumley, A. (2012). Exploring compassion: A meta-analysis of the association between self-compassion and psychopathology. *Clinical Psychology Review, 32*, 545-552.

Mahler, H. I., Kulik, J. A., Gerrard, M., & Gibbons, F. X. (2010). Effects of upward and downward social comparison information on the efficacy of an appearance-based sun protection intervention: A randomized, controlled experiment. *Journal of Behavioral Medicine, 33*, 496-507.

Marshall, S. L., Parker, P. D., Ciarrochi, J., Sahdra, B., Jackson, C. J., & Heaven, P. C. (2015). Self-compassion protects against the negative effects of low self-esteem: A longitudinal study in a large adolescent sample. *Personality and Individual Differences, 74*, 116-121.

Mecca, A. (1990). *Toward A State of Esteem: The Final Report of the California Task Force to Promote Self-Esteem and Personal and Social Responsibility*. California Department of Education.

Mor, N., & Winquist, J. (2002). Self-focused attention and negative affect: a meta-analysis. *Psychological Bulletin, 128*, 638-662.

Moretti, M. M., & Higgins, E. T. (1990). Relating self-discrepancy to self-esteem: The contribution of discrepancy beyond actual-self ratings. *Journal of Experimental Social Psychology, 26*, 108-123.

Mori, M., & Tanno, Y. (2015). Mediating role of decentering in the associations between self-reflection, self-rumination, and depressive symptoms. *Psychology, 6*, 613-621.

Neff, K. (2003). Self-compassion: An alternative conceptualization of a healthy attitude toward oneself. *Self and Identity, 2*, 85-101.

Neff, K. D. (2011). Self-compassion, self-esteem, and well-being. *Social and Personality Psychology Compass, 5*, 1-12.

Prochaska, J, O, & Norcross, J, C. (2013). *Systems of psychotherapy: A transtheoretical analysis (8th ed.)*. Belmont, CA: Brooks/Cole Cengage Advantage Books.

Pyszczynski, T., & Greenberg, J. (1987). Self-regulatory perseveration and the depressive self-focusing style: A self-awareness theory of reactive depression. *Psychological Bulletin, 102*, 122-138.

Renaud, J. M., & McConnell, A. R. (2007). Wanting to be better but thinking you can't: Implicit theories of personality moderate the impact of self-discrepancies on self-esteem. *Self and Identity, 6*, 41-50.

Rogers, C. (1959). A theory of therapy, personality and interpersonal relationships as developed in the client-centered framework. In (ed.) S. Koch, *Psychology: A study of a science. Vol. 3: Formulations of the person and the social context*. New York, NY: McGraw Hill.

Rosenberg, M. (1979). *Conceiving the self*. New York, NY: Basic Books.

Safran, J. D., & Segal, Z. V. (1990). *Interpersonal process in cognitive therapy*. Lanham, MD: Rowman & Littlefield.

Sarason, I. G. (1988). Anxiety, self-preoccupation and attention. *Anxiety Research, 1*, 3-7.

Scott, L., & O'Hara, M. W. (1993). Self-discrepancies in clinically anxious and depressed university students. *Journal of Abnormal Psychology, 102*, 282-287.

Svendsen, J. L., Kvernenes, K. V., Wiker, A. S., & Dundas, I. (2017). Mechanisms of mindfulness: Rumination and self-compassion. *Nordic Psychology, 69*, 71-82.

Teasdale, J. D., Moore, R. G., Hayhurst, H., Pope, M., Williams, S., & Segal, Z. V. (2002). Metacognitive awareness and prevention of relapse in depression: empirical evidence. *Journal of Consulting and Clinical Psychology, 70*, 275-287.

In: Social Psychology and Counseling
Editors: D. A. Kleiber and E. Delgado-Romero
ISBN: 978-1-53616-548-7

Chapter 11

COMBATTING BODY IMAGE DISSATISFACTION IN AFRICAN AMERICAN GIRLS

Courtney Williams

Social psychology is a field that seeks to understand how human behavior is influenced by other individuals, groups, and social contexts and systems (DeLamater, Collett, & Myers, 2014). Social influence research suggests that individuals often identify with the influencer; and the *attractiveness* of the influencer is one of the many reasons for that identification (Aronson, 2012). But the attractiveness of the influencer may also lead to dissatisfaction when comparing oneself; and this is the focus of this chapter.

In the United States mass media have often shaped what is considered physically attractive (Kelch-Oliver & Ancis, 2011), and these ideals can become an issue when they reflect age and racial bias. Women in general have identified distorted body ideals as a problem through *objectification theory* (Moradi, 2010) that posits that one outcome of objectification can be issues like eating disorders. For many years it was a widely held misconception that ethnic minority women were immune from the negative impacts of objectification. Given a long history of rape and objectification of Black women in the U.S. (Wyatt, 1998), researchers have encouraged professionals to consider how racism and sexism have an impact on the way a Black female relates to her body (Cho, Crenshaw, & McCall, 2013; Collins & Bilge, 2016).

Swann (2010) asserted that people's sense of self is related to how they think others see them, i.e., their *perceived appraisal*. Internalization of an observer's appraisal leads to self-objectification and is manifested by persistent body surveillance (Moradi, 2010), which can easily lead to a distorted body image. Shroff and Thompson (2010) report that a girl's internalized appraisal of her body based on social ideals can have a major impact on her self-worth, interaction with peers, and her eating behaviors, which could have implications for self-enhancement (i.e., maintaining self-esteem, motivation towards self-improvement).

Body image pathology has been a growing problem in the United States (National Institute of Mental Health, 2012). Body image is defined as the thoughts and feelings that an individual holds towards his or her body (Flowers, Levesque, & Fischer, 2012). According to Mendelson, Mendelson, and White (2001), body image has three components: *body-esteem appearance*, *body-esteem weight*, and *body-esteem attribution*. Body-esteem appearance is one's overall feeling about one's outward appearance. Body-esteem weight assesses an individual's weight satisfaction. And body-esteem attribution is defined by one's assessment of others' evaluations of one's body and appearance (Mendelson et al., 2001). Clearly the construct of body-esteem attribution involves constantly assessing one's body based on the opinions of others which are themselves based primarily on cultural norms and standards.

The Eurocentric versions of beauty consistently challenges the self-image of ethnic minority women, and in particular Black females (Kelch-Oliver et al., 2011). Black women are subjected to beauty standards that dictate that lighter skin and longer straight hair are seen as beautiful while darker skin and natural hair are seen as unattractive (Kelch-Oliver et al., 2011). Although the Black community has been found to embrace a more voluptuous body type (Gordon et al., 2010), mainstream Eurocentric culture values thinness and defines what is normal and attractive according to White beauty ideals (Kelch-Oliver et al., 2011), which generally includes thinness to the degree that it is unhealthy (Kring et al., 2012).

As a result of the ubiquitous nature of White beauty ideals, body dissatisfaction has become a norm among Western cultures among all women regardless of race or ethnicity (National Eating Disorders Collaboration, 2017). Studies show that while Black females do not strive to be as thin as their White counterparts, they still desire to have a slender body (Baugh et al., 2010). These findings suggest that there are culturally specific factors that impact a Black female's body image (Capodilupo & Kim, 2014; Henrickson, Harrington, & Crowther, 2010; Hesse-Biber et al., 2010; Watson, Robinson, Dispenza, & Nazari, 2013). Given the rise in body image pathology in the U.S. and the specific factors affecting body image among Black women and girls, this chapter will explore how social influence, mass media, and other related factors impact body image among members of this population. Furthermore, the chapter will discuss social and group-based intervention efforts to reduce body dissatisfaction among Black women and girls including a model program designed by the author.

Black Females, Body Image and the Media

Adolescence is a pivotal period for mental, social, and emotional wellbeing where girls encounter factors that impact their cognitive and physical development (World Health Organization, 2018). During this period of development, others' evaluations have a significant impact on how an adolescent girl judges her level of attractiveness and potentially her level of worth (Caughy, Nettles & Lima, 2011; Salomon et al., 2019; Talleyrand et al., 2017). Lowered self-esteem and negative body image are common issues that adolescent girls struggle with during this period (Talleyrand, 2010). Research has frequently associated negative body image and low self-esteem with White girls (Bagley, Character & Shelton, 2003; Roberts, Feingold, Cash & Johnson, 2006; Talleyrand, 2010). However, factors specific to the African American experience may put African American girls at even greater risk for body image and self-esteem issues given the often-ignored history of racism and slavery and the reality of modern-day aversive racism (Gaertner et al., 2005).

Stanley and Brown (2015) reconsidered *self-discrepancy theory* (Higgins, 1987; Rogers, 1959) to further address how people use knowledge about themselves to fit into social standards. This theory holds that people have multiple self-guides, or standards, that they follow in order to regulate their behavior. There is the *actual self* (who one is right now) and the *ideal self* (who a person wants to be) (Stanley & Brown, 2015; see also, Oh, this volume). In the social imagery of Black female beauty, lighter skin and longer, curly hair have been regarded as more positive than darker skin and course, "kinky" hair (Kelch-Oliver et al., 2011; Talleyrand et al., 2017). Therefore, a Black girl may conclude that the darker she is and the more natural her hair is, the less attractive she is. Vandiver and colleagues (2001) refer to this effect as *miseducation*, a social referent status where a Black person has internalized negative and racist beliefs about themselves.

Awad and colleagues (2014) found that Black women were dissatisfied by the limited examples of Black women's beauty represented in the media. Pressures to be thin, coming from numerous sources, have induced anxiety and confusion in Black females (Awad et al., 2014; Watson et al., 2019). The media, male validation, family, and peer groups have all been found to be influential in how Black adolescent girls shape their own definition and perceptions about physical attractiveness (Kelch-Oliver et al., 2011; Talleyrand, Gordon, Daquin, & Johnson, 2017). In several studies Black females reported pressure to conform to the thin ideal promoted in popular media (Awad et al., 2014; Muhammed & McArthur, 2015; Watson, Lewis, & Moody, 2019).

A significant relationship exists between media images and body image dissatisfaction among adolescent girls especially in the era of widespread social media (Muhammed & McArthur, 2015; Salomon & Spears Brown, 2019). Darker skinned Black women report that an overwhelmingly high preference for lighter skin negatively impacts their feelings and thoughts about themselves (Awad et al., 2014). Images promoted in the media, and those often admired by Black males, reflect fairer skinned females with curly or long hair (Awad et al., 2014). In a qualitative study (Muhammad & McArthur, 2015) Black girls described the dichotomy of "good hair" (silky, soft, wavy) and "bad hair" (tightly coiled, coarse). One participant observed that making assumptions about a Black female based on her hair texture is a part of a larger system of racial profiling. Given that Black girls are more likely to struggle with issues related to body shape, hair texture, and skin color, factors that increase resilience and bolster racial/cultural pride are necessary.

For adolescents much of social learning and social comparison occurs in the school context, where self-concept and social competence both have a rapid growth trajectory (Harter, 2013). Diamond and Lee (2011) argued that social-emotional competence develops early on in the form of self-regulation and problem-solving. Thus, *social-emotional learning* (SEL) programs have been implemented in schools to foster these competencies and academic success simultaneously (McCormick et al., 2015). The SEL framework has been used to address the needs of young people as well as the fragmentation that typically characterizes the response of schools to those needs (Jones & Doolittle, 2017; McCormick, Cappella, O'Connor, & McClowry, 2015). SEL programming focuses on underlying causes of problem behavior while supporting academic achievement. Through developmentally- and culturally-appropriate classroom instruction and application of learning to everyday situations, SEL programming builds children's skills to identify and control their emotions, understand the viewpoint of others, create constructive goals, make responsible choices, and handle interpersonal situations effectively (Jones & Doolittle, 2017; McCormick et al., 2015). In addition to producing students who are culturally literate, intellectually reflective, and committed to lifelong learning SEL dictates that high-quality education should teach young people to: (a) interact in socially skilled and respectful ways, (b) practice positive, safe, and healthy behaviors, (c) contribute ethically and responsibly to their peer group, family, school, and community, and (d) acquire basic competencies, work habits, and values as a foundation for meaningful employment and engaged citizenship (Elias, 2003).

Though the literature is mixed with respect to academic implications, programs that foster SEL are regarded as foundational to adolescent development (McCormick et al., 2015). SEL is thought to boost critical thinking skills, compassion and empathy, interpersonal skills, decision making, positive relationships, and healthy self-image (McCormick et al., 2015). SEL programming may be best applied within the context of school-based youth interventions.

Today schools are faced with a multitude of high demands while being severely under resourced. According to Biag (2016), teachers often serve as counselors to their students, attending to each student's educational and emotional needs and serving as surrogate parents for students, having an open-door policy, providing school supplies, and supplementing other needs that students may not get met outside of school. However, these expectations are often met without adequate resources and are particularly challenging in schools with different racial and ethnic mixes (Duncan & Murnane, 2011; Nasir, Jones, & McLaughlin, 2011). Risk and protective factors may manifest differently in the lives of different ethnic groups (Duncan & Murnane, 2011). Furthermore, the evidence is that schools have difficulty involving community members in the implementation process of the newer holistic health models (Centers for Disease Control and Prevention, 2009; 2014), which then require partnering with communities to promote student health and academic success (Hunt, Barrios, Telljohann, Mazyck, & 2015; Lee et al., 2019).

The Whole School, Whole Community, Whole Child Model (WSWC; Hunt et al., 2015) was developed to achieve optimal student health outcomes through educational and health organizational partnerships. This model takes an integrated and collaborative approach to education and health that is intended to combat common challenges faced by both students and school systems. Wright, Giger, Norris, and Suro (2012) found a school-community partnership to be effective in health promotion among minority youth. A study by Akintobi and colleagues (2010) found that school-community partnerships were successful in enhancing health-related behaviors among African American adolescents, particularly around sexual activity. They found that establishing trust and working relationships among community partners, as well as creating a both culturally and developmentally relevant intervention was paramount in encouraging sexual health among African American youth. These findings suggest that creating an intervention with an inter-professional framework can provide holistic health benefits for youth. Moreover, infusing culturally adaptive components, while enhancing educator-participant relationships, may have particularly beneficial effects in addressing the self-esteem challenges that face students, including that of body dissatisfaction.

The school social environment affects students' attendance, academic achievement and behavior and health practices. A safe and healthy school environment promotes student engagement and protects against risky behaviors and dropping out (Rose-Clark, Bentley, Marston, & Prost, 2019). Research has demonstrated that facilitating social connectedness influences health and well-being in many ways, and that social connectedness can promote multiple health objectives, as well as lead to broader community and societal benefits (DeKoker et al., 2014; Salam et al., 2016; Shackleton et al., 2016). The Center for Disease Control (2009) reported that the more likely students feel connected at school the less likely they will be to display emotional distress and issues related to body image.

Developing a culturally relevant school-based intervention specifically for African American girls is also an innovative way to address the mental health needs of this population. The Office of the Surgeon General noted that ethnic minorities are less likely to have access to or utilize mental health care services; so it is important to reduce risk factors that lead to mental health among these populations while also altering modes of service delivery to increase accessibility (U. S. DHHS, 2001).

The majority of interventions in social service practice in the U.S. that are targeted towards combatting body image dissatisfaction for women are created for White women by implication. That is, culture and race is inferred rather than addressed and although body ideals are critiqued as unhealthy, the racist aspects of body image are not addressed. To impact body image, health and wellbeing, and self-esteem issues in Black girls' experience, *culturally adapted* interventions should be implemented. *Cultural adaptation* refers to "program modifications that are culturally sensitive and tailored to a cultural group's traditional world views" (Castro et al., 2004. p. 43). Cabassa and Baumann (2013) argued that when an intervention is culturally adapted it enhances recruitment, relevance, retention, and program effectiveness. Literature has shown that infusing factors such as cultural values, cultural history, and contemporary culture are important aspects in creating positive development among Black girls. Furthermore, culturally adapted interventions have been found to have a significant impact on improving prosocial behavior in this population (Peterson, Villarreal, & Castro, 2017). Researchers have defined prosocial behaviors as a relatively selfless action implemented to encourage or benefit another person or group of people (Afolabi, 2014; Fiske, 2004; Ringdahl, this volume). Moreover, prosocial behaviors are viewed as a selfless act to provide assistance or guidance to others (Afolabi, 2014). The literature has indicated ways in which intervention programs can be useful in increasing pro-social behaviors around more favorable body images of youth (Das et al., 2016; De Koker, Mathews, Zuch, Bastien, Mason-Jones, 2014; Office of Disease Prevention & Health Promotion, 2014; Salam, et al., 2016; Shackleton et al., 2016), even as they take a more general approach to various health issues. Furthermore, prosocial behavior has been linked to self-esteem, particularly among females (Afolabi, 2014). These findings suggest that group interventions can be useful in encouraging peer-to-peer learning, as well as create opportunities for peers to encourage and support each other involving difficult issues such as body image and self-esteem, issues that are impacted by social processes. The following is an example of such a program.

P.O.I.S.E. (Providing Outreach and Intervention through Sisterhood and Education)

Utilizing an action research, mixed method approach, the author implemented a culturally-adapted, school-based group intervention for eleven African American sixth and seventh grade (middle school) girls to explore the impact of the intervention on their body image and self-esteem (Williams, 2019). The program utilized peer-to-peer education, mentorship, and process groups to encourage compassion, critical thinking, connectedness, and confidence (some of the key components of SEL type programs). The program was based in a middle school, had sponsorship of the school administration and was implemented by a trained group of Black women facilitators from the community.

Over the course of eight weeks, participants worked closely with trained group facilitators, Black (undergraduate and graduate level) women, to discuss topics like body image, self-esteem and sociocultural influences. More specifically, the P.O.I.S.E. curriculum was designed to engage participants in experiential learning, team building, skill building, creative arts, and group processing to discuss hair-esteem, colorism, media influence, as well as relationships with peers and family.

Quantitative analysis of the results of the intervention revealed an increase in skin color satisfaction and hair-esteem as a result. The author used the *Sociocultural Attitudes Toward Appearance Questionnaire* (SATAQ-3) to assess body image within her sample. This measure was originally developed to measure the societal influences on body image disturbances. Results of administration of the SATAQ-3 before and after the program indicated a decline in scores on the *Pressures* and *Internalization* general subscales from time one (pre) to time two (post). These two scales assess the extent to which an individual feels pressured to ascribe to societal prescriptions for beauty and the extent to which an individual internalizes said influences. Participants' scores declining from pretest to posttests suggests that those in the program felt less pressure and less inclination to internalize such standards of beauty after completing the P.O.I.S.E. program.

In the qualitative parts of the study, the following themes were also observed: (a) Salient Identities: "Who you are"- participants reflected on their most significant identities, highlighting both physical and non-physical characteristics; (b) Peers & Media: "Because the DM [direct messages] tells me"- participants identified social media as a main source of information about beauty standards, as well as relational aggression experienced among peers for their appearance; (c) Resilience: "Don't let nobody bring you down"- participants described how they overcome adversity related to relational aggression, mentioning support from loved ones; (d) Covering new ground: "Before P.O.I.S.E., I wasn't really thinking about it"- participants shared how participation in P.O.I.S.E. fostered new insights and experiences.

As outlined by DeLamater et al., (2014), interactions with others can have a major impact on how one navigates the world; this was true of the P.O.I.S.E. participants as well. Girls shared how prevalent social influence had been in their lives through media, peers, and family interactions. Participants discussed the negative stereotypes projected onto Black girls, with many of the issues being related to skin tone. They also discussed how peer-to-peer relations often included ridicule about appearance- body shape, hair, and skin tone. Moreover, social media was discussed as a key factor in how participants defined their beauty, stating that the number of "likes" on a post or the number of "direct messages" they received translated into an affirmation of one's beauty. While many girls highlighted how positive affirmations from family and friends served as buffers to negative self-image, participants still seemed to regard the media as a significant source of information for self-appraisal.

IMPLICATIONS

Findings from the P.O.I.S.E group indicate that body image issues are indeed especially relevant to Black women and girls. Additionally, findings from that project and others clearly highlight how paramount social influence is in one's self-image. The stories from the interventions reviewed, as well as the author's own intervention, support the argument of Mendelson and colleagues (1997) that it is crucial to assess body image and body dissatisfaction in Black women and girls in more nuanced ways. Indeed, Williams, Livingston, and Waters (2013) found significant effects of their intervention on some body image constructs but not others. Therefore, in future studies it may be inappropriate to make global statements about body image without a clear conceptualization of its variations.

Additionally, such research offers researchers and health professionals a stronger foundation for understanding differences across ethnically diverse populations. The findings of the P.O.I.S.E study explored the culturally-specific pressures Black girls face related to their hair, skin, and physique. Participants in these studies reflected a lack of (accurate) representation of Black women and girls in society, often combating stereotypes. If researchers and health professionals are more knowledgeable about body image related to Black women and girls, cultural biases and racial stereotypes may have less of an impact on the detection and diagnosis of body image pathology among this population.

Implications from these findings may also prove valuable in the development of body image measures and intervention programs that specifically address issues that Black females may face regarding body image and self-esteem. To date, literature on body image has been focused on European American cultural influences. However, future research and intervention studies should include the diverse experiences of Black women and girls from other cultures with respect to body image and self-esteem. More specifically, hierarchies related to skin color, facial features, hair type, and body type should be reflected on assessment measures. Considering all of the literature that suggests that interventions should not take a "one size fits all" approach, keeping an eye out for cultural, racial and ethnic differences is clearly warranted. Culturally-adapted considerations are necessary when developing youth interventions. Particularly for Black girls, interventionists should consider how Black girls make meaning and incorporate those factors into programming strategies.

Nevertheless, the research reviewed here should be of use to communities, families, and schools in recognizing mechanisms, resources, and strategies already in place to help foster positive perspectives on body image and self-esteem among Black girls. Findings reported above reflect how school-community partnerships can maximize and supplement their resources to foster optimal health among students. Findings from the author's own intervention study highlight the resilience of Black girls amidst adversity, buoyed by the encouragement and support of family and loved ones in response to negative messages. This further suggests that mental health professionals, parental figures, and school officials should continue to encourage young girls to be critical of media influences that perpetuate real-ideal self-discrepancies. Moreover, communities must continue to endorse positive messages and images that enhance Black girls' self-confidence.

REFERENCES

Afolabi, O. A. (2014). Do self-esteem and family relations predict prosocial behaviour and social adjustment of fresh students? *Higher Education of Social Science*, 7(1), 26-34.

Akintobi. T. H., Trotter, J. C., Evans, D., Johnson, T., Laster, N., Jacobs, D., & King, T. (2010). Applications in bridging the gap: A community-campus partnership to address sexual health disparities among African-American youth in the south. *Journal of Community Health*, 36, 486-494.

Awad, G. H., Norwood, C., Taylor, D. S., Martinez, M., McClain, S., Jones, B., Chapman-Hilliard, C. (2014). Beauty and body image concerns among African American college women. *The Journal of Black Psychology, 41*(6), 540–564. doi:10.1177/0095798414550864.

Baugh, E., Mullis, R., Mullis, A., Hicks, M., & Peterson, G. (2010). Ethnic identity and body image among black and white college females. *Journal of American College Health, 59*, 105-109.

Biag, M. (2016). A descriptive analysis of school connectedness: The views of school personnel. *Urban Education, 51*(1), 32-59.

Cabassa, L. J., & Baumann, A. A. (2013). A two-way street: Bridging implementation science and cultural adaptations of mental health treatments. *Implementation Science, 8*, 90. doi:10.1186/1748–5908–8-90.

Capodilupo C. M., Kim S. (2014). Gender and race matter: The importance of considering intersections in Black women's body image. *Journal of Counseling Psychology, 61*, 37-49.

Castro, F. G., Barrera Jr., M., Martinez Jr., C. R. (2004). The cultural adaptation of prevention interventions: Resolving tensions between fidelity and fit. *Prevention Science*, 5, 41-45.

Center for Disease Control and Prevention (2009). *School connectedness: Strategies for increasing protective factors among youth*. Atlanta, GA: U.S. Department of Health and Human Services.

Center for Disease Control and Prevention (2014). *Youth risk behavior surveillance-United States 2013,* 63 (4), 1-168. Atlanta, GA: U.S. Department of Health and Human Services.

Cox, T. L., Zunker, C., Wingo, B., Thomas, D. M., & Ard, J. D. (2010). Body image and quality of life in a group of African American women. *Social Indicators Research, 99*, 531-540.

Das, J. K., Salam, R. A., Arshad, A., Finkelstein, Y., Bhutta, Z. A. (2016). Interventions for adolescent substance abuse: an overview of systematic reviews. *Journal of Adolescent Health, 59*(4), S61–S75.

Das JK, Salam RA, Lassi ZS, Khan MN, Mahmood W, Patel V, et al., (2016). Interventions for adolescent mental health: an overview of systematic reviews. *Journal of Adolescent Health, 59*(4):S49–S60.

De Koker P, Mathews C, Zuch M, Bastien S, Mason-Jones AJ. (2014). A systematic review of interventions for preventing adolescent intimate partner violence. *Journal of Adolescent Health, 54*(1):3–13. https://doi.org/10.1016/j.jadohealth.2013.08.008 PMID: 24125727.

DeLamater, J. D., Collett, J. L., Myers, D. J. (2014). *Social psychology*. 8th ed. New York, NY. Routledge Publishing.

Duncan, G. J., & Murnane, R. (Eds.). (2011). *Whither opportunity? Rising inequality, schools, and chidren's life chances*. New York, NY: Russell Sage.

Fiske, S. T. (2004). *Social beings: A core motives approach to social psychology*. New York City: Wiley.

Flowers, K. C., Levesque, M. J., & Fischer, S. (2012). The relationship between maladaptive eating behaviors and racial identity among African American women in college. *Journal of Black Psychology, 38*, 290-312.doi: 10.1177/0095798411416459.

Gaertner, S. & Dovidio, J. F. & Nier, J. & Hodson, G. & Houlette, M. A. (2005). *Aversive Racism: Bias without Intention*. 10.1007/1-4020-3455-5_19.

Gordon, K. H., Sitnikov, L., Castro, Y., & Holm-Denoma, J. M. (2010). Cultural body shape ideals and eating disorder symptoms among White, Latina, and Black college women. *Cultural Diversity and Ethnic Minority Psychology, 16*, 135-143. doi: 10.1037/a0018671.

Guthrie, R. V. (2003). *Even the rat was White: A historical view of psychology* (2nd ed.). Boston, MA: Pearson.

Harter (Harter, S. (2013) *The construction of the self: Developmental and sociocultural foundations*. New York, NY: Gilford Press.).

Henrickson H. C., Harrington E. F., Crowther J. H. (2010). Ethnic identity and maladaptive eating: Expectancies about eating and thinness in African American women. *Cultural Diversity & Ethnic Minority Psychology, 16*, 87-93.

Hesse-Biber S., Livingstone S., Ramirez D., Barko E. B., Johnson A. L. (2010). Racial identity and body image among Black female college students attending predominately White colleges. *Sex Roles, 63,* 697-711. doi:10.1007/s11199-010-9862-7.

Higgins, E. T. (1987). Self-discrepancy: A theory relating self and affect. *Psychological Review, 94*, 319-340.

Hughes, D., Hagelskamp, C., Way, N., Foust, M. D. (2009). The role of mothers' and adolescents' perceptions of ethnic-racial socialization in shaping ethnic-racial identity among early adolescent boys and girls. *Journal of Youth Adolescents*, *38*, 605-626.

Hunt P, Barrios L, Telljohann SK, Mazyck D. A whole school approach: collaborative development of school healthpolicies, processes, and practices. *Journal of School Health. 85*: 802-809.

Jemmott, J. B., Jemmott, L. S., Fong, G. T., & Morales, K. H. (2010). Effectiveness of an HIV/STD Risk-Reduction Intervention for Adolescents When Implemented by Community-Based Organizations: A Cluster-Randomized Controlled Trial. *American Journal of Public Health*, *100*(4), 720–726. doi:10.2105/AJPH.2008.140657.

Kelch-Oliver, K., Ancis, J. R. (2011). Black women's body image: An analysis of culture-specific influences. *Women & Therapy*, 34, 345-358.

Kring, A. M., Johnson, S. L., Davison, G. C., & Neale, J. M. (2012). *Abnormal psychology*. (12 ed., pp. 94-95). New York: John Wiley & Sons.

Lee, S. M., Miller, G. F., Brener, N., Michael, S., Jones, S. E., Leroy, Z. Merlo, C., Robin, L. and Barrios, L. (2019), Practices that support and sustain health in schools: An analysis of SPSS data. *Journal of School Health, 89*: 279-299. doi:10.1111/josh.12742.

Linton, M (n.d.). "Teens & self-esteem: Your teen's self-esteem dependent on you." *Examiner.com*. Accessed November 13, 2014. http://www.examiner.com/article/teens-self-esteem-your-teen-s-self-esteem-dependent-on-you.

McCormick, M. P., Cappella, E., O'Connor, E. E., & McClowry, S. G. (2015). Social-emotional learning and academic achievement: Using causal methods to explore classroom-level mechanisms. *AERA Open*. https://doi.org/10.1177/2332858415603959.

Moradi, B. (2010). Addressing gender and cultural diversity in body image: Objectification theory as a framework for integrating theories and grounding research. *Sex Roles, 63*,138-148.

Muhammad, G. E., & McArthur, S. A. (2015). "Styled by their perceptions": Black adolescent girls interpret representation of Black females in popular culture. *Multicultural Perspectives, 17*(3), 133-140.

Nasir, N. S., Jones, A., & McLaughlin, M. W. (2011). School connectedness for students in low-income urban high schools. *Teachers College Record, 113*, 1755-1793.

National Eating Disorders Collaboration. (2017). *What is body image?*

National Institute of Mental Health (2012). *Eating disorders*. Retrieved from http://www.nimh.nih.gov.

Office of Disease Prevention and Health Promotion (2014). *Adolescent health*. Retrieved from https://www.healthypeople.gov/2020/topics-objectives/topic/Adolescent-Health

Peterson, L. S., Villarreal, V., & Castro, M. J. (2017). Models and frameworks for culturally responsive adaptations of interventions. *Contemporary School Psychology, 21*, 181–190. doi: https://doi-org.proxy.cc.uic.edu/10.1007/s40688–016–0115–9.

Rogers, C. (1959). A theory of therapy, personality and interpersonal relationships as developed in the client-centered framework. In (ed.) S. Koch, Psychology: *A study of a science. Vol. 3: Formulations of the person and the social context*. New York, NY: McGraw Hill.

Salam, R. A., Faqqah, A., Sajjad, N., Lassi, Z. S., Das, J. K., Kaufman, M., et al., (2016). Improving adolescent sexual and reproductive health: a systematic review of potential interventions. *Journal of Adolescent Health, 59*(4):S11–S28.

Salomon, I., & Spears Brown, C. (2019). The selfie generation: Examining the relationship between social media and early adolescent body image. *Journal of Early Adolescence, 39*(4), 539-560.

Shackleton N, Jamal F, Viner RM, Dickson K, Patton G, Bonell C. (2016) School-based interventions going beyond health education to promote adolescent health: systematic review of reviews. *Journal of Adolescent Health, 58*(4):382–96. https://doi.org/10.1016/j.jadohealth.2015.12.017 PMID: 27013271.

Shapiro, H. (n.d.). Dove's Campaign for Real Beauty boosts girls' self-esteem for Back to School. *Examiner.com*. Accessed November 13, 2014. http://www.examiner.com/article/dove-s-campaign-for-real-beauty-boosts-girls-self-esteem-for-back-to-school.

Stanley, M., & Brown, A. L. (2015). The distance between selves: The influence of self-discrepancy on purpose of life. *Self and Identity, 14*(4), 441-452.

Stice, E., Shaw, H., & Marti, C. N. (2006). A meta-analytic review of obesity revention programs for children and adolescents: The skinny on interventions that work. *Psychological Bulletin, 132,*667–691. doi:10.1037/0033-2909.132.5.667.

Striegel-Moore, R. H., Schreiber, G. B., Pike, K. M., Wilfley, D. E. and Rodin, J. (1995), Drive for thinness in black and white preadolescent girls. *International Journal of Eating Disorders*, 18, 59–69. doi:10.1002/1098-108X(199507)18:1<59::AID-EAT2260180107>3.0.CO;2-6.

Sue, D. W., Arredondo, P., & McDavis, R. J. (1992). Multicultural counseling competencies and standards: A call to the profession. *Journal of Multicultural Counseling and Development, 20,* 64–68.

Swann, William. 2010. Self and Identity. *Handbook of social psychology.* DO:10.1002/9780470561119.socpsy001016.

Talleyrand, R. M. (2010). Eating disorders in African American girls: Implications for counselors. *Journal of Counseling & Development*, *88*, 319-324.

Talleyrand, R. M., Gordon, A. D., Daquin, J. V., & Johnson, A. J. (2017). Expanding Our Understanding of Eating Practices, Body Image, and Appearance in African American Women: A Qualitative Study. *Journal of Black Psychology, 43*, 464–492. https://doi.org/10.1177/0095798416649086.

Taylor, J., & Tomasic, M. (1996).Taylor's measures of dysphoria, anxiety, anger, and self-esteem. In R. L. Jones (Ed.), *Handbook of Tests and Measurements for Black Populations* (Vol. 2). Hampton, VA: Cobb & Henry.

U.S. Department of Health and Human Services (2012). Office of Disease Prevention and Health Promotion. *Healthy People 2020.* Washington, DC. Available at [http://healthypeople.gov/2020/topicsobjectives2020/overview.aspx?topicid=2]. Accessed [April 10, 2012].

Van den Berg, P. A., Mond, J., Eisenberg, M., Ackard, D., & Neumark-Sztainer, D. (2010). The link between body dissatisfaction and self-esteem in adolescents: Similarities across gender, age, weight status, race/ethnicity, and socioeconomic status. *The Journal of Adolescent Health : Official Publication of the Society for Adolescent Medicine*, 47(3), 290–296. doi:10.1016/j.jadohealth.2010.02.004.

Van Tergouw, M. (2011). Peer influences on the body satisfaction of adolescent girls: Where do we go from here? *Social Cosmos, 2*, 104-110.

Vandiver, B. J., Fhagen-Smith, P. E., Cokley, K. O., Cross, Jr., W. E. & Worrell, F. C. (2001). Cross's Nigrescence Model: From theory to scale to theory. *Journal of Multicultural Counseling and Development, 29*, 174-200.

Watson, J. C. (2017). Examining the relationship between self-esteem, mattering, school connectedness, and wellness among middle school students. *Professional School Counseling, 21*(1), 108-118.

Watson L. B., Robinson D., Dispenza F., Nazari N. (2013). African American women's sexual objectification experiences: A qualitative study. *Psychology of Women Quarterly, 36*, 458-475. doi:10.1177/0361684312454724.

Watson, L. B., Lewis, J. A., & Moody, A. T. (2019). A sociocultural examination of body image among Black women. *Body Image*. https://doi.org/10.1016/j.bodyim.2019.03.008.

Williams, C. (2019). *P.O.I.S.E.: Investigating the impact of group intervention on body image and self-esteem among African American middle school girls*. Unpublished doctoral dissertation. University of Georgia, Athens, GA.

World Health Organization (2018, September). *Adolescent mental health*. Retrieved on April 25, 2019. https://www.who.int/news-room/fact-sheets/detail/adolescent-mental-health.

Wright, K., Norris, K., Giger, J. N., & Suro, Z. (2012). Improving health dietary behaviors, nutrition knowledge, and self-efficacy among underserved school children with parent and community involvement. *Childhood Obesity*, 8, 347-36.

Wyatt, G. (1998). *Stolen women: Reclaiming our sexuality, taking back our lives*. New York: Wiley & Sons.

In: Social Psychology and Counseling
Editors: D. A. Kleiber and E. Delgado-Romero
ISBN: 978-1-53616-548-7

Chapter 12

POSITIVE MASCULINITY: COUNSELING MEN THROUGH A PROSOCIAL AND STRENGTHS-BASED LENS

Bret A. Ringdahl

Researchers in the field of men and masculinity question how well the existing counseling approaches and theoretical frameworks inform interventions that enhance interpersonal functioning, increase help-seeking behaviors, and encourage strengths and values-based living to support the physical and mental health of men and foster an individual's unique social identity (Addis & Mahalik, 2003; Kiselica, Benton-Wright, & Englar-Carlson, 2016). Contextual factors (e.g., family relations, aging, social inequities, retirement) that influence how men perceive their ability to control and monitor their overall mental and physical health have been studied (O'Neil, 2015; World Health Organization and Calouste Gulbenkian Foundation, 2014; Wong & Wester, 2016). Additionally, many men do not seek treatment when necessary and are even more reluctant to engage in gender-sensitive forms of therapy (Mahalik, Good, Tager, Levant, & Mackowiak, 2012). The positive and negative outcomes of these factors ultimately influence how health care providers and counselors approach these sensitive topics with men socially and interpersonally.

Existing literature on the long-term impacts of early developmental male socialization and men's gender role conflict (GRC) is extensive (Levant & Richmond, 2016; O'Neil, 2015; Pleck, 1995), and focuses mainly on the negative consequences and outcomes on health, family, interpersonal relationships, restricted emotional affect, and power and work preoccupation (O'Neil, 2008, 2012, 2015; Smiler, 2004). The endorsement of rigid and restrictive masculine ideologies, resulting in gender role strain, appears to construct a significant hurdle that can negatively impact both men and boys (Levant & Richmond, 2016; O'Neil, 2015).

The positive psychology positive masculinity paradigm (PPPM; Englar-Carlson & Kiselica, 2013; Kiselica, 2011; Kiselica et al., 2016) redirects the research and clinical goals for the study of men and masculinity and challenges the field to consider healthy qualities men possess that enable many to enhance intimacy, group belonging, altruism, and community with self and others. New conceptualizations of theoretical and clinical models indicate men can be receptive to psychotherapy and can encompass a positive view of wellness and prosocial behaviors (Nahon & Lander, 2016). The clinical implications for treating the behavioral and psychological components of men's health in the context of intersecting masculine identity, include enhancing the attributes of "positive masculinity" (e.g., responsibility, leadership, generativity, stability, strength, and stoicism) to foster self-efficacy and improve individual and societal well-being. A broader discourse within social contexts emerges for practitioners on how to balance accentuating the positive and more functional aspects of masculinity while deconstructing negative masculine role norms that demonstrate barriers to overall mental and physical wellness.

THEORETICAL AND HISTORICAL BACKGROUND

The early study of masculinity led researchers to the conclusion that certain aspects of being socialized into traditional male gender roles could have negative social and psychological consequences for men (Deutch & Gilbert, 1976; O'Neil, 2015; Pleck, 1981; Thompson & Pleck, 1986). Deviations from the adherence to these culturally defined norms have negative outcomes as internalizing rigid masculinity ideologies produce distorted gender role schemas that are damaging to men socially and interpersonally. This stress is not benign or transient, showing that indeed, gender role socialization places men at greater risk than women for mortality by somatic disease, mental health issues, alcoholism, aggression, and relationship difficulties (Gove, 1979; Moore & Stuart, 2005; O'Neil, 2015; Levant & Richmond, 2016).

Pleck's gender role strain model described how gender role restrictions can be detrimental to the psychological health of men (Pleck, 1981, 1995). In Pleck's early model, he described specific gender role strain propositions that men often violate which lead to negative evaluations from others and contended that men who violate masculine gender norms are subject to harsher societal judgments than are women who violate feminine gender norms (Pleck, 1981). Masculinity was thought to be associated with violence, the subjugation of women, and aggressive traits. The later model of male role strain was related to masculine ideology in that men have "beliefs about the importance of men adhering to culturally defined standards for male behavior" (Pleck, 1995, p. 19).

O'Neil (1981) outlined a synopsis of "The Masculine Mystique and Value System" (p. 205) that summarized the myths of ideal masculinity in society. Masculine mystique is the assumption that vulnerability and intimacy with other men is a form of weakness; feelings and emotions are signs of weakness; masculinity rather than femininity is the preferred gender identity; logical communication is preferred to emotional communication; sex is a means to prove manhood; and success and power are a measure of a man's worth. It has been theorized that men are prone to feel a certain amount of anxiety or stress if they cannot conform to the edicts of the masculine mystique.

Despite the assertions that gender role socialization has iatrogenic effects for men, no measures for investigating stress associated with gender socialization existed until development of the Masculine Gender Role Stress Scale (MGRS; Eisler & Skidmore, 1987). Prior to that research exploring the negative effects of being socialized into a "masculine" gender role did not distinguish the effects of being socialized into traditionally "masculine" roles from the stress associated with failure to conform to such social standards. Indeed, one thing these researchers had seemingly not considered was that perhaps socialization into culturally-sanctioned masculine roles itself was not the problem; perhaps the failure to conform to this socialization was more problematic than the socialization itself. The MGRS was constructed to assess the stress men seem to encounter when their ability to conform to masculine gender roles is stymied or challenged. This unique scale was designed to measure men's cognitive appraisal of stressfulness in specific, gender-sensitive, situations. MGRS is a term developed by these authors to define the stress that men experience when they are unable to meet the expectations and imperatives of the traditional male role or when certain situations are viewed as requiring stereotypically "feminine" behavior. Such situations may include comforting a crying woman, needing to disclose personal feelings, failing to perform in work or another important life area.

Eisler and Skidmore (1987) noted that men with high scores on socially desirable traits of masculinity were not at high risk for unhealthy or maladaptive behavior. This finding was contrary to previous work detailing the negative effects of "masculinity" for men. Rather, these authors found "trait measures of masculinity seem to be related to positive personal and social adjustment" (p. 134). Some men experience significant stress and anxiety surrounding the fulfillment (or lack of fulfillment) of these masculine roles, leading to negative cognitive appraisals. It was hypothesized that the strong negative evaluation and anxiety associated with these thoughts and subsequent interpretation of stressful situations are affected by gender socialization processes, leading to the aforementioned maladaptive outcomes. Most notably, it was contended that such stress and anxiety may be a strong contributor to violence in romantic relationships; this line of research has been subsequently investigated by other researchers over the last two decades.

Gender Role Conflict

The psychology of men emerged as an important area for scientific inquiry and clinical intervention over 30 years ago (Addis & Mahalik, 2003; Blazina, 2003; Brooks & Good, 2001a; Cochran & Rabinowitz, 2000). James O'Neil's historic issue of *The Counseling Psychologist* described how men's psychological problems are related to masculine gender role conflicts. It was further hypothesized that men are oppressed by rigid gender role socialization processes that limit them from being fully functioning human beings (O'Neil, 1981). More than 230 studies have been completed using the Gender Role Conflict Scale (GRCS; O'Neil, Helms, Gable, David, & Wrightsman, 1986), and more attention is being directed to men and the so-called "crisis" in men's health (Gough, 2006). Many studies have examined men's gender roles as related to depression, anxiety, violence, suicide, poor health care, homophobia, academic failure, bullying, racial and ethnic oppression, and dysfunctional relations with women, men, and children (O'Neil, 2015).

Gender role conflict occurs when rigid, sexist, or restrictive gender roles result in the restriction, devaluation, or violation of others or self (O'Neil, 2015; O'Neil, Good, & Holmes, 1995). The outcome of this conflict is a restriction of one's potential or the restriction of another person's potential leading to negative consequences for the person or others (O'Neil et al., 1995). Gender role conflict occurs within situational contexts when men experience a gender role transition or face difficult developmental tasks over the lifespan (O'Neil & Egan, 1992a). Conflict can also arise when men experience discrepancies between their real self-concepts and their ideal self-concepts, based on gender role stereotypes and masculinity ideology (Garnets & Pleck, 1979; Liu, Rochlen, & Mohr, 2005). Men's fears about appearing feminine are linked to the four patterns of GRC - Success/Power/Competition (SPC), Restrictive Emotionality (RE), Restrictive Affectionate Behavior Between Men (RABBM), and Conflict Between Work and Family Relations (CBWFR) – which have been isolated and rigorously supported with psychometric research (O'Neil, 2015; O'Neil et al., 1986).

Other mediator studies have been conducted using the gender role conflict paradigm to examine the relationship between greater GRC and negative outcome variables. Shepherd and Rickard (2012) specified that men with higher gender role conflict tend to exhibit a variety of body image concerns, including a drive for muscularity. Results demonstrated that GRC mediated the relationship between the drive for muscularity and help-seeking intentions, explaining why men with body image concerns may be less likely to utilize or seek out treatment services and recommendations (Shepherd & Rickard, 2012). Other studies have been able to link gender role conflict to moderator and mediator variables that influence men's attitudes toward seeking psychological help (Levant et al., 2013; Murray & Lewis, 2014; Robinson & Brewster, 2014; Vogel, Wester, Hammer, & Downing-Matibage, 2014)

Liu et al. (2005) examined the relationship between real and ideal gender role conflict and the impact on psychological distress. Results showed some men may not fully embrace the rigid gender-role ideals to which they are socialized, and the differences between real and perceived ideals of GRC may be related to feelings of conflict and distress. The results were positively related in that real life GRC was correlated with strong values in the ideal life. The highest levels of distress were correlated with high levels of GRC in both real and ideal life situations (Liu et al., 2005).

O'Neil's (2008) prescribed model for future research uses a contextual perspective to answer GRC questions using moderator and mediator variables. The contextual domains of GRC include: "(a) age, developmental stage, resolving developmental tasks, and gender role transitions; b) family interaction patterns, interpersonal situations, and peer relationships; c) masculinity ideology, norms, and conformity; d) psychological and physical health variables; e) men's diversity – race, ethnicity, culture, class, religious, and sexual orientation - as well as identity issues related to these categories; f) vulnerability related to violence, oppression, and abuse; and g) methods to help men resolve GRC through therapy and psychoeducational and preventative interventions" (O'Neil, 2008, p. 44).

POSITIVE PSYCHOLOGY AND THE POSITIVE MASCULINITY PARADIGM

The positive psychology-positive masculinity (PPPM) paradigm is a growing field for research and clinical work in counseling and has flourished over the past decade (Englar-Carlson & Kiselica, 2013). Both counseling and positive psychology share mutual admiration for growth, development, excellence, and authentic goodness. Researchers have explored the intersection of positive psychology in counseling, school psychology, and rehabilitation and physical medicine (Chapin & Boykin, 2010; Harris, Thoresen, & Lopez, 2007; Park & Peterson, 2008). Empirical support from positive psychology literature underpins the focus of counseling on the remediation of suffering and alleviation of symptoms; however, a focus on positivity and building strengths has been valuable as well (Seligman, 2008; Seligman, Rashid, & Parks, 2006).

Recently, calls to action for the inclusion of courses about the psychology of men and masculinity in training programs have been met with resistance. White males have been the traditional dominant reference group for biased and exclusionary research until the 1970s (O'Neil & Renzulli, 2013). Men themselves are rarely classified as a marginalized group and consequently, the psychology men is traditionally associated with male patriarchy, privilege, aggression, dominance, sexism, and the devaluation of women. The new psychology of men and masculinity aligns closely with pro-feminist values of activism, an equal balance of power, reduced sexism and dominance, and a restructure of masculinity itself (Englar-Carlson & Kiselica, 2013). For many counselors, the idea of capitalizing on male strengths and positive masculinity may perpetuate the impact of negative masculinity and support historically patriarchal ideals. Additionally, positive masculinity is often stringently criticized for focusing on male gender-specific interventions that reinforce gender roles and stereotypes and negate feminist ideals of gender deconstruction (Addis, Mansfield, & Syzdek, 2010).

Existing models and previous research attend to the negative characteristics and impacts that traditional masculinity has on men in Western societies (O'Neil, 2015). Conversely, positive masculinity is a term used to describe "Qualities of traditional masculine roles that are more positive, strength-based, and potentially used to improve the lives of men and those around them (Isacco, Talovic, Chromik, & Yallum, 2012). Positive masculinity encompasses working with men on pre-existing strengths, potentials, skills, capacities, encouragement of possibilities, and a focus on who men are, rather than who they are not (Englar-Carlson & Kiselica, 2013). Counselors can shift a client's attitude and outlook by encouraging hope, concentrating on positive contributions, and focusing on aspects of the client that are kind, creative, capable, and not limited by rigid societal stereotypes (O'Neil, 2015).

Masculine identity is deeply embedded within cultural and contextual factors. The definitions, expressions, and displays of male strengths are complicated constructs which are dictated by race, sexual orientation, socio-economic status, religion, ability, and other salient identities (Shields, 2008). Therefore, positive-psychology and strengths-based counseling approaches frame positive masculinity within the constructs of one's own cultural and contextual identity. For instance, masculinity is strongly associated with family and an important value for what it means to be a man in Latino and African-American culture (Hurtado & Sinha, 2008; Hammond & Mattis, 2005); however, this dimension of masculinity is not as salient for other groups. A growing body of literature suggests men develop qualities of positive masculinity in adaptive and prosocial ways by creating communities, role modeling, living authentically, enacting non-violent conflict resolution, expressing emotion appropriately, and developing egalitarian relationships (Hernandez, 2002; Riggle & Rostosky, 2011; Rochlen, McKelley, & Whittaker, 2010; Rochlen, Suizzo, McKelley, & Scaringi, 2008).

Enhancing prosocial behaviors in men is not without challenges. One study examined gender differences in prosocial behavior with economic games and found social framing tends to increase prosocial behavior in women but not men, and encouragement of reflection decreases the prosocial behavior of males (Espinosa & Kovářík, 2015). These findings suggest positive, prosocial behaviors are malleable, but males and females respond to different aspects of the social context. Literature in the study of men and masculinity considers that an array of cultural norms, ideologies, and gender roles shape intrapersonal differences specific to the individual and play a part in discouraging men's help-seeking behaviors (Addis & Mahalik, 2003). Gilmore (1990) noted that "macho" styles of masculine expressions do benefit society in some respects and are a necessary function of humanity's perceived need for protection against aggressors. Increased levels of testosterone to preserve this function allow men to aggress physically and violently, whereas women are more prone to engage in relational aggression (Aronson, 2012). The interplay between gender and psychological functioning is intricate and subtle. The role gender plays in the lives of men affects how they manage, control, and seek assistance when issues arise (Broom & Lenagh-Maguire, 2010).

Implications for Counseling and Psychological Practice

The recent dissemination of the *APA Guidelines for Psychological Practice with Boys and Men* (2018) has stirred debate among many in the field. APA's position states that the development of guidelines for psychological practice with boys and men may help attend to barriers that historically, research has demonstrated, lead to the disparities discussed earlier. The American Psychological Association (APA) has released guidelines for psychologists working with specific populations such as gay/lesbian/bisexual clients (APA, 2012), racial and ethnic minority clients (APA, 2017), older adults (APA, 2014), transgender and gender-non-conforming persons (APA, 2015a), and girls and women (APA, 2007). Additional guidelines have been released in healthcare delivery systems (APA, 2013a), professional practice (APA, 2015b), and specialty areas of forensic psychology (APA, 2013b) and psychological evaluations in child protection matters (APA, 2013c). The stated purpose for these guidelines is to (a) improve service delivery, (b) stimulate public policy initiatives, and (c) provide professional guidance based on advances in the field (APA, Boys and Men Guidelines Group, 2018).

Opponents of the guidelines have been vocal, stating the guidelines lack a broader scientific base, fail to report biological contributors to gender identity, and include stereotyped terms such as "traditional masculinity" that are conceptually ill-defined and socio-political in nature rather than based in scientific theory (Ferguson, 2019). Other critics have staunchly rejected the notion of "toxic masculinity" stating, "It is harmful to all members of our society and dangerous to our national security. Masculine qualities like rugged individualism, courage, stoicism, ambition, and a willingness to protect and sacrifice for others helped secure the freedom and prosperity that so many now take for granted (Frueh, 2019)."

Many men hold expectations of the need to be independent, stoic, and self-determined, which are presumed to be biologically helpful characteristics. A recent column in *The Washington Post* responded to the APA guidelines, cited that "troubles may arise when rugged individualistic characteristics men hold are the only tools they believe they have, when help is needed and [men] are afraid to ask for it, or when [men] experience emotions they can't even name, much less express (Hesse, 2019)." Hesse continued that when men ultimately blame themselves for being unable to make those insufficient tools work, the results are negative consequences in physical, psychological, and interpersonal domains.

Within the context of positive masculinity, traditional masculinity is not seen as the problem; instead, it can be part of a solution to the problems that plague many modern boys and men. Guidance from positive male role models and institutions that instill a purpose-providing moral system which gives men a code to live by can play a vital role in developing healthy men. For example, martial arts training involves a dose of traditional masculinity—aggression, stoicism, confidence, and competitiveness, and the traditional military-style teaching methods. Training takes advantage of traditional masculinity philosophy to build positive characteristics such as dignity, restraint, personal responsibility, and a sense of duty toward others (Routledge, 2019).

Kiselica et al. (2016) define positive masculinity as "prosocial attitudes, beliefs, and behaviors of boys and men that produce positive consequences for self and others (p. 126)." Positive characteristics are not necessarily inherent; rather, they are learned traits which are internalized through socialization processes in which boys and men develop masculine beliefs and attitudes, promoting healthy development and fostering a sense of duty to others and the greater society. The positive psychology-positive masculinity paradigm is a shift in the psychology of men and masculinity from a focus on male pathology and identifying men's deficits while overlooking the qualities of masculine strengths, adaptive and evolutionary behaviors, and positive aspects of being a man (Kiselica, Englar-Carlson, & Fisher, 2006; Kiselica, Englar-Carlson, Horne, & Fisher, 2008). The wide body of research on gender role strain and its emphasis on restrictive masculinity and gender-linked problems for men has contributed to a lack of awareness of positive characteristics of masculinity, shared through intergenerational history, that benefit men, their partners, and society (Kiselica, 2011).

Clinical application of PPPM promote 11 healthy and adaptive characteristics of masculinity that may enhance a clinician's understanding of and facilitate clinical work with boys and men: male relational styles, male ways of caring, generative fatherhood, forms of male self-reliance, the worker-provider tradition, respect for women, courage-daring-and risk-taking, styles of group orientation, male forms of service, men's use of humor, and male heroism (see Kiselica et al., 2016, for full review). A critical component of PPPM requires the ability to be flexible in the enactment of male strengths and the knowledge to recognize when a strength is adaptive or problematic (Kiselica & Englar-Carlson, 2010).

The Integrity Model

Clinical psychologists working with men in various counseling settings lack a sound theoretical basis for exploring the ways men address and communicate issues of intimacy, belonging, and sense of self (Nahon & Lander, 2013, 2016). A number of voices in psychology have suggested that phrases such as "fear of intimacy," "restrictive emotionality," and "low emotional intelligence" foster a sense of defectiveness in men's ability for emotionality and inaccurately depict intimate experiences of men by attempting to feminize their nature (Heesacker & Prichard, 1992).

Nahon and Lander (2013) adapted the Integrity model of psychotherapy from Mowrer's Integrity Therapy Group Approach (Mowrer, 1953) and developed it as a values-based wellness approach to therapy with men. The Integrity model is existential in nature and encompasses four basic components: (1) men's clarification of their values and value clashes, (2) mindfulness of the three pillars of Integrity (e.g., honesty, responsibility, & emotional closure), (3) a concept of the "I-Thou" relationship (e.g., a deep and meaningful relationship between therapist and client), and (4) "movement towards, away from, or against others" in conflict resolution. Through this framework, clinicians are challenged to consider that men do have the capacity to build meaningful relational experiences, emotional faculties, and ability to focus on reflection, value clarification, integrity, and intimacy through existential therapy (Schermer & Holmes, 2018).

Generational Strength-Based Positive Masculinity

Generational approaches to positive psychology and positive masculinity (PPPM) promote counseling that focuses on identifying, affirming, and developing male strengths that are passed down across generations (Kiselica & Englar-Carlson, 2010). Counseling techniques that focus on strength-based positive masculinity include: exploration of male heroes, integrating male humor, positive companionship though male humanitarian organizations, capitalizing on male group orientation, being sensitive to the cultural expectation of the "worker-provider" tradition, fostering healthy male self-reliance and problem-solving, recognizing and promoting the ways in which male clients care for others, conducting sessions while participating in action-oriented activities, and affirming generative fatherhood and positive parenthood experiences. Strength-based therapy, in addition to other interventions, can reframe negative, stereotypical, oppressive, and dysfunctional attitudes and behaviors of men and replace them with honorable and principled notions of masculinity and prosocial behaviors that facilitate growth and wellness (Englar-Carlson & Kiselica, 2013).

Men are considerably less likely than women to seek counseling or visit a physician's office (Centers for Disease Control and Prevention, 2015). The role of counseling is geared towards helping individuals gain insight about connecting rational patterns of thoughts, feelings, and behaviors. Men who ascribe to traditional masculine norms may have difficulty fulfilling intimate relationship expectations such as vulnerability, negotiation, and interdependence (Tager, Good, & Brammer, 2010; Williams & Justice, 2010). Psychologists and counselors are encouraged to increase psychoeducation about restrictive masculine ideologies and how they relate to health-risk behaviors. Additionally, counseling professionals are able to help men build health-promoting behaviors such as resisting social pressures, engaging in self-acceptance, fostering a positive identity, engaging in preventative health-related services, and developing positive habits (APA, 2018).

Improvements in delivery systems for mental health services in integrated health care settings have increased access for patients to direct (often same-day) referrals for both individual and group psychosocial interventions. Group therapies for diabetes focus on coping strategies, social skills, problem-solving, goal-setting, adherence to anti-depressants/anxiolytic medications, group sharing, and mind-body health. Mind-body work draws attention to the intimate connection between physical and psychological symptoms of diabetes, relaxation training, yoga, emotional processing of physical and psychological symptoms (Parks, 2017). A recent study by Blizzard and Heckman (2018) examined mindfulness, meditation, personality characteristics, and frequency of engagement with mindfulness practice. The study reported that men spent more days in meditation practice during the intervention. Researchers hypothesized that men may not feel that the practice of meditation challenges their explicitly or implicitly held beliefs about masculinity. Additionally, mindfulness practice may be viewed as a solitary practice, as opposed to a social engagement like psychotherapy. Mindfulness may also provide men an effective release from shame and blame that have historically impeded men's likelihood of seeking psychotherapy.

There has been a growing focus on applying strengths-based approaches to counseling and psychotherapy (Chapin & Boykin, 2010; Kosine, Steger, & Duncan, 2008; Smith, 2008). The APA guidelines (2018) suggest that psychologists should make every effort to recognize the influence of masculine gender role socialization on some men's reluctance to seek help. Although certain psychological diagnoses are more common among women (e.g., depression, anxiety), these discrepancies may be due to gender role socialization (Addis, 2008), which impacts men's help-seeking behaviors and how they may present physical and psychological distress (Cochran & Rabinowitz, 2000). Clinicians who capitalize on strengths throughout their work with men communicate to their clients a sense of hope about the clients' potential and future. Furthermore, a focus on positive masculinity may increase the utility and appeal of therapy and health-related services for more therapy-resistant men (Hammer & Good, 2010; Kiselica et al., 2016).

From a social justice perspective, psychologists are situated to help men obtain the necessary knowledge, attitudes, and behaviors to use their own social influence to promote positive behaviors in other boys and men (American Psychological Association, Boys and Men Guidelines Group, 2018). Furthermore, psychologists are encouraged to promote information to reshape attitudes about men and mental health. Public information campaigns highlighting depression as a normative problem for men are needed to reduce continued mental health stigma among men (Lynch & Kilmartin, 2013; National Institute of Mental Health, 2017; Rabinowitz & Cochran, 2008; Rochlen, Whilde, & Hoyer, 2005).

Implications for Training

The importance of diversity in counseling psychology programs is well-documented (American Psychological Association, 2017; Campbell et al., 2012; Fouad et al., 2009; Fuertes, Spokane, & Holloway, 2013; Mintz & Bieschke, 2009; Packard, 2009; Society for the Psychological Study of Men and Masculinities, 2019). Given that the psychology of men is rarely taught at either undergraduate or graduate levels (O'Neil & Renzulli, 2013), including multicultural counseling courses (Liu, 2005), research suggests that attaining adequate knowledge of men's gender role socialization processes, and acquiring skill in clinical work with males, have important implications for psychological practice with boys (Bruchmüller, Margraf, & Schneider, 2012) and men (Mahalik et al., 2012). Counseling programs offer limited training in men's issues and have relatively no training in men's health-related issues. Clinicians often feel uncomfortable discussing the most relevant men's health-related concerns with their clients such as diabetes, heart disease, erectile dysfunction, testicular cancer, prostate inflammation, lung cancer, and trauma (Neukrug, Britton, & Crews, 2013). The implications for practice and research that have been noted are of importance to counseling psychology trainees as they enter practicum, internship, and careers as early psychologists.

Traditional interventions that focus on classical counseling skills may be insufficient for working with men in the context of enhancing prosocial behaviors and adopting a framework of positive masculinity (Levant, 1995; Rowan, 1997). Counseling models have been created now that attract men and keep them engaged in counseling, as well as to effectively communicate with health care professionals (e.g., Addis & Mahalik, 2003; Englar-Carlson, Evans, & Duffey, 2014; McKelley & Rochlen, 2007; Robertson, 2005). Some of the techniques described include: 1) reframing the counseling service to conceptualize it as a learning process 2) to use a male-friendly counseling model which validates a man's understanding of his gender identity, 3) to have men talk with men and promote group activities and social support structures and 4) to help men navigate help-seeking and counseling in hopes of easing frustration, worry, and fear of mental health and medical services (Addis & Mahalik, 2003). Recommendations for providers engaging in male-friendly counseling have included: 1) gaining and maintaining competencies in the knowledge of men, masculinity, and socialization; 2) therapist critical self-awareness and commitment; 3) knowledge and execution of masculinity-informed treatment adaptations; and 4) masculinity-informed tasks and goals (i.e., assessment, client conceptualization, strategies, intervention, and goals). These themes were identified across 44 literature sources written over a 21-year period on how to enhance engagement and therapeutic change for men in counseling (Beel, Jeffries, Brownlow, Winterbotham, & du Preez, 2018).

Conclusion

Men are detrimentally impacted by rigid gender socialization processes, cultural and contextual expectations of masculine gender performance, and gender role conflict. Men who adhere to the restrictions of masculine expectations experience direct and indirect negative mental and physical health consequences. As the fields of counseling psychology and positive psychology continue to integrate theoretically and clinically, outcome studies are necessary to demonstrate the efficacy of positive masculinity on individual, group, and systematic levels. Social psychologists are responsible for supporting and validating the broad role that the psychology of men and masculinity plays in Western and other societies. Clinicians and health service professionals can integrate positive psychology and positive masculinity to enhance wellness and facilitate the ideological and societal shift towards a more generative and values-based prosocial masculinity.

References

Addis, M. E. (2008). Gender and depression in men. *Clinical Psychology: Science and Practice*, *15*, 153-168. doi:10.1111/j.1468-2850.2008.00125.x.

Addis, M. E. & Mahalik, J. R. (2003). Men, masculinity, and the context of help-seeking. *American Psychologist*, *58*, 5-14.

Addis, M. E., Mansfield, A. & Syzdek, M. (2010). Is "masculinity" a problem?: Framing the effects of gendered social learning in men. *Psychology of Men& Masculinity*, *11*, 77-90. doi: 10.1037/ aOO18602.

American Psychological Association, Boys and Men Guidelines Group. (2018). *APA guidelines for psychological practice with boys and men*. Retrieved from http://www.apa.org/about/policy/psychological-practice-boys-men-guidelines.pdf.

American Psychological Association. (2007). Guidelines for psychological practice with girls and women. *American Psychologist*, *62*(9), 949–979. doi:10.1037/0003-066X.62.9.949.

American Psychological Association. (2012). Guidelines for psychological practice with the lesbian, gay, and bisexual clients. *American Psychologist*, *67*(1), 10–42. doi:10.1037/a0024659.

American Psychological Association. (2013a). Guidelines for psychological practice in healthcare delivery systems. *American Psychologist*, *68*(1), 1–6. doi:10.1037/a0029890.

American Psychological Association. (2013b). Specialty guidelines for forensic psychology. *American Psychologist*, *68*(1), 7–19. doi:10.1037/a0029889.

American Psychological Association. (2013c). Guidelines for psychological evaluations in child protection matters. *American Psychologist*, *68*(1), 20–31. doi:10.1037/a0029891.

American Psychological Association. (2014). Guidelines for psychological practice with older adults. *American Psychologist*, *69*(1), 34–65. doi:10.1037/a0035063.

American Psychological Association. (2015a). Guidelines for psychological practice with transgender and gender nonconforming people. *American Psychologist*, *70*, 832–864. doi:10.1037/a0039906 .

American Psychological Association. (2015b). Professional practice guidelines: Guidance for developers and users. *American Psychologist*, *70*(9), 823 831. doi:10.1037/a0039644.

American Psychological Association. (2017). *Multicultural Guidelines: An Ecological Approach to Context, Identity, and Intersectionality*. Retrieved from: http://www.apa.org/about/policy/multicultural-guidelines.pdf.

Aronson, E. (2012). *The social animal* (11th ed.). New York: Worth Publishers.

Beel, N., Jeffries, C., Brownlow, C., Winterbotham, S. & du Preez, J. (2018). Recommendations for male-friendly individual counseling with men: A qualitative systematic literature review for the period 1995–2016. *Psychology of Men & Masculinity, 19*(4), 600-611. http://dx.doi.org/10.1037/men0000137.

Blazina, C. (2003). *The cultural myth of masculinity*. New York: Praeger.

Blizzard, J. R. & Heckman, B. D. (2018). *Personality and mindfulness practice: Does personality predict engagement in mindfulness?* (Unpublished Doctoral Dissertation). University of Georgia, Athens, GA.

Brooks, G. R. & Good, G. E. (2001a). Introduction. In G. R. Brooks & G. E. Good (Eds.), *The new handbook of psychotherapy and counseling with men: A comprehensive guide to settings, problems, and treatment approaches* (pp. 3-21). San Francisco: Jossey-Bass.

Broom, D. H. & Lenagh-Maguire, A. (2010). Gendered configurations of diabetes: from rules to exceptions. *Journal of Gender Studies*, *19*(2), 195-209.

Bruchmüller, K., Margraf, J. & Schneider, S. (2012). Is ADHD diagnosed in accord with diagnostic criteria? Overdiagnosis and influence of client gender on diagnosis. *Journal of Consulting and Clinical Psychology*, *80*(1), 128–138. doi:10.1037/a002658.

Campbell, L., Fouad, N., Grus, C., Hatcher, R., Leahy, K. & McCutcheon, S. (2012, July). A *Practical Guidebook for the Competency Benchmarks*. Retrieved from https://www.apa.org/ed/graduate/guide-benchmarks.pdf.

Centers for Disease Control and Prevention. (2015). Health, United States, 2015. Retrieved from http://www.cdc.gov/diabetes/statistics/prev/national/figbysex.htm.

Chapin, M. & Boykin, R. (2010). Gray matter: Integrating positive psychology techniques into rehabilitation counselor education. *Rehabilitation Education*, *24*, 25-34.

Cochran, S. V. & Rabinowitz, F. (2000). *Men and depression: Clinical and empirical perspectives*. San Diego, CA: Academic Press.

Deutch, C. J. & Gilbert, L. A. (1976). Sex role stereotypes: Effect on perceptions of self and others and on personal adjustment. *Journal of Counseling Psychology*, *23*, 373-379.

Eisler, R. M. & Skidmore, J. R. (1987). Masculine gender role stress: Scale development and component factors in the appraisal of stressful situations. *Behavior Modification*, *11*(2), 123-136.

Englar-Carlson, M., Evans, M. P. & Duffey, T. (Eds.). (2014). A counselor's guide to working with men. Alexandria, VA, US: American Counseling Association.

Englar-Carlson, M. & Kiselica, M. S. (2013). Affirming the Strengths in Men: A Positive Masculinity Approach to Assisting Male Clients. *Journal of Counseling & Development*, *91*, 399-409. doi:10.1002/j.1556-6676.2013.00111.x.

Espinosa, M. P. & Kovářík, J. (2015). Prosocial behavior and gender. *Frontiers in Behavioral Neuroscience*, *9*.

Ferguson, C. (2019, February 4). Twelve scholars respond to the APA's guidance for treating men and boys. *Quillette Magazine*. Retrieved from https://quillette.com/2019/02/04/psychologists-respond-to-the-apas-guidance-for-treating-men-and-boys/.

Fouad, N. A., Grus, C. L., Hatcher, R. L., Kaslow, N. J., Hutchings, P., Madson, M. B. & Crossman, R. E. (2009). Competency benchmarks: A model for understanding and measuring competence in professional psychology across training levels. *Training and Education in Professional Psychology*, *3*(4, Suppl), S5-S26. doi:10.1037/a0015832.

Frueh, C. (2019, February 4). Twelve scholars respond to the APA's guidance for treating men and boys. *Quillette Magazine.* Retrieved from https://quillette.com/2019/02/04/psychologists-respond-to-the-apas-guidance-for-treating-men-and-boys/.

Fuertes, J. N., Spokane, A. R. & Holloway, E. (2013). *Specialty competencies in counseling psychology.* New York: Oxford University Press.

Garnets, L. & Pleck, J. (1979). Sex role identity, androgyny, and sex role transcendence: A sex role strain analysis. *Psychology of Women Quarterly*, *3*, 270-283.

Gilmore, D. D. (1990). *Manhood in the making: Cultural concepts of masculinity.* New Haven, CT: Yale.

Gough, B. (2006). Try to be healthy, but don't forgo your masculinity: Deconstructing men's health discourse in the media. *Social Science & Medicine*, *63*, 2476–2488.

Gove, W. R. (1979). Sex differences in epidemiology of mental disorder: Evidence and explanations. In E.S. Gomberg & V. Franks (Eds.), *Gender and disordered behavior: Sex differences in psychopathology* (p. 23-68). New York: Brunner/Mazel.

Hammer, J. H. & Good, G. (2010). Positive psychology: An empirical examination of beneficial aspects of endorsement of masculine norms. *Psychology of Men & Masculinity, 11,* 303-318. doi:10.1037/a0019056.

Hammond, W. P. & Mattis, J. S. (2005). Being a man about it: Manhood meaning among African American men. *Psychology of Men & Masculinity*, *6*, 114-126. doi:10.1037/1524-9220.6.2.114.

Harris, A. H. S., Thoresen, C. E. & Lopez, S. J. (2007). Integrating positive psychology into counseling: Why and (when appropriate) how. *Journal of Counseling & Development*, *85*, 3-13. doi:10.1002/j.1556-6678.2007.tb00438.x.

Heesacker, M. & Prichard, S. (1992). In a different voice, revisited: Men, women and emotion. *Journal of Mental Health Counseling*, *14*, 274-290.

Hernandez, R. (2002). *Fatherwork in the crossfire: Chicano teen fathers struggling to take care of business.* East Lansing, MI: Michigan State University, Julian Samora Research Institute. (ERIC Document Reproduction Service No. ED471926).

Hesse, M. (2019, January 13). How 'traditional masculinity' hurts the men who believe in it most. *The Washington Post.* Retrieved from https://www.washingtonpost.com/lifestyle/style/how-traditional-masculinity-hurts-the-men-who-believe-in-it-most/2019/01/12/.

Hurtado, A. & Sinha, M. (2008). More than men: Latino feminist masculinities and intersectionality. *Sex Roles*, *59*, 337-349. doi:10.1007/sl 1199-008-9405-7.

Isacco, A., Talovic, E., Chromik, L. & Yallum, N. (2012). Addressing men's mental health through a strength-based approach. In J. M. Rippe (Ed.), *Lifestyle medicine* (2nd ed., pp. 369-382). Boca Raton, FL: CRC Press.

Kiselica, M. S. (2011). Promoting positive masculinity while addressing gender role conflict: A balanced theoretical approach to clinical work with boys and men. In C. Blazina, D. S. Shen-Miller, C. Blazina, & D. S. Shen-Miller (Eds.), *An international psychology of men: Theoretical advances, case studies, and clinical innovations*, (pp. 127–156). New York, NY: Routledge/Taylor & Francis Group.

Kiselica, M. S., Benton-Wright, S. & Englar-Carlson, M. (2016). Accentuating positive masculinity: A new foundation for the psychology of boys, men, and masculinity. In Y. J. Wong, S. R. Wester, Y. J. Wong, & S. R. Wester (Eds.), *APA handbook of men and masculinities*, (pp. 123–143). Washington, DC: American Psychological Association. http://dx.doi.org/10.1037/14594-006.

Kiselica, M. S. & Englar-Carlson, M. (2010). Identifying, affirming, and building upon male strengths: The positive psychology/positive masculinity model of psychotherapy with boys and men. *Psychotherapy: Theory, Research, Practice, Training*, *47*, 276-287. doi:10.1037/a0021159.

Kiselica, M. S., Englar-Carlson, M. & Fisher, M. (2006). A positive psychology framework for building upon male strengths. In M. S. Kiselica (Chair), *Toward a positive psychology of boys, men, and masculinity.* Symposium presented at the 114th Annual Meeting of the American Psychological Association, New Orleans, LA.

Kiselica, M. S., Englar-Carlson, M., Horne, A. M. & Fisher, M. (2008). A positive psychology perspective on helping boys. In M. S. Kiselica, M. Englar-Carlson, & A. M. Horne (Eds.), *The Routledge series on counseling and psychotherapy with boys and men. Counseling troubled boys: A guidebook for professionals*, (pp. 31-48). New York, NY: Routledge/Taylor & Francis Group.

Kosine, N. R., Steger, M. F. & Duncan, S. (2008). Purpose-centered career development: A strengths-based approach to finding meaning and purpose in careers. *Professional School Counseling*, *12*(2), 133-136. https://doi.org/10.1177/2156759X0801200209.

Levant, R. F. (1995). Toward the reconstruction of masculinity. In R. F. Levant & W. S. Pollack (Eds.), *A new psychology of men* (pp. 229-251). New York, NY, US: Basic Books. (Reprinted in modified form from the *Journal of Family Psychology*, *1992*, 5, 379–402).

Levant, R. F. & Richmond, K. (2016). The gender role strain paradigm and masculinity ideologies. In Y. J. Wong, S. R. Wester, Y. J. Wong, & S. R. Wester (Eds.), *APA handbook of men and masculinities* (pp. 23– 49). Washington, DC: American Psychological Association. http://dx.doi .org/10.1037/14594-00.

Levant, R. F., Stefanov, D. G., Rankin, T. J., Halter, M. J., Mellinger, C. & Williams, C. M. (2013). Moderated path analysis of the relationships between masculinity and men's attitudes toward seeking psychological help. *Journal of Counseling Psychology*, *60*(3), 392-406. doi:10.1037/a0033014.

Liu, W. M. (2005). The study of men and masculinity as an important multicultural competency consideration. *Journal of Clinical Psychology*, *61*(6), 685–697. doi:10.1002/jclp.20103.

Liu, W. M., Rochlen, A. B. & Mohr, J. (2005). Real and ideal gender role conflict: Exploring psychological distress among men. *Psychology of Men and Masculinity*, *6*, 137-148.

Lynch, J. & Kilmartin, C. (2013). *Overcoming masculine depression: The pain behind the mask*. New York: Routledge.

Mahalik, J. R., Good, G. E., Tager, D., Levant, R. F. & Mackowiak, C. (2012). Developing a taxonomy of helpful and harmful practices for clinical work with boys and men. *Journal of Counseling Psychology, 59*(4), 591-603. Retrieved from http://dx.doi.org/10.1037/a0030130.

McKelley, R. A. & Rochlen, A. B. (2007). The practice of coaching: Exploring alternatives to therapy for counseling-resistant men. *Psychology of Men & Masculinity, 8*, 53-65. http://dx.doi.org/10.1037/1524-9220.8.1.53.

Mintz, L. B. & Bieschke, K. J. (2009). Counseling psychology model training values statement addressing diversity: Development and introduction to the major contribution. *The Counseling Psychologist*, *37*, 634-640. doi:10.1177/0011000009331923.

Moore, T. M. & Stuart, G. L. (2005). A review of the literature on masculinity and partner violence. Psychology of Men and Masculinity, 6, 46 – 61. http://dx.doi.org/10.1037/1524-9220.6.1.46.

Mowrer, O. H. (1953). *Psychotherapy: Theory and research.* New York, NY: Ronald Press Company. http://dx.doi.org/10.1037/10572-000.

Murray, T. & Lewis, V. (2014). Gender role conflict and men's body satisfaction: The moderating role of age. *Psychology of Men and Masculinity*, *15*, 40-48.

Nahon, D. & Lander, N. R. (2013). Working with men in groups from an Integrity model perspective. *The Journal of Men's Studies*, *21*, 162-177.

Nahon, D. & Lander, N. R. (2016). The integrity model. *Journal of Men's Studies*, *24*(1), 89-116. doi:10.1177/1060826515600459.

National Institute of Mental Health (NIMH). (2017, February 17). Mission. Retrieved from https://www.nih.gov/about-nih/what-we-do/nih-almanac/national-institute-mental-health-nimh.

Neukrug, E., Britton, B. S. & Crews, R. C. (2013). Common health-related concerns of men: implications for counselors. *Journal of Counseling & Development*, *91*(4), 390-397. doi:10.1002/j.1556-6676.2013.00109.x.

O'Neil, J. M. (1981). Male sex-role conflict, sexism, and masculinity: Implications for men, women, and the counseling psychologist. *The Counseling Psychologist*, *9*, 61-80.

O'Neil, J. M. (2008). Summarizing 25 years of research on men's gender role conflict using the gender role conflict scale: New research paradigms and clinical implications. *The Counseling Psychologist*, *36*, 358-445.

O'Neil, J. M. (2012). The psychology of men. In E. Altmaier & J. Hansen (Eds.), *The Oxford handbook of counseling psychology*, (pp. 375-08). New York, NY: Oxford University Press.

O'Neil, J. M. (2015). *Men's gender role conflict: Psychological costs, consequences, and an agenda for change.* Washington, DC: American Psychological Association. http://dx.doi.org/10.1037/14501-000.

O'Neil, J. M. & Egan, J. (1992a). Men's and women's gender role journeys: Metaphor for healing, transition, and transformation. In B. Wainrib (Ed.), *Gender issues across the life cycle*, (pp. 107-123). New York: Springer.

O'Neil, J. M. & Renzulli, S. (2013). Introduction to the special section: Teaching the psychology of men — A call to action. *Psychology of Men & Masculinity*, *14*(3), 221-229. doi:10.1037/a0033258.

O'Neil, J. M., Good, G. E. & Holmes, S. (1995). Fifteen years of theory and research on men's gender role conflict: New paradigms for empirical research. In R. Levant & W. Pollack (Eds.), *The new psychology of men*, (pp. 164-206). New York: Basic Books.

O'Neil, J. M., Helms, B., Gable, R., David, L. & Wrightsman, L. (1986). Gender Role Conflict Scale (GRCS): College men's fears of femininity. *Sex Roles*, *14*, 335-350.

Packard, T. (2009). The 2008 Leona Tyler Award Address: Core values that distinguish counseling psychology: Personal and professional perspectives. *The Counseling Psychologist*, *37*(4), 610-624. doi:10.1177/0011000009333986.

Parks, J. (2017). *Interactions and outcomes of co-morbid diabetes and depression* [PowerPoint slides]. Retrieved from https://www.integration.samhsa.gov/about-us/May_Webinar_Depression_and_Diabetes_05.23.17.pdf.

Park, N. & Peterson, C. (2008). Positive psychology and character strengths: Application to strengths-based school counseling. *Professional School Counseling*, *12*, 85-92. doi: 10.5330/ PSC.n.2010-12.85.

Pleck, J. H. (1981). *The myth of masculinity*. Cambridge, MA: MIT Press.

Pleck, J. H. (1995). The gender role strain paradigm: An update. In R. F. Levant & W. S. Pollack (Eds.), *A new psychology of men*, (pp. 11-32). New York: Basic Books.

Rabinowitz, F. E. & Cochran, S. V. (2008). Men and therapy: A case of masked male depression. *Clinical Case Studies*, *7*(6), 575–591. https://doi.org/10.1177/1534650108319917.

Riggle, E. & Rostosky, S. (2011). *A positive view for LGBTQ: Embracing identity and cultivating well-being*. Lanham, MD: Rowman & Littlefield.

Robertson, J. M. (2005). Counseling men in college settings. In Brooks G. R., Good G. E., editors. (Eds.), *The new handbook of psychotherapy and counseling with men*, (pp. 70-87). San Francisco, CA: Jossey-Bass.

Robinson, M. A. & Brewster, M. E. (2014). Motivations for fatherhood: Examining internalized heterosexism and gender role conflict with childless gay and bisexual men. *Psychology of Men and Masculinity.*, *15*, 49-59.

Rochlen, A. B., McKelley, R. A. & Whittaker, T. A. (2010). Stay-at-home fathers' reasons for entering the role and stigma experiences: A preliminary report. *Psychology of Men & Masculinity*, *11*(4), 279-285. doi:10.1037/a0017774.

Rochlen, A. B., Suizzo, M., McKelley, R. & Scaringi, V. (2008). "I'm just providing for my family": A qualitative study of stay-at-home fathers. *Psychology of Men & Masculinity*, *9*, 193-206. doi:10.1037/a0012510.

Rochlen, A. B., Whilde, M. R. & Hoyer, W. D. (2005). The real men. Real depression campaign: Overview, theoretical implications, and research considerations. *Psychology of Men & Masculinity*, *6*(3), 186-194.

Routledge, C. (2019, February 4). Twelve scholars respond to the APA's guidance for treating men and boys. *Quillette Magazine.* Retrieved from https://quillette.com/2019/02/04/psychologists-respond-to-the-apas-guidance-for-treating-men-and-boys/.

Rowan, J. (1997). *Healing the male psyche: Therapy as initiation.* London: Routledge.

Schermer, T. W. & Holmes, C. N. (2018). Will to masculinity: An existential examination of men's issues. *The Journal of Humanistic Counseling*, *54*(7), 191-207.

Seligman, M. E. (2008). Positive health. *Applied Psychology: An International Review*, 3–18.

Seligman, M. E. P., Rashid, T. & Parks, A. C. (2006). Positive psychotherapy. *American Psychologist*, *61*, 774–788.

Shepherd, C. B. & Rickard, K. M. (2012). Drive for muscularity and help-seeking: The mediational role of gender role conflict, self-stigma, and attitudes. *Psychology of Men & Masculinity*, *13*(4), 379-392. doi:10.1037/a0025923.

Shields, A. (2008). Gender: An intersectionality perspective. *Sex Roles*, *59*, 301-311. doi:10.1007/sl1199-008-9501-8.

Smiler, A. P. (2004). Thirty years after the discovery of gender: Psychological concepts and measures of masculinity. *Sex Roles*, *50*, 15-26. doi:10.1023/B:SERS.0000011069.02279.4c.

Smith, C. (2008). *Positive Psychology Mind Map.* Retrieved from http://www.positivepsychology.org.uk/images/stories/files/Claire_Smith_MM.pdf.

Society for the Psychological Study of Men and Masculinities. (2019). *Special Interest Groups*. Retrieved from https://www.division51.net/special-interest-groups.

Tager, D., Good, G. E. & Brammer, S. (2010). "Walking over 'em": An exploration of relations between emotion dysregulation, masculine norms, and intimate partner abuse in a clinical sample of men. *Psychology of Men & Masculinity, 11*(3), 233-239. http://dx.doi.org/10.1037/a0017636.

Thompson, E. H. & Pleck, J. H. (1986). The structure of the male norms. *American Behavioral Scientist*, *29*, 531-543.

Vogel, D. L., Wester, S. R., Hammer, J. H. & Downing-Matibage, T. (2014). Referring men to seek help: The influence of gender role conflict and stigma. *Psychology of Men and Masculinity*, *15*, 60-67.

Williams, A. & Justice, M. (2010). Attitudes of African American Males Regarding Counseling in Four Texas Universities. *Education*, *131*(1), 158-168.

Wong, Y. J. & Wester, S. R. (Eds.). (2016). *APA handbooks in psychology series. APA handbook of men and masculinities.* Washington, DC, US: American Psychological Association. Retrieved from http://dx.doi.org/10.1037/14594-000.

World Health Organization and Calouste Gulbenkian Foundation. (2014). *Social determinants of mental health. World Health Organization*, Geneva, 2014. Retrieved from https://www.who.int/mental_health/publications/gulbenkian_paper_social_determinants_of_mental_health/en/.

SECTION VI.
HUMAN AGGRESSION

In: Social Psychology and Counseling
Editors: D. A. Kleiber and E. Delgado-Romero
ISBN: 978-1-53616-548-7

Chapter 13

AGGRESSION IN OFFENDERS: A BIOPSYCHOSOCIAL APPROACH AND IMPLICATIONS FOR TREATMENT

Brittany A. Field and Katie K. Robinson

One of the domains that social psychologists have spent an extensive amount of time studying and attempting to understand is the area of aggression and violence. According to Aronson (2012), aggression is defined as "intentional behavior aimed at causing either physical or psychological pain" (pg. 250). This definition is often further delineated into many different forms, the most commonly referenced being hostile, instrumental, and reactive aggression. Hostile aggression is conceptualized as acts of aggression that are rooted in emotions such as anger with the goal of causing harm. Instrumental aggression is often defined as acts of aggression that are working towards a certain goal (Goldstein & Naglieri, 2011). Reactive aggression most often occurs as a response to an actual or alleged threat or when someone is provoked (Marsee & Frick, 2007). Whatever form it may take, aggression and violence have a negative impact on millions of people each year, creating a vested interest from researchers and society-at-large in attempting to understand the roots of human aggression and its susceptibility to treatment and reduction.

Social psychology's attempt to understand violence has led researchers to approach this topic from many different angles. Early studies focused on the notion that aggression was an instinct, which led to a large amount of research being conducted with nonhuman species such as chimps or rats (Kuo, 1961). Well-known figures in the field have examined the connection between aggression and the basic social psychological concepts of social learning and modeling (Bandura, Ross, & Ross, 1961). Others have attempted to understand how reactions to frustration or being excluded (see Ford & Ocampo, this volume) result in the expression of aggression (Harris, 1974).

THE BIOPSYCHOSOCIAL MOVEMENT

Concurrent with these seminal studies on aggression, a conceptual model emerged that significantly impacted the body of literature on aggression. In 1977, psychiatrist George Engel suggested a shift away from a medical model of understanding illness that focused exclusively on biological determinants, advocating for the development of a biopsychosocial approach which provided space for the inclusion of psychological and social factors. Engel's (1977) original work was intended for the medical and psychiatric community, but the notion of a biopsychosocial approach to understanding human behavior quickly found itself in the research programs of social psychologists around the world.

In a review of the biopsychosocial approaches to understanding human aggression, Berman (1997) concluded that researchers have now come to understand and operate from the framework that aggressive behaviors are best understood when viewed through a multifactor lens. Therefore, if the goal is to create a well-rounded and thorough model of aggression then that model must include aspects of biology and psychology as well as consideration of the social context within which an individual exists. However, due to the complex nature of studying all three components of the biopsychosocial model simultaneously, much of the current research on aggression tends to focus on only one of the three domains.

Individuals involved in the criminal justice system are often targeted by researchers as prime examples of the manifestation of aggression since aggression has most often been a prominent part of their experience. With this in mind, the authors will provide a preliminary review of the biopsychosocial conceptualizations of aggression in adult offenders. It is the hope of the author that this work will clarify the individual explanations of aggression in each of the biopsychosocial realms and provide suggestions for mental health treatment aimed at understanding and reducing aggression in adult offenders.

The Biological Domain

The biological domain of the biopsychosocial framework includes areas of functioning that can be out of an individual's control. As an example, a study by Bertsch et al., (2013) investigated potential brain structural abnormalities in prison inmates that were diagnosed with antisocial personality disorder compared to normal controls. Results indicated that inmates with antisocial personality disorder displayed distinct differences in brain structure than the control group. Further, inmates with comorbid antisocial and borderline personality disorder had structural variations in the components of the brain that impact emotion regulation, reactive aggression, and the interpretation of others' motives. Participants displaying high levels of both antisocial and psychopathic traits showed significant differences in areas of the brain that facilitate self-reflection and the understanding of others' emotions.

A study by Prehn et al., (2013) was designed to reveal the neural connections of inmates who had been convicted of violent crimes. The researchers had inmates engage in a financial decision-making task that consisted of low-risk and high-risk options while being assessed with functional magnetic resonance imaging (fMRI) to measure brain activity based on changes in blood flow. The results suggested that inmates who had a history of instrumental aggression showed decreased neural activation when faced with uncertainty and decreased prefrontal cortex activity when attempting to regulate their behavior. Prehn et al., (2013) suggested that these decreases could lead to difficulties in understanding the consequences of choices, particularly regarding impulsive decision making. This study suggests that when faced with uncertainty, the brain of an adult offender can slow down in the areas that control decision-making and forward thinking, which may contribute to increases in impulsive and aggressive activity.

A large cross-section of biological research on aggression involves investigating the connection between certain genes and the manifestation of aggression. One such gene that has received extensive attention is the monoamine oxidase A gene (MAOA). The MAOA gene is responsible for breaking down neurotransmitters such as dopamine, serotonin and norepinephrine, all of which are connected to behavior patterns and movement. Interestingly, both high and low frequency variants of this gene have been associated with aggressive behavior (Manuck, Flory, Ferrell, Mann, & Muldoon, 2000; Meyer-Lindenberg et al., 2006). Researchers suggest that understanding the interaction of psychological and social factors alongside this gene is key to linking both high and low variants of MAOA to aggression. This line of research paves the way for further development of a psychosocial model of aggression among adult offenders.

The Psychological Domain

The psychological domain of the biopsychosocial approach to understanding aggression focuses on the role of individual differences. Understanding individual difference requires understanding the key concepts of attribution tendencies, problem solving skills, emotion regulation, internal motivation, self-concept, and self-esteem. Each of these unique individual aspects impact how one interacts with the world. Social psychology has extensively studied the role of attributions on behavior (Hewstone, 1983; Kelley, 1967; Quan et. al., 2019). An attribution is the way in which one perceives and explains the behavior of others (Godleski & Ostrov, 2010; cf. Aronson, 2012). Considering that people are likely to interpret others' actions based on their own personal experiences and insights, individual levels of aggression may result from their attribution for the reason for another's behavior. This leads to the concept of hostile attributional bias (HAB). The hostile attribution bias is seen as a tendency to interpret the behavior of others as hostile or aggressive (Tuente, Bogaerts, & Veling, 2019). A study by Seager (2005) found that in a sample of federally incarcerated adult males, individuals that had been charged with more violent crimes such as assault were more likely to endorse items in a questionnaire that indicated views of the world as a hostile and threatening place, indicating a potential hostile attribution bias. The endorsement of HAB by other adult offenders also correlates with a tendency to act more aggressively (Lim, Day, & Casey, 2011). This body of research seems to indicate that adult offenders who engage in aggressive acts toward others may do so because they increasingly interpret the actions of others as being disrespectful if not overtly aggressive (see also Ford & Ocampo, this volume).

In contrast to studies linking HAB patterns to increased aggressive acts among adult offenders, Kelty (2013) argued that the tendency to endorse a hostile attribution bias is not the core reason for engaging in aggressive behavior; instead, he found that it was an adult offender's lack of effective problem-solving skills that led directly to aggressive behavior (Kelty, 2013). When comparing situational problem-solving between violent adult offenders with non-offenders of similar age, race, and socio-economic status, the results of his study indicated that offenders generated a similar number of ways to solve a problem compared to non-offenders. However, the problem-solving options generated by the offender group consisted more of verbal and physical acts of aggression instead of more peaceful or assertive options, especially in situations that involved a dispute between offenders and their families or friends. Kelty's (2013) study proposes a focus less on how offenders interpret the behavior of others and more on what they will do to solve interpersonal problems as linked to aggressive action.

Another skill that plays a notable role in the expression of aggression broadly among individuals is the ability to regulate emotions (Garofalo & Velotti, 2017; Garofalo, Velotti, & Zavattini, 2018; Holley et. al., 2017; Kuzcu, 2016). Contemporary criminology and psychology literature on aggression highlights the need to increase focus on emotion regulation and its impact on aggressive behavior among offenders (Garofalo & Velotti, 2017). A study of adult offenders by Roberton, Daffern, and Bucks (2015) found that difficulty attending to emotions was a significant predictor of aggressive behavior within their sample. This study suggests that being aware of and understanding any kind of emotion, including the ability to label specific emotions, is a predictor of less aggressive behaviors among adult offenders.

Another key social psychological concept that exists throughout adult offender literature is motivation. Specifically, researchers have continually questioned the internal motives for aggression among this population, as external motivators tend to be clearer cut. Reiss (2012) describes motives as the way in which individual's perceptions, attention, cognition, emotions, and behaviors come together to determine a person's actions (See also Varley & Zito, this volume). Adding to this, Ohlsson and Ireland (2011) identified four core motives that underlie aggression: protection, social recognition, perceived positive outcome, and pleasure (p. 278). When comparing violent and non-violent adult offenders, their investigation indicated that violent offenders reported higher levels of the perceived positive outcomes and pleasure motives of aggressive behavior (Ohlsson & Ireland, 2011).

One of the most notable individual differences explored within aggression research is self-esteem (Durand, 2016; Khodabandeh, Khalilzadeh, & Hemati, 2018; Mier & Ladny, 2018). Self-esteem is often viewed as the positive or negative ways in which a person views himself or herself or the attitudes they hold about themselves (Walker & Knauer, 2011). The research on self-esteem and aggression is equivocal; some literature suggests low self-esteem contributes to violence while others purport that inflated self-esteem leads to aggressive acts (Baumeister et. al., 1996; Walker, 2009). Part of the explanation may be that individuals who present with an inflated sense of self-esteem and positive perceptual bias may be engaging in impression management, a protective factor to hide the experience of very low levels of self-worth (Smith, Lynch, Stephens, & Kistner, 2015). A recent review of the literature of self-esteem and aggression among male offenders supports the connection between low self-esteem and violent behavior (Walker & Bright, 2009). There is consensus among several authors noted in the review that when adult offenders with low self-esteem perceive a threat or the potential for humiliation, they are likely to engage in aggressive behavior to protect themselves physically and mentally. In this way, violence is seen as way to protect a fragile view of the self and, perhaps even to maintain some form of pride, dignity, or self-respect. In forensic settings where pride and respect are viewed as key aspects of survival, adult offenders with low self-esteem may not identify any other options than to be aggressive (Garofalo, Holden, Ziegler-Hill, & Velotti, 2016). Understanding aggression as a potential protective factor among adult offenders is an important avenue of social psychological research.

The Social Domain

The final domain of the biopsychosocial approach, the social domain, consists of larger systems within which the individual is involved. The social domain examines how environmental, social, community, and familial contexts contribute to the development of aggressive behavior (Lehman, David, & Gruber, 2017). Two such social contexts that have received extensive attention in adult offender literature are the impact of the family of origin and the neighborhood or community where the individual was raised (Kernsmith, 2006; Wang et al., 2008).

Much of this literature is rooted in the principles of modeling and social learning theory, focusing on the idea that individuals will learn, model, and imitate the behaviors observed in their environment (Bandura, Ross, & Ross, 1961). As a more specific example, work by Wang, Horne, Holdford and Henning (2008) examined two groups of adult male offenders who reported engaging in violent behavior. The first group consisted of men who were charged with aggressive acts against people outside of their home, while the second consisted of men who only engaged in violent acts against people in their family. Results indicated that experiences of childhood family violence were a significant predictor of violent behavior in both groups of men. Further, men in the group who only engaged in violent acts against members of their own family reported witnessing more father-initiated violence growing up. As noted by the authors, the results of this study provide support for the social learning interpretation and its connection to the development of aggression in adulthood. If an offender was raised in a home where violence was modeled as a way to resolve conflict, then it is reasonable to believe that the individual would then use this form of problem solving as an adult.

Another consideration with regard to family context and its relationship to aggression is exposure to adverse childhood experiences (ACEs). Adverse childhood experiences (ACEs) is a broad term that is used interchangeably with childhood trauma and includes experiences of childhood abuse and neglect and other challenges at home and in society more generally (Feltti et al., 1998). Literature on this connection is consistent in highlighting a link between early childhood traumatic experiences and the later development of aggressive behavior. The current body of research suggests multiple potential explanations for this link. Work by Matsuura, Hashimoto, and Toichi (2013) postulates that early family trauma leads to the development of depression and low self-esteem which contributes to aggressive behavior. In a similar vein, Sarcbiapone et al. (2009) pointed out that early traumatic experiences have been connected to the development of Post-Traumatic Stress Disorder (PTSD) and symptoms related to a number of personality disorders, many of which heighten an individual's propensity to engage in violent acts.

Moving outside of the home and into the context of neighborhoods and community has been an important step in the research on the development of aggression in adult offenders. This line of inquiry has sought to determine what influences community and neighborhood contexts have with respect to the amount and type of aggression displayed by adult criminal offenders. In his seminal work, social psychologist Elijah Anderson (2000) took an ecological view of the development of violence and focused on an individual's attitudes, beliefs, and behaviors regarding violence in the context of specific communities. His work suggests that if an individual is raised in a community in which one gains value and respect by being tough or violent, and where aggression is viewed as acceptable behavior, then the individual is more likely to adopt "street code values," which are defined as a set of informal rules governing interpersonal behavior (public and private) including violence (Anderson, 2000; Burgason, 2014). The internalization of street code values represents an individual's acceptance of the values, beliefs, and behaviors regarding street code. This acceptance can develop out of choice when an individual connects with his or her culture. According to Anderson (2000), assimilation, safety, or other protective traits may lead to further internalization of street code values to decrease the likelihood that an individual will be put in dangerous situations. In both cases, Anderson (2000) notes that street code values lead to an increased likelihood that an individual will engage in violent acts.

The role of street culture, street codes, and street values have been widely researched in the field of aggression. Stewart and Simons (2010) conducted a multicity analysis of acceptance of street culture and violence among adolescent offenders. Results demonstrated that individuals who lived in neighborhoods with well-established and entrenched street values incorporating violence were more likely to engage in violent criminal behaviors. The study found that adolescents' acceptance of the street codes increased their likelihood to engage in violent acts by 25% (Stewart & Simons, 2010). Similar results were obtained in another study examining the relationship between street culture and gun usage in criminal acts. Individuals who endorsed a higher level of street culture mentality (acceptance of the informal, unwritten rules of a community) were more likely to use a gun in the commission of a crime (Burgason, Thomas, Berthelot, & Burkey, 2014). It is necessary to highlight the role that adoption of street culture has on the identity development among both adolescent and adult offenders. For many individuals in the criminal justice system who come from marginalized communities, the acceptance of violence as a way of life can be adaptive. Acceptance of and engagement in violent acts may actually prove to serve a psychologically self-protective function within their more violent community (Weierstall et al., 2013). Individuals in these communities may view aggression as a way to physically and mentally survive (or even thrive).

Research has collectively shown that individuals, particularly those within the criminal justice system, are negatively impacted by exposure to community violence (Baskin & Sommers, 2015; Burgason, 2014; Hotton et al., 2019; Richters et al., 2003). When assessing the impact of trauma exposure, development of PTSD symptomology, and later aggressive behavior, the number one traumatic event reported by male juvenile offenders was witnessing community violence (Stimmel, Cruise, Ford, & Weiss, 2014). Among these young men, this exposure went on to contribute to the development of PTSD symptoms and accounted for a significant portion of self-reported reactive episodes of aggression (Stimmel, Cruise, Ford, & Weiss, 2014). This connection, which likely stretches across the lifespan, suggests that even if the individual is not an active participant in community violence (or any type of street culture), witnessing such violence can have a negative psychological impact.

CLINICAL UTILITY

Connecting each domain of the biopsychosocial perspective on aggression among adult offenders suggests a multidimensional therapeutic approach to treatment with this population. Following are foundational suggestions for such integration, offered with the hope of building a more thorough clinical knowledge-base for supporting this population while simultaneously addressing potential obstacles.

The most obvious obstacle in translating research into concrete therapeutic intervention appears within the biological domain as, at present, genes and brain structure cannot be altered to tailor behavior. However, the line of biological inquiry does provide beneficial information in suggesting that some aspects of aggression are outside of an individual's control. When working with adult offenders, it may be beneficial to integrate psychoeducation in order to demonstrate the potential origins of aggressive behavior. In doing so, individuals have the opportunity to better understand how the brain and the body respond to threats and, as a result, how behaviors become instinctive and potentially protective. The goal of such education would be less focused on assigning responsibility for aggressive actions and more focused on gaining insight into the relationship between the body, the brain, the environment, and behavior.

Research within the psychological domain actively connects genetics, brain structure, and neural activity to psychological and behavioral manifestations of skills including emotion regulation, problem solving, and attributional tendencies (Garofalo, Velotti, & Zavattini, 2018; Garofalo & Velotti, 2017). Each of these skills can be directly targeted and integrated into active therapeutic interventions. For example, attribution biases, which describe the act of interpreting the behavior of self or others, connect with the basic Cognitive Behavioral Therapy (CBT) objective of addressing cognitive distortions (Beck, 1976; Kelty, 2013). When working with offender populations, CBT interventions can be structured to help individuals identify their own cognitive distortions and how they shape their worldviews (See also Edner and Casiello-Robbins, this volume.). Once identified, the individual can work in treatment to replace potentially hostile attributions and cognitive distortions with more adaptive cognitive mechanisms.

Cognitive Behavioral Therapy is often viewed as the "go to" form of treatment for adult offenders (Landenberger & Lipsey, 2005; Tagrate & Mitchell, 2014), but it should not be seen as the only avenue for effective therapy. A review of psychological literature revealed that focusing on the development of certain skills and more affective approaches to treatment may also prove beneficial (Carriere, 1995; Howells, 1987; Shortt et al, 2014). The connection between lack of problem-solving abilities and aggression among adult offenders is of particular importance within this literature. The ability to effectively and efficiently solve problems is a skill, and a skill is something that can be learned. Therefore, the integration of interventions that clarify, practice, and support problem-solving skills have the potential to enhance therapeutic efficacy. This could be accomplished through the use of group interventions that teach individuals to identify the problem, generate solutions, quickly identify risks and benefits of each solution, and then choose a solution that will move them closer to their long-term goals. A group therapy model makes room for members to connect and practice skills with each other as well as receive feedback regarding the development of those skills.

Affective-focused interventions would not be affective without a spotlight on emotion regulation and self-esteem. As noted previously, offender populations are shown to have difficulties identifying, attending to, understanding, and processing their emotional experiences (Garofalo & Velotti, 2017; Garofalo, Velotti, & Zavattini, 2018; Holley et. al., 2017; Kuzcu, 2016). This suggests that there is room for more emotion-focused and mindfulness-based therapies among adult offender populations. Acceptance and mindfulness-based interventions encourage an individual to tune into their internal experiences without judgment (Schauss, Zettler, & Russell, 2019; Villagra-Lanza et al., 2014). Among adult offenders, these techniques could encourage the disconnection of emotions such as anger and frustration with behaviors such as violent acts. Emotion-focused interventions with this population may seek to improve emotional intelligence by promoting an understanding of one's own emotional experience, as well as by working to separate or decouple certain emotional experiences from their association with specific behaviors.

It is important to note that relying solely on cognitive behavioral and skills-based interventions will not fully address an individual's view of self, which is one of many potential roots to aggression among offender populations. (Smith, Lynch, Stephens, & Kistner, 2015) note the importance of self-esteem and self-awareness within therapeutic interventions with adult offenders. Humanistic approaches to this type of intervention may prove to be especially important when working with adult offenders with low self-esteem (Smith, Lynch, Stephens, & Kistner, 2015). When working with individuals in this population that show particularly low levels of self-esteem, clinicians may have success when actively operating from a present-focused stance of warmth and unconditional positive regard. In doing so, clinicians may invite adult offenders to "come as they are" and experience less judgement about their past experiences, resulting in a therapeutic alliance within which the individual (or group) can focus on the present need for self-compassion. Integration of these elements into therapeutic intervention allows for a more holistic acknowledgement of thinking, behavior, and emotion.

When designing appropriate and effective mental health treatment for adult offenders' family of origin, childhood community, and present community must all be considered. Because incarcerated individuals are not presently living in their typical environment, the relationship between environmental factors and thoughts, feelings, and behavior can remain unacknowledged. This "out of sight, out of mind" mentality fails to consider the importance of environmental and social context to treatment interventions, especially when considering an incarcerated offender's future reintegration with society.

There are many ways contextual and social influence on aggression can inform therapy. An awareness of how an individual's family of origin and community context may influence aggressive behavior provides a lens through which a clinician can begin to understand a client. Building upon this, active assessment of the social, familial, and community environments of an adult offender can prove vital to not only understanding a client's experiences, but for using them as mechanisms for growth in a psychoeducational way. This type of assessment may also prove to be integral in assessing for potential trauma. Seeking out information from the adult offender client regarding their past and present communities, culture, and family dynamics provides a foundation from which to conceptualize experiences using a multicultural framework (Kapoor, Dike, & Griffith, 2013; Okembe-RA Imani, 2011). Additionally, this framework could help clinicians avoid making assumptions about the many, varied values, morals, and rules that exist in different families, communities, and cultures. The integration of the contextual elements of an adult offender's experience lends itself to the use of systemic, multicultural, and feminist theories in therapy. Each of these therapeutic approaches works to illuminate how different social, cultural, and even political factors impact an individual's thoughts, feelings, and behaviors (Leibmann, 2007). Each operates from an egalitarian framework with an ultimate goal of client empowerment (Leibmann, 2007). Encouraging adult offender clients to consider their personal context as it relates to society may be vital in activating therapeutic work. There is hope from these frameworks that when individuals have a clearer view of self (both individually and in various contexts, including societal), they are more empowered to make choices that support their growth.

In summary, the work of understanding the development and manifestation of aggression in adult offender populations is incomplete. This is evidenced by the active and growing body of literature focusing on violent criminal offenders (DeLisi & Conis, 2018; Larden et al., 2018; Moore et al., 2018). Presently, social, clinical, and counseling psychologists alike are well advised to view aggression through the biopsychosocial perspective (Berman, 1997), providing a framework for addressing all aspects of an individual when considering effective treatment interventions.

REFERENCES

Anderson, E. (2000). *Code of the Street: Decency, Violence, and the Moral Life of the Inner City.* New York: W. W. Norton & Company.

Aronson, E. (2012). *The social animal* (11th ed.). New York: Worth Publishers.

Bandura, A., Ross, D., & Ross, S. A. (1961). Transmission of aggression through imitation of aggressive models. *Journal of Abnormal and Social Psychology*, 63, 575-582.

Baskin, D., & Sommers, I. (2015). Trajectories of exposure to community violence and mental health symptoms among serious adolescent offenders. *Criminal Justice and Behavior*, 587.

Baumeister, R. F., Smart, L., & Boden, J. M. (1996). Relation of threatened egotism to violence and aggression: The dark side of high self-esteem. *Psychological Review*, 103(1), 5-33. doi:10.1037/0033-295X.103.1.5.

Berman, M. E. (1997). Biopsychosocial approaches to understanding human aggression: The first 30 years. *Clinical Psychology Review*, 17, 585-588.

Bertsch, K., Grothe, M., Prehn, K., Vohs, K., Berger, C., Hauenstein, K., Herpertz, S. C. (2013). Brain volumes differ between diagnostic groups of violent criminal offenders. *European Archives of Psychiatry and Clinical Neuroscience*, 263, 593-606.

Burgason, K. A., Thomas, S. A., & Berthelot, E. R. (2014). The Nature of Violence: A Multilevel Analysis of Gun Use and Victim Injury in Violent Interpersonal Encounters. *Journal of Interpersonal Violence*, 29, 371-393.

Burgason, K. A., Thomas, S. A., Berthelot, E. R., & Burkey, L. C. (2014). Gats and gashes: Street culture and distinctions in the nature of violence between youth and adult offenders. *Deviant Behavior*, 35(7), 534-554. doi:10.1080/01639625.2013.862032.

Carriere, P. L. (1995). *Engaging the violent offender in group treatment: A case study*. (1995-95017-081).

Deffenbacher, J. L., Oetting, E. R., Thwaites, G. A., Lynch, R. S., Backer, D. A., Stark, R. S….Eiswerth-Cox, L. (1996). State-trait anger theory and the utility of the Trait Anger Scale. *Journal of Counseling Psychology*, 43, 131-148.

DeLisi, M., & Conis, P. J. (2018). Violent offenders: Theory, research, policy, and practice. Burlington, Massachusetts: Jones & Bartlett Learning, 2018; Third edition.

Durand, G. (2016). A replication of "Using self-esteem to disaggregate psychopathy, narcissism, and aggression (2013)." *Tutorials in Quantitative Methods for Psychology*, (2), r1. doi:10.20982/tqmp.12.2.r001.

Engel, G. L. (1977). The need for a new medical model: A challenge for biomedicine. *Science*, 196, 129-136.

Felitti, V. J., Anda, R. F., Nordenberg, D., Williamson, D. F., Spitz, A. M., Edwards, V., ... Marks, J. S. (1998). Relationship of childhood abuse and household dysfunction to many of the leading causes of death in adults: The adverse childhood experiences (ACE) study. *American Journal of Preventive Medicine*, 14(4), 245-258. doi:10.1016/S0749-3797(98)00017-8.

Garofalo, C., Holden, C. J., Zeigler-Hill, V., & Velotti, P. (2016). Understanding the connection between self-esteem and aggression: The mediating role of emotion dysregulation. *Aggressive Behavior*, 42(1), 3-15. doi:10.1002/ab.21601.

Garofalo, C., & Velotti, P. (2017). Negative emotionality and aggression in violent offenders: The moderating role of emotion dysregulation. *Journal of Criminal Justice,* 51, 9-16. doi:10.1016/j.jcrimjus.2017.05.015.

Garofalo, C., Velotti, P., & Zavattini, G. C. (2018). Emotion regulation and aggression: The incremental contribution of alexithymia, impulsivity, and emotion dysregulation facets. *Psychology of Violence, 8(*4), 470-483. doi:10.1037/vio0000141.

Godleski, S. A., & Ostrov, J. M. (2010). Relational Aggression and Hostile Attribution Biases: Testing Multiple Statistical Methods and Models. *Journal of Abnormal Child* Psychology, 38, 447-458.

Goldstein, S., & Naglieri, J. A. (Eds.). (2011). *Encyclopedia of Child Behavior and Development.* New York, NY: Springer Publisher.

Harris, M. B. (1974). Mediators between frustration and aggression in a field experiment. *Journal of Experimental Social Psychology*, 10, 561-571.

Hewstone, M. (1983). *Attribution theory: Social and functional extensions*. Oxford, England: B. Blackwell, 1983.

Holley, S. R., Ewing, S. T., Stiver, J. T., & Bloch, L. (2017). The relationship between emotion regulation, executive functioning, and aggressive behaviors. *Journal of Interpersonal Violence*, 32(11), 1692-1707. doi:10.1177/0886260515592619.

Hotton, A., Quinn, K., Schneider, J., & Voisin, D. (2019). Exposure to community violence and substance use among black men who have sex with men: Examining the role of psychological distress and criminal justice involvement. *AIDS Care*, 31(3), 370-378. doi:10.1080/09540121.2018.1529294.

Howells, K. (1987a). Social skills training and criminal and antisocial behaviour in adults. In C. R. Hollin, & P. Trower (Eds.), *Handbook of social skills training, Vol. 1: Applications across the life span* (pp. 185-210). Elmsford, NY: Pergamon Press.

Kapoor, R., Dike, C. Burns, C., Carvalho, V., & Griffith, E. E. H. (2013). Cultural competence in correctional mental health. *International Journal of Law & Psychiatry*, 36(3), 273-280. doi:10.1016/j.ijlp.2013.04.016.

Kelly, H. H. (1967). Attribution theory in social psychology. *Nebraska Symposium on Motivation*, 15, 192-238.

Kelty, S. F. (2013). You have to hit some people! Why problem-solving skills are more criminogenic than hostile attribution biases for adult male violent offenders. *Psychiatry, Psychology, and Law*, 5, 713-734.

Kernsmith, P. (2006). Gender differences in the impact of family of origin violence on perpetrators of domestic violence. *Journal of Family Violence*, 21(2), 163-171. doi:10.1007/s10896-005-9014-y.

Khodabandeh, F., Khalilzadeh, M., & Hemati, Z. (2018). The impact of adverse childhood experiences on adulthood aggression and self-esteem-A study on male forensic clients. *Novelty in Biomedicine*, (2), 85. doi:10.22037/nbm.v6i2.20695.

Kuo, Z. Y. (1961). Genesis of the cat's response to the rate. In E. Aronson (Ed.), *Instinct (p. 24)*. Princeton, NJ: Van Nostrand.

Kuzucu, Y. (2016). Do anger control and social problem-solving mediate relationships between difficulties in emotion regulation and aggression in adolescents? *Educational Sciences: Theory and Practice,* 16(3), 849-866.

Landenberger, N., & Lipsey, M. (2005). The positive effects of cognitive–behavioral programs for offenders: A meta-analysis of factors associated with effective treatment. *Journal of Experimental Criminology*, 1(4), 451-476. doi:10.1007/s11292-005-3541-7.

Larden, M., Norden, E., Forsman, M., & Langstrom, N. (2018). Effectiveness of aggression replacement training in reducing criminal recidivism among convicted adult offenders. *Criminal Behaviour and Mental Health*, 28(6), 476-491. doi:10.1002/cbm.2092.

Lehman, B. J., David, D. M., & Gruber, J. A. (2017). Rethinking the biopsychosocial model of health: Understanding health as a dynamic system. *Social and Personality Psychology Compass*, 11(8), n/a. doi:10.1111/spc3.12328.

Liebmann, M. (2007). *Restorative justice: How it works* Philadelphia, PA: Jessica Kingsley Publishers, 2007.

Lim, L., Day, A., & Casey, S. (2011). Social cognitive processing in violent male offenders. *Psychiatry, Psychology, and Law*, 18, 177-189.

Manuck, S. B., Flory, J. D., Ferrell, R. E., Mann, J. J., & Muldoon, M. F. (2000). A regulatory polymorphism of the monoamine oxidase-A gene may be associated with variability in aggression, impulsivity, and central nervous system serotonergic responsivity. *Psychiatry Research*, 95, 9-23.

Marsee, M. A., & Frick, P. J. (2007). Exploring the cognitive and emotional correlates to proactive and reactive aggression in a sample of detained girls. *Journal of Abnormal Child Psychology,* 35, 969-981.

Matsuura, N., Hashimoto, T., & Toichi, M. (2013). Associations among adverse childhood experiences, aggression, depression, and self-esteem in serious female juvenile offenders in Japan. *The Journal of Forensic Psychiatry and Psychology*, 24, 111-127.

Meyer-Lindenberg, A., Buckholtz, J. W., Kolachana, B., Hariri, A. R., Pezawas, L., Blasi, G., & ... Weinberger, D. R. (2006). Neural Mechanisms of Genetic Risk for Impulsivity and Violence in Humans. *Proceedings of the National Academy of Sciences of the United States of America*, 103, 6269-6274.

Mier, C., & Ladny, R. T. (2018). Docs self-esteem negatively impact crime and delinquency? *A meta-analytic review of 25 years of evidence* doi:10.1080/01639625.2017.1395667.

Moore, K. E., Milam, K. C., Folk, J. B., & Tangney, J. P. (2018). Self-stigma among criminal offenders: Risk and protective factors. *Stigma and Health*, 3(3), 241-252. doi:10.1037/sah0000092.

Nilsson, I. M., & Ireland, J. L. (2011). Aggression and offender motivation in prisoners: Exploring the components of motivation in an adult male sample. *Aggressive Behavior*, 37, 278-288.

Okembe-RA Imani, N. (2011). *Head games: De-colonizing the psychotherapeutic process*. Lanham, MD: UPA.

Prehn, K., Schlagenhauf, F., Schulze, L., Berger, C., Vohns, K., Fleischer, M., … Herpertz, S. C. (2013). Neural correlates of risk taking in violent criminal offenders characterized by emotional hypo-and hyper-reactivity. *Social Neuroscience*, 8, 136-147.

Quan, F., Zhu, W., Dong, Y., Qiu, J., Gong, X., Xiao, M., ... Xia, L. (2019). Brain structure links trait hostile attribution bias and attitudes toward violence. *Neuropsychologia*, 125, 42-50. doi:10.1016/j.neuropsychologia.2019.01.015.

Reiss, S. (2012). Intrinsic and Extrinsic Motivation. *Teaching of Psychology*, 39, 152-156.

Richters, J. E., Saltzman, W., Rosario, M., Salzinger, S., Feldman, R. S., & Ng-Mak, D. (2003). Survey of exposure to community violence. *Journal of Community Psychology*, 31, 489-512.

Roberton, T., Daffern, M., & Bucks, R. S. (2015). Beyond anger control: Difficulty attending to emotions also predicts aggression in offenders. *Psychology of Violence*, 5, 74-83.

Sarcbiapone, M., Carli, V., Cuomo, C., Marchetti, M., & Roy, A. (2009). Association between childhood trauma and aggression in male prisoners. *Psychiatry Research,* 165, 187-192.

Schauss, E., Zettler, H. R., & Russell, A. (2019). Examining ACTV: An argument for implementing neuroscience-based and trauma- informed treatment models in offender treatment programs. *Aggression and Violent Behavior*, 46, 1-7. doi:10.1016/j.avb.2019.01.002.

Seager, J. A. (2005). Violent Men: The Importance of Impulsivity and Cognitive Schema. *Criminal Justice and Behavior*, 32, 26-49.

Shortt, J. W., Eddy, J. M., Sheeber, L., & Davis, B. (2014). Project home: A pilot evaluation of an emotion-focused intervention for mothers reuniting with children after prison. *Psychological Services*, 11(1), 1-9. doi:10.1037/a0034323.

Stewart, E. A., & Simons, R. L. (2010). Race, code of the street, and violent delinquency: A multilevel investigation of neighborhood street culture and individual norms of violence. *Criminology*, 48, 569-605.

Stimmel, M. A., Cruise, K. R., Ford, J. D., & Weiss, R. A. (2014). Trauma exposure, posttraumatic stress disorder symptomatology, and aggression in male juvenile offenders. *Psychological Trauma: Theory, Research, Practice, and Policy*, 6, 184-191.

Smith, S. D., Lynch, R. J., Stephens, H. F., & Kistner, J. A. (2015). Self-perceptions and their prediction of aggression in male juvenile offenders. *Child Psychiatry and Human Development*, 46, 609-621.

Speilberger, C. D. (1988) *Manual for the State-Trait Anger Expression Inventory*. Odessa, FL: Psychological Assessment Resources.

Tafrate, R. C., & Mitchell, D. (2014). In Tafrate R. C., Mitchell D. (Eds.), Forensic CBT: *A handbook for clinical practice Wiley-Blackwell.* Retrieved from http://proxy-remote.galib.uga.edu/login?url=http://search.ebscohost.com/login.aspx?direct=true&db=psyh&AN=2013-40476-000&site=eds-live.

Tuente, S. K., Bogaerts, S., & Veling, W. (2019). Hostile attribution bias and aggression in adults - a systematic review. *Aggression and Violent Behavior*, doi:10.1016/j.avb.2019.01.009.

Villagra Lanza, P., Fernandez Garcia, P., Rodriguez Lamelas, F., & Gonzalez-Menendez, A. (2014). Acceptance and commitment therapy versus cognitive behavioral therapy in the treatment of substance use disorder with incarcerated women. *Journal of Clinical Psychology*, 70(7), 644-657. doi:10.1002/jclp.22060.

Walker, J. S. & Bright, J. A. (2009). False inflated self-esteem and violence: A systematic review and cognitive model. *The Journal of Forensic Psychiatry and Psychology*, 20, 1-32.

Walker, J., & Knauer, V. (2011). Humiliation, self-esteem and violence. *The Journal of Forensic Psychiatry and Psychology*, 5, 724-741.

Wang, M., Horne, S. G., Holdford, R., & Henning, K. R. (2008). Family of origin violence predictors of IPV by two types of male offenders. *Journal of Aggression, Maltreatment, and Trauma,* 17, 156-174.

Weierstall, R., Hinsberger, M., Kaminer, D., Holtzhausen, L., Madikane, S., & Elbert, T. (2013). Appetitive aggression and adaptation to a violent environment among youth offenders. *Peach and Conflict: Journal of Peace Psychology*, 19, 138-149.

In: Social Psychology and Counseling
Editors: D. A. Kleiber and E. Delgado-Romero
ISBN: 978-1-53616-548-7

Chapter 14

MANAGING ANGER AND RELATIONAL AGGRESSION

Bailey J. Nevels

Aggression in dating relationships is both prevalent and costly. The Department of Justice (2014) reported when compared to other age groups, people between the ages of 18 and 24 experienced the highest rates of domestic violence and intimate partner violence. In a recent study, 72% of college students in dating relationships had engaged in relational aggression and 20% in physical aggression (Bilton, et al. 2016). Interpersonal violence led women to miss 8 million paid days of work per year at a cost of $8.3 billion dollars per year nationwide (Rothman, et al. 2007). The rates of psychological aggression between partners are staggering with 48.4% of women and 48.8% of men reporting they have experienced at least one psychologically aggressive act from a partner (NCADV 2015). Regarding diverse populations, the 2015 US Transgender Survey reported that 54% of transgender people experienced some form of interpersonal violence (James, et al. 2015). Understanding relational aggression, particularly in emerging adults, is an important step to preventing interpersonal violence and increasing healthy relationship behaviors.

Relational aggression has changed as technology use has become prevalent. While the use of social media and text messaging enable instant social connection, particularly for marginalized communities, they can also be used as platforms for cyber-aggression (Marganski and Melander 2015). Research suggests that people are often less inhibited online, willing to post things that they would be unlikely to say when face-to-face, because they are less aware of how such comments negatively affect the recipient. The prevalence of cyber aggression is astounding, given that 73% of students reported experiencing cyber aggression from an intimate partner, which was much more prevalent than in-person acts of aggression. Mishna and colleagues (2018) found that intimate partners are the second most likely perpetrators of some forms of cyber aggression, and they suggested that approximately 33% of college students who reported experiencing cyber aggression also reported that such aggression negatively impacted their mental health (Mishna, et al. 2018). Understanding relational aggression and its antecedents may result in the prevention of relational aggression. The following research and case illustrations attempt to shed light on how emotional expression relates to aggressive behavior in order to equip mental health providers with knowledge about how to treat clients with these concerns.

Research on the underpinnings of aggressive behavior begins with the *frustration-aggression hypothesis*, which essentially argued that aggression follows frustration and is the most common consequence of it (Miller 1941). But Berkowitz (1989) argued that frustration as a concept is vague. He clarified how in the frustration-aggression theory frustration refers to an external factor impeding a goal directed action. A toddler pushes another child out of the way to get to the front of the ice cream line, for example. Miller noted further that the frustration-aggression hypothesis needed more specification as many people experience frustration without acting out on aggressive urges. Traffic jams are usually frustrating for people, but most people do not express such frustration by physically aggressing the people they perceive to be responsible for the hold up. However, the important piece of this framework is that aggression is often a consequence of people not getting what they want.

Emotional catharsis emerged as a theory to better understand how emotions relate to aggressive behavior. Freud was one of the first Western psychologists to theorize that aggressive urges build up like a 'pressure cooker,' which, unless redirected somehow, lead to aggressive behavior (Aronson 2012). For example, aggressive behavior occurs when a person ignores anger for a significant amount of time. Freud speculated that this aggressive energy needs to be expressed in order to prevent violence or illness. Also called the *hydraulic theory*, this idea has become widely accepted, such that people are encouraged to release angry energy incrementally to prevent themselves from exploding into a rage (Bushman 2002). In fact, entrepreneurs have created businesses like smash or rage rooms where people can unload their aggressive energy by, for example, throwing dishes or breaking electronics (Pitofsky 2018). Similarly, parents are encouraged to enroll their children in contact sports to help them dissipate pent up aggressive energy. Although prevalent and popular, there is little empirical support for the catharsis/hydraulic theory. Bushman notes, in fact, venting anger is "like using gasoline to put out a fire—it only fuels the flame" (p. 729). He found that participants who did nothing after experiencing an anger-provoking stimulus were less aggressive than those who punched a punching bag. So, although this assumption is widespread and feels true anecdotally, the catharsis theory lacks the support of empirical research.

Robert Allan (2009), a cardiac psychologist, used one of his clinical cases and related research to refute the popular theory about expressing anger in an essay for the *New York Times*. He detailed how one of his group counseling clients reported satisfaction after lashing out at an aggressive driver during a traffic argument. However, the client suffered from financial strain and job insecurity, so according to Allan, reacting aggressively did not produce long term life satisfaction or even enhance his short term adjustment. He also cited meta-analytic research that demonstrates a relationship between anger and hostility and Coronary Heart Disease and noted that anger can trigger a small percentage of heart attacks (Chida & Steptoe 2009). Chida and Steptoe provide no context for how subjects responded to their anger, only that heart health negatively correlates with anger and hostility, whereas Allan contends that expressing anger was of "no benefit" to the patient in question.

Allan's (2009) argument, while compelling to a point, is not entirely well supported by research and raises questions about generalizing the effects of expressing anger. My own clinical experience suggests that suppressing such emotion may have equally deleterious effects. Allan implies a dichotomy: either people express their anger through aggressive and unhealthy means, or they do not express anger at all. While I agree with Allan that "giving way to an angry impulse makes nearly any situation worse," (para. 5), my own experience in a college counseling center leads me to the conclusion that refusing to deal with or express anger can be detrimental to mental health.

Perhaps there is a middle ground between the two positions, such that someone may feel the urge to aggress but can successfully express the anger underlying that urge in a meaningful, healthy manner. Finkel and Eckhardt (2011) attempted to shed light on what leads someone to act aggressively in interpersonal relationships. They suggest the I^3 Model to increase understanding of risk factors of interpersonal aggression consisting of three factors: *instigation*, or events activating aggressive urges; *impellance*, aspects of a person that contribute to someone's likelihood of having an aggressive urge (e.g., alcohol use), and *inhibition,* factors that decrease the chances someone will act on an aggressive urge. Finkel and Eckhardt theorize that when inhibition factors are greater than instigation and impellance, one will not act aggressively. However, when impellance and instigation are stronger than inhibition, aggressive acts ensue. Another interesting note is how someone's impellance factors do not lead to aggressive behavior in the absence of instigation. This research sheds light on ways to reduce aggressive behavior, such as teaching adolescents how to respond to or ignore negative social media interactions in a healthy way, or practicing ways to increase inhibition, such as meditation or exercise to manage anger, when instigation intersects with impellance.

Maldonado and colleagues (2015) demonstrated how learning skills to manage emotions can help with reducing interpersonal aggression. Based on the I^3 Model, they taught college students how to view situations instigating anger and aggression more positively, and as a result, the participants verbalized aggression less frequently than those who were not taught any skills and those who were taught to ignore or suppress their emotions. For example, participants read scenarios designed to provoke anger, then later were instructed to think positively about additional scenarios designed to instigate aggressive urges. The researchers analyzed the participants' spoken responses to the scenarios and demonstrated how learning emotion regulation skills can reduce verbal aggression, and they observed that some participants who had been taught to suppress their emotions were more inclined to verbalize aggression than the other groups. And there was no statistically significant difference between male and female participants despite the prevailing view that males are less likely than females to engage in verbal aggression. These findings also lend support to the notion that regulating anger, as opposed to suppressing it, could help reduce aggression. They also instill hope that interventions aimed at emotion regulation can positively impact clients and relationships at risk for aggressive behavior.

Consider the following from my own clinical experience: Ben [pseudonym]

> Ben was a college student who presented to individual psychotherapy with anxiety and depression that spanned multiple areas of his life: social, career, romantic and family relationships. Ben's father communicated messages of his inadequacy, and over time, Ben internalized the core belief he is not good enough (Beck 2011). This core belief drove his anxiety. Ben seemed to have learned to ignore his emotions from his father who regarded any emotional expression in Ben as 'unmanly.' Accordingly, Ben displayed a pattern of holding in feelings such as frustration and anger. These unexamined feelings resulted in self-reported irritability and relationally aggressive urges. They also led him to experience interpersonal conflict, particularly with his girlfriend at the time.
>
> Although there was no physical aggression reported between Ben and his girlfriend, much relational aggression, or a social form of aggression including social exclusion, damaging others' reputations, or spreading gossip, co-occurred with his unwillingness to express unpleasant emotion. In fact, Ben and his girlfriend would often engage in the forms of relational aggression common in dyadic relationships as described by Archer and Coyne (2005), such as withdrawing attention, flirting to encourage jealousy, or threatening to end the relationship if the partner is non-compliant. Ben and his girlfriend would exclude or ignore one another at social outings, refuse to call one another if they had argued that day, or would either flirt with others or engage in infidelity which seemed more a function of punishing the partner than seeking the attentions of another. Also noteworthy was that much of their unhealthy communication occurred via text message. This is consistent with evidence that people are more inclined to act aggressively when they do not have to immediately face the consequences of their actions in person as is the case with digital communication (Marganski and Melander 2015).
>
> This pattern of relational aggression led to an unhealthy cycle. Ben's anxiety about the relationship led him to aggress against his girlfriend in an attempt to regain power in the relationship. This aggression led to more arguing in their relationship, which led to increased symptoms of anxiety and depression, such as increased sadness and irritability,

suicidality, loneliness, and lack of motivation. And rather than dissipating the anger, their fighting and expressions of anger only seemed to increase in ways consistent with the 'aggression fuels more aggression' view discussed earlier.

Ben struggled to express his emotions to his partner in a healthy way; therefore, a large portion of therapy focused on increasing emotional awareness and facilitating communication about his feelings. Learning what triggered anger, such as someone activating his core beliefs of inadequacy (Beck 2011), and how to express anger in an adaptive way in therapy enabled him to begin to effectively communicate and manage anger in healthier ways outside of therapy. He was able to talk directly with his girlfriend more frequently rather than engaging in relational aggression to feel more secure. While expressing anger through aggressive behavior is unhealthy and unproductive, this case shows the value of learning to identify and express anger adaptively. It seems that previous research minimizes the possibility of learning to manage anger and instead focuses on the mere presence of anger automatically leading to aggression. Essentially, this case example demonstrates the benefits of expressing emotions in healthy ways, such as journaling, writing or performing music, seeking social support, or communicating calmly with people who have hurt their feelings.

The case of Ben is only marginally supportive of Allan's (2009) ideas about expressing anger in that Ben and his partner expressing anger through aggressive means was ultimately destructive to the relationship. Ben's situation also highlighted the harmful effects of suppressing anger. However, as he learned to manage anger by communicating it directly and engaging in pleasurable activities, like exercise, he eventually reported more life satisfaction and his relationship improved. So, to modify Allan's argument: experiencing and expressing *anger* can be detrimental only if expressed through aggressive actions.

Furthermore, Ben's case offers a contrast to research reported by Aronson (2012) about gender differences… that men are less likely to engage in verbal aggression compared to women. Ben's relationship is consistent with other research conducted by Burton, Hafetz, and Henninger (2007) who found no gender differences among college students when examining relational aggression, noting certain personality characteristics and self-reported aggressive tendencies were more predictive of relational aggression than gender. And Archer and Coyne's (2005) review of the literature regarding sex differences and relational aggression showed that while differences were found between girls and boys in childhood and adolescence, the effect sizes in these studies were quite small and such gender differences have not been detected among adults and college students. They point out that females tend to use relational aggression more than physical aggression which may be why people tend to perceive this gender difference to be more pronounced than the research has demonstrated. Bilton and colleagues (2016) discovered that college aged females engaged in relational aggression more than their male counterparts, but emotional dysregulation significantly predicted interpersonal violence within dating relationships for both genders. In the case reviewed above both Ben and his girlfriend engaged in relational aggression, and both struggled with emotion regulation.

Self-control may be the mediating factor affecting the outcomes of Ben's case and Dr. Allan's cardiac group therapy client. To review, Allan's (2009) client did not seem to benefit from expressing anger aggressively, whereas Ben showed the possibility of coping with anger without engaging in a cycle of aggression. Baumeister, Vohs and Tice (2007) defined self-control as enabling a person "to restrain or override one response, thereby making another response possible" (p. 351). They explained self-control as being like a muscle that loses strength due to limited energy resources. Baumeister and colleagues (2007) described the loss of psychological resources after exercising self-control as "ego depletion" (p. 352). Basically, as one engages in self-control throughout the day, the ability to continue controlling responses to impulses fatigues and energy is directed elsewhere for conservation. Allan's cardiac patient perhaps suffered from ego depletion, leaving aggression to be the only response after a day of resisting unhealthy impulses. In fact, researchers delineated "aggression after being provoked" (p. 353) as a behavior sensitive to ego depletion. Ben's relational aggression could be explained by ego depletion after hours of attending to course material during the college semester or other frustrations.

How can counseling address ego depletion? Interestingly, Allan (2009) mentioned that his client terminated treatment after one group session, and thus the opportunity for therapeutic intervention with that client was minimal. However, Ben attended treatment for a full academic year and reported progress regarding improved interpersonal relationships and decreased anxiety and depression, which may be related to developing ways to mitigate ego depletion and manage anger. Baumeister and colleagues (2007) identified several techniques to buffer against ego depletion, including such social goals as "wanting to be a good relationship partner" (p. 353). A large portion of therapy with Ben consisted of examining motivation for continuing in the relationship; so it is possible that therapy illuminated his social goal of being a strong relationship partner. Another technique listed is implementation intentions, such as "if then" plans. Ben and I worked on how to respond to his girlfriend if she behaved in certain ways, which perhaps gave a sense of preparedness when entering into conflict with her in the future, thus making it less ego depleting.

The available research demonstrates how interventions targeting an increase in self-control in treatment may help clients who struggle with aggressive behavior. Baumeister and colleagues (2007) suggested several ways to use therapy to offset effects of ego depletion such as using humor, for example, to increase positive emotions, which prior research has established as a way to alleviate depressive symptoms (e.g., Seligman, et al. 2006). Therefore, when faced with clients who struggle with managing their responses to anger and frustration, interventions focused on examining positive aspects of their lives to increase gratitude, or prescribing homework such as watching a humorous television show as a mechanism for self-care, might help build the strength of their self-control "muscles".

Increased motivation would be another viable treatment goal for someone struggling with regulating their emotions and aggressive behavior (Hagger et al. 2010). A meta-analysis regarding self-control and ego depletion found that motivation might explain suppressed performance on a second task requiring self-control. Offering incentives counteracted the effects of ego depletion. Therefore, if clients present with dysregulated anger or report frequent aggressive outbursts, therapy from a motivational interviewing perspective, or working towards contingency management may be helpful interventions to build awareness of internal motivation and self-control (Beck 2011; Miller and Rollnick 2013; see also Varley and Zito, this volume).

In conclusion, research refutes the theory that anger builds up over time and needs to be expressed, even through aggressive means. Research also shows suppressed anger is detrimental for both mental and physical health (Chida and Steptoe 2009). The clinical examples reported above demonstrate that expressing anger aggressively is unproductive but suppressing anger can also be harmful. Allan's client (2009) attended one therapy session; Ben attended a year of therapy; so future research needs to address longer term benefits of expressing anger in productive ways and the value of more extended therapy. Overall, however, available research and clinical experience suggests that working with clients to improve self-control and reduce ego-depletion are viable therapeutic interventions to regulate anger and reduce the likelihood of acting aggressively.

REFERENCES

Allan, R. (2009). When the heart pays the price of anger. *New York Times.* Published June 25, 2009. http://opinionator.blogs.nytimes.com/2009/06/25/when-the-heart-pays-the-price-of-anger/.

Archer, J. and Coyne, S. M. (2005). An integrated review of indirect, relational, and social aggression. *Personality and Social Psychology Review, 9.* 212 - 230. doi: 10.1207/s15327957pspr0903_2.

Aronson, E. (2012). *The Social Animal.* 11th ed. New York, NY: Worth Publishers.

Baumeister, R. F., Tice, D. M. and Vohs, K. D. (2018). The strength model of self-regulation: Conclusions from the second decade of Willpower Research. *Perspectives on Psychological Science, 13*, 141 - 145. doi: 10.1177/1745691617716946.

Bauermeister, R. F., Vohs, K. D., Tice, D. M. (2007). The strength model of self-control. *Current Directions in Psychological Science, 16*, 351 - 355. doi: 10.1111/j.1467-8721.2007.00534.x.

Beck, J. S. (2011). *Cognitive Therapy: Basics and Beyond.* 2nd ed. New York: Guilford.

Berkowitz, L. (1989). Frustration-aggression hypothesis: Examination and reformulation. *Psychological Bulletin, 106*, 59 - 73. doi: 10.1037/0033-2909.106.1.59.

Bliton, C. F., Wolford-Clevenger, C., Zapor, H., Elmquist, J., Brem, M. J., Shorey, R., C. and Stuart, G. L. (2016). Emotion dysregulation, gender, and intimate partner violence perpetration: An exploratory study in college students. *Journal of Family Violence, 31*, 371 - 377. doi: 10.1007/s10896-015-9772-0.

Burton, L. A., Hafetz, J. and Henninger, D. (2007). Gender differences in relational and physical aggression. *Social Behavior and Personality, 35*, 41 - 50. doi: 10.2224/sbp.2007.35.1.41.

Bushman, B. J. (2002). Does venting anger feed or extinguish the flame? Catharsis, rumination, distraction, anger, and aggressive responding. *Personality and Social Psychology Bulletin, 28*. 724 - 731. doi: 10.1177/0146167202289002.

Chida, Y. and Steptoe, A. (2009). The association of anger and hostility with future coronary heart disease: a meta-analytic review of prospective evidence. *Journal of the American College of Cardiology, 53*. 936 - 946. doi: 10.1016/j.jacc.2008.11.044.

Department of Justice. (2014). *Nonfatal Domestic Violence*, 2003 - 2012. Retrieved from: https://www.bjs.gov/content/pub/pdf/ndv0312.pdf.

Finkel, E. J. and Eckhardt, C. I. (2011). Intimate partner violence. J. A. Simpson and L. Campbell (Eds.), *The Oxford Handbook of Close Relationships,* 452 - 474. Oxford: New York.

Hagger, M. S., Wood, C., Stiff, C., Chatzisarantis, N. L. D. (2010). Ego depletion and the strength model of self-control: A meta-analysis. *Psychological Bulletin, 136*, 495 - 525. doi: 10.1037/a0019486.

James, S. E., Herman, J. L., Rankin, S., Keisling, M., Mottet, L. and Anafi, M. (2016). *The Report of the 2015 U.S. Transgender Survey*, Washington, DC: National Center for Transgender Equality.

Maldonado, R., DiLillo, D. and Hoffman, L. (2015). Can college students use emotion regulation strategies to alter intimate partner aggression-risk behaviors? An Examination Using I^3 Theory. *Psychology of Violence, 5*. 46 - 55. doi: 10.1037/a0035454.

Marganski, A. and Melander, L. (2015). Intimate partner violence victimization in the cyber and real world: Examining the extent of cyber aggression experiences and its association with in-person dating violence. *Journal of Interpersonal Violence, 33*, 1071 - 1095. doi: 10.1177/0886260515614283.

Miller, N. E. (1941). The frustration-aggression hypothesis. *Psychological Review, 48*, 337 - 342. https://doi-org.libproxy.clemson.edu/10.1037/h0055861.

Miller, W. R. and Rollnick, S. (2013). *Motivational Interviewing: Helping People Change* 3rd. Ed. New York: Guilford.

Mishna, F., Regehr, C., Lacombe-Duncan, A., Daciuk, J., Fearing, G, and Van Wert, M., (2018). Social media, cyber-aggression and student mental health on a university campus. *Journal of Mental Health*, *27,* 222 - 229. doi: 10.1080/09638237.2018.1437607.

NCADV. (2015). *Domestic violence national statistics*. Retrieved from www.ncadv.org.

Pitofsky, M. (2018). Rage rooms: Why recreational smashing could be good for your mental health. *USA Today*, Retrieved from: https://www.usatoday.com/story/news/2018/11/11/rage-rooms-what-might-surprise-you-growing-trend/1754653002/.

Rothman, E. F., Hathaway, J., Stidsen, A. and de Vries, H. F. (2007). How employment helps female victims of intimate partner violence: A qualitative study. *Journal of Occupational Health Psychology, 12*, 136 - 143. doi:10.1037/1076-8998.12.2.136.

Seligman, M. E. P., Rashid, T. and Parks, A. C. (2006). Positive psychotherapy. *American Psychologist, 61*, 774 - 788. oi: 10.1037/0003-066X.61.8.774.

In: Social Psychology and Counseling
Editors: D. A. Kleiber and E. Delgado-Romero
ISBN: 978-1-53616-548-7

Chapter 15

DEALING WITH AGGRESSION IN THERAPY

Anthony W. Hansen

THE CASE OF CHRISTOPHER

> Christopher is a 19-year-old, mixed-ethnicity (White and LatinX), male, cisgender, gay man currently in his second-year in a major state university. He presented to therapy to discuss his familial and social relationships after feeling repeatedly "out of control" in his life and "frustrated by everything". He noted that he recently decided to end a 2-year long-term committed relationship and acknowledged that he felt like he could no longer sustain the relationship in a healthy manner. Christopher described himself as "tired" and "frustrated" at everything in his life and feels that life is "worthless" and wishes everything would just "end" but denied an active desire or intent to end his life himself. He reported that he feels like he is "too much" for everything in his life and feels misunderstood and excluded by anyone in his family and social circle. He stated that he has "plenty of friends" and feels capable of "putting on a mask" in front of others but knows that "none of it matters in the end". As he described his feelings, he often aggressively clenched his fists and tensed his muscles in his arms, face, and neck in an overt display of anger and frustration, and at one point motioned with his arms as if to strike something in the room. He denied any history of physical harm against others but noted that he feels like he has to "contain" himself and his anger almost "constantly".

Therapists in varied mental health occupations are reporting a significant increase in the number of clients who present initially with anger and aggression problems (DiGuseppe & Tafrate, 2003; Glancy & Saini, 2005; see also Field & Robinson, Ford & Ocampo, and Nevels, this volume). One national survey of psychologists and psychiatrists found that angry clients presented as frequently as anxious clients (Glancy & Saini, 2005). Aggressive behavior is commonly viewed as harmful to the self and other individuals, and aggression is widely considered to be an ever-present societal issue that impacts interpersonal relationships, social services, and education across the globe. While aggression is consistently observed across many other species, human aggression is seen as more complex and multifaceted, often stemming from a wide variety of causes. Human aggression is also associated with important costs and repercussions to both the aggressor and victims of the aggressive behavior. Causes of aggressive behavior are complex and not fully understood, often times rooted in learned experiences and driven by emotion. The human experience varies greatly, which makes the prediction of aggressive behaviors difficult, and successful interventions for aggressive behavior have proven to be elusive. Nevertheless, aggressive thoughts and behaviors can show up in therapy, and a skilled therapist may use tools to unpack the various contributing emotions and experiences that give rise to aggression, while some therapists may attempt to use aggression as a tool for intervention. This chapter will discuss relevant information and issues related to anger and aggression in therapy. First, what is aggression and how might aggression and aggressive behavior show up in a therapeutic space? Secondly, how is aggressive behavior addressed and ameliorated in the therapeutic setting, and what do we do if the client exhibits aggression in the room?

WHAT IS AGGRESSION AND WHAT CAUSES IT?

There is no clear academic consensus as to how aggression should be defined. In recent literature, scholars have referred to differences in aggression as distinct yet inconsistent and often overlapping forms, either differentiating between overt and indirect aggression, physical, verbal, and relational aggression, premeditated and impulsive aggression, proactive and reactive aggression, and/or numerous other terms (Aime, Paquette, Dery, & Verlaan, 2018; Bass, Saldarriaga, Cunha, Chen, Santo, & Bukowski, 2018; Dodge, 2006, Worthington, 2012;). For the purposes of this chapter, overt aggression is described in terms of physical manifestations of behavior in addition to other forms of non-physical confrontation such as bullying and malicious intent to harm, while indirect aggression is described as non-confrontational behaviors that may include passive-aggression, gossip, and coordinated isolation by peers (Aime et al., 2018). Moreover, some scholars further divide forms of aggression into separate categories that include physical, verbal, and relational aggression. It appears that the differences between physical and verbal aggression refer to forms of overt aggression, but delineate between actual physical force versus harsh language, taunting, and verbal threats (Garcia-Sancho, Dhont, Salguero, & Fernandez-Berrocal, 2017). Relational aggression, however, is likely more associated with above-mentioned definitions of indirect aggression, and has been described as harm that specifically targets relationships, social status and general acceptance by others, and usually causes harm via indirect means (e.g., gossip, harmful rumors, social exclusion; Bass et al., 2018; Bjorkvqvist, 2001; Card, Stucky, Sawalani, & Little, 2008; Garcia-Sancho et al., 2017; see also Nevels, this volume). Furthermore, Dodge (2006) described aggressive behaviors in terms of *proactive* versus *reactive* aggression. In their manuscript, Lui, Barry, and Schlosser described proactive aggression as instrumental in nature, stating that "proactive aggression is unprovoked aggression for instrumental gain or dominance" (p. 1299), while reactive aggression is described as hostile in nature and a usually as a response to a threat that is real or perceived (Lui & Barry, 2017; See also Crick & Dodge, 1996; Dodge, 2006).

Aronson (2012) claims that aggressive action is *intended* to cause physical or psychological pain. He described a distinction between *hostile aggressive acts* and *instrumental aggressive acts*. In a *hostile aggressive act*, a person acts from a feeling of anger aimed at inflicting pain or injury. An *act of instrumental aggression* occurs when the intent to hurt others manifests through means not inherently driven by anger and hostility (Aronson, 2012). In a review on anger and aggression by Taft, Creech, and Kachadourian (2012) the authors identified aggression as a behavior (or a set of behaviors) that are intended to cause harm to another person, including acts of verbal abuse, threats, or violence. They note that anger is often a precursor to aggression; yet not all aggression stems from anger and those who are angry are not always prone to aggression.

Initial theories of aggression were related to many well-known psychological theories such as social learning theory, cognitive neoassociation theory, and script theory (Bandura, 1973; Berkowitz, 1963; Huesmann, 1988; Mishcel, 1999), but it wasn't until Anderson and Bushman developed the General Aggression Model (GAM) in 2002 that a specific, unified theory of aggression was proposed The GAM proposed that precursors to aggression are multi-modal and therefore resulting interventions should be designed with all aspects of aggression in mind. Worthington (2012) found that specific inputs such as personality traits, attitudes, gender, and genetic predispositions have all been identified as factors which contribute towards aggression (Anderson & Bushman, 2002; Bushman & Baumeister, 1998; Huesmann & Guerra, 1997; White, 2001). Furthermore, Anderson and Bushman (2002) state that those with more positive attitudes toward general forms of violence are in effect "prepared" to act more aggressively (see also Field & Robinson, this volume).

Aggression is viewed as an instrumental trait, linked to survival behaviors in many species, and many scholars have linked human aggression to Charles Darwin's theory of evolution and the idea of "survival of the fittest" (Darwin, 1900). However, with modern humans, aggression is not interpreted as a vital characteristic for life, and, more often than not, aggressive tendencies are interpreted as negative and in most cases maladaptive.

Ashley Montagu (1966) explained that the American mind seems to generally misconstrue the relevance of Darwin's theories to American life, especially as a society that has relied on entrepreneurial capitalism (Aronson, 2012). Indeed, the ethologist Konrad Lorenz (1966) discussed the differences between aggressive behaviors exhibited by a wide-range species and found that a major distinction between cold-blooded predation and frenzied anger. He described the former as behavior that lacks emotion and is tied to a specific outcome or goal while the latter is typically viewed as an emotional outburst that is often defensive in nature (e.g., response to threat or provocation). Lorenz viewed this reactive anger as inherently more violent but less controlled and predictable and, where possible, should be unlearned or controlled through development (Dodge, 2006). Dodge suggested that given that retaliatory and justified aggression are core to human behavior (as evidenced by evolutionary biology and deep-rooted neural pathways), humans are likely born with an aggressive retaliatory response potential and must in turn learn skills to inhibit that response (See also De Quervain et al., 2004; Knutson, 2004; McClure et al., 2004).

Sigmund Freud (1948) believed that aggression was innate, and his "hydraulic" theory asserted that built up aggressive energy produced illness unless released through a cathartic act. Theories about innate aggressive urges and how aggression is expressed are plentiful in the literature, yet there is no clear explanation as to why some humans are more aggressive than others. Nor has the hydraulic theory gained much empirical support. In some contrast, Worthington (2012) discussed the impact of trauma and social learning on the potential development for aggression.

SOCIAL LEARNING

Social learning theory proposes that aggression is a learned behavior that is reinforced over time by observation and repetition, and is often governed by rules (Bandura, 1973; Dodge, 2006). Huesmann (1988) stated that conditions that are "most conducive to the learning of aggression seem to be those in which the child has many opportunities to observe aggression, in which the child is reinforced for his or her own aggression, and in which the child is the object of aggression" (p. 14). It is thought that individuals who display overtly benign or hostile attitudes and attributions towards others in front of children and adolescents may be *modeling* those attitudes and behaviors for a young person. In contrast, children who repeatedly observe parental prosocial behaviors are more likely to attribute positive intent to others in novel situations while discounting discrepant information that would favor aggression or hostile attributions (Bruner, 1957; Aime et al., 2018).

Sex-Specific Differences in Development of Aggression

Research seems to find a clear difference in inclination toward aggressive behavior when delineated by gender, at least with regard to physical and overt aggression, with boys seemingly the more likely to exercise aggressive behaviors (see also Nevels, this volume). Aime and colleagues (2017) found that differences between genders on physically aggressive behavior may be due to more prevalent individual vulnerabilities, low effortful control, or hyperactivity in boys, while girls are likely encouraged by parents and guidance figures to cooperate and be more attentive to others' needs and emotions (Barkley, Fischer, Smallish, & Fletcher, 2006; Bennett, Farrington, & Huesmann, 2005; Else-Quest, Hyde, Goldsmith, & Van Hulle, 2006; Keenan & Shaw, 1997; Morgan & Lilienfeld, 2000). While gender differences are pronounced with respect to overt and physical aggression, there seems to be mixed evidence supporting similar distinctions between genders when discussing relational aggression (Bass et al., 2018; see also Nevels, this volume). Stereotypes delineated by gender may increase the belief that women and girls are more prone to relational aggression despite the literature that finds otherwise. It is often argued that gender-based societal norms contribute to the differences in social expectations and result in differing evaluations of behaviors based on gender; and despite mixed evidence for increased relational aggression in girls, it is still commonly seen as more normative in behavior of girls while physical aggression is more normative for boys (Bass et al., 2018).

Initial Assessment with Aggressive Clients

According to Citrome and Volavka (2011), aggressive behavior is caused by a multitude of factors such as impulse and others factors. Clients might have trouble controlling anger or might agitate easily within the therapy session. It is important to consider the impact that an aggressive client may have on the therapist's comfort in session and the potential impact on the therapeutic alliance. As stated earlier, two studies have documented psychotherapists' perceptions of aggression in therapy, and found that a therapist who perceived aggression toward the therapist was second only to statements of suicide as the most stressful behavior to be enacted in session (Deutsch, 1984; Farber, 1983; Glancy & Saini, 2005; Norcross & Kobayashi, 1999). Clients who present with a history of violence and aggression should be carefully assessed through comprehensive clinical interview and through the administration of appropriate clinical assessments. Benzodiazepines, mood-stabilizers, and/or antipsychotic medications are often used to help combat the potential dangers of an aggressive client (Citrome & Volavka, 2011). Some clients with a history of aggression may already be prescribed medications to treat mood and/or psychotic symptoms, and it may be important for the therapist to obtain a release of information to collaborate with medical professionals responsible for medication management in order to ensure informed, ethical, and comprehensive care.

Treating Aggression in a Clinical Setting

The literature regarding aggressive clients in therapeutic settings does not appear to reach a consensus on one specific treatment plan to remediate aggression or anger in either short-term or long-term therapy. Moreover, there is little relevant academic research that addresses the problem of aggressive behavior within the therapeutic space. This issue may be of concern to many therapists as angry clients are becoming increasingly likely to present to therapy (at least as frequently as anxious clients), while many therapists have deemed aggressive behavior in the therapy room to be stressful and uncomfortable (Glancy & Saini, 2005; Lachmund & DiGiuseppe, 1997). Below are the treatment modalities that have been validated by peer-reviewed studies to show efficacy in the therapeutic treatment of anger and aggression. Note that little has been said to address the interpersonal experience of the therapist while sitting with an aggressive client.

Cognitive-Behavioral Therapies

Beck and Fernandez found that in a recent review of literature, a majority of the outcome studies treating anger used a form of *Cognitive-Behavioral-Therapy* (CBT) (1998). Using Michenbaum's *Stress Inoculation Training* (SIT) intervention based in CBT (Michenbaum, 1975), the client is exposed to three phases of treatment: cognitive preparation, skill acquisition, and application training. Novaco's (1975) adaptation of Michenbaum's SIT method allows a client struggling with anger and aggression to participate in the three SIT phases while becoming familiar with classic CBT tenets such as cognitive reframing, relaxation training, imagery, modeling, and role-playing as a way to boost coping skills (Beck & Fernandez, 1998; see also Edner & Casiello-Robins, this volume). In theory, clients struggling with anger can identify the triggers for the anger and aggression and ameliorate them by reframing their thoughts and feelings with self-statements that provide a healthier response (see also, Nevels, this volume). The SIT treatments are also enhanced with relaxation techniques that can be paired with the cognitive self-statements to allow such clients to "mentally and physically soothe themselves" (Beck & Fernandez, 1998). Research has validated the effectiveness of SIT in the reduction of inappropriate expression of anger, improving self-esteem, and perceived stress (Cary & Dua, 1999; Deffenbacher, Thwaites, Wallace, & Oetting, 1994; Glancy et al., 2005; Hains, 1992; Hains & Szyjakowski, 1990; Nugent, Champlin, &

Winimaki, 1997; Rose, West, & Clifford, 2000; Timmons, Oehlert, Sumerall, Timmons, & Borgers, 1997;

Glancy and associates (2005) also found cognitive-behavioral treatments to be efficacious in a meta-analysis, noting that while other interventions may also be as helpful no others have received the extensive empirical support that CBT has garnered in recent years. He found that CBT-based interventions have shown promise in both anger suppression and for reducing general anger, anger from diverse provocations, anger-related physiological arousal, and dysfunctional coping tendencies (Deffenbacher, McNamara, Stark, & Sabadell, 1990b; Fernandez & Beck, 2001; Galovski & Blanchard, 2002; Siddle, Jones, & Awenat, 2003; Stermac, 1987; Whitfield, 1999; Willner, Jones, Tams, & Green, 2002).

Another helpful CBT-based treatment for aggression in adolescents is *aggression replacement therapy*, which utilizes CBT elements of modeling, role-playing, skill building, anger arousal awareness, and education (Ray et al., 2009). Glick and Goldstein (1987) and Ray et al. (2009) found that individuals who follow the aggression replacement therapy protocol demonstrated a statistically significant increase in social skills and increased functioning in relationships. Kazdin (2003) also supports use of cognitive-behaviorally-based *Problem-Solving Skills Training* as an effective intervention with children with "serious aggressive conduct problems," noting that the effects can be maintained over time.

Other Forms of Therapy

Ireland and colleagues (2008) found that the *Unified Model of Information Processing* approach proposed by Huesmann (1998) can help reduce the expression of anger if focused on the following four areas: social scripts, normative beliefs, emotions, and perception errors. It is important to note that the above listed four areas are considered to be active simultaneously and are to be treated as such within treatment (Worthington, 2012). Other treatment options for adults struggling with anger and aggression include mindfulness therapy and *Dialectical-Behavior-Therapy* (DBT; Wupperman et al., 2011). A review of mindfulness-based treatments for aggression found consistent reductions in aggressive behaviors, although the sample size of studies completed is small (Fix & Fix, 2013). Both Talfrate (1995) and Bowman-Edmondson & Cohen-Congers' (1996) meta-analytic studies on effective treatments for anger and aggression found that relaxation-based interventions showed the most potential for improvements, with reports of less general anger and less anger across varied situations as compared to control groups (Deffenbacher & Stark, 1992; Glancy et al., 2005). However, some scholars point to methodological problems present in many of the studies that give pause to clinicians about using the findings with full confidence (Glancy et al.,

2005). For severe cases including self-injury and violence, *Electroconvulsive Therapy* (ECT) is sometimes used under close supervision as a way to stabilize mood with some indicationss of success (Wachtel, Jaffe & Kellner, 2010). However, treatments such as ECT are beyond the scope of most practitioners.

Anger management programs have become increasingly common and available, allowing clients to explore their anger and aggressive behaviors in both group and individual services (see also Nevels, this volume). Previous theories of anger and aggression focused on the therapist helping clients let out or "vent" their anger in a more controlled environment (Del Veccio & O'Leary, 2004; Glancy et al., 2005). A therapist skilled in the treatment of anger and aggression may choose to allow a client to express aggression in a therapeutic manner. Therapists must be careful how and when they choose to use aggression as a therapeutic tool in session. Some therapists believe that cathartic release of aggression removes a hostile impulse from a potentially aggressive and dangerous client (Shaefer & Mattei, 2005). Some even advocate for clients to strike objects out of aggression, however the literature has shown that when a client vents anger and aggression the level of aggression actually increases (Aronson, 2012). Shaefer and Mattei (2005) posit that the debate about catharsis stems from two theories of psychology; social learning theory and psychoanalytic theory. While social learning theory claims that catharsis provokes emotion, psychoanalytic theory claims that catharsis purges the passions. The literature regarding catharsis in therapy all concur with the belief that cathartic release of aggression is not therapeutic and can produce a contrary effect (Aronson 2012; Bushman, Baumeister, & Phillips, 2001; Shaefer & Mattei, 2005; Warren & Kurlychek, 1981; see also Nevels, this volume).

Glancy and colleauges (2005) found that ample research exists that focuses on the efficacy of group therapy as a treatment for anger and aggression. DiGiuseppe (1999) stated that 80% of all research studies on treatments of anger and aggression used a form of group intervention, which may be skewed by the selection of participants (e.g., in hospitals, correctional facilities or residential centers). There is evidence, in fact, that individual therapy may be more efficacious than group services for clients who are particularly angry and resistant to change (Glancy et al., 2005; Tafrate, 2003).

POTENTIAL ISSUES IN THERAPY

Kalogerakis (2004) and Tyson and Tyson (1986) discuss the potential for transference and countertransference issues when dealing with angry and aggressive clients. He warns that clients in therapy could invariably interact with their "habitual mode of relating" and succumb to a hostile attribution of the therapist or view the therapist as an idealized other who may be a savior figure. These clients may also invoke powerful countertransference reactions, including an irrational fear that the client's display of anger may suddenly transform into rage or become retaliatory in some nature if the client were to feel discomfort (Kalogerakis, 2004). Many clinical training programs fail to teach therapists to deal with aggression or angry clients, and therefore clinicians may feel unprepared to deal with aggressive clients and may learn to fear aggression to the point that they avoid taking such clients.

It is important to note that some scholars believe that a critical factor in the success of therapeutic services in dealing with anger and aggressive behavior is in targeting clients' beliefs that their behaviors are problematic while enhancing their sense of responsibility for their own recovery (Deegan, 1996; Singh et al., 2007;). In plain terms, clients committed to changing their anger and aggression must commit to the belief that change can happen and that the behavior-modification techniques being taught (e.g., CBT, SIT, mindfulness) are helpful and worthy of practice with discipline.

RETURNING TO THE CASE OF CHRISTOPHER

While it may have appeared that Christopher was prone to exhibit aggressive behavior in his daily life and even potentially in the therapeutic space itself, we can highlight various contextual factors that may allow us to understand the basis for his aggressive and angry tendencies and why he chooses anger as a default emotion to display. After initial assessment, it was learned that Christopher has been hospitalized for suicidal thoughts on multiple occasions, one by self-referral. It is standard practice to ask for a release of information to gather records on those visits and to ascertain what the medical professionals have diagnosed and possibly prescribed. In the interview, Cristopher reported that he was not taking medications currently and could not remember the name of the medication he was prescribed by his psychiatrist. He was immediately referred to a local psychiatrist for evaluation and continuity of care and was later placed on lamictal (lamotrigine), a mood-stabilizing anticonvulsant.

It appears that Christopher was displaying overt forms of aggression in the room despite his attempts to conceal or minimize it, and he even alluded to "putting on a mask" as a metaphor to his concealment. It does not appear that he exhibits instrumental or relational aggression in either his self-report or via observable cues in the room (e.g., negative "gossip" against others, evidence of "bullying" behaviors, etc.), but his overt anger in the counseling room would give many experienced therapists reason to feel caution. Through careful exploration of his familial life, it was learned that Christopher was "never enough" for his father who, in his patriarchal orientation, often showed "tough love" to him and avoided direct praise for anything positive. To Christopher, he only received feedback when he was wrong or failed, and as per social learning theory, he learned that the only acceptable emotion to display was anger. He admitted that his father offered the mildest of praise when he suspended from school as a child after getting into a physical altercation with another student. He stated that his father told him that he "did the right thing" by defending himself after another child pushed him and took his book.

Using cognitive-behavioral therapy as a basis for treatment, the therapist can investigate client self-conceptions that may have been shaped and formed throughout life. In the case of Christopher, it seems that he has learned that he is "not enough" for others, and regardless of his actions, he has been unable to find sources of validation and acceptance. Furthermore, it is likely that he has learned that being a "man" means being "tough" by showing an acceptable amount of anger and aggression. It seems that one of the only sources for reward from his social model, his father, came after he became aggressive in self-defense; and the idea of aggression being "good" was then further reinforced by the lack of rewards stemming from any other (less aggressive) behavior. Through careful attending, listening, and reflecting, a therapist can identify and shine a light on these beliefs with the client in session. The therapist can combine cognitive reframing of the beliefs with mindfulness/relaxation practice to help the client become more aware of his anger in the moment and work to challenge those automatic aggressive impulses with a new, healthier response. Improvements in reducing aggression using cognitive behavioral therapy will take time and practice, as Christopher learns a new way of relating; and the therapist can also examine the automatic thoughts that may get in the way of successful application of a new behavior. Therapists using a more interpersonal process approach can also use their own feelings about clients' apparent aggression as a therapeutic tool, as long as the clients are able to understand how observable aggression impacts others around them. As stated previously, seeking out clinical supervision for those unfamiliar with working with aggressive clients is very important.

Over time, with constant work on the therapeutic alliance and by mindfully challenging his own beliefs and behaviors, Christopher may learn how to negotiate difficult situations without defaulting to his comfortable aggressive responses. As stated earlier in the chapter, Christopher has navigated a critical factor in the potential success of his treatment: through the process of therapy he has come to understand that his aggressive behaviors are problematic and learned, and he has come to find that his own aggression has only served to inhibit his growth. In trusting the therapeutic process, he has come to believe that he can change and is more mindful of his emotions in everyday life. As he learns to understand his tendency for frustration, anger, and aggression, Christopher may also become open to exploring other difficult emotions in the therapy room with the guidance of the therapist. While Christopher's treatment is unfinished, the therapeutic space has given him a chance to remediate his default expression of anger and aggression and given him permission to share his more complicated and difficult feelings about his father, his family, and his social world.

CONCLUSION

Clients who present to therapy with aggressive tendencies can be overwhelming due to the complex and often substantial number of factors that contribute to their aggression. As stated earlier, many therapists find working with aggressive clients to be stressful and yet increasingly common. Often, a primary collaboration with psychiatric staff is necessary to rule out medical causes or to collaborate on a treatment plan that includes medication. Using aggression as a tool for intervention in therapy can be difficult as the literature shows little evidence for the effectiveness of aggressive catharsis. However, many treatments, such as CBT, mindfulness therapy, and dialectical-behavioral therapy, do exist, and the body of research supporting their use with aggressive and violent clients is growing. Above all, a healthy and supportive collaborative relationship and a strong working alliance are a therapist's best bet for a suitable environment for change.

REFERENCES

Aimé, C., Paquette, D., Déry, M. & Verlaan, P. (2018). Predictors of childhood trajectories of overt and indirect aggression: An interdisciplinary approach. *Aggressive Behavior*, *44*(4), 382–393. doi:10.1002/ab.21759.

Anderson, C. A. & Bushman, B. J. (2002). Human aggression. *Annual Review of Psychology*, *53*(1), 27–51. doi:10.1146/annurev.psych.53.100901.135231.

Aronson, E. (2011). *The social animal*. New York, New York: Worth Publishers

Bandura, A. (1973). Aggression: A social learning analysis. *Stanford Law Review*, *26*(1), 239. doi:10.2307/1227918.

Barkley, R. A., Fischer, M., Smallish, L. & Fletcher, K. (2006). Young adult outcome of hyperactive children: Adaptive functioning in major life activities. *Journal of the American Academy of Child and Adolescent Psychiatry*, *45*, 192–202. doi:10.1097/01.chi.0000189134.97436.e2.

Bass, E. C., Saldarriaga, L., Cunha, J., Chen, B. B., Santo, J. B. & Bukowski, W. M. (2018). A cross-cultural analysis of the relations of physical and relational aggression with peer victimization. *International Journal of Behavioral Development*, *42*(1), 132–142. doi:10.1177/0165025416677846.

Beck, R. & Fernandez, E. (1998). Cognitive-behavioral therapy in the treatment of anger: A meta analysis. *Cognitive Therapy and Research*, *22*(1), 63–74. doi:10.1023/a:1018763902991.

Bennett, S., Farrington, D. P. & Huesmann, L. R. (2005). Explaining gender differences in crime and violence. *Aggression and Violent Behavior*, *10*, 263–288. doi:10.1016/j.avb.2004.07.001.

Berkowitz, L. (1963). *Aggression: A social psychological analysis*. New York: McGraw–Hill.

Björkqvist, K. (2001). Different names, same issue. *Social Development*, *10*(2), 272–274. doi:10.1111/1467-9507.00164.

Bowman Edmondson, C. & Cohen Conger, J. (1996). A review of treatment efficacy for individuals with anger problems: conceptual, assessment, and methodological issues. *Clinical Psychology Review*, *16*(3), 251–275. doi:10.1016/s0272-7358(96)90003-3.

Bruner, J. S. (1957). On perceptual readiness. *Psychological Review*, *64*(2), 123–152. doi:10.1037/h0043805.

Bushman, B. J. & Baumeister, R. F. (1998). Threatened egotism, narcissism, self-esteem, and direct and displaced aggression: Does self-love or self-hate lead to violence? *Journal of Personality and Social Psychology*, *75*(1), 219–229. doi:10.1037/0022-3514.75.1.219.

Bushman, B. J., Baumeister, R. F. & Phillips, C. M. (2001). Do people aggress to improve their mood? Catharsis beliefs, affect regulation opportunity, and aggressive responding. *Journal of Personality and Social Psychology*, *81*(1), 17–32. doi:10.1037/0022-3514.81.1.17.

Card, N. A., Stucky, B. D., Sawalani, G. M. & Little, T. D. (2008). Direct and indirect aggression during childhood and adolescence: A meta-analytic review of gender differences, intercorrelations, and relations to maladjustment. *Child Development*, *79*(5), 1185–1229. doi:10.1111/j.1467-8624.2008.01184.x.

Cary, M. & Dua, J. (1999). Cognitive-behavioral and systematic desensitization procedures in reducing stress and anger in caregivers for the disabled. *International Journal of Stress Management*, *6*(2), 75–87. doi:10.1023/a:1022962409572.

Citrome, L. & Volavka, J. (2011). Pharmacological management of acute and persistent aggression in forensic psychiatry settings. *CNS Drugs*, *25*(12), 1009-1021. doi:10.2165/11596930-000000000-00000.

Crick, N. R. & Dodge, K. A. (1996). Social information-processing mechanisms in reactive and proactive aggression. *Child Development*, *67*(3), 993. doi:10.2307/1131875.

Darwin, C. (1900). *Origin of species*/Charles Darwin. doi:10.5962/bhl.title.959.

Deffenbacher, J. L., Thwaites, G. A., Wallace, T. L. & Oetting, E. R. (1994). Social skills and cognitive-relaxation approaches to general anger reduction. *Journal of Counseling Psychology*, *41*(3), 386–396. doi:10.1037/0022-0167.41.3.386.

Deffenbacher, J. L., McNamara, K., Stark, R. S. & Sabadell, P. M. (1990). A comparison of cognitive-behavioral and process-oriented group counseling for general anger reduction. *Journal of Counseling & Development*, *69*(2), 167–172. doi:10.1002/j.1556-6676.1990.tb01480.x.

Deffenbacher, J. L. & Stark, R. S. (1992). Relaxation and cognitive-relaxation treatments of general anger. *Journal of Counseling Psychology*, *39*(2), 158–167. doi:10.1037/0022-0167.39.2.158.

De Quervain, D. J. F., Treyer, V., Schellhammer, M., Schnyder, U., Buck, A. & Fehr, E. (2004). The neural basis of altruistic punishment. *Science*, *305*(5688), 1254–1258. doi:10.1126/science.1100735.

Deegan, P. (1996). Recovery as a journey of the heart. *Psychiatric Rehabilitation Journal*, *19*(3), 91–97. doi:10.1037/h0101301.

Del Vecchio, T. & O'Leary, K. D. (2004). Effectiveness of anger treatments for specific anger problems: A meta-analytic review. *Clinical Psychology Review*, *24*(1), 15–34. doi:10.1016/j.cpr.2003.09.006.

Deutsch, C. J. (1984). Self-reported sources of stress among psychotherapists. *Professional Psychology: Research and Practice*, *15*(6), 833–845. doi:10.1037/0735-7028.15.6.833.

DiGiuseppe, R. & Tafrate, R. C. (2006). Anger treatment for adults: A meta-analytic review. *Clinical Psychology: Science and Practice*, *10*(1), 70–84. doi:10.1093/clipsy.10.1.70.

DiGiuseppe, R. (1999). End piece: Reflections on the treatment of anger. *J. Clin. Psychol.*, *55*, 365-379. doi:10.1002/(SICI)1097-4679(199903)55:3<365::AID-JCLP8>3.0.CO;2-3.

Dodge, K. A. (2006). Translational science in action: Hostile attributional style and the development of aggressive behavior problems. *Development and Psychopathology*, *18*(03). doi:10.1017/s0954579406060391.

Else-Quest, N. M., Hyde, J. S., Goldsmith, H. H. & Van Hulle, C. A. (2006). Gender differences in temperament: A meta-analysis. *Psychological Bulletin*, *132*, 33. doi:10.1037/0033-2909.132.1.33.

Farber, B. A. (1983). Psychotherapists' perceptions of stressful patient behavior. *Professional Psychology: Research and Practice*, *14*, 697–705. doi:10.1037//0735-7028.14.5.697.

Fernandez, E. & Beck, R. (2001). Cognitive-behavioral self-intervention versus self-monitoring of anger: Effects on anger frequency, duration, and intensity, *Behavioral and Cognitive Psychotherapy*, *29*(3), 345–356. doi:10.1017/s1352465801003071.

Fix, R. L. & Fix, S. T. (2013). The effects of mindfulness-based treatments for aggression: A critical review. *Aggression and Violent Behavior*, *18*(2), 219–227. doi:10.1016/j.avb.2012.11.009.

Freud, S. (1948). *Beyond the pleasure principle*. London: Hogarth Press and Institute of Psycho-Analysis.

García-Sancho, E., Dhont, K., Salguero, J. M. & Fernández-Berrocal, P. (2017). The personality basis of aggression: The mediating role of anger and the moderating role of emotional intelligence. *Scandinavian Journal of Psychology, 58*(4), 333–340. doi:10.1111/sjop.12367.

Glancy, G. & Saini, M. A. (2005). An evidenced-based review of psychological treatments of anger and aggression. *Brief Treatment and Crisis Intervention, 5*(2), 229–248. doi:10.1093/brief-treatment/mhi013.

Glick, B. & Goldstein, A. P. (1987). Aggression Replacement Training. *Journal of Counseling & Development, 65*(7), 356–362. doi:10.1002/j.1556-6676.1987.tb00730.x.

Galovski, T. E. & Blanchard, E. B. (2002). The effectiveness of a brief psychological intervention on court-referred and self-referred aggressive drivers. *Behavior Research and Therapy, 40*(12), 1385–1402. doi:10.1016/s0005-7967(01)00100-0.

Hains, A. A. (1992). Comparison of cognitive-behavioral stress management techniques With adolescent boys. *Journal of Counseling & Development, 70*(5), 600–605. doi:10.1002/j.1556-6676.1992.tb01668.x.

Hains, A. A. & Szyjakowski, M. (1990). A cognitive stress-reduction intervention program for adolescents. *Journal of Counseling Psychology, 37*(1), 79–84. doi:10.1037/0022-0167.37.1.79.

Huesmann, L. R. (1998). 'The role of social information processing and cognitive schema in the acquisition and maintenance of habitual aggressive behavior, in Geen, R. and Donnerstein, E. (Eds), *Human Aggression: Theories, Research and Implications for Policy*. Academic Press, New York, NY, pp. 73-109.

Huesmann, L. R. & Guerra, N. G. (1997). "Social norms and children's aggressive behavior", *Journal of Personality and Social Psychology*, Vol. *72*, pp. 408-19. doi: 10.1037/0022-3514.72.2.408.

Huesmann, L. R. (1988). An information-processing model for the development of aggression. *Aggressive Behavior., 14*, 13–24. doi: 10.1002/1098-2337(1988)14:1<13::AID-AB2480140104>3.0.CO;2-J.

Ireland, J. L., Ireland, C. A. & Birch, P. (Eds) (2008). *The assessment, treatment and management of violent and sexual offenders*. Willan: Devon, UK.

Kalogerakis, M. G. (1997). Adolescent analyzability reconsidered. *Adolescent Psychiatry, 21*, 271–288. Hillsdale, NJ: The Analytic Press.

Kazdin, A. E. (2003). Problem-solving skills training and parent management training for conduct disorder. In A. E. Kazdin & J. R. Weisz (Eds.), *Evidenced-based psychotherapies for children and adolescents*, (pp. 241–262). New York: Guilford Press.

Keenan, K. & Shaw, D. (1997). Developmental and social influences on young girls' early problem behavior. *Psychological Bulletin, 121*, 95. doi: 10.1037/0033-2909.121.1.95.

Knutson, B. (2004). Behavior: Sweet revenge? *Science, 305*(5688), 1246–1247. doi:10.1126/science.1102822.

Kobayashi, M. & Norcross, J. C. (1999). Treating anger in psychotherapy: Introduction and cases. *Clinical Psychology*, *55*, 275–282. doi:10.1002/(SICI)1097-4679(199903)55:3<275::AID-JCLP1>3.0.CO;2-M.

Lachmund, E. & DiGiuseppe, R. (1997, August). *How clinicians assess anger: Do we need an anger diagnosis?* In R. DiGiuseppe (Chair), Advances in the diagnosis, assessment, and treatment of angry clients. Symposium conducted at the 105th annual convention of the American Psychological Association, Chicago.

Lorenz, K. (1966). *On aggression*. New York: Harcourt.

Lui, J. H. L., Barry, C. T. & Schoessler, M. (2017). The indirect effects of adolescent psychopathic traits on aggression through social-cognitive factors. *Journal of Child and Family Studies*, *26*(5), 1298–1309. doi:10.1007/s10826-017-0667-y.

Mischel, W. (1999). Personality coherence and dispositions in a cognitive-affective personality system (CAPS) approach. In: Cervone, D.; Shoda, Y., editors. *The coherence of personality: Social–cognitive bases of consistency, variability, and organization*. New York: Guilford Press; 1999. p. 37-60.

Montagu, A. (1966). *On being human*.

McClure, S. M., Laibson, D. I., Loewenstein, G. & Cohen, J. D. (2004). Separate neural systems value immediate and delayed monetary rewards. *Science*, *306*(5695), 503–507. doi:10.1126/science.1100907.

Morgan, A. B. & Lilienfeld, S. O. (2000). A meta-analytic review of the relation between antisocial behavior and neuropsychological measures of executive function. *Clinical Psychology Review*, *20*, 113–136. doi:10.1016/S0272-7358(98)00096-8.

Meichenbaum, D. H. (1975). *Stress inoculation training*. New York: Pergamon Press.

Novaco, R. W. (1975). *Anger control: The development and evaluation of an experimental treatment*. Lexington, MA: D.C. Health.

Nugent, W. R., Champlin, D. & Wiinimaki, L. (1997). The Effects of Anger Control Training on Adolescent Antisocial Behavior. *Research on Social Work Practice*, 7(4), 446–462. doi:10.1177/104973159700700402.

Ray, D. C., Blanco, P. J., Sullivan, J. M. & Holliman, R. (2009). An exploratory study of child-centered play therapy with aggressive children. *International Journal of Play Therapy*, *18*(3), 162–175. doi:10.1037/a0014742.

Rose, J., West, C. & Clifford, D. (2000). Group interventions for anger in people with intellectual disabilities. *Research in Developmental Disabilities*, *21*(3), 171–181. doi:10.1016/s0891-4222(00)00032-9.

Schaefer, C. E. & Mattei, D. (2005). Catharsis: Effectiveness in children's aggression. *International Journal of Play Therapy*, *14*(2), 103–109. doi:10.1037/h0088905.

Siddle, R., Jones, F. & Awenat, F. (2003). Group cognitive behavior therapy for anger: A pilot study. *Behavioral and Cognitive Psychotherapy*, *31*(1), 69–83. doi:10.1017/s1352465803001073.

Singh, N. N., Lancioni, G. E., Singh Joy, S. D., Winton, A. S. W., Sabaawi, M., Wahler, R. G. & Singh, J. (2007). Adolescents with conduct disorder can be mindful of their aggressive behavior. *Journal of Emotional and Behavioral Disorders*, *15*(1), 56–63. doi:10.1177/10634266070150010601.

Tafrate, R. (1995). Evaluation of treatment strategies for adult anger disorders. In H. Kassinove (Ed.), *Anger disorders: Definition, diagnosis, and treatment*. Washington, DC: Taylor and Francis.

Taft, C. T., Creech, S. K. & Kachadourian, L. (2012). Assessment and treatment of posttraumatic anger and aggression: A review. *Journal of Rehabilitation Research & Development*, *49*(5), 777-788. doi:http://dx.doi.org.proxy- remote.galib.uga.edu/10.1682/JRRD.2011.09.0156.

Timmons, P. L., Oehlert, M. E., Sumerall, S. W., Timmons, C. W. & Borgers, S. B. (1997). Stress inoculation training for maladaptive anger: Comparison of group counseling versus computer guidance. *Computers in Human Behavior*, *13*(1), 51–64. doi:10.1016/s0747-5632(96)00029-5.

Tyson, R. L. & Tyson, P. (1986). The concept of transference in child psychoanalysis. *Journal of the American Academy of Child Psychiatry*, *25*(1), 30–39. doi:10.1016/s0002-7138(09)60596-3.

Wachtel, L., Jaffe, R. & Kellner, C. (2011). Electroconvulsive therapy for psychotropic-refractory bipolar affective disorder and severe self-injury and aggression in an 11-year- old autistic boy. *European Child & Adolescent Psychiatry*, *20*(3), 147-152. doi:10.1007/s00787-010-0155-z.

Warren, R. & Kurlychek, R. T. (1981). Treatment of maladaptive anger and aggression: Catharsis vs. behavior therapy. *Corrective & Social Psychiatry & Journal of Behavior Technology, Methods & Therapy*, *27*(3), 135-139.

Whitfield, G. W. (1999). Validating school social work: An evaluation of a cognitive-behavioral approach to reduce school violence. *Research on Social Work Practice*, *9*(4), 399–426. doi:10.1177/104973159900900402.

Willner, P., Jones, J., Tams, R. & Green, G. (2002). A randomized controlled trial of the efficacy of a cognitive-behavioural anger management group for clients with learning disabilities. *Journal of Applied Research in Intellectual Disabilities*, *15*(3), 224–235. doi:10.1046/j.1468-3148.2002.00121.x.

White, J. W. (2001). Gendered aggression across the lifespan. In J. Worell, (Ed.), *Encyclopedia of Gender*. San Diego, CA: Academic Press.

Worthington, R. (2012). Dealing with trauma as an intervention for aggression: a review of approaches and the value of reprocessing. *Journal of Aggression, Conflict and Peace Research*, *4*(2), 108–118. doi:10.1108/17596591211208319.

Wupperman, P., Marlatt, G., Cunningham, A., Bowen, S., Berking, M., Mulvihill-Rivera, N. & Easton, C. (2012). Mindfulness and modification therapy for behavioral dysregulation: results from a pilot study targeting alcohol use and aggression in women. *Journal of Clinical Psychology*, *68*(1), 50-66. doi:10.1002/jclp.20830.

In: Social Psychology and Counseling
Editors: D. A. Kleiber and E. Delgado-Romero
ISBN: 978-1-53616-548-7

Chapter 16

SOCIAL EXCLUSION, HOSTILE ATTRIBUTION BIAS, AND OTHER CONTRIBUTORS TO SCHOOL VIOLENCE

Dontavious Ford and Paloma Ocampo

School shootings and school violence have occurred in other countries, but with such events becoming more frequent within the United States in recent decades, government officials and others have been searching widely for ways to prevent further tragedies from happening. In 2001, the United States Congress requested that the National Research Council study the phenomenon of school violence that had been occurring increasingly between the years of 1992 and 2001 (Moore, Petrie, Braga & McLaughlin, 2003). The report focused on specific situations that included school shootings in which one or more students or teachers had been injured or killed and looked at information such as the perpetrator, the school situation, the community in which it occurred, and the events leading up to the incidents of violence. Although the committee was unable to reach scientific conclusions about the causes of the shootings, the information gathered provided insights into the psychological, emotional, and social dynamics present in the lives of both the shooters and the communities in which they lived. The data highlighted areas such as experiences of alienation, teasing/bullying in schools, dysfunctional family relationships, and relationships within the school system between teachers and students and among students, to name a few (Moore, Petrie, Braga & McLaughlin, 2003).

During the 2015–16 school year, 79 percent of public schools recorded one or more incidents of violence, theft, or other crimes, amounting to 1.4 million crimes. These statistics translate to a rate of 28 crimes per 1,000 students enrolled during that school year. During the same school year, 47 percent of schools reported one or more of these particular crimes to the police, amounting to 449,000 crimes, or 9 crimes per 1,000 students enrolled (National Center for Education Statistics, 2018). During the 2016 school year, the percentage of public schools that recorded incidents of violent crime, serious violent crime, theft, and other incidents varied depending on school characteristics. For example, the National Center for Education Statistics (2018) reported 57 percent of elementary schools recorded violent incidents compared with 88 percent of middle schools and 90 percent of high schools. Overall, a lower percentage of elementary schools recorded serious violent incidents (9 percent) compared to middle and high schools (23 and 30 percent, respectively). A lower percentage of elementary schools recorded incidents of theft (23 percent) than middle and high schools (55 and 76 percent, respectively), and a lower percentage of elementary schools recorded other incidents (43 percent) than middle and high schools (77 and 88 percent, respectively).

Thus, school violence is a social problem that is affecting a growing number of children, adolescents, teachers, and staff. Violent behaviors among students in an educational setting are usually acts of aggression exerted toward a classmate with whom there is an imbalance of power (Marsh et al., 2011). These aggressive and social behaviors can vary in that they can be physical (pushing, hitting, etc.), verbal (insulting, threatening, etc.), or can be relational violence (spreading false rumors, excluding from activities, etc.). The perpetrator's intention is to dominate and exert control over the other person (Marsh et al., 2011), thereby creating a dynamic of violence in which the victims are usually unable to defend themselves due to this imbalance of power (Garaigordobil & Oñederra, 2010).

Schools are often seen as being responsible for providing a positive environment for students to develop academically, emotionally, and socially. Successful school environments are those schools that promote positive norms and values, academic achievement, social competence, and prosocial behavior (Gage, Larson, Sugai, & Chafouleas, 2016). The National School Climate Center (2016) defines school climate as the quality and character of school life as it relates to norms and values, interpersonal relations and social interactions, and organizational processes and structures. Loukas (2007) further described the school climate as "a multidimensional construct that includes physical, social, and academic dimensions" that are based on students' perceptions and experiences. This can be further understood by exploring the norms and goals of the school, the interpersonal relationships between students and school staff, practices of teaching and learning, and the structural environment of the school (Cohen et al., 2009). A healthy school climate promotes individual growth, provides students with norms and expectations for prosocial behavior, and fosters a respectful and collaborative atmosphere (National School Climate Center, 2016).

A positive school climate relates to lower rates of school disorder and therefore lower rates of school violence (Bear, Gaskins, Blank, & Chen, 2011; Bryson & Childs, 2018; Estevez, Jimenez, & Cava, 2016). Studies have shown that students who report positive perceptions of school climate are less likely to engage in aggressive behavior toward peers at school (Shukla, Konold, & Cornell, 2016). Currently, there is no national consensus on the number of dimensions that make up a school climate or which ones are most important in creating a positive school environment. This has led to the use of an array of measures to represent school climate with studies measuring anywhere from three to ten different dimensions (Steffgen, Recchia, & Viechtbauer, 2013; Voight, Hanson, O'Malley, & Adekanye, 2015; Zullig, Koopman, Patton, & Ubbes, 2010). Most studies that measure student perceptions usually measure five areas which include the quality of student–teacher relationships, physical and emotional safety, established rules and norms for behavior, student connectedness and institutional environment, and equality and respect for differences (Bryson & Childs, 2018). As a result, there has been an increase in school climate research as a "viable, data driven school improvement strategy that promotes safer, more supportive, and more civil" school environments (Thapa, Cohen, Guffey, & Higgins-D'Alessandro, 2013). If we also consider violence towards teachers, research suggests that certain school characteristics such as staffing, size, resources, and educational and social climate make a difference in the amount of teacher victimization in the school. More teaching resources, smaller school size, more proficiency in teaching, and sensible disciplinary measures appear to prevent teacher victimization (Rose, 2009.) But what are the factors that contribute to school violence to begin with?

Factors Contributing to School Violence

The Columbine High School shooting in the United States has been one of the deadliest school shootings to occur, and has ultimately set the stage for others to come. One of the common themes of the various school shootings has been that the perpetrators have usually experienced social rejection repeatedly and/or been bullied by their peers (Twenge, Baumeister, Tice, & Stucke, 2001). However, research is still being conducted to determine other factors that are prevalent before a shooting occurs, as well as suggested explanations that causes perpetrators to terrorize and commit horrendous acts in schools. A few factors that consistently appear in the literature with regard to why adolescents commit violent crimes include: (1) being socially excluded (i.e., lack of belonging and acceptance due to factors that make children feel more socially vulnerable such as being poor), (2) developing a hostile attribution bias (i.e., the tendency to interpret the behaviors of others across situations as threatening or aggressive), (3) having social/emotional problems that impact day to day functioning with others (e.g., emotional behavioral disorder), and (4) having been affected by their environment, including exposed to violence at home, online or elsewhere (e.g., continuous community violence).

Having a history of aggression is another contributing factor to school violence. The most reliable predictor of violent crimes conducted by adolescents is a *history of elevated aggression* (Loeber, Burke, & Pardini, 2009; Reingle, Jennings, & Maldonado-Molina, 2012). Trajectory studies by Nagin and Tremblay (1999) and replicated by Broidy et al., (2003) across six, cross-national, longitudinal data-sets found that boys' violent crime in late adolescence was best predicted by showing the highest trajectory of physical aggression in the preceding years. Similarly, other studies have shown higher levels of childhood physical aggression in samples of previously violent adolescents than those who committed nonviolent crimes or no offenses (Lai, Zing, & Chu, 2015; Reingle et al., 2012). Elevated aggression and the emergence of violence have been linked with social and emotional difficulties for adolescents who commit violent acts.

In a study conducted by Kalvin and Bierman (2017), risk for future violent crime was indicated by a childhood profile that included emotional and social dysfunction, as well as aggressive behavior. Individuals who later became violent are likely to have had aggressive tendencies including fighting, physically attacking others, destroying things and being interpersonally hostile (teasing, threatening others) as younger children. They were also frequently angry and volatile emotionally, having difficulties tolerating frustration, calming down when upset, and controlling anger. Issues with social isolation reflecting social discomfort (prefers to be alone, shy) and social demoralization (sulks, unhappy) were also predictors. The results are consistent with studies showing robust associations between later violent offending and both childhood aggression (Broidy et al, 2003; Lai et al., 2015) and childhood emotional dysregulation and social isolation (Hawkins et al., 2000).

Nonetheless, adolescence is a tumultuous developmental period. The burgeoning autonomy associated with adolescence results in a flood of new experiences, including the exposure to risk factors that may increase vulnerability. A tendency toward aggressive reactivity is one such risk factor that has major developmental consequences. Developmental theorists have speculated that elevated childhood aggression often reflects reactivity in the more primitive neural circuits associated with the processing of fear and rage, evoked when children feel threatened (Vitaro, Brendgen, & Trembley, 2002). Consistent with this developmental analysis, research has shown that difficulties regulating emotions and managing anger in childhood may portend becoming violent later on.

Social Isolation and Rejection

Social exclusion is a contributing factor for increased violence, but oftentimes social exclusion and isolation are confused. Isolation is not always the result of exclusion; some youth may be in a state of self-imposed isolation. These youth, often referred to a socially withdrawn youth, generally fall into two categories: socially disinterested or socially avoidant. Socially disinterested youth avoid peer interaction because of a lack of motivation to engage in social relationships. In other words, these youth have the ability to engage in meaningful relationships but choose to remain in solitude (Coplan, Prakash, O'Neil, & Armer, 2004). Socially avoidant youth, on the other hand, exhibit a combination of poor social skills and high avoidance motivations (Asendorpf, 1993). Both groups avoid contact with the broader peer network and prefer to remain in isolation.

Peer-rejected youth, those who have been forced into a state of isolation as a result of peer rejection or social exclusion, have also been studied in developmental psychology (Nino, Ignatow, & Cai, 2017). Peer-rejected youth, also known as "active isolators," have been shown to be at an increased risk for aggressive behavior; and as peer rejection increases as youth age, so does aggressive behavior (Kupersmidt, Burchinal, & Patterson, 1995). It is also important to note that studies suggest that the rejection-aggression relationship is bidirectional: youth who are aggressive also are inclined to be actively isolated because their aggressive behavior is offensive and alienating to their respective peers (French, 1988; Hymel, Bowker, & Woody, 1993).

Aggressive children who are emotionally dysregulated are particularly likely to experience peer rejection and social isolation, and thereby become excluded from positive peer socialization opportunities that facilitate the growth of communication skills, empathy, and general social competence (Bierman, 2004). Social isolation, in turn, increases the risk for later violence (Hawkins et al., 2000). Most youth are able to develop and maintain peer relationships during adolescence, but a small portion either are unable to establish friendships or prefer being alone. Recent estimates indicate roughly 10% of adolescent youth are socially isolated from their peers (Vaquera & Kao, 2008). Social isolation also places youth at increased risk for a myriad of negative health and mental health outcomes such as low self-worth, depression, anxiety, loneliness, and suicide. Furthermore, children who are isolated from mainstream peers often play with other aggressive children who encourage rebellious behavior and reinforce antisocial norms (Powers & Bierman, 2013). Peer-rejected children appear particularly vulnerable to developing a heightened vigilance for social threat and cues of impending conflict, choosing to act hostilely rather than experience vulnerability. For these reasons, the combination of childhood aggression, emotion dysregulation, and social isolation may reflect dysfunction in social-emotional development that primes children for later violence, making them more angry, reactive, and easily activated to attack compared to aggressive children without the same level of concurrent emotional risk.

Social Learning

It is well established that children who grow up in contexts characterized by high levels of exposure to conflict and violence are also more likely to display aggression and develop anti-social behavior than children growing up in more protected environments (Dodge, Greenberg, Malone, & Conduct Problems Prevention Research Group, 2008). Largely this has been explained by social learning and social control theories that emphasize the role that parents and peers play in modeling, normalizing, and reinforcing aggression (Dishion, 2014; Loeber et al., 2009). Social learning theory has established itself as one of the most prominent criminological theories concerning marginalized youth and delinquent behavior. At the core of social learning theory is the notion that violent behavior is learned through social relationships, and, based on this framework, learning theorists argue that violent delinquency is learned through a reciprocal process of exposure, imitation of peers, and the observation of positive and negative consequences of behavior.

Exposure to environments with high levels of conflict, stress, and violence may teach aggressive behavior that undermines the development of emotion regulation, empathy, and self-control. The result of these conditions may result in a transactional process in which emotion dysregulation, aggressive behavior, and social alienation interact and are socially reinforced over time to increase the propensity for violence. For example, frustrated and/or emotionally dysregulated children are less able to modulate their feelings of anger or inhibit their aggressive impulses. Consequently, they are prone to react aggressively when upset, eliciting negative reactions from others, limiting opportunities for positive social interactions, and exacerbating feelings of social alienation (Bierman, 2004; Dodge et al., 2008). These various contextual influences may even cause changes in thought patterns compared with those lacking such exposure. In particular, an orientation called "hostile attribution bias" may result.

Hostile Attribution Bias

The hostile attribution bias is the propensity to interpret the behavior of others, across situations, as either threatening, aggressive, or both (Dodge, 1980). People who exhibit a hostile attribution bias think that ambiguous behavior of others is hostile and often directed toward them, while those who do not exhibit a hostile attribution bias interpret the behavior and actions of others in a non-hostile, nonthreatening way. Furthermore, people who may have a hostile attribution bias respond to the other person's behavior in an aggressive manner because they perceive it as a personal threat. When they respond aggressively, this action is often viewed as inappropriate because the other person's original behavior was not intended to be aggressive. For example, someone may accidently step on a young man's foot and apologize; if the one whose foot was stepped on has a hostile attribution bias, he will interpret the accident as hostile and a personal threat towards him, regardless of an apology (Aronson, 2012). When hostile intent is presumed, both aggressive and nonaggressive children respond with more hostility.

However, when the intent is ambiguous or unclear, nonaggressive children respond as though the intent was benign while aggressive children respond as though the intent was hostile.

Hostile attributions in unintentional situations have been extensively implicated in samples of youth who exhibit antisocial behavior. Several studies (e.g., Sorge, Skilling, & Toplak, 2015) have suggested that clinical samples of adjudicated youth display immature moral reasoning and make more hostile attributions in ambiguous situations than community comparison groups were prone to do. In Sorge and colleagues' study, noted group differences were found in the unintentional hostile attribution bias scenarios but not in the intentional aggression situations. The clinical group reported experiencing more anger and intentionality in social situations where there was no evidence of hostile intent than the community comparison group but comparable anger and intentionality in situations where the hostile intent was salient. These findings suggest that the clinical group made hostile attributions when they were not warranted. Some research has suggested that the group difference in the hostile attribution bias is due to a decision-making failure that may stem from a more specific misunderstanding of social information processing. It has also been suggested in the clinical literature that offending youth may have failed to internalize critical rules and social conventions in our society (Stams, et al., 2006). Hostile attributions in unintentional situations may be a failure to internalize certain social conventions in combination with a heuristic to infer negative intent. In a meta-analysis, Stams et al. (2006) found that a sample of justice-involved youth scored significantly lower on measures of moral judgment than their non-offending counterparts.

Hostile attributions of intention have been discussed in relation to the development and maintenance of aggressive behavior in children for over thirty years (Martinelli, Ackermann, Bernhard, Freitag, Schwenck, 2018). In particular, ascribing hostile intention to a behavior is associated with an increased likelihood to engage in aggressive responses. According to Martinelli and colleagues, aggression can be divided into two types based on its function: reactive or proactive. Reactive aggression is considered highly related to the emotion of anger, occurs in reaction to frustration, and is impulsive or automatic. Proactive aggression[1], in contrast, is considered premeditated. It serves to achieve an anticipated reward for the aggressor. Specifically, it has been proposed that children high in reactive aggression interpret hostile intention in the actions of others, while children high in proactive aggression evaluate aggression more positively and expect positive outcomes for aggression (anticipated reward) (Dodge, 2006; and for more on this idea, see Field & Robinson, this volume). The majority of evidence to date supports that notion that physically aggressive children display hostile attribution bias in

[1] Proactive aggression is also referred to as "instrumental" aggression (e.g., Aronson, 2012), though reactive aggression is arguably also instrumental in the sense of causing harm or hurt to another, if only for self-protection.

response to physically provocative situations (for example, being hit with a ball or having one's toy broken). Individuals engaging in physical aggression correspondingly show physical hostile attribution bias while those engaging in relational aggression show relational hostile attribution bias (Crick, Grotpeter, & Bigbee, 2002). Arguably, hostile attribution bias acts as a mediator between relational and physical victimization and development of the respective type of aggression.

Research by DeWall et al., (2009) examined participants who experienced social exclusion along with a control group and a group of participants who experienced social acceptance with respect to hostile cognitive bias. Results from the study indicated that when given measures to complete (mood measures, measures of hostile cognition), those who experienced social exclusion showed a higher level of in hostility-related cognitions. The researchers interpreted these findings as indicating that social exclusion makes individuals feel betrayed by others and that this sense of betrayal causes individuals to perceive neutral information as hostile, which then has consequences for their aggressive treatment of others.

In a similar study by Twenge and colleagues (2001), the authors conducted several experiments that examined social exclusion and rejection and its effects on aggressive behavior. In one of the experiments, the researchers gave feedback to participants supposedly based on a personality test whether they would end up alone for most of their adult lives or end up having a large social network. In the other, the researchers told participants that either no one in the group, or everyone in the group, had chosen them to work together on a task. Afterwards, aggression was measured by participants giving an evaluation of others or administering blasts of stressful noise. Results showed that, overall, participants who experienced social rejection were more aggressive. For example, participants who had been told they would be alone for most of their lives (social exclusion), followed by receiving an insult, showed an increase in aggression. And socially excluded participants who had to administer a blast of stressful noise chose a higher intensity and tended to select a longer duration of the noise. However, if the participants received some sort of praise, even after experiencing social exclusion, there was no increase in aggression towards others. But the researchers also found that those participants who were rejected or excluded did not try to do anything to win friends or win the social approval or acceptance of others and were still aggressive towards others who were considered a "neutral target" (i.e., had neither insulted nor praised them).

It is important to think about these findings as we look back to school shootings in which many are targeted and not necessarily anyone who has done anything towards the perpetrator. Research shows generally that humans are social creatures and crave a sense of belonging and a need to be with others. The final comments of Twenge and her colleagues (2001) in their study are worth noting: "if intelligent, well-adjusted, successful university students can turn aggressive in response to a small laboratory experience of social exclusion, it is disturbing to imagine…what might arise from a series of important rejections or chronic exclusion from desired groups in actual social life" (p. 23).

The tendency to attribute hostile intention has been shown to correlate positively with aggressive behavior in community children and adolescents, in children with clinical levels of aggressive or delinquent behavior, and with clinical diagnoses of conduct disorder, oppositional defiant disorder, or attention deficit/hyperactivity disorder. A meta-analysis of 41 studies and 6017 participants, 8 to 12-years-old, on degree of hostile attribution bias and the experience of social rejection, reported the highest effect size between aggressive behavior and hostile attribution bias in multiple areas of society (Martinelli, et al, 2018). Also, one of the most common findings in the clinical literature that has examined antisocial youth is misattribution or hostile attribution bias in social settings (Sorge et al., 2015).

An Evidence-based Model of Factors Leading to School Violence

A chain of events that may lead to aggression can be initiated by input variables influencing affect, cognition, and arousal. *The General Aggression Model* (Anderson & Bushman, 2011) offers a model for understanding how school violence may erupt from input variables such as factors related to the person (e.g., high irritability, certain attitudes or beliefs about violence, and hostile attribution bias) and situation (exposure to others behaving aggressively, continuously being insulted, or other environmental factors). Outcomes from these inputs received by adolescents can involve thoughtful actions or reactions or impulsive actions of aggression toward others. Figure 1 represents key aspects of an early version of the General Aggression Model (it has since been updated to include more factors, but the basics are still the same). Unpleasant experiences and situational cues can trigger negative affect, high arousal, and aggression-related thoughts in children. Due to individual differences, some children are more likely than others to experience these feelings and thoughts. Higher order thinking then shapes these feelings and thoughts into well-defined emotions and behavioral intentions. Depending on the outcome of this thinking, which can occur beneath the child's conscious awareness and can be affected by factors such as stress, the individual may choose to aggress. Although the general aggression model has been used to explain the development of aggression in individuals, further empirical research is needed to support the unique development of aggression in schools. There is limited research using a particular model to offer more understanding about school violence or dynamics that influence aggression in school environments.

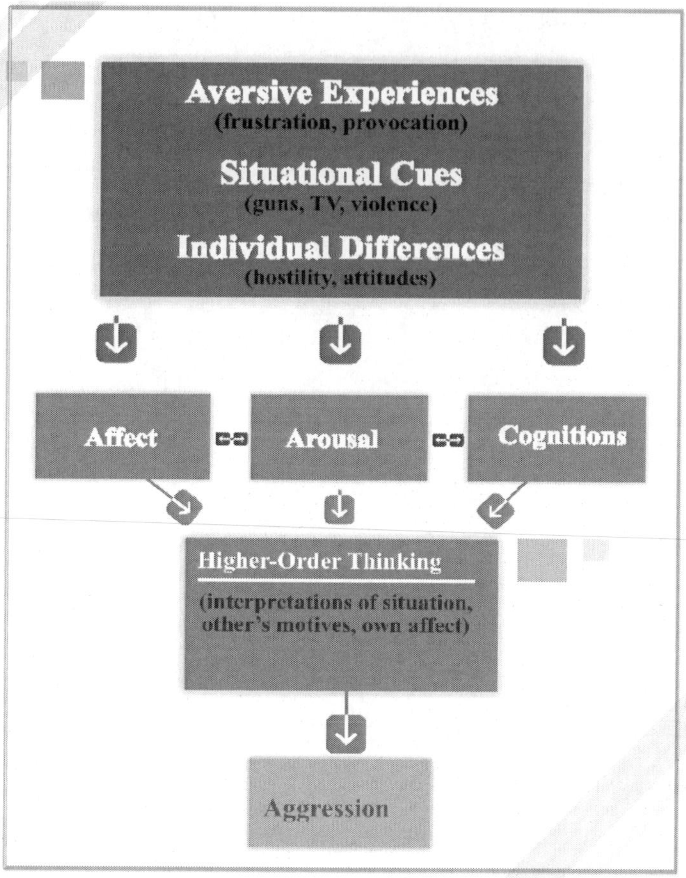

Figure 1. General Aggression Model (adapted from Anderson, Anderson, & Deuser, 1996).

IMPLICATIONS FOR PRACTICE AND FURTHER RESEARCH

The experiments conducted by Twenge and her colleagues (2007) also enabled the investigators to examine ways to *reduce* aggression among those who had been socially excluded. They discovered that by having participants write about a close friend or family member or having a positive social interaction soon after being excluded reduced aggression to the same level as those who had not experienced any social exclusion or rejection. Thus, these findings suggest that any positive, social interaction or thinking about positive social connections can help reduce aggression towards others. The results from this study can be useful in helping schools and communities find ways in which to increase positive social interactions with students who are bullied or rejected. It would be useful for teachers, principals, and staff to include trainings that are geared towards helping them identify students who are being excluded or rejected by peers so that they can perhaps intervene and have a positive social interaction with the student in order to reduce the impact of exclusion and any possible aggression. These results are consistent with Aronson's (2012) use of the "Jigsaw Method," for example, that was shown to reduce intergroup prejudice and hostility by utilizing a cooperative task approach to learning.

Social acceptance, especially during middle school and high school years, is important, and therefore being excluded or rejected during this time can have devastating effects on the individual. Anti-bullying campaigns and commercials have been gaining attention and usually encourage students to stand up against those who are bullying and to stand with those who are being bullied. These commercials and campaigns have the right idea in that students who are being socially excluded or rejected can perceive the student standing up for them as a positive social interaction. It would be wise for schools to have similar campaigns with anti-bullying strategies in order to help reduce social exclusion and/or rejection. Finally, DeWall and colleagues (2009) stated that being socially excluded caused their research participants to feel betrayed and angry, while the research by Twenge amd collaborators (2001) demonstrated that having positive social interactions or thinking about positive social relationships can help a person feel more trusting and have a more positive attitude towards others, which in turn reduces aggression and a tendency to perceive people as hostile.

The findings of those studies also suggest that children at high risk for later violence might be identified by late childhood; interventions to reduce violent crime may be more powerful when they start earlier in childhood (Kalvin and Bierman, 2017). The current research also suggests that preventive interventions would benefit by focusing concurrently on the emotional and social difficulties of children at high risk, as well as those with accelerating levels of aggressive behavior. Fostering stronger parent-youth communication bonds and structuring free time to reduce opportunities for unstructured deviant peer activity, as has been shown to reduce *nonviolent* crime, may also help in the prevention of violent crimes. Also, child social-emotional development seems to be a key factor in preventing violent crimes later on.

Today's reality is that school counselors, school psychologists, school social workers, and other mental health professionals in the community need to have training on warning signs and therapeutic treatment for children who are at risk to commit a violent act. Furthermore, mental health professionals should also be prepared and have knowledge about responding to school violence in the event of an emergency and plans to deal with the aftermath of violent acts in the school and community.

For school violence prevention, it is imperative that school personnel pay attention to the day-to-day issues that affect a school's safety, from racial microaggressions and bullying to dating and relationship violence and to be present and visible. Students should know who they can confide in when they are upset, feeling angry, or concerned about a situation. School counselors, school social workers, and school psychologists are a resource for children to talk to, and they can travel from classroom to classroom to talk with students about their role in the school building. More importantly, they can foster safe environments in which each student has at least one positive relationship with a staff member of their choice (e.g., teacher-student mentorship). Also, school personnel should be responsible for making sure that all students feel heard and that there are trusted adults in the building waiting to listen. Teachers can be trained by mental health professionals to do a weekly "check-in" in their classes to determine the climate. Weekly "check-ins" are important because students know of issues that may be happening that staff members don't. If you ask a teacher if bullying is happening in class, he or she might respond "no," but if you ask students individually, they may well respond in the affirmative. Teachers and school personnel have to understand as adults that they may be naïve to situations that are very apparent to children at school. Check-ins are equally important once a child who is struggling has been identified. Regularly meeting with that student is an important intervention to continue monitoring the issue that the student is faced with and maintaining school safety.

Schools can create advisory councils that include student leaders, parents, school staff members, and mental health professionals to understand issues going on in the school and the community at large. Mental health professionals can work with parents to gain a better understanding about resources to send to other parents regarding warning signs that might indicate their child needs a little bit more attention around bullying or being bullied, social withdrawal or isolation, feeling suicidal, and outbursts of uncontrolled anger. Also, mental health professionals can create a forum to understand and know situations that may be happening in the community and escalating in the school. Mental health professionals can work with student leaders on spotting "friends" who may be bullied, feeling "unheard," or having a difficult time at school. These student leaders can be trained on how to befriend these students especially if the student feels more comfortable talking to a peer instead of an adult. Finally, having a team approach in which all school staff members in the building are responsible for student safety may be necessary. To prevent school violence school personnel should be focused on building rapport with students in the building and promoting openness and prosocial behavior toward fellow classmates.

REFERENCES

Asendorpf, J. B. (1993). Abnormal shyness in children. *Journal of Child Psychology and Psychiatry, 34*, 1069-1083.

Bear, G. G., Gaskins, C., Blank, J., & Chen, F. F. (2011). Delaware School Climate Survey-Student: Its factor structure, concurrent validity, and reliability. *Journal of School Psychology, 49*, 157–174.

Bierman, K. L. (2004). *Peer rejection: Developmental processes and intervention strategies*. New York, NY: Guilford Press.

Broidy, L. M., Tremblay, R. E., Brame, B, Fergusson, D., Horwood, J. L. Laird, R., Vitaro, F. (2003). Developmental trajectories of childhood disruptive behaviors and adolescent delinquency: A six-site, cross-national study. *Developmental Psychology, 39*, 222-245.

Bryson, S. L., & Childs, K. K. (2018). Racial and ethnic differences in the relationship between school climate and disorder. *School Psychology Review, 47,* 258-274.

Burt, S. A. (2012). How do we optimally conceptualize the heterogeneity within antisocial behavior? An argument for aggressive versus nonaggressive behavioral dimensions. *Clinical Psychology Review. 32,* 263-279.

Cohen, J., McCabe, E. M., Michelli, N. M., Pickerall, T. (2009). School climate: Research, policy, practice, and teacher education. *School Climate Research and Educational Policy*, *111*, 180-213.

Coplan, R. J., Prakash, K., O'Neil, K., & Armer, M. (2004). Do you "want" to play? Distinguishing between conflicted shyness and social disinterest in early childhood. *Developmental Psychology, 40*, 244-258.

Cornell, D., Shukla, K., & Konold, T. R. (2016). Authoritative school climate and student academic engagement, grades, and aspirations in middle and high schools. *AERA Open, 2* (2).

Crick, N. R., & Grotpeter, J. K., & Bigbee, M. A. (2002). Relationally and physically aggressive children's intent attributions and feelings of distress for relational and instrumental peer provocations. *Child Development, 73,* 1134-1142.

DeWall, C., Twenge, J. M., Gitter, S. A., & Baumeister, R. F. (2009). It's the thought that counts: The role of hostile cognition in shaping aggressive responses to social exclusion. *Journal of Personality & Social Psychology*, *96*, 45-59.

Dishion, T. J. (2014). Developmental model of aggression and violence: Microsocial and macrosocial dynamics within an ecological framework. *Handbook of developmental psychopathology* (pp. 449-466.) New York, NY: Springer.

Dodge, K. (1980). Social cognition and children's aggressive behavior. *Child Development, 51* (1), 162.

Dodge, K. (2006). Translational science in action: Hostile attributional style and the development of aggressive behavior problems. *Development and Psychopathology, 18*, 791-814.

Dodge, K. A. Greenberg, M. T., Malone, P. S., & Conduct Problems Prevention Research Group. (2008). Testing an idealized dynamic cascade model of the development of serious violence in adolescence. *Child Development. 79, 1907-1927.*

Estevez, E., Jimenez, T. I., & Cava, M. (2016). A cross-cultural study in spain and mexico on school aggression in adolescence: Examining the role of individual, family, and school variables. *Cross-Cultural Research, 50*(2), 123-153.

Gage, N. A., Larson, A., Sugai, G., & Chafouleas, S. M. (2016). Student perceptions of school climate as predictors of office discipline referral *American Educational Research Journal*, *3*, 492 - 499.

Garaigordobil, M., & Onederra, J. A. (2008). Bullying: Incidence of peer violence in the schools of the Autonomous Community of the Basque Country. *International Journal of Psychology and Psychological Therapy, 8*, 51-62.

Goodrum, S., Thompson, A. J., Ward, K. C., & Woodward, W. (2018). A case study on threat assessment: Learning critical lessons to prevent school violence. *Journal of Threat Assessment and Management, 5*(3), 121-136.

Hawkins, J. D., Herrenkohl, T. I., Farrington, D. P., Brewer, D., Catalano, R, F. Harachi, T. W., & Cothern, L. (2000). *Predictors of youth violence*. Washington, DC: Office of Juvenile Justice and Delinquency Prevention.

Hymel, S., Bowker, A., & Woody, E. (1993). Aggressive versus withdrawn unpopular children: Variations in peer and self-perceptions in multiple domains. *Child Development*, *3*, 879-896.

Kalvin, Carla B., Bierman, Karen. (2017). Child and adolescent risk factors that differentially predict violent versus nonviolent crime. *Aggressive Behavior*, *43*, 568-577.

Konold, T., Cornell, D., Shukla, K., & Huang, F. (2017). Racial/ethnic differences in perceptions of school climate and its association with student engagement and peer aggression. *Journal of Youth and Adolescence, 6*, 1289-1302.

Kupersmidt, J. B., Burchinal, M., & Patterson, C. J. (1995). Developmental patterns of childhood peer relations as predictors of externalizing behavior problems. *Development and Psychopathology*, 7, 825-843.

Lai, V., Zeng, G., & Chu, C. M. (2015). Violent and nonviolent youth offenders: Preliminary evidence on group subtypes. *Youth Violence and Juvenile Justice, 14,* 313-329.

Loeber, R., Burke, J., & Pardini, D. A. (2009). Perspectives on oppositional defiant disorder, conduct disorder, and psychopathic features. *Journal of Child Psychology and Psychiatry, 50*, 133-142.

Loukas, A. (2007) What Is School Climate? High-quality school climate is advantageous for all students and may be particularly beneficial for at-risk students. *Leadership Compass, 5*, 1-3.

Marsh, H. W., Nagengast, B., Morin, A. J. S., Parada, R. H., Craven, R. G., & Hamilton, L. R. (2011). Construct validity of the multidimensional structure of bullying and victimization: An application of exploratory structural equation modeling. *Journal of Educational Psychology, 103*, 701-732.

Martinelli A., Ackerman, K., Bernhard, A., Freitag, C. M., Schwenck, C. (2017). Hostile attribution bias and aggression in children and adolescents: A systematic literature review on the influence of aggression subtype and gender. *Aggression and Violent Behavior*, 39, 25-32.

Moore, M. H. (2003). Deadly lessons: Understanding lethal school violence. *Case studies of school violence committee* Washington, DC: National Academy Press.

Nagin, D., & Tremblay, R. E. (1999). Trajectories of boys' physical aggression, opposition, and hyperactivity on the path to physically violent and nonviolent juvenile delinquency. *Child Development, 70*, 1181-1196.

National Center for Education Statistics U.S. Department of Education. *Crime, Violence, Discipline, and Safety in U.S. Public Schools: Findings from the School Survey on Crime and Safety in U.S. Public Schools 2015–16.*

Nino, M., Ignatow, G., Cai, T. (2017). Social isolation, strain, and youth violence. *Youth Violence and Juvenile Justice, 15*, 299-313.

Powers, C. J. & Bierman, K. L. (2013). The multifaceted impact of peer relations on aggressive-disruptive behavior in early elementary school. *Developmental Psychology*, *49*, 1174-1186.

Reingle, J. M., Jennings, W. G., & Maldonado-Molina, M. M. (2012). Risk and protective factors for trajectories of violent delinquency among a nationally representative sample of early adolescents. *Youth Violence and Juvenile Justice*, *10*, 261-277.

Rose, I. (2009). *School violence: Studies in alienation, revenge and redemption*. London: Routledge.

Stams, G. J., Brugman, D., Dekovic, M., van Rosmalen, L., van der Laan, P., & Gibbs, J. C. (2006). The moral judgment of juvenile delinquents: A meta-analysis. *Journal of Abnormal Child Psychology, 34*, 697-713.

Steffgen, G., Recchia, S., & Viechtbauer, W. (2013). The link between school climate and violence in school: A meta-analytic review. *Aggression and Violent Behavior, 18*, 300-309.

Sorge, G. B., Skilling, T. A., Toplak, M. E. (2015). Intelligence, executive functions, and decision making as predictors of antisocial behavior in an adolescent sample of justice-involved youth and a community comparison group. *Journal of Behavioral Decision Making, 28*, 477-490.

Thapa, A., Cohen, J., Guffey, S., & Higgins-D'Alessandro, A. (2013). A review of school climate research. *Review of Educational Research, 83*, 357-385.

Twenge, J. M., Baumeister, R. F., Tice, D. M., & Stucke, T. S. (2001). If you can't join them, beat them: Effects of social exclusion on aggressive behavior. *Journal of Personality & Social Psychology*, *81*, 1058-1069.

Twenge, J. M., Liqing, Z., Catanese, K. R., Dolan-Pascoe, B., Lyche, L. F., & Baumeister, R. F. (2007). Replenishing connectedness: Reminders of social activity reduce aggression after social exclusion. *British Journal of Social Psychology*, *46*, 205-224.

Vitaro, F., Brendgen, M., & Tremblay, R. E. (2002). Reactively and proactively aggressive children: Antecedent and subsequent characteristics. *Journal of Child Psychology and Psychiatry*, *43*, 495-505.

Viataro, F., Brendgen, M., & Barker, E. D. (2006). Subtypes of aggressive behavior: A developmental perspective. *International Journal of Behavioral Development, 30*, 12-19.

Voight, A., Hanson, T., O'Malley, M., & Adekanye, L. (2015). The racial school climate gap: Within-school disparities in students' experiences of safety, support, and connectedness. *American Journal of Community Psychology*, *56*, 252-267.

Zullig, K. J., Koopman, T. M., Patton, J. M., & Ubbes, V. A. (2010). School Climate: Historical Review, Instrument Development, and School Assessment. *Journal of Psychoeducational Assessment, 28*, 139–152.

SECTION VII.
PREJUDICE AND DISCRIMINATION

In: Social Psychology and Counseling
Editors: D. A. Kleiber and E. Delgado-Romero
ISBN: 978-1-53616-548-7

Chapter 17

IMPLICATIONS OF RESEARCH ON PREJUDICE FOR COUNSELING PRACTICE

Rebekah Estevez

The American Psychological Association (APA) declares in both its bylaws and ethical codes a commitment to social justice for creating a better world (Vasquez, 2012). From this commitment social justice commitment came numerous policy statements, practice guidelines, and research programs aimed at the reduction of prejudice, discrimination, and injustice in society. APA's Division 17, the Society of Counseling Psychology is among the leading divisions in this regard. As delineated by Delgado-Romero and colleagues (Delgado-Romero, Lau, & Shullman, 2012), the core values of counseling psychology include a holistic and contextualized understanding of the world, the celebration of diversity of human nature, and engagement in social justice pursuits. Thus, research and practice produced by those in this field are closely aligned with the project of advancing equality and fairness for all in modern society.

Similarly, understanding prejudice has historically been a fundamental objective for the field of social psychology (Legault, Green-Demers, & Eadie, 2009). Through the examination of topics such as human aggression, conformity, prejudice, stereotype threat, and social cognition, social psychologists have aided in the collective understanding of the insidious nature and underlying mechanisms of prejudice that pervade modern society. Thus, the field of counseling psychology can learn much from its colleagues in social psychology towards the advancement and expression of its core values. The aim of this chapter is to review recent research in the field of psychology as it relates to prejudice and bias, using Aronson's chapter on prejudice in *The Social Animal* (2012) as a guide for relevant topics. The brief literature review will be examined for the emergence of implications for the field of counseling psychology. Counseling Psychology is an extremely broad specialty within the field of psychology, leading to Counseling Psychologists to integrate research, supervision, education training programs, practice, assessments, and public relation activities (Delgado-Romero et al., 2012). Thus, implications and recommendations drawn from the literature can be applied to any of these areas.

THE DEFINITION AND NATURE OF PREJUDICE

Aronson (2012) defined prejudice as "a hostile or negative attitude toward a distinguishable group on the basis of generalizations derived from faulty or incomplete information" (p. 299). Contributing to its insidious nature is the fact that prejudice contains cognitive, emotional, and behavioral components. Stereotypes constitute the cognitive level process and are defined as the act of "generaliz[ing] characteristics or motives to a group of people" (Aronson, 2012, pg. 300). Discrimination is the behavioral component of prejudice and is defined as action taken against people based on their belonging to a particular social group (Casas, Suzuki, Alexander, & Jackson, 2017). The emotional component is captured in the definition of prejudice.

Multiple Forms of Prejudice

As research on prejudice has continued to unfold, the emergence of multiple forms of this construct led to several important findings that are critical to the field of psychology in general. Aronson asserts that "[prejudice] can be conscious and intentional or unconscious and unintentional. And it can fall somewhere in between these extremes" (2012, p. 302). Research has found that while most people have been culturally conditioned to avoid overt forms of prejudice, they may continue discriminatory behaviors in more subversive ways. In other words, most people are motivated to avoid *explicit bias*, or discriminatory attitudes and beliefs that a person can consciously recognize (Casas, et al., 2017). However, due to the socialization processes, people are also subject to *implicit biases*, which are defined as prejudicial beliefs that work beneath one's consciousness (Spencer, Charbonneau, & Glaser, 2016). Commenting on the insidious nature of implicit biases, counseling psychologist Derald Sue and colleagues note that implicit biases are difficult to "identify, quantify, and therefore rectify because of their subtle, nebulous, and unnamed nature" (Sue et al., 2007, pg. 272).

With respect to the social justice priorities shared by both the social and counseling psychology communities, research shows that the nature of prejudice makes it virtually unchangeable in the face of information alone (Aronson, 2012). This immutability is due in part to the fact that cognition is conservative in nature, making people resistant to changing the nature of their beliefs and values. Further, it is necessary to point out that even psychologists hold some degree of unacknowledged prejudice and bias as products of the same racist macro-level social environment. Guthrie (2004) chronicled the deeply racist history of psychological thinking, ranging from the influence of the pseudo-science of eugenics to the exclusion of ethnic minority viewpoints form mainstream psychology. Even within APA, examples have been reported of ways APA can be perceived as unwelcoming to persons from marginalized communities (APA, 2005). Thus, it is paramount that all research and practicing psychologists be reflective about their own biases and prejudicial beliefs.

APPLICATION TO COUNSELING PSYCHOLOGY

Therapy

Counseling psychologists are committed to the integration of science and practice. A major charge to Counseling Psychologists is to become multiculturally competent in working with diverse populations (APA, 2017). Multicultural competence encompasses two aspects that speak directly to the issue of prejudice and bias: a) awareness of the self as a product of certain cultural values, beliefs, and assumptions, and b) awareness that clients are also products of certain cultural values, beliefs, and assumptions that may be similar or different from that of the clinician (Sue et al., 2007). The failure of counselors to practice in culturally competent ways has been linked to premature termination and underutilization of therapy by persons of color (Sue et al., 2007). Studies on the role of counselor bias and prejudice in the context of therapy have largely focused on what psychiatrist Chester Pierce and later Derald Wing Sue termed *microaggressions*. In his seminal work, Sue defined microaggressions as "brief, commonplace daily verbal, behavioral, or environmental indignities that communicate hostile, derogatory, or negative racial slights and insults toward people of color" (Sue et al., 2007, pg. 278). These acts, commonly experienced in the forms of dismissive snubs, gestures, and tones, are so pervasive in everyday life that they are often dismissed as being innocent when brought to the perpetrator's attention (Sue et al, 2007).[1]

Perhaps one of the most powerful research studies on microaggressions in the context of therapy centers around their impact on the therapeutic relationship. The working alliance has been demonstrated to be incredibly important to the overall success of the therapeutic endeavor. For example, Asay and Lambart (1999) reported that 30% of

[1] It is important to note, however, that the existence of microaggressions is not universally accepted within psychology. Some scholars have experienced serious reservations about the concepts and resultant research and policy (see Lillenfield, 2017).

the total variance in therapy outcome is attributable to the therapeutic relationship. Davis and colleagues (2016) examined microaggressions in the context of the therapeutic alliance and identified them as identity-related ruptures in the therapeutic relationship, which can damage the therapeutic relationship and produce subsequent negative outcomes such as early termination (Davis et al., 2016). Other research has found that microaggressions are correlated negatively with intention to see a counselor in the future, as well as negatively related to perceiving one's therapist as generally competent (Crawford, 2011; Constantine, 2007).

Microaggression research in the context of counseling has extended to sexual minorities and gender-nonconforming clients as well. As with all types of biases, even psychologists who disagree with heterosexism and cissexism (the belief that there are two genders and that sexual and/or partnership activities should occur only between opposite genders) contribute to the social stigmatization of the LGBT population. Indeed, the field of psychology itself has put forth many heterosexist ideas, such as the pathologizing of same-sex attraction until it was removed from the *Diagnostic and Statistical Manual of Mental Disorders* (DSM) III-R in 1987, and the current pathologizing of the transgender identity in the DSM 5. Shelton and Delgado-Romero (2011) found that LGB-identified clients identified subtle and covert forms of heterosexism as microaggressions. Several alarming themes that emerged from focus groups of former clients included making stereotypical assumptions about LGB clients ("You don't look like a lesbian."), and warnings about the dangers of identifying as LGBT ("This lifestyle brings certain problems with it"). Thus, although psychologists may not be aware of the ways in which they convey prejudiced beliefs to clients, the clients in the Shelton and Delgado-Romero study were deeply aware of these messages and in many cases tolerated the prejudice in order get some type of much needed support. Indeed, psychologists may express prejudiced beliefs across a variety of intersectional identities.

Assessment

Psychological assessment is another area in which psychologists can aid or harm clients given the high stakes of most clinical, intellectual and personality assessment. If psychologists fail to consider intersectional aspects of culture in the construction, administration and implementation of psychological testing, then the client may experience a range of negative outcomes (Casas et al., 2017). As stated previously, cultural competence speaks directly to the issue of prejudice and bias as it involves the work of uncovering one's own prejudicial beliefs and working to eradicate them in order to work with diverse populations (Sue et al., 2007). In order to promote a culturally competent clinical interview, the *Cultural Formulation Interview* is included in the *Diagnostic and Statistical Manual 5*, which includes standardized questions aimed at addressing cultural factors related to the client's support and coping systems (American Psychiatric Association, 2013). In diagnosing clients, the writers of the *Handbook of Multicultural Counseling* (Casas et al., 2017) warn practitioners to remember that the etiology of pathology differs among diverse groups, and they urge psychologists to strive to identify possible culture-bound syndromes that can be overlooked or misdiagnosed by Western-focused therapists. These scholars likewise critique the current field of psychological testing, asserting that the most widely used assessments have been the same for 50 years and thus do not reflect the increased emphasis on multicultural concerns in psychology (Casas et al., 2017). As an example, they state that the *Minnesota Multiphasic Personality Inventory*, or MMPI, was developed in a White American context and was not originally designed to be multiculturally sensitive. In order to correct this problem, calls for more research attending to ethnic group differences, the role of language and acculturation, and perceived minority status should be undertaken and included in the construction of all psychological assessments (Casas et. al, 2017). Without doing so, psychologists could be perpetuating biased diagnoses and subsequent interventions which can be harmful to minority clients and extend a long history of the misuse of psychological assessment to the detriment of minority populations (Guthrie, 2002).

Policy and Consultation

Often, counseling psychologists can be found in roles directly related to the creation of law and policy, as well as working as consultants with business and government agencies. For example, counseling psychologists have been called upon to produce research and intervention programs to understand and combat police brutality and the mass incarceration of Black and Brown persons (Lowery, 2016; Spencer, Charbonneau, & Glaser, 2016). Toward an understanding of potential causes of staggering inequality in the criminal justice system, Hall, Hall, and Perry (2016) explored the potential psychological determinants of law enforcement killings of unarmed Black males. Specifically, they examined the role implicit biases and stereotypes might have in the decision of officers to use deadly force in interactions with Black males. Several pervasive, empirically supported stereotypes reported in this review include Black youth as adult-like, Blacks as sub-and superhuman, and Blacks as violent and criminal threats (Hall, Hall & Perry, 2016). Collectively, the authors report that the existence of these stereotypes informs the degree to which Black persons are seen socially as human beings, and subsequently the extent to which their lives matter (Hall, Hall, & Perry, 2016).

Hall and colleagues also reported studies that found pervasive racial bias and stereotypes in the context of use of force scenarios with police trainees. In shooter bias experiments, participants must make rapid decisions about whether to shoot or not shoot

Black or White targets, either holding a gun or non-gun object, via computer simulation. Multiple studies have shown that Whites choose to shoot armed Black men more quickly than armed White men and choose not to shoot unarmed White men more quickly than unarmed Black men, thus falling prey to shooter bias (Hall, Hall, & Perry, 2016). Interestingly, in one replication of this finding, participants were also given the *Modern Racism Scale*, which found that their explicit prejudices against Blacks were unrelated to their actions (Correll, Park, Judd, & Wittenbrink, 2002, as cited in Hall, Hall, & Perry, 2016). This finding points to the enhanced possibility that implicit bias and prejudices, rather than explicit beliefs, are triggered in the decision to use deadly force. This fact is often mitigated by the circumstances around decisions to use deadly force -- which are often ambiguous and intensely stressful, -- that can lead to the brain's reliance on stereotypes in order to make rapid decisions (Casas et al., 2017).

In addition to exploring the pervasive racial stereotypes that might be exercising influence over police decisions to use force in the community, Hall and colleagues report several aspects of the nature of law enforcement culture that can also contribute to the unequal killings of Black men by police officers. These include a) a collective identity orientation, which can lead to a strong "us vs them" worldview, the use of labels such as "suspect" and "perpetrator" which can lead to police viewing civilians as threats to their safety, b) distinct ideology, including adherence to a organizational structure governed by hierarchy, and c) distinct values, such as conformity, loyalty, and adherence to social norms and expectations (Hall, Hall, & Perry, 2016). Interestingly, Hall and colleagues also write about the large reported proportion of officer trainees who hold a high *social dominance orientation* (SDO), which values maintaining hierarchical group norms in interpersonal interactions (Hall, Hall, & Perry, 2016). Importantly, persons with high SDO tend to favor severe punishments when group members who are below them on the hierarchy fail to comply. The SDO orientation, as well as other reported characteristics of law enforcement culture, seem in line with what Aronson terms authoritarian personalities, who in the literature have a greater predisposition toward being prejudiced and endorsing punishment (Aronson, 2012). Persons with authoritarian personalities have rigid belief systems, conventional attitudes, an intolerance of weakness, act in highly punitive and suspicious ways, with a more-than-normal respectful attitude towards authority figures (Aronson, 2012). Aronson reports that persons who are high on authoritarianism show a consistently high degree of prejudice against all minority groups (Aronson, 2012). Taken together, it is possible that the distinct culture of law enforcement is attractive to (and attracts) people with a high SDO and/or authoritarian personalities, traits which are then reinforced the longer the person is employed in the world of law enforcement. Thus, it is possible that the nature of law enforcement in some contexts, individual characteristics of police, and the pervasive racial stereotypes and biases in society collide to create the staggering inequality of police killings of Black males. With this information, counseling psychologists can intervene through the implementation of implicit bias training and the provision of psychological testing to help identify those with high SDO and/or authoritarian personality traits. Further, Hall and colleagues recommend that psychologists continue to help the larger community address racial prejudice at a younger age through research and diversity training initiatives (Hall, Hall, & Perry, 2016).

STEREOTYPES AND STEREOTYPE THREATS

Harkening back to the definition of prejudice, the psychological community has developed a line of research centering on stereotypes and the role they play in areas such as job performance and academic achievement. In fact, a recent article found that more than 300 peer-reviewed studies centered around a phenomenon called *stereotype threat* (Block, Koch, Liberman, Merriweather, & Roberson, 2011). Renowned social psychologist Claude Steele took up the project of examining prejudice and bias in order to make sense of the disparate academic performance gap between Black and White students (Aronson, 2012). While there are a great many historical and societal-based explanations for this gap's existence, Steele argued that they did not account for the gaps' persistence when taking into account high preparation and low preparation (Aronson, 2012). Thus, some psychological process must be occurring that prevents well-prepared, bright, and motivated Black students from performing as well as their White peers when matched in ability and preparation (Aronson, 2012). Through his research, Steele (1997) defined stereotype threat as "the event of a negative stereotype about a group to which one belongs becoming self-relevant, usually as a plausible interpretation for something one is doing...that has relevance to one's self-definition" (pg. 616). Steele argued that stereotype threat is so insidious that a person doesn't have to actually personally believe the stereotype in order to experience the impact of stereotype threat (Steele, 1997). Stereotypes are often setting-specific, meaning that the task of disproving a stereotype associated with one's group is persistent, recurrent, and in some situations, a futile task.

Scholarly research on stereotype threat in both the social psychology and counseling psychology fields has continued Steele's inquiry into the impact of this processes on the lives of students of color. For example, stereotype threat has been found to result in lower performance for women (of all races) on math tests, as well as decreased performance for Black and Latino persons on standardized tests (Block et al., 2011). Due to the requirements of entering college including high scores on standardized tests, this means that students of color are at a disadvantage in college admissions.

Once in undergraduate or graduate school, stereotype threat continues to operate in the lives of students of color and may result in such effects as *the imposter syndrome*. The literature describes the imposter syndrome as being the "subjective experience of perceived intellectual phoniness… [in persons who] despite objective successes, fail to internalize these successes" (Kolligian & Sternberg, 1991, pg. 309). Moxley (2014; this volume) reviews multidisciplinary research on students of color that documents a relationship between intrapersonal and interpersonal experiences within the academy, an environment that is full of stereotypes, microaggressions, and systemic racism which act as barriers to internalizing identification with academic institutions. As a result of this inability to truly believe oneself as capable of being admitted to and graduating from programs in higher education, the presence of imposter syndrome in university students of color has positively predicted psychological distress (Moxley, 2014; see also Joseph & Atilano, this volume.).

Unfortunately, minority students are not the only group of persons who fall victim to stereotype threat and subsequent consequences on performance within the academy. Research has found that in addition to macro-level systemic racism, stereotype threat operates on faculty of color as well (Niemann, 2003). Thus, obstacles faced by faculty of color involve both facing systemic racism, as well as the interactive process of undermining the self through internalized beliefs about incompetence (Niemann, 2003). Thus, both students and faculty of color are at significant disadvantages for succeeding in higher education due to the impacts of stereotype threat and imposter syndrome.

Stereotype threat has likewise been found to operate within work environments outside of higher education, with studies finding that stereotypes attributing a lack of qualities necessary for good leadership success are pervasive for women, Black, and Latino persons when compared to men and White persons (Block et al., 2011). Also, the workplace itself often perpetuates such stereotypes, since in many professions women and people of color are minorities (Block et al., 2011). Further, in some workplace environments, 'token' minority workers are hired, which can lead to increasing the salience of negative stereotypes about these groups to which they belong. This is evidenced by studies showing that being in the demographic minority in a workplace setting conjures stronger experiences of stereotype threat (Block et al., 2011).

Recent psychological research has expanded this line of inquiry into the lives of other marginalized groups, including the LGBT population. Though research suggests an overall trend towards increased social acceptance of LGBT persons, negative stereotypes and stigmatizing beliefs about this subset of society are still prevalent. Collins (2007) was interested in the experience of workplace discrimination for LGBT individuals and produced a dissertation study examining the impact of negative stereotype threat for LGBT workers on subsequent job performance. He found that two dimensions of stereotype threat: stereotyped evaluations (the belief that one's job evaluation will be negatively influenced by their boss' perception of their sexual orientation) and stereotyped perceptions (concerns regarding others' perception of the self due to one's sexual orientation) were positively endorsed to varying degrees as being apparent in the job life of the participants (Collins, 2007). Certain mitigating circumstances, such as the employer having a diversity policy in place but being rarely mentioned, or the employee being "out" to coworkers but it never being talked about, impacted these findings differently for both males and females (Collins, 2007).

Attempts to understand the underlying mechanisms through which stereotype threat operates have found that this process negatively impacts performance through heightened physiological arousal, reduced working memory capacity, impaired self-regulation, and lowered performance expectations (Block et. al, 2011). This means that when minority group members are faced with stereotype threat their cognitive resources used for self-regulation, which include managing task-related worries and negative projections about future performances, are readily depleted (Block et al., 2011). As a result, minority group members can become involved in a cognitive and behavioral cycle of lowered expectations and lowered subsequent performance in their work or academic settings that is difficult to escape. When faced with such circumstances, research has found that individuals respond in several ways including disengagement from activities in which stereotype threat is experienced, deidentifying with the group being stereotyped, and self-sabotaging in ways that would keep them from making appropriate external attributions for their poor performance (Block et al., 2011; see also Moxley and Joseph & Atilano, this volume).

Further Applications to Counseling Psychology

Teaching and the Academy

One of the primary settings within which counseling psychologists work is "the ivory tower" of U.S. higher education. Serving as both undergraduate and graduate-level professors, counseling psychologists are charged with teaching, advising, and mentoring the next generation of scientist-practitioners. The scholarly community's knowledge about the impact of stereotype threat and imposter syndrome can help make sense of the fact that the graduation rates of students of color continue to lag far behind those of their fellow White students (Thomas, 2010). Thus, counseling psychologist professors face the task of keeping bright, motivated minority students in class in order to achieve graduation. Steele (1997) offers some insights into ways professors can achieve this task, which include affirming teacher-student relationships, giving challenging work in the place of remedial tasks, and emphasizing the expandability of intelligence in order to disconfirm the belief that a person's intellectual abilities are fixed and unchangeable. Additionally, McClain (2016) reviewed research that suggested further strategies professors can use to ameliorate the effects of stereotype threat on minority students. These include explicitly discussing stereotype threat with students, holding students to high standards and offering effective feedback, presenting students with similar role models, normalizing the difficulties that come with being in the academy, and the encouragement of mindfulness-based practices throughout one's academic career (McClain, 2016; see also, Steele, 1997, on "Wise schooling").

Research

Often, counseling psychologists' roles within the academy include both teaching and the production and dissemination of scholarly research. Using a social justice orientation and knowledge about processes such as stereotype threat and imposter syndrome in education, counseling psychologists in the academy can use research as a means to address educational and health inequity. In addition to traditional quantitative methods of research (which also have a history of racism; see Guthrie, 2002), faculty can embrace a variety of methods and theories to competently study minority populations. For example, qualitative research has risen in popularity and is seen as a potentially culturally competent method to study minority populations (see Delgado-Romero, Singh & de los Santos, 2019). Qualitative research can be guided by critical theories that presuppose the ubiquitous nature of racism. For example, Moxley (2014) writes about the potential usefulness and applicability of critical race theory to the graduate education experiences of minority students. Indeed, critical race theory's overall goal applied to graduate education is to "develop…[strategies] that accounts for the role of race and racism in US graduate education...toward the elimination of racism as part of a larger goal of eliminating forms of subordination (Solorzano & Yosso, 2001, p. 472; see also Moxley, this volume). Counseling psychologists can use critical race research strategies such as centering the voices of the oppressed in research, soliciting and disseminating counter narratives, and utilizing scholarly work to uncover places ripe for change through activism (Denzin, 2016).

CONCLUSION

Counseling and social psychologists typically act as agents of change. Both the social and counseling psychology fields have produced a robust body of knowledge about prejudice, biases, and their seemingly ubiquitous manifestations and implications. As scientist-practitioners, counseling psychologists are charged with integrating science and practice to work towards social justice and equality in society through practice, such as engaging in therapy, consultation, and assessment activities. Thus, counseling psychologists' activities and goals can be informed by the research and investigations conducted by those in social psychology who have a long history of studying important contemporary and controversial processes such as prejudice. Together, these domains of psychology can and should work hand in hand towards one of the main aims of psychology: a commitment to social justice and a better world.

REFERENCES

American Council on Education. (2011). *Minorities in higher education: Twenty-fourth status report: 2011 supplement*. Retrieved from http://diversity.ucsc.edu/resources/images/ace_report.pdf.

American Psychiatric Association. (2013). *Diagnostic and statistical manual of mental disorders: DSM-5*. Washington, D.C: American Psychiatric Association.

American Psychological Association. 2017. *Multicultural Guidelines: An Ecological Approach to Context, Identity, and Intersectionality*. Retrieved from: http://www.apa.org/about/policy/multicultural-guidelines.pdf.

American Psychological Association. (2005a). *APA Presidential Task Force on Enhancing Diversity: Final Report*. Washington, DC: Author. Retrieved from http://www.apa.org/pi/oema/resources/taskforce-report .pdf.

Aronson, E. (2012). *The social animal.* (11th ed). New York: Worth.

Asay, T. P., & Lambert, M. J. (1999). The empirical case for the common factors in therapy: Quantitative findings. In M. A. Hubble, B. L. Duncan, S. D. Miller, M. A. Hubble (Ed), B. L. Duncan (Ed), & S. D. Miller (Ed) (Eds.), *The heart and soul of change: What works in therapy.* (pp. 23–55). Washington, DC, US: American Psychological Association. https://doi.org/10.1037/11132-001.

Block, C. J., Koch, S. M., Liberman, B. E., Merriweather, T. J., & Roberson, L. (2011).

Contending with stereotype threat at work: A model of long-term responses 1Ψ7. *The Counseling Psychologist*, *39*(4), 570-600.

Casas, J. M., Suzuki, L. A., Alexander, C. M., & Jackson, M. A. (2017). *Handbook of multicultural counseling*. Los Angeles: SAGE.

Collins, G. M. (2007). Encountering stereotype threat in the workplace: how lesbian, gay, bisexual, and transgender employees meet the challenge of negative stereotyping.

Constantine, M. G. (2007). Racial microaggressions against African American clients in cross-racial counseling relationships. *Journal of Counseling Psychology, 54*, 1–16. doi:10.1037/0022-0167.54.1.1.

Correll, J., Park, B., Judd, C. M., & Wittenbrink, B. (2002). The police officer's dilemma: Using ethnicity to disambiguate potentially threatening individuals. *Journal of Personality and Social Psychology, 83*, 1314-1329.

Crawford, E. P. (2011). *Stigma, racial microaggressions, and acculturation strategies as predictors of likelihood to seek counseling among Black college students.* (Unpublished doctoral dissertation). Oklahoma State University, Stillwater, OK.

Davis, D. E., DeBlaere, C., Brubaker, K., Owen, J., Jordan, T. A., Hook, J. N., & Van Tongeren, D. R. (2016). Microaggressions and perceptions of cultural humility in counseling. *Journal of Counseling & Development*, *94*, 483-493.

Delgado-Romero, E. A., Lau, M. Y. & Shulman, S. (2012). The society of counseling psychology: Historical values, themes, and patterns viewed from the American Psychological Association presidential podium. In N. Fouad, J. Carter & L. Subich (Eds.) *APA Handbook of Counseling Psychology: Vol. 1 Theories, Research, and Methods*. Washington, DC: APA Books.

Delgado-Romero, E. A., Singh, A. & De Los Santos, J. (2018). *Cuéntame*: The Promise of Qualitative Research with Latinx Populations. *Journal of Latina/o Psychology*, *6*, 318-328. DOI: 10.1037/lat0000123.

Denzin, N. K. (2016). Critical qualitative inquiry. *Qualitative Inquiry, 23*, 8-16.

Guthrie, R. V. (2004). *Even the rat was white: A historical view of psychology*. Boston, MA: Pearson Education.

Hall, A. V., Hall, E. V., & Perry, J. L. (2016). Black and blue: Exploring racial bias and law enforcement in the killings of unarmed black male civilians. *American Psychologist*, *71*(3), 175.

Kolligian Jr, J., & Sternberg, R. J. (1991). Perceived fraudulence in young adults: Is there an 'Imposter Syndrome'?. *Journal of Personality Assessment*, *56*, 308-326.

Legault, L., Green-Demers, I., & Eadie, A. L. (2009). When internalization leads to automatization: The role of self-determination in automatic stereotype suppression and implicit prejudice regulation. *Motivation and Emotion*, *33*, 10-24.

Lilienfeld, S. O. (2017). Microaggressions: Strong claims, inadequate evidence. *Perspectives on Psychological Science*, *12*, 138-169.

Lowery, Wesley. (2016, July 11). Aren't more white people than black people killed by police? Yes, but no. *The Washington Post.* Retrieved from https://www.washingtonpost.com/news/post-nation/wp/2016/07/11/arent-more-white-people-than-black-people-killed-by-police-yes-but-no/?utm_term=e00396150fd2.

McClain, R. A. (2016). Helping our students reach their full potential: The insidious consequences of ignoring stereotype threat. *Rutgers Race & L. Rev.*, *17*, 1.

Moxley, R. E. (2014*). Stereotype threat, microaggressions, and the imposter syndrome, oh my! Minority student resilience in academia.* Unpublished doctoral dissertation. University of Georgia, Athens, GA

Niemann, Y. F. (2016). The social ecology of tokenism in higher education. *Peace Review*, *28*(4), 451–458.

Prasad, P. (2005). *Crafting qualitative research : Working in the postpositivist traditions*. Armonk, N.Y.: M. E. Sharpe.

Shelton, K., & Delgado-Romero, E. A. (2011). Sexual orientation microaggressions: the experience of lesbian, gay, bisexual, and queer clients in psychotherapy. *Journal of Counseling Psychology*, *58*, 210-221.

Solorzano, D., & Yosso, T. J. (2001). Critical race and LatCrit theory and method: Counter-storytelling—Chicana and Chicano graduate school experiences. *International Journal of Qualitative Studies in Education*, *14*, 471-495. doi:10.1080/09518390110063365.

Spencer, K. B., Charbonneau, A. K., & Glaser, J. (2016). Implicit bias and policing. *Social and Personality Psychology Compass*, *10*, 50-63. doi:10.1111/spc3.12210.

Steele, C. M. (1997). A threat in the air: How stereotypes shape intellectual identity and performance. *American Psychologist*, *52*, 613-629.

Sue, D. W., Capodilupo, C. M., Torino, G. C., Bucceri, J. M., Holder, A., Nadal, K. L., & Esquilin, M. (2007). Racial microaggressions in everyday life: implications for clinical practice. *American Psychologist*, *62*, 271-284.

Thomas, Evan. (2010, Feb 2). Why minority students don't graduate from college. *Newsweek.* Retrieved from http://www.newsweek.com/why-minority-students-dont-graduate-college-75143.

Vasquez, M. J. (2012). Psychology and social justice: Why we do what we do. *American Psychologist*, *67*, 337-346.

In: Social Psychology and Counseling
Editors: D. A. Kleiber and E. Delgado-Romero
ISBN: 978-1-53616-548-7

Chapter 18

NOT BY THE JOB, NOR THE DAY, BUT BY MY LIFE: BLACK STUDENT RESILIENCE IN ACADEMIA

Reisha E. Moxley

The contemporary discourse on systemic impediments to the successful matriculation and graduation of students of color, particularly Black-identified students, in academe is now quite extensive (Boysen, Vogel, Cope & Hubbard, 2009; Cokley, McClain, Enciso, & Martinez, 2013; Dortch, 2016; Cokely, et al., 2017; Ewing, Richardson, James-Myers & Russell, 1996; Lewis, Mendenhall, Harwood & Huntt, 2016; Solórzano, Ceja & Yosso, 2000). In this chapter I will examine the impact of racial stereotype threat, microaggressions and the subsequent internalization of these prejudicial social phenomena, commonly referred to as "the impostor phenomenon" (Clance, 1985; Clance & Imes, 1978; Stone et al., 2018), within the academic domain, including a culturally-informed model of the phenomenon for Black graduate students in particular. Suggestions for and examples of circumvention of these obstructions through teaching strategies framed by critical race theory will also be explored.

The examination of these dynamics will be facilitated thorough a narrative approach, counter-storytelling, that allows for the telling of personal experiences from those on the margins of the social domain being studied (Delgado, 1993). This approach is further informed by a critical race philosophical perspective and is useful as "a tool for analyzing and challenging the stories of those in power" (Solórzano & Yosso, 2001, pp. 475). This challenge is facilitated by the presentation of experiences counter to traditionally published accounts of more dominant group members. This approach will be explicated through an analysis of my own experience as a former graduate student and current psychologist working in an academic professional setting. The narrative presented in this article is a personal one; it details one specific experience I had as a Black woman enrolled in a graduate training program at a large southeastern, predominately White institution (PWI). I begin my narrative with a historical context that will serve to highlight the potency of impostor feelings I had studying within a PWI in the United States.

THE COUNTER-NARRATIVE: A STRANGER IN THE HOUSE

> [Billy Hull] was for years the [enslaved] college carpenter. Dr. Church stopped at [Billy's] bench once and watching him push his plane said, Billy, what makes you work so slowly? Stopping to spit on his hands — a habit he always had before speaking — Billy replied, Mass Church, I am not working by the job, nor by the day; but by my life (Hull, 1906, p. 174).

The above quote is taken from a historical account of an enslaved man, toiling as a carpenter for the university granting me access to a doctoral education over 150 years later. Billy, the enslaved Black man is being casually observed by a White man affiliated with the university and asked why he seemed to work so slowly. Billy, in tendering a response, referred to the White man as "Mass," short for "Master," which was a colloquialism often used by the enslaved to denote a White man's authority, whether the owner of slaves or not, during the antebellum period in the southern United States. Billy, with all due respect to his White male authority figure, lets Dr. Church know that the pace of his work could not be hastened by the near completion of the task itself, nor with anticipation of the close of a work day. Billy let 'Mass' Church know that his labor, and by extension his enslavement, would not be complete, as far as Billy knew, until he drew his last breath.

While I did not know this bit of institutional history while enrolled as a doctoral student at this same university well over a century later, I certainly felt the weight of this history each day that I went to class. The weight of the historical context of Billy's labor and our shared racial/ethnic background was not always crushing, and yet on some days, it felt as though I could barely breathe from the pressure of it. I did not know, at the time, the extent to which I internalized this weighted pressure. I do not think there was one day, over the course of my graduate training or any formative training experience up until that point, during which I stopped to consider the historical context in which I studied. Yes, I did study aspects of history, mostly facts and figures to satisfy tests purportedly designed to assess my ability to grasp advanced concepts, or more accurately, tests designed to assess my ability to retain and recall information. Very rarely, if ever, did these tests assess my awareness, not of facts and figures, but of blood and bones. Particularly the blood and bones of those that toiled before me, who were never granted access to the education I sought, if they were even regarded as more than 3/5ths a human being.

I am the great-great granddaughter of slaves. This subordinate status and those that followed during the Gilded Age, the Progressive Era and later in the Jim Crow south, did not diminish the value of education in my family. If anything, status as a slave, then a freedman, then a 'Colored' and next a Negro, catapulted the value of education in my family context. For those who could not obtain formal education, they vicariously did so through their sacrifice of time and resources so that a chosen few, could. My great-grandmother went to normal school and eventually taught grade school to Black children in her west Tennessee farm community. Although my grandmother did not go to college, her daughter, my mother, did and later earned a master's degree. Her daughter (the writer) went on to earn a doctoral degree and has not yet left the hallowed (and sometimes seemingly haunted) halls of academia. I currently work in support of students' mental and emotional health as they pursue the very education only the privileged in my family were able to obtain. While my perspective has certainly changed since my own period as a graduate student, I still recall the experiences that elicited impostor feelings, survivor's guilt, compounded by the pressure to succeed, which often culminated in crippling self-doubt and fear. This period in pursuit of higher education was marked, paradoxically, with as many microaggressions and macroassaults (See Sue and Sue, 2008, for elaboration of the microaggression perspective.), as it was appropriate challenge and support. One particular experience highlights the interplay of the aforementioned and taught me how self-advocacy often starts with a desire to be seen and to feel connected. This experience taught me that self-advocacy has the power to extend beyond the individual to inspire change by and for others at the broadest systemic levels.

This particular part of my narrative account begins during a site visit in which a national professional organization gathered data to inform the renewal of accreditation for the academic program in which I was enrolled. It was during this site visit that a wayward comment by a seemingly well-meaning member of the accreditation committee sent shock waves through the small group of students and faculty gathered to hear the results of a two-day inquiry. This particular committee member, one of three older White men, was designated as the authoritative representative examining the status of multicultural and diversity related matters in my program. He stated, during his closing remarks, that while there had been a great deal of progress made to address the matriculation and subsequent needs of students of color in the program, "if the faculty *really* wanted to attract the *star minority students*, they must consider different recruitment strategies." As I looked around the room for an indication that someone – anyone – had heard the statement and internalized it in the way that I had, I noticed, first, the diverse group of talented students and faculty present in the room. As I continued to search the room for acknowledgment and connection, I noticed next the visible identities of the site visitors – three older White men - and particularly the visitor charged with judging my program's efforts related to "diversity matters." While my recognition of the phenotype of the visitors was fleeting in that moment, it occurred to me much later that the power bestowed upon these White male visitors by the accrediting body went well beyond their professional affiliation. Their real and perceived power spoke directly to the intricacies of the dynamics they were charged with judging. Finally, during the last moments of my search around the room, I noticed downward glances and uncomfortable squirms from my White counterparts before I locked eyes with several Black women, who were fellow students and my friends. In the relatively brief moment of connection and eye contact with these women, I was able to receive and convey feelings of outrage and hurt, later confirmed by our heated discussion at the culmination of the event. As we processed what the site visitor could have possibly meant by "star minority students" and the implication that our hard working and successful group of "minority students" where not 'star material,' a familiar feeling rushed over me. In that moment, I acknowledged feelings of shame and guilt and an odd sense of relief as I recognized that I had finally been discovered and exposed as a fraud. I considered my most salient identities as a Black woman, reared in the southern United States by a middle-class family who valued education, but had limited access to the financial resources required to obtain higher education. During this period of my life, I did not see my status as the great-great granddaughter of slaves as a particular point of privilege. Instead, I compared my family history to those of my White counterparts and considered the results. While we were granted access to the same rooms, I often felt as though I came up short in these shared spaces. And it was this White man, the designated authoritative representative of the governing body of my profession who was able to, in only two days, discover what my faculty members had not seen in several years of close work with me: I was not a 'star student;' in fact, I was not even a 'star *minority* student.' I struggled to keep my composure as I simultaneously and sincerely informed my colleagues that this statement was likely not in reference to them. Although I did not say it, I knew that the comments must have been informed by tangible data. Because of the respect I held for my colleagues and their talents and, quite frankly, the unchallenged deference I had for authority figures, particularly White men in authority, during that time in my life, I suspected that the tangible data and the subsequent comment were likely informed by and directed at me.

Later, in an effort to quell my growing discomfort, I took to the literature in another attempt to make a connection, this time with scholars who may have endured the indignity of what I had internalized as a very personal indecent exposure of my flaws. What I found outraged and encouraged me. It was as if the authors that I found had not only suffered the indignity of that experience with me, but that they were there in that moment, consoling me and providing invaluable support through shared experience as I read,

> Perhaps the most salient issue that the participants in this study raised was the concern about being viewed as unintelligent. This has long been an issue for Blacks in the United States. Beginning with slavery, Blacks were depicted as a race with an inability to learn who were inferior to Whites. In the academy, women of color, despite their advanced educations, are still subject to this racist ideology used to subordinate Blacks and other people of color (Woods, 2011).

As my search continued, I found,

> Women of Color in the academy are not commonplace we are an aberration – outliers. We often ask ourselves, how is it that I 'arrived' when so many others like me haven't? Will someone discover that a mistake was made, and I don't really belong here? How long will it take for 'them' to realize that I am an impostor, an 'other,' I'm not 'one of them? (Solórzano & Yosso, 2001, p. 485).

As I considered the latter authors and their extensive body of work on critical race theory and the impact of racism, microaggressions and systemic oppression on the educative experiences of graduate students of color (Solórzano, 1993, 1994, 1998; Solórzano, Ceja & Yosso, 2000; Solórzano & Yosso, 2001), I begin to reassess my feelings of inadequacy as I considered that perhaps I was not an impostor. I began to recognize that this experience and my subsequent reactions had, in fact, placed me in very good company. While my initial search was for narrative accounts, subsequent searches led and continue to lead me to extant empirical literature on the structural components and subsequent individual and group implications of microaggressions, impostor phenomenon and stereotype threat in higher education.

ACADEMIC IMPEDIMENTS TO SUCCESS FOR STUDENTS OF COLOR

In studying impediments to the intellectual functioning of African American students in the collegiate environment, Steele and Aronson (1995) define *stereotype threat* and posit this social-psychological predicament as a likely contributor to research that highlights the underachievement phenomenon in African American students as compared to their White counterparts. Specifically, the authors define stereotype threat as a self-evaluative "risk of confirming, as self-characteristic, a negative stereotype about one's group" (Steele & Aronson, 1995, pp. 797). One of the most compelling components of stereotype threat, particularly as it relates to minority students' self-esteem and identification within their academic environments, is that the existence and activation of a widely known negative stereotype frustrates a minority student's intellectual abilities during diagnostic ability tasks. This frustration becomes apparent and maladaptive as the student attempts to divide cognitive resources between the intellectual task(s) at hand and the anxiety aroused by the potential that their performance may inadvertently conform to stereotypes in the eyes of others, and paradoxically, in their own eyes (Steele, 1997; Steele & Aronson, 1995).

Research suggests that the experience of stereotype threat adversely impacts minority students as it can generate fear of being reduced to a negative stereotype about these students' racial/ethnic (and in some cases gender) groups, without regard to individual characteristics that disprove these ill-informed assumptions (Cokley, 2002; Steele, 1997; Steele & Aronson, 1995). An unfortunate extension of the activation of stereotype threat is its tendency to affect the vanguard of students of color within the academic domain as those students with the skills and self-confidence to have developed identification within their academic fields begin to question the merit of their own positions within these competitive environments (Aronson, 2012; Steele, 1997). This internalization process often leads to negative academic outcomes fueled by microaggressions and perceived fraudulence, or impostor phenomenon, as a member of the identified academic domain.

Impostor Phenomenon, Microaggressions and Stereotype Threat in Academe

The impostor phenomenon is a construct derived from personality research on perceived fraudulence (Clance, 1985; Clance & Imes, 1978). It is described as a "subjective experience of perceived intellectual phoniness that is held by certain high-achieving adults who, despite their objective successes, fail to internalize these successes" (Kolligian & Sternberg, 1991, pg. 309). Kolligian and Sternberg found that this perception of fraudulence was comprised of a "complex interplay of inauthentic ideation, depressive tendencies, self-criticism, social anxiety, high self-monitoring skills and strong pressures to excel and achieve (pg. 323)." These authors explored this phenomenon in primarily White undergraduate students at an Ivy League institution over forty years ago. Since that time, there has been a multidisciplinary study of imposter phenomenon in students of color, particularly at the graduate level (Cokley, McClain, Enciso, & Martinez, 2013; Dortch, 2016; Cokely, et al., 2017). These lines of inquiry examine the impact of intrapersonal experiences coupled with minority students' interpersonal experiences within the social environments in which they study. Unfortunately, this social environment is replete with racism, racial and gender microaggressions, stereotyping and systemic barriers that continue to pose an impediment to identification with academic institutions, thusly posing a threat to successful matriculation and graduation (Cokley, McClain, Enciso & Martinez, 2013; Solórzano, 1998; Solórzano & Yosso, 2001; Steele, 1997). Cokley et al., (2013) found that impostor feelings in minority students significantly predicted psychological distress and was a much stronger predictor of that distress than the stress generally associated with being a minority student alone (pp. 91). Further research on the experiences of minority students in higher education highlight racial and gender *microaggressions*. Pierce (1974) described these racial and gender assaults to dignity and hope as an incessant, cumulative and under-researched social problem (Solórzano, 1998).

Microaggressions "are brief and commonplace daily verbal or behavioral indignities, whether intentional or unintentional, that communicate hostile, derogatory, or negative racial slights and insults that potentially have a harmful or unpleasant psychological impact on the target person or group" (Sue & Sue, 2008, pg. 110).

Sue and Sue (2008) suggest that there are four assumptions that can be made about the nature of microaggressions: That they (1) are typically unintentional and indirect, (2) occur in a context in which alternate explanations are possible, (3) are emblematic of unconscious biased beliefs and/or attitudes, and (4) "are more likely to occur when people pretend not to notice differences, thereby denying that race, gender, or sexual orientation had anything to do with their actions" (pp. 110). These authors go on to describe three specific types of microaggressions, the most salient, in regard to the current chapter, is defined as a microinsult. Sue and Sue (2008) define a *microinsult* as "an unintentional behavior or verbal comment that conveys rudeness or insensitivity or demeans a person's racial heritage identity…" (pp. 111).

A closer look at the narrative account provided in this chapter will provide practical examinations of the experience of a specific type of racial/gender microaggression, a microinsult, and the subsequent impact on me, a female student of color. While the site visitor's comment did not appear to be informed by a conscious effort to undermine the academic merit and potential of the minority students in the program, his identity as an older White man in an official capacity as a representative of the governing body of a national professional organization presented a complicated confluence of power, prejudice and inferential racism (Hartlep, 2013). This confluence was implied by the notion that the faculty had not succeeded in attracting 'star' or model minority students. Inferential racism, according to Prashad (2000) entails a naturalized presentation of remarks, "whether 'factual' or 'fictional,' that have racist premises and propositions inscribed in turn as a set of unquestioned assumptions" (pp. 170) and are typically 'invisible' because it is not considered offensive. In this case, the 'star minority' assertion implied that there were some undetermined and/or unacknowledged criteria catapulting certain students into 'star status' that eluded the minority students currently enrolled in the program. This inference is the hallmark of microaggressive sentiment and is felt most keenly by those in the perceived power down position, e.g., cisgender female identifying students, LGBT+ students and or/students of color. These types of comments and experiences often induce the experience of stereotype threat in the aforementioned student populations as they grapple with the allegation of inability presented by a powerful member of their identified academic/professional domain (Steele & Aronson, 1997).

Stereotype threat has been described as the experience of extra pressures that can potentially affect the performance and academic identities of African Americans and women in White male dominated branches of science, technology, engineering and mathematics (Steele, 1998). While the activation of stereotype threat has been proven to significantly diminish the intellectual abilities of racial/ethnic and gender minority students on specific diagnostic tasks (Spencer, Steele & Quinn, 1999; Steele; 1995; Steele & Aronson, 1997; Stoet & Geary, 2012), the most distressing component appears to be that the threat of being stereotyped only impairs the student's academic performance if that student cares enough about the performance domain to be upset by the prospect of being negatively stereotyped in it (Steele, 1998, pp. 681). That is, the threat of being negatively stereotyped is not particularly menacing to students who do not have a vested interest or sincere connection and identification with the environment in which they are being judged. In my case, the investment of nearly a decade of graduate study and practical experience, as well as my conformity to a professional identity in an associated field of study left me particularly vulnerable to, and perhaps more perceptive of, negative evaluations of my presence in the academic environment. This threat contributed to a brief dis-identification with my academic program as there appeared to be a glaring event, albeit precipitated by an outsider, that confirmed impostor feelings which felt incessantly perched in wait to threaten my self-esteem in the academic domain.

In an effort to affect change and circumvent the negative experiences posing a constant and real threat to the matriculation of students of color, critical race theorists, psychologists and educators have considered practical tools that will potentially affect change at the individual, group and systemic levels (Solórzano, 1998; Solórzano & Yosso, 2001; Steele, 1997; Taylor & Antony, 2000). This change is grounded in social justice advocacy (Solórzano & Yosso, 2001) and is described in greater detail in the following section.

Critical Race Theory as a Tool for Change

In describing the utility of critical race theory and its applicability to graduate education, Solórzano and Yosso (2001) explain that the overall goal is "to develop a theoretical, conceptual, methodological and pedagogical strategy that accounts for the role of race and racism in US graduate education and works toward the elimination of racism as part of a larger goal of eliminating forms of subordination..." (p. 472). Towards this end, the authors posit five themes that are the foundation for basic perspectives, research methods and pedagogy in education which are: (1) the centrality of race and racism and their intersectionality with other forms of subordination; (2) the challenge to dominant ideology; (3) the commitment to social justice; (4) the centrality of experiential knowledge and (5) the transdisciplinary perspective.

While an exhaustive explanation of critical race theory is beyond the scope of the current chapter, the most salient themes as it relates to the experience of microaggressions, stereotype threat and the impostor phenomenon in students of color are important to consider in relation to the personal account shared earlier in this chapter. When considering the centrality of race and historical racism in US academic settings, they are almost impossible to examine without consideration of other forms of subordination. With regards to the experience of microaggressions, stereotype threat and the imposture phenomenon in the academic setting, the intersection of race and gender has been found to be a central factor as female students and students of color are consistently identified as the most vulnerable to these experiences (Solórzano & Yosso, 2001; Spencer, Steele & Quinn, 1999; Steele; 1995; Steele & Aronson, 1997; Stoet & Geary, 2012). In order to gain a critical understanding of racial and gender subordination in education, Solórzano and Yosso (2001) explain the importance of the experiential knowledge of female students and students of color. The authors explain that research methodology that centralizes personal accounts and narratives are critical to the understanding and analysis of marginalized voices. Towards this end, Solórzano and Yosso (2001) explain that critical race theory in education demonstrates a commitment to social justice as it leads to the elimination of racism, sexism and poverty and simultaneously towards the empowerment of underrepresented groups in academia.

In his analysis of the ways in which stereotype threat shapes the intellectual identity and performance of female students and students of color, Steele (1997) introduces the modification of situational factors in the academic environment as a method to reduce or eliminate the threat. Specifically, Steele posits that "wise" schooling methods (a term the author explained was derived from sexual minorities in the 1950s to designate allies) offers an opportunity to offset the activation of stereotype threat for students most susceptible to its impact. For domain-identified students, Steele (1997) suggests the following wise strategies: (1) Optimistic teacher-student relationships, where intentional effort is made in the creation and development of potential-affirming relationships between faculty/authority figures within the academic environment and the students at the greatest risk for experiencing stereotype threat; (2) challenge over remediation, where students who are underperforming are given challenging work (with respect to their current skill level) rather than remedial assignments, in an effort to convey respect for their potential; (3) stressing the expandability of intelligence, where students are encouraged to view human intelligence as a trait that is responsive to experience and training as opposed to being fixed or limited based on racial and or gender identification. Steele (1997) further explains that when creating opportunities to implement the final wise strategy, stressing the expandability of intelligence, it is most prudent to consider whether or not the student identifies with the environment in which she studies. Steele proposes three specific strategies for emphasizing the dynamic nature of intelligence for those whom he defined as "domain-identified students" (p. 625). These strategies are: (1)

affirming domain belongingness whereby direct affirmation of the student's belonginess is based on their intellectual potential; (2) valuing multiple perspectives which is defined as the employment of strategies that deliberately place value on both academic substance and the academic culture in which said substance is considered; and (3) identification of role models whom are successful members from the stereotyped group within the academic domain. Taylor and Antony (2000) expanded the conceptual framework and practicality of Steele's wise schooling strategies by conducting a study that examined the experience of stereotype threat in African American students with wise methods as an intervention. The results of the study offered early support for wise interventions as tools for "successful socialization of African American graduate students in education" (p. 194).

Revisiting the Narrative: A Stranger No More

When taken together, focused interventions framed by a critical race perspective and informed by wise strategies can facilitate the disruption of the internalization of microagressions that often contribute to activation of stereotype threat and impostor feelings for Black students studying in predominantly White academic spaces. As I reflect on the events shared in my narrative account in this chapter, particularly the site visitor's comment about successful recruitment of "star minority students," I recognize and appreciate the immediate and sincere actions of influential members of my program. These actions offer a case example of several wise schooling strategies, particularly optimistic teacher-student relationships, affirmation of domain belongingness, valuation of multiple perspectives and the presence and accessibility of role models.

Directly after the incident, a listserv email was sent on behalf of the faculty denouncing the derogatory statement and encouraging all students. As a result of this email, many students agreed to formulate a response addressing the statement and its impact on the student body. One of the most heartening aspects of this faculty and student reaction is that the individuals who volunteered were representative of our entire student body and consisted of students with various gender, sexual and racial/ethnic identities. This show of support and camaraderie captured many of Steele's wise strategies and served to facilitate re-identification with my academic program and my professional discipline as a whole. The experience and subsequent reactions added a collective fuel and a renewed passion for social justice advocacy on behalf of the students enrolled in the program at the time of the incident and those potentially impacted by the triple threat of microaggressions, stereotype threat and the impostor phenomenon, as we navigated the hallowed halls of academia. An excerpt from the correspondence sent on behalf of my program's faculty captures this sentiment as it affirmed my subjective experience and simultaneously moved our student body toward collective action:

I want to address a comment made during the site visit exit interview [regarding] going after the "star minority students." I realize that this comment was inappropriate and offensive to all of us. I don't know what exactly [was] meant by the comment, but I know he didn't get that from our faculty. You cannot on the one hand celebrate our rich diversity and then tell us there are better minority students out there. That's clearly wrong. Our strength is our diversity; no student is "less than" any other, and certainly not on the basis of gender, race, ability, sexual orientation, religious belief or non-belief or any other aspect of diversity. We ALREADY have stars in the program. The outcomes support this, our interactions support this, and our basic respect for each other supports the fact that once you are in the program, we view you all as stars. I'm deeply sorry that a very important and positive message was undermined by a microaggression. I also appreciate all the constructive criticism I heard today. I'm glad we can identify ways to make the program better. Here is what I propose we do about the comment…

REFERENCES

Aronson, E. (2012). *The social animal* (11th ed.). New York, NY: Worth.

Boysen, G. A., Vogel, D. L., Cope M. A. & Hubbard, A. (2009). Incidents of bias in college classrooms: Instructor and student perceptions. *Journal of Diversity in Higher Education*, *2*, 219-231.

Clance, P. R. (1985). *The imposter phenomenon.* Atlanta: Peachtree.

Clance, P. R. & Imes, S. A. (1978). The impostor phenomenon in high achieving women: Dynamics and therapeutic intervention. *Psychotherapy: Theory, Research and Practice*, *15*, 241-247.

Cokley, K. (2002). Ethnicity, gender, and academic self-concept: A preliminary examination of academic disidentification and implications for psychologists. *Culture, Diversity and Ethnic Minority Psychology*, *8*(4) 378-388.

Cokley, K., McClain, S., Enciso, A. & Martinez, M. (2013). An examination of the impact of minority status stress and impostor feelings on the mental health of diverse ethnic minority college students. *Journal of Multicultural Counseling & Development*, *41*(2), 82-95.

Cokely, K., Smith, L., Bernard, D., Hurst, A., Jackson, S., Stone, S., Awosogba, O., Saucer, C., Bailey, M. & Roberts, D. (2017). Impostor feelings as a moderator and mediator of the relationship between perceived discrimination and mental health among racial/ethnic minority college students. *Journal of Counseling Psychology*, *64*, 141-154.

Delgado, R. (1993). On telling stories in school: A reply to Farber and Sherry. *Vanderbilt Law Review*, *46*, 665-676.

Dortch, D. (2016). The strength from within: A phenomenological study examining the academic self-efficacy of African American women in doctoral studies. *Journal of Negro Education*, *85*, 350-364.

Ewing, K. M., Richardson, T. Q., James-Myers, L. & Russell, R. K. (1996). The relationship between racial identity attitudes worldview and African American graduate students' experience of the impostor phenomenon. *Journal of Black Psychology*, *22*, 53-66.

Hartlep, N. (2013). *Model minority stereotype: Demystifying Asian American success*. Charlotte, NC: Information Age Pub.

Hull, A. L. (1906). *The annals of Athens*. Athens, GA: Athens Banner Job Office. Retrieved from https://digihum.libs.uga.edu.

Kolligian, Jr. J. & Sternberg, R. J. (1991). Perceived fraudulence in young adults: Is there an 'Imposter Syndrome'? *Journal of Personality Assessment*, *56*(2), 308.

Lewis, J., Mendenhall, R., Harwood, S. A. & Huntt, M. B. (2016). "Ain't I a woman?" Perceived gendered racial microaggressions experienced by Black women. *Counseling Psychologist*, *44*, 758-780.

Prashad, V. (2000). *The karma of brown folk*. Minneapolis, MN: University of Minnesota Press.

Solórzano, D. (1993). *The career paths of Chicana and Chicano doctorates: A study of Ford Foundation minority fellows in California*. Berkely, CA: The California Policy Seminar.

Solórzano, D. (1994). The Baccalaureate organs of Chicana and Chicano doctorates n the Physical, Life and Engineering Sciences: 1980-1990. *Journal of Women and Minorities in Science and Engineering*, *1*, 253-272.

Solórzano, D. (1998) Critical race theory, race and gender microaggressions, and the experience of Chicana and Chicano scholars. *International Journal of Qualitative Studies in Education*, *11*(1), 121-136, DOI: 10.1080/095183998236926.

Solórzano, D., Ceja, M. & Yosso, T. (2000). Critical race theory, racial microaggressions, and campus racial climate: The experiences of African American college students. *Journal of Negro Education*, *69*, 60-73.

Solórzano, D. & Yosso, T. J. (2001). Critical race and LatCrit theory and method: Counter-storytelling—Chicana and Chicano graduate school experiences. *International Journal of Qualitative Studies In Education*, *14*, 471-495. doi:10.1080/09518390110063365.

Spencer, S. J., Steele, C. M. & Quinn, D. M. (1999). Stereotype threat and women's math performance. *Journal of Experimental Social Psychology*, *35*, 4-28.

Steele, C. M. (1997). A threat in the air: How stereotypes shape intellectual identity and performance. *American Psychologist*, *52*, 613-629.

Steele, C. M. (1998). Stereotyping and its threat are real. *American Psychologist*, *53*, 680-681.

Steele, C. M. & Aronson, J. (1995). Stereotype threat and the intellectual test performance of African Americans. *Journal of Personality and Social Psychology*, *69*(5), 797-811.

Stoet, G. & Geary, D. C. (2012). Can stereotype threat explain the gender gap in mathematics performance and achievement? *Review of General Psychology*, *16*(1) 93-102.

Stone, S., Saucer, C., Bailey, M., Garba, R., Hurst, A., Jackson, S., Krueger, N. & Cokley, K. (2018). Learning while Black: A culturally informed model of the Impostor Phenomenon for Black graduate students. *Journal of Black Psychology*, *44*, 491-531.

Sue, D. W. & Sue, D. (2008). *Counseling the culturally diverse: Theory and practice* (5th edition). Hoboken, NJ: Wiley.

Taylor, E. & Antony, J. S. (2000). Stereotype threat reduction and wise schooling: Towards the successful socialization of African American doctoral students in education. *The Journal of Negro Education*, *69*, 184-198.

Woods, R. L. (2011). Invisible women: The experiences of Black female doctoral students at the University of Michigan. In R. Mabokela & A. Green (Eds.). *Sisters of the academy: Emergent Black women scholars in higher education* (1st ed.). Sterling, Va.: Stylus.

In: Social Psychology and Counseling
Editors: D. A. Kleiber and E. Delgado-Romero

ISBN: 978-1-53616-548-7

Chapter 19

MANAGING STEREOTYPE THREAT IN LATINX AND AFRICAN AMERICAN COLLEGE STUDENTS

Cindy Joseph and Ruben Atilano

According to the National Science Foundation (2017), Latinx (N = 3,038,278) and African-American (2,296,900) college students make up 30% of the college student population in 2014 (National Science Foundation, 2017a), yet only 21% of them graduated at institutions of higher education in 2016 (NSF 2017b). Latinx and African-American college students continue to demonstrate lower numbers in earning their bachelor degrees when compared with White college students (NSF 2017c). The underrepresentation of Latino and African-American males in U.S. higher education is more apparent when comparing the percentages of Latinx and African American students enrolled according to gender. More specifically, 60% and 64% of the bachelor's degrees awarded in 2016 were earned by Latina and African-American females, respectively (NSF 2017d); this is a stark discrepancy that begs the question, "Why?" The statistics make it clear that Latino and African-American male college students are at an increased risk of not enrolling and completing their college degree compared with their female counterparts. The findings also suggested that institutions would benefit from taking into consideration gender-specific experiences as they work to meet the needs of male students from underrepresented groups.

One factor rooted in the lack of representation of Latinx and African-American college students is in *stereotype threat*. Claude Steele (1997) introduced the concept, stereotype threat, which he defined as "the event of a negative stereotype about a group to which one belongs becoming self-relevant, usually as a plausible interpretation for something one is doing, for an experience one is having, or for a situation one is in, that has relevance to one's self-definition" (p. 616). Steele explained that if stereotype threat is experienced in the area of performance, then the emotional reaction interferes with that performance (Steele 1997; see also Moxley, this volume).

Steele and associates (2002) also presented the concept *social identity contingencies*, which are perceptions, stereotypes, and treatments that are tied to one's social group in a given setting (Steele, Spencer & Aronson 2002, as cited in Purdie-Vaughns, Steele, Davies, Ditlman & Crosby 2008). Purdie-Vaughn and colleagues (2008) noted that a given setting may present nuances of devaluation of one's group identity. Hence, stereotypes present a threat for both the individual and the individual's group. Researchers have extensively studied the impact of stereotype threat on the individual's self-concept. This is heavily demonstrated in studies of Latinx and African American students in college. Attending college is considered more of an *elective* decision when compared to attending high school. For this reason, Latinx and African American students entering college are considered a selective group that possess characteristics of self-identification and values that may be different from those who choose not to attend college. Consequently, it can be inferred that Latinx and African American students who choose to attend college are more likely to be individuals who have some level of positive academic self-concept integrated into their overall sense of self. Therefore, this demonstrates the importance of researching the impact of stereotype threat on academic performance among Latinx and African American students.

This chapter will examine various studies relevant to the Latinx and Black college experience including how their academic journey influences their career expectations and experiences. We will consider evidence and arguments relevant to a more complete understanding of how Latino and African-American male students balance both their professional and racial/ethnic identities, and how this balance influences their career persistence. Additionally, this chapter aims to provide concrete recommendations and suggestions to improve Latino and African-American males' academic and career outcomes as well as recommendations and directions for future studies.

MANAGING STEREOTYPE THREAT ON COLLEGE CAMPUS

College students of color encounter a number of issues during their college experiences. This includes being one of relatively few students from their racial/ethnic group to attend college, and encountering racial stereotype threats related to their integration into institutions of higher education (Quaye, Griffin & Museus 2015). For example, one study found that students of color encounter additional barriers compared to those of White college students, including implicit and explicit discrimination (Bertrand, Chugh & Mullainathan, 2005). According to Yosso et al. (2009), students of color encounter negative perceptions of the campus racial climate due to feelings of alienation and isolation; this is likely to contribute to their lack of persistence. Alienation and isolation establish the thought of "them" versus "we". They are also more susceptible to feeling different and like the "other" and therefore more susceptible to greater awareness of stereotypes and stereotype threat. Moreover, others (e.g., Aronson, 2012) have recognized that such conditions directly impact one's self-esteem. Even more nuanced than self-esteem is the construct of *self-efficacy*. Self-esteem is a product of one's self-evaluation, including self-acceptance and self-respect, while self-efficacy represents one's belief in one's ability (Fiske, 2004; Oates, 2004). Self-efficacy is more specific to context and domain. Self-efficacy is especially important for students of color since it is likely to mediate their reactions to stereotype threat. Those who have greater academic self-efficacy are less likely to experience stereotype threat in general; however, simply identifying with the subject (e.g., academics) puts one at risk for stereotype self-awareness. Consequently, it is also important to consider self-efficacy when examining the experiences of Latinx and African American college students throughout academic and career pursuit.

The university environment plays a significant role in the academic and career pursuit of Latinx and African Americans. Roscoe (2015) highlighted the importance of social support networks in the acclimation of Latinx and African American students to college campuses. The author indicated that social support on college campus is a vital factor as it influences commitment to their academic aspiration. Specifically, support from peers, family, faculty, and institution helps to ensure that Latinx and African-American students will have the necessary support structure in place immediately upon entering college to be able to make the right choices (Roscoe, 2015). This support is also key when students of color feel displaced or alienated. Social support on college campuses ensures that these students feel connected with their college experience and helps to buffer against negative experiences, deepening their self-esteem. Moreover, feeling *truly* supported helps to soften their experiences of stereotype threat.

Of the individuals who provide social support to students of color, academic and peer mentors are paramount for the college experience. Academic and peer mentors provide a safe learning environment for Latinx and African American college students to discuss academic stressors (Roscoe, 2015). Academic mentors possess a number of responsibilities and accountabilities, including fostering a relationship with students. One study found faculty mentorship and self-efficacy were significantly related to academic achievement (DeFreitas & Bravo, 2012).

Most importantly, mentors support students in the development of their professional and career identities. Researchers found that Latinx and African-American college students who received mentorship gain a better understanding of how their college education could prepare them for the job market. These relationships offer opportunities for Latinx and African American students to have candid conversations about stereotype threat and its impact on their performance and perceived academic and career progress.

This is especially important for students who identify academic achievement as a part of their self-concept or identity.

Therefore, it is important that university faculty and staff provide a welcoming environment to enable Latinx and African American college students to cultivate a sense of belonging on college campus. Without these supports in place, Latinx and African American college students may be more resistant to finishing their academic education. Additionally, Steele (1997) introduces the concept of "wise schooling" to assist instructors in reducing the effects of stereotype threat (see also Jean, 1995, and Moxley, this volume).

For groups that have negative stereotypes related to academic achievement, Steele mentioned that instructors should present intelligence as an expandable construct instead of a fixed one; one that can be built upon. In doing so, the instructor establishes not only rapport, but also trust and faith in the students' self-efficacy, which can significantly reduce stereotype threat in the classroom.

He also identified ways to reduce stereotype threat by establishing relationships with targeted students, providing challenges in the subject area to promote growth in ability, and establishing group study to demonstrate variety in ability. Steele also believed that residential education, that is residences that incorporate academics into day to day living, was helpful in establishing communities that value cross-cultural communication with regards to peer-learning.

University faculty and staff are not always representative of the marginalized communities who attend the institution. For this reason, faculty and staff may have fewer opportunities to engage with Latino and African American male students and learn more about their unique college experiences. At predominantly White institutions, many college students of color must learn to navigate a hostile campus climate plagued with racial and gender microaggressions received in an academic setting (McCabe, 2009). In building a better community for Latino and African-American males, it is important to have their values incorporated (Ratts, 2016).

The incorporation of these values is likely to assist with dismantling stereotypes. For instance, creating community learning environments allows Latino and African American male college students to have shared experiences in understanding their academic strengths and weakness. This establishes a sense of community and highlights that no one person knows everything, but rather; each individual has his own academic strength and potential to learn more. Rewards for sharing knowledge or assisting another student with overcoming an academic hurdle is a great reinforcer of positive self-concept and self-efficacy. Moreover, this social support will create a climate of trust, which essentially allows Latino and African-American students to develop a sense of achievement in their academic and career journey.

Stereotype Threat in the Work Environment

A major aspiration post college is to secure employment in one's chosen area of study. However, associated with being marketable for employment is one's level of competence and performance. Even for Latinx and African Americans who attend Historically Black Colleges and University (HBCUs) or Hispanic Serving Institutions (HSIs) and benefit from a racial/ethnic integrated college environment that is likely to foster positive racial self-image and identity, it is possible that seeking employment re-introduces awareness and confrontation with perceptions of negative racial stereotypes. This is likely due to the fact that the workforce re-introduced their demographic minority status while attending institutions of higher learning with a higher concentration of minority students presented a welcomed break from this awareness. Indeed, there is evidence that Latinx and African-American college students also face various challenges in their entry to the workforce. According to Flores, Li, and May (2017), youth and adults from diverse backgrounds are more likely to be unemployed, incarcerated, and underrepresented in STEM fields. Specifically, due to the educational disparities, among Latinx and African Americans, a higher percentage are found in low wage employment situations (Flores, Li and May 2017). For example, Chung, Ehrhart, Ehrhart, Hattrup, and Solamon (2010) confirmed the notion of performance stereotype threat for African American employees in a testing situation study where a written job knowledge examination was utilized, African Americans were more likely to perceive that their performance confirmed a negative stereotype about their race. Arguably, stereotype threat in the workplace may be greater than in an academic setting as the need for employment and financial stability may be greater than the desire to attain good grades. This illustrates that despite one's achievement of attaining a college degree, minorities may continue to struggle with stereotype threat.

Latino and African American College *Male* Students

As previously mentioned, Latino and African American males may be under even greater threat and in need of more support and intervention than their female counterparts in avoiding the consequences of stereotype threat in college environments and in the workplace. Not only are Latino and African American males confronted with stereotypes of their racial group, but this is confounded with stereotypes of their gender as well.

Stereotypes of African American males include being overly aggressive, shiftless, lazy, threatening, and unfriendly. Further, Owens, Lacey, Rawls, and Holbert-Quince (2010) described African American male students as a unique population who are also likely disadvantaged by inadequate educational preparation, low high school and college attendance rates, in addition to high unemployment and incarceration rates. Therefore, the stereotypes of African American males as being shiftless and lazy are compounded by stereotypes of high unemployment and deviant behaviors.

Similarly, Latinos are often stereotyped as lazy, unreliable, illegal in the United States, and criminals (Delgado-Romero, Galván, Hunter & Torres, 2008, p. 331). Factors such as school suspensions have been cited as having a negative influence on Latino and African-American male school achievement (Fergus and Noguera 2010). For these reasons, it is plausible that the plight of Latinos and African American males in college and post-college is one that is distinctly *different* from Latinx and African American females. This is not to be misunderstood as Latinos and African American males having a "worse" experience than African American females. However, it is important to underscore the disservice of collapsing the African American college experience under one umbrella, and the importance of studying gender differences. It would be equally important to explore the resiliency factors in Latina and African American women that may contribute to the gender gap in academics.

One factor to consider is women's greater tendency to gather and discuss emotional struggles. These communal spaces are likely to create opportunities to utilize peer feedback to challenge negative thoughts and perceptions stemming from stereotype threat. Men tend to have less open patterns of expressing their feelings and utilize coping strategies that are a part of society's gender expectations (i.e., deflecting or the use of aggression) or culturally expected (e.g., machismo). For example, Latino and African American male college students who encounter stereotype threat and underperform academically may become frustrated, deflect, and assert that they are better with their hands than in the classroom.

IMPLICATIONS FOR COLLEGE COUNSELING

In providing psychotherapy to college students, it is always challenging grappling with a "perfect way" to help a male client of color because of the different cultural values for each community. It is simple and disserving to think that everyone from the same racial/ethnic group is similar. The counselor holds a range of responsibilities and accountabilities, including maintaining high standards of professional competence and ethical behavior. Unfortunately, multicultural training tends to be an elective in counselor training. Therefore, it's important that clinicians take into consideration the differences in cultural values and beliefs that may impact the individuals from varying communities distinctively.

Counseling psychology's distinct contribution to the field is multicultural counseling and addressing multicultural issues (American Psychological Association 2017). Its hallmark in multiculturism has allowed counseling psychology to have an imprint in multicultural advocacy, service, and research. A therapist role in serving Latino and African-American males is to provide a supportive environment to explore their personal issues. Ratts and colleagues (2016) highlighted the importance of multicultural competence in the counseling process. Factors that improve counselors' efficacy in providing quality counseling to marginalized communities include counselor self-awareness, client worldview, counseling relationship, and counseling and advocacy interventions. Effective counseling requires a strong and trusting therapeutic relationship. Thus, the right positive experiences can shape the individual's intrinsic characteristics in a way that will build his/her resilience. Consequently, it is important that counselors, in their training, explore culturally-sensitive topics, such as stereotype threat, to better understand the experiences of minorities and explore the impact of stereotype threat on self-efficacy and self-esteem.

CONCLUSION

A primary reason for this examination is the need to better serve Latino and African American males in their academic and career pursuit. The information presented in this chapter was intended to be useful to researchers, faculty, staff, and counselors on college campuses. Institutions of higher education need to provide males of color with services and resources including mentorship and cultural enrichment programming. The findings of this chapter may not apply to every male of color, but these issues are more widespread than universities typically acknowledge. While this chapter primarily focused on challenges faced by male Latinx and African Americans, it is important to note that researchers should also consider taking into account other minority identities such as those of women and the LGBT community, as they relate to the impact of stereotype threat.

REFERENCES

American Psychological Association. (2017). *Multicultural Guidelines: An Ecological Approach to Context, Identity, and Intersectionality*, Retrieved from: http://www.apa.org/about/policy/multicultural-guidelines.pdf.

Bertrand, M., Chugh, D., & Mullainathan, S. (2005). Implicit discrimination. *The American Economic Review, 95*(2), 94 - 98.

Chung, B. G., Ehrhart, M. G., Ehrhart, K. H., Hattrup, K., & Solamon, J. (2010). Stereotype threat, state anxiety and specific self-efficacy as predictors of promotion exam performance. *Group and Organization Management, 35*(1), 77 - 107.

DeFreitas, S. C., & Bravo, Jr., A. (2012). The influence of involvement with faculty and mentoring on the self-efficacy and academic achievement of African American and Latino college students. *Journal of the Scholarship of Teaching and Learning, 12*(4), 1 - 11.

Delgado-Romero, E. A., Galván, N., Hunter, M. R., & Torres, V. (2008). Latino/Latina Americans. *Culturally alert counseling: A comprehensive introduction*, 223 - 283.

Fergus, E., & Noguera, P. (2010). Doing what it takes to prepare black and Latino males in college. In C. Edley & J. Ruiz (Eds.), *Changing places: How communities will improve the health of boys of color,* (pp. 97 - 139). Berkeley and Los Angeles, CA: University of California Press.

Flores, L. Y., Li, F., & May, S. F. (2017). Overview of career and workforce profiles among diverse US racial/ethnic groups. *The Handbook of Career and Workforce Development: Research, Practice, and Policy*.

Jean, T. (1995). Wise Words: Steele's Strategy for change. *Stanford Daily,* 208 (45), 1, 12.

McCabe, J. (2009). Racial and gender microaggressions on a predominantly-White campus: Experiences of Black, Latina/o and White undergraduates. *Race, Gender and Class*, *16,* 133 - 151.

National Science Foundation (2017a). *Undergraduate enrollment at all institutions, by citizenship, ethnicity, race, sex, and enrollment status: 2004 - 14*. Retrieved March 14, 2018, from https://www.nsf.gov/statistics/2017/nsf17310/static/data/tab2-1.pdf.

National Science Foundation (2017b). *Bachelor's degrees awarded, by citizenship, ethnicity, race, sex, and field, 2014*. Retrieved March 14, 2018, from https://www.nsf.gov/statistics/2017/nsf17310/static/data/tab5-7.pdf.

National Science Foundation (2017c). *Bachelor's degrees awarded, by citizenship, ethnicity, race, sex, and field, 2014*. Retrieved March 14, 2018, from https://www.nsf.gov/statistics/2017/nsf17310/static/data/tab5-7.pdf.

National Science Foundation (2017d). *Bachelor's degrees awarded, by citizenship, ethnicity, race, sex, and field, 2014*. Retrieved March 14, 2018, from https://www.nsf.gov/statistics/2017/nsf17310/static/data/tab5-7.pdf.

Oates, G. L. S. C. (2004). The color of the undergraduate experience and the Black self-concept: Evidence from longitudinal data. *Social Psychology Quarterly, 67*(1), 16 - 32.

Purdie-Vaughns, V., Steele, C. M., Davies, P. G., Ditlman, R., & Crosby, J. R. (2008). Social identity contingencies: How diversity cues signal threat or safety for African Americans in mainstream institutions. *Journal of Personality and Social Psychology, 94*(4), 615 - 630.

Quaye, S. J., Griffin, K. A., & Museus, S. D. (2015). Engaging students of color. *Student engagement in higher education: Theoretical perspectives and practical approaches for diverse populations, 56* (3), 15 - 35.

Ratts, M. J., Singh, A. A., Nassar-McMillan, S., Butler, S. K., & McCullough, J. R. (2016). Multicultural and social justice counseling competencies: Guidelines for the counseling profession. *Journal of Multicultural Counseling and Development, 44*(1), 28 - 48.

Roscoe, J. L. (2015). Advising African American and Latino students. *Research and Teaching in Developmental Education, 31*(2), 48 - 60.

Steele, C. M. (1997). A threat in the air: How stereotypes shape intellectual identity and performance. *American Psychologist, 52*(6), 613 - 629.

Yosso, T., Smith, W., Ceja, M., & Solorzano, D. (2009). Critical Race Theory, racial microaggressions, and campus racial climate for Latina/o undergraduates. *Harvard Educational Review, 79*, 659 - 690.

SECTION VIII.

LIKING, LOVING AND INTERPERSONAL SENSITIVITY

In: Social Psychology and Counseling
Editors: D. A. Kleiber and E. Delgado-Romero

ISBN: 978-1-53616-548-7

Chapter 20

NAVIGATING ROMANTIC RELATIONSHIPS: CONSIDERATIONS FOR COUNSELORS

Katherine Crosby Gross

Relationship distress has historically been the most frequently cited reason individuals seek help from psychotherapists and counselors (Veroff, Douvan, & Kulka, 1981, as cited in a study by Reis, Aron, Clark, & Finkel, 2013). Satisfaction in relationships has widespread impact across areas of functioning, including physical health and emotional well-being. Contrastingly, relationship dissatisfaction contributes to feelings of loneliness and depression, and can lead to relationship dissolution and negative coping behaviors. Although differences in treatment goals exist, such as whether to end the relationship or repair the relationship, the act of seeking therapy may reflect an implicit commitment to address the relational distress. Thus, it is important for clinicians to understand factors contributing to dissatisfaction among couples who seek therapy for such issues.

To understand relational distress and clinical considerations for counselors working with couples, it is important to first determine the nature of the relationship itself. A discussion defining romantic love and a brief overview of selected theories and frameworks follow. Given the decades of research on romantic relationships, the theories included represent only a segment of the social science perspectives and were selected according to their relevance to the clinical considerations included in the discussion.

It is also important to note that a majority of studies cited focus on a specific type of couple, typically White, monogamous, heterosexual, married couples who voluntarily seek therapy services. Research to date provides a narrow representation of couples in committed relationships. Although demographic exceptions to sample populations are noted, the implications and clinical considerations may be limited in terms of application and relevancy to couples who do not fit these classifications (but see Clarke & Harper, this volume for treatment of intimacy in African-American couples).

Given the clinical considerations, distinguishing between marriage therapy and couple therapy is important. The shift in language from marriage therapy to couple therapy is intentional, in an effort to encompass individuals in long-term, committed, romantic relationships whose partnerships are not legally acknowledged. This may include same-sex couples, cohabitating couples, couples in common-law marriages, and individuals in consensual non-monogamous relationships. Although couples fitting these identities are included in some of the studies described, there is a paucity of literature focused on relationship trends and implications for treatment specific to these couples. Given the importance of cultural competency, the prevalence of couples in the United States who fit these descriptions follows.

As mentioned, the understanding of marriage and romantic relationships in the United States is changing. According to the Pew Research Center, overall marriage rates in the United States are falling as individuals tend to marry later in life, if at all (as cited in Wang & Parker, 2014). A 2012 analysis of U.S. Census Bureau data revealed one in five adults, or roughly 42 million people, ages 25 years and older had never been married, as opposed to approximately one in ten adults in 1960 (Wang & Parker, 2014). The UCLA Williams Institute (2019) reported there are approximately 646,500 same-sex couples in the United States. This includes lesbian and gay couples in committed, romantic relationships, who may or may not be legally married.

Divorce rates among married adults ages 50 and older has nearly doubled since 1990, with an estimated 10 of every 1,000 married people, per census data (as cited in Stepler, 2017b). Additionally, the rate of unmarried Americans who live with their partner continues to rise. In an analysis of census data, Stepler (2017a) reports there were an estimated 18 million cohabitating couples in 2016 as compared to 14 million in 2007. This means approximately 7% of the United States population reported being unmarried and living with their partner.

There are also growing rates of individuals who engage in consensual non-monogamous relationships, which include open relationships, swinging, polygamy, and polyamory, and are characterized by an open agreement between partners to have more than one sexual or romantic relationship (Rubin, Moors, Matsick, Ziegler, & Conley, 2014). According to Haupert, Gesselman, Moors, Fisher, and Garcia (2017), nearly one-fifth of the United States population has engaged in consensual non-monogamous sex. In a 2014 study, Rubin, Moors, Matsick, Ziegler, and Conley estimated the current number of people engaging in consensual non-monogamous relationships totaled 4 to 5% of the United States population. Changes in the marriage, divorce, and cohabitation rates have important implications for therapists, as the profile of couples who seek therapy may shift as well.

Defining Love

Defining love remains elusive, in part due to the complexity of mental, emotional, and physiological frameworks from which it is has been studied. In a seminal piece, Ellen Berscheid and Elaine (Hatfield) Walster (1969) identified four central principles of interpersonal attraction: similarity, familiarity, reciprocity, and physical attraction. These core principles have shaped social scientists' understanding of love, which can be understood as "the emotion experienced in the presence of a heightened degree of physiological arousal, such as passion and excitement, combined with relevant social cues" (Anderson & Sabatelli, 2007, p. 119). Relevant social cues include factors such as trust, commitment, and intimacy, or a sense of closeness and connectedness (Berscheid & Walster, 1974). It is reasonable, therefore, to view love as both a factor contributing to the pursuit of a relationship, as well as a desired outcome of the relationship.

Aron and Aron (1991) defined love as "the constellation of behaviors, cognitions, and emotions associated with a desire to enter or maintain a close relationship with a specific other person" (p. 26). Reis and Aron (2008) defined love as "a desire to enter, maintain, or expand a close, connected, and ongoing relationship with another person" (p. 80). These definitions implicate the dual roles of an individual and another person in the experience of love, and underscore the experience of entering in to and maintaining a degree of closeness without specifying romantic, companionate, or even reciprocated love. Although the concept of love as "including each other in each other's self" (Aron & Aron, 1996, p. 48) has been cited in Aron and Aron's research, the field of psychology has long been influenced by the notion of an individual's closeness and overlap with another being as reflected in the writings of Jung, Buber, James, and Maslow, among others.

As cited in Reis, Aron, Clark, and Finkel (2013) the work of Berscheid and Hatfield (Walster) in the 1970s and 1980s pioneered a foundation for better understanding romantic love by distinguishing between passionate love and companionate love. Passionate love, or "a state of intense longing for union with another" (Berscheid & Walster, 1969, p. 9), is characterized by "strong emotions, sexual desire, and intense preoccupation with the beloved" (Aronson, 2012, p. 390). It is associated with changes in cognition, emotion, and behavior, and is assumed to decrease over time, particularly following the first few years of marriage among couples who marry. Its onset is typically rapid, and the intensity subsides with time.

In contrast to passionate love, companionate love is "the affection we feel for those with whom our lives are deeply intertwined" (Berscheid & Walster, 1969, p. 9) and is characterized by "a milder, more stable experience marked by feelings of mutual trust, dependability, and warmth" (Aronson, 2012, p. 390). It is associated with "mutual expectations that oneself and a partner will be responsive to each other's needs" (Reis & Aron, 2008, p. 83). Companionate love is believed to be longer lasting than passionate love and deepens over time. Couples who share companionate love are believed to experience social relatedness, good health, and positive well-being as a result of feeling understood, appreciated, supported, and cared for (Reis & Aron, 2008).

In sum, Berscheid and Walster's definitions contrasted the degree of emotionality present in the two types of love identified and associated passionate love with more intense emotions that possibly wane overtime. Building upon the extensive work of Berscheid and Walster (Hatfield), Robert Sternberg (1988) developed the *Triangular Theory of Love*, which includes three essential components for a long-lasting relationship: intimacy, passion, and commitment. Intimacy is defined as feeling close, connected, and bonded in a loving relationship. It includes feelings of warmth, such as the shared experience of happiness with one's partner, sharing and receiving emotional support, and sharing oneself and possessions with another. Passion is defined as "drives that lead to romance, physical attraction, sexual consummation, and the like" within a romantic relationship (Sternberg, 1988, pp. 120-121). Commitment is comprised of two important aspects: the short-term decision to love someone and the long-term commitment to maintain that love. Together, these three components comprise a type of complete love Sternberg (1988) refered to as 'consummate love' (pp. 120-121).

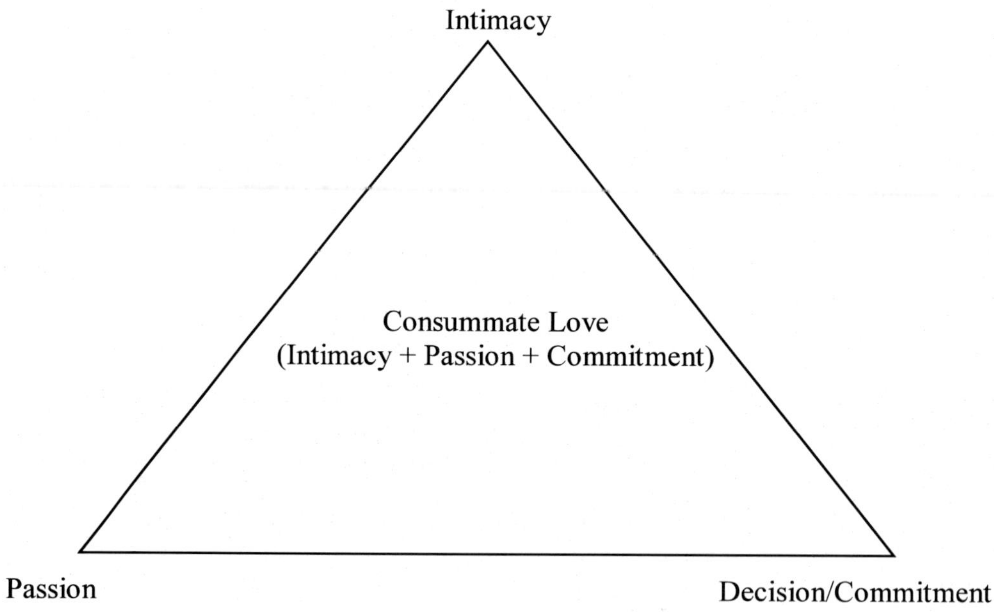

Figure 1. Sternberg's Triangular Theory of Love. Adapted from Sternberg (1988).

FRAMEWORKS FOR UNDERSTANDING LOVE

Social Exchange Theories

Social exchange theories, including *Interdependence Theory* (Ogolsky, Monk, Rice, Thiesen, & Maniotes, 2017) and *Social Learning Theory* (Bandura, 1971), incorporate an economic metaphor to understand romantic relationships. Individuals act out of self-interest in order to maximize their profits and minimize their costs. An important distinction between the economy and relationships, though, is the presence of interdependence within romantic relationships. Interdependence assumes one's personal satisfaction in a relationship depends on the partner's satisfaction as well and fosters a tendency to act in the best interest of one's partner.

Interdependence deepens as partners shift from a self-focus to a we- or us-focus and partners' outcomes become more intertwined. Interdependence helps foster trust and commitment, which builds intimacy. When this type of sacrifice (i.e., putting the needs of one's partner before their own) is mutual, trust and commitment are strengthened (Ogolsky et al., 2017). Ogolsky, Monk, Rice, Theisen, and Maniotes explain, "as interdependence builds, individuals begin to see benefits to the relationship as benefits to the self, because partners have become mutually reliant on each other for rewarding outcomes" (2017, p. 278). Failing to act in the best interest of one's partner leads to decreased trust and reduced reciprocity, which can then impact one's own commitment or perception of the other's commitment to the relationship (Anderson & Sabatelli, 2007; Meuwly & Schoebi, 2017).

Social learning theory defines romantic partners as sources of rewards and costs, based on the exchange of behaviors between partners (Meuwly & Schoebi, 2017). Exchanging positive behaviors leads to better relationship quality, whereas exchanging negative behaviors negatively impacts the relationship. The learning process occurs through the frequent interactions and experiences between partners, and guides individuals when making behavioral decisions to do so in a way that maximizes rewards and minimizes costs. Within this theory, repairing and improving the relationship often rests in partners learning constructive communication skills (Meuwly & Schoebi, 2017).

Within social exchange theories, rewards refer to positive benefits attained through the relationship, such as experiences that lead to feelings of pleasure, satisfaction, and gratification. Costs include drawbacks or expenses associated with the relationship, such as negative feelings and the real or perceived rewards available outside the relationship. Outcomes within relationships include the balance of rewards and costs; attraction to the relationship is enhanced by rewards and hindered by costs (Anderson & Sabatelli, 2007; Meuwly & Schoebi, 2017).

The strength of a relational bond hinges on the presence of alternatives to the current relationship. This concept is referred to as the "comparison level for alternatives,"

(Anderson & Sabatelli, 2007, pp. 116-117) and includes factors such as: relationship status (e.g., being single or entering a new relationship); material, social, or symbolic resources (e.g., money, friendships, or values); expected costs of leaving the relationship; and influences from one's family of origin, information gained from observing others' relationships, and one's own relationship history (Anderson & Sabatelli, 2007; Meuwly & Schoebi, 2017).

Ogolsky and colleagues (2017) described previous studies that found positive associations between individuals who engaged in spiritual behaviors, such as partner-focused prayer, and individual well-being, relational well-being, and in one longitudinal study, greater relationship enhancement. It is important to note partner-focused prayer includes praying for their well-being, and is not focused on fixing the person or the problems. For individuals or couples who practice prayer, clinicians may consider integrating spiritual practices into discussion on repairing the romantic relationship. Ogolsky and colleagues also suggested that couples can mitigate potential threats to their relationship, or alternatives, through a process called derogation. Derogation entails devaluation of the attractiveness of others or even the existence of others, which results in the conservation of cognitive resources for their current relationship. Derogation of alternatives is more common in long-term, highly committed relationships, and is associated with higher levels of commitment, love, a stronger relationship identity, secure attachment, and self-regulation (Ogolsky et al., 2017).

Attachment Theory

Adult romantic relationships have also been studied through the lens of John Bowlby's infant attachment theory (Meuwly & Schoebi, 2017), which suggests the capacity to form emotional relationships with others is developed within the parent-child relationships during infancy and early childhood. As infants experience adequate attention, responsiveness, and proximity from their caregivers, they experience feelings of safety and security. When infants do not experience these things from their primary caregiver, however, they feel anxious and insecure (Bowlby, 1979, as cited in Meuwly & Schoebi, 2017). Individuals who experience a warm, responsive caregiver are characterized by having a secure attachment style. They generally view themselves as being worthy of love and respect, perceive others as being trustworthy and dependable, and see the social world as being reliable and consistent (Anderson & Sabatelli, 2007). They are comfortable getting close to, depending on, and trusting others, and typically do not experience fears of abandonment or concerns about others depending on them.

In contrast, when infants' needs are not consistently met by caregivers, the children subsequently tend to experience negative feelings within their interpersonal relationships such as feelings of unworthiness, unreliability, distrust, and a lack of self-respect. As adults, their attachment style may be insecure and described as either avoidant or anxious-ambivalent. An avoidant attachment style is characterized by a lack of trust in others and a tendency to avoid closeness with others. An anxious-ambivalent attachment style includes a tendency to view others as unreliable and non-committal, such as perceiving others as reluctant to get as close as the anxious-ambivalent individual would like them to be. As adults, these individuals may worry their partners do not really love them or will want to leave them.

Studies on attachment in adult relationships indicate individuals with a secure attachment style are generally more attracted to one another than are individuals with an insecure attachment style (Feeney & Noller, 1996, as cited in Anderson & Sabatelli, 2007; Simpson, 1990, as cited in Anderson & Sabatelli, 2007). Similar, individuals with insecure attachment seem to match up with one another. Within romantic relationships, securely-attached individuals tend to perceive and provide more support to their partners, solve problems more effectively, and have the ability to be close to their partners (Sesemann, Kruse, Gardner, Broadbent, & Spencer, 2017). Conversely, couples with insecure attachment styles tend to have less satisfying and shorter-lasting relationships (Feeney & Noller, 1996, as cited in Anderson & Sabatelli, 2007). Relationships in which one or both partners have an insecure attachment style typically have more conflict, have less effective relationship functioning when stressed, may focus on their own emotions to help manage stress, and distance themselves from their partner through denial or disengagement (Sesemann et al., 2017).

Attachment theory emphasizes the role of emotional regulation and expression within romantic relationships. Attunement, or the mutual understanding of each other on a core emotional level, is an important aspect of emotional regulation and expression for couples (Gottman, 2011). The task for therapists is to help individuals understand how their families of origin and past relationships shape their current behaviors in romantic relationships. Better understanding one's own attachment style may increase insight into their attachment needs and their partner's emotional experience of them. Attention to each individual within the dyad helps therapists address couple issues as well (Sesemann et al., 2017).

Clinicians who incorporate attachment theory into an understanding of adult romantic relationships may approach therapy with couples similarly to how they approach individual therapy. They may view themselves as needing to create a secure base so individuals and couples feel safe to explore new ways of relating. Such clinicians may prioritize sensitivity, empathy, availability, and being capable of handling challenging issues that cause fear and/or anxiety (Byng-Hall, 2001). Because clinical work with couples provides unique challenges, especially related client fear that the therapist will take a side or determine who is at fault, it is important for therapists to monitor reactions in the room and connect with each person present.

RELATIONSHIP DISSATISFACTION

Predictors of Dissolution and Divorce

John Gottman's extensive research on romantic relationships has contributed to a better understanding of factors that promote long-term success and those that predict of dissolution and divorce (Gottman, 2011; Gottman & Silver, 2015). His "Four Horsemen of the Apocalypse," *Criticism, Defensiveness, Contempt*, and *Stonewalling,* are types of negativity that, when consistently present, are considered lethal to a relationship. Criticism is distinguished from complaining in that it is global and focuses on the partner's character or personality. Defensiveness, albeit an understandable response to feeling attacked, shifts blame to one's partner and further escalates conflict. Contempt is a form of disrespect that is rooted in a sense of superiority over one's partner, and includes sarcasm, mockery, cynicism, hostile humor, belligerence, and behaviors such as eye-rolling and name-calling. It is the single best predictor of divorce and also impacts physical health, as contemptuous couples have higher rates of infectious illnesses, such as the flu and colds (Gottman, 2011, 2015). Stonewalling entails disengaging from one's partner, such as walking away or facing the opposite direction during an argument, and not displaying cues indicative of listening, such as making eye contact, nodding one's head, or minimal vocalizations.

Gottman's studies (Gottman & Silver, 2015) revealed the ability to predict divorce with 85% accuracy by examining the presence of these four behaviors. Gottman (2011) suggested the presence of conflict or argument does not predict divorce; rather, the *way* in which couples argue leaves them susceptible to increased negativity and distrust. The antidote to contempt, he suggested, is fondness and admiration. The absence of belief that one's partner is worthy of honor and respect and the inability to recognize the positive qualities of one's partner doom a relationship and lead to dissatisfaction. As cited in Gottman and Silver (2015), researchers Elizabeth Robinson and Gail Price found couples who described themselves as unhappily married were less likely to notice positive interactions with their partners. It seems such couples were so focused on their partners' mistakes, they each missed 50% of their partner's positive actions.

Relational Boredom

Individuals in long-term, committed relationships often report 'relational boredom,' or a lack of novelty and stimulation, as a barrier for maintaining relationship satisfaction over time (Harasymchuk & Fehr, 2010, 2012). Couples who report experiencing relational boredom typically describe the relationship using features such as "[a] lack of interest in partner" or "[the relationship is] no longer exciting," and not "[we have] nothing in common" or "[we are] too similar" (Harasymchuk & Fehr, 2012, p. 627). Relational boredom is characterized by the absence of positivity, rather than the presence of negativity, in a relationship (Harasymchuk & Fehr, 2012).

In a study of dating relationships among college-aged students, Harasymchuk and Fehr (2010) found the most commonly endorsed causes of relational boredom were repetition, a lack of arousal, a lack of intrinsic meaning, and constraint, or feeling limited or confined. In response to those experiences, participants reported that the most frequently experienced emotions were unexcited, frustrated, tired, anxious, and depressed. To cope with relational boredom, dating participants most frequently identified active relationship-focused strategies, such as trying new things, talking to one's partner, and engaging in spontaneity.

A second study by Harasymchuk and Fehr (2010) focused on adult couples who had been married at least three years. In contrast to the previous study, external factors contributed to relational boredom, such as work obligations and stress, limited income, and having children; however, similar to the college sample of dating participants, married couples also reported a lack of novelty and a lack of stimulation as contributing to boredom. Interestingly, the breadth of emotions endorsed by married participants suggested the emotional cost of boredom is higher for people who endure it over a prolonged period of time (Harasymchuk & Fehr, 2010). Married participants reported feeling restless, tired, frustrated, lonely, and low energy, as well as numb, disconnected, ignored, and resentful, which were not endorsed by dating couples.

Lack of Self-Expansion

The self-expansion model operates on three main principles: (1) people seek to expand the self, (2) by attempting to include others in the self through close relationships, and (3) people seek situations and experiences that have become associated with experiences of expansion of the self (Aron and Aron, 1996). Through shared experiences, such as trying out new ways of being in diverse social situations after having rehearsed them with a partner and received acceptance, there is a mutual process of personal growth that serves to enhance intimacy and closeness. Whereas self-expansion theory suggests people are innately motivated to broaden their sense of self, within romantic relationships, self-expansion includes the extent to which a partner facilitates and provides opportunities for novel experiences, new perspectives, and gaining new skills (Aron & Aron, 1996; Muise et al., 2018).

The perception of an opportunity to expand oneself through the closeness with another person has been linked to what causes attraction to the other person (Aron & Aron, 1996). Consequently, as a couple becomes more well-established and intimate, including taking on the other's identity as one's own, the opportunities for expansion lessen. Sheets (2014) described the lessening of opportunities for self-expansion as contributing to feelings of dissatisfaction in a relationship overtime, despite the closeness and similarities shared between partners. One way to combat this experience is to continue engaging in self-expanding activities in the context of daily life (Muise et al., 2018). Because self-expansion is often associated with earlier stages of a relationship, which is also characterized by higher levels of passion, continuing to seek out and engage in novel activities promotes the positive feelings associated with engaging in self-expansion activities.

The somewhat paradoxical notion that closeness and similarities contribute to relationship dissatisfaction (Aron & Aron, 1996; Sheets, 2014) poses a dilemma with important implications for clinicians working with couples. Harasymchuk and Fehr (2010) noted self-reported relational boredom among married couples was typically not an internalized feeling or partner-blaming expression, but rather an externalized attribution, such as children, work demands, and busyness of household chores and duties. While acknowledging the demandingness of those tasks, it is equally crucial to explore strategies to combat such demands in order to optimize martial satisfaction. Additionally, in response to the presence of relational boredom among married couples in particular, it is important to note that experiencing boredom can be viewed as adaptive in that it can signify a problem area and motivate individuals to respond to it in a proactive way (Harasymchuk & Fehr, 2010). Experiences of boredom within a romantic relationship may be exacerbated by the increased availability of social media and pornography, which serve as distractions.

One proposed method of combating the feeling of boredom within a romantic relationship involves associating experiences of expansion with one's partner, such as engaging in expanding activities together that are novel and arousing (Aron & Aron, 1996). Participation in such activities is linked to reduced levels of relational boredom (Harasymchuk & Fehr, 2010), a known contributor to marital dissatisfaction. It is important to note that researchers studying arousal within the self-expansion context agree that "arousal" in activities should be perceived as high, yet tolerable, in order to promote enjoyment, attraction, expansion, and competence (McNeal & Aron, 1995, as cited in Aron & Aron, 1996; Dutton & Aron, 1974, as cited in Aron & Aron, 1996). Muise et al. (2018) suggested that involving one's partner in self-expanding activities can be beneficial for the relationship even if the other partner is not experiencing self-expansion. This finding relates to the interdependence of romantic relationships, and suggests simply witnessing a partner's self-expansion, and not personally experiencing self-expansion, can still promote desire and connection among romantic partners.

In a survey of dating and married couples, Harasymchuk and Fehr (2010) found more similarities than differences among genders and relationship types regarding experiences of and coping strategies for relational boredom. Active relationship-focused enhancement strategies included communicating and engaging in novel self-expansion with one another. Active self-focused enhancement strategies included engaging in personal hobbies and seeking social contact outside the relationship, especially among married couples.

ADDITIONAL CLINICAL CONSIDERATIONS

Although conflict is inevitable in romantic relationships, its presence signifies the need to examine relationship strategies and rules in order to develop effective conflict-management strategies that promote improved communication, increased understanding, resolution of differences, and thereby, foster intimacy. Couples report similarities in the sources of conflict experienced, including among gay, lesbian, and heterosexual couples (Kurdek, 1993, as cited in Anderson & Sabatelli, 2007). Given these similarities, rather than understanding the content of conflict, understanding its underlying sources may be more important for clinicians when providing couple therapy (Anderson & Sabatelli, 2007). Clinicians also have opportunities to help individuals and couples develop ideas and plans of action to implement activities outside of therapy sessions.

Relationship-Defining Memories

Relationship-defining memories are "recollections about specific significant events that occur during the course of an interpersonal relationship and are vividly and emotionally remembered" (Alea & Vick, 2010, p. 730). Once activated, such memories can affect one's well-being, intentions, and behaviors (Guilbault & Philippe, 2017). They typically reflect an enduring theme and remain salient due to the frequency with which they are recalled and the intensity of emotions that results. Memories that satisfy three basic psychological needs – autonomy, competence, and relatedness (see also Varley & Zito, this volume) – predict relationship quality and well-being among romantic partners (Guilbault & Philippe, 2017). Additional studies indicate the recollection of positive memories about romantic relationships leads to an increase in warmth towards one's partner (Alea & Bluck, 2007, as cited in Guilbault & Philippe, 2017) and to increased relationship satisfaction, especially when couples recall an experience involving shared laughter (Bazzini et al., 2007, as cited in Guilbault & Philippe, 2017).

First encounter memories are highly specific, emotionally rich, and vivid memories of a brief moment in which a couple first recalls feeling in love, and, as such, they typically represent the current and future hopes of a relationship. Support for having couples recall positive memories and first-encounters in romantic relationships as a way to increase intimacy was described as bidirectional; that is, recalling positive memories fostered intimacy and deeper intimacy in turn led to recalling memories with more vividness, emotional content, and rehearsal (Alea and Vick, 2010). Important gender differences exist between men and women as related to the encoding and recollection of memories; compared to men, women tend to recall more emotional memories, remember more vivid and specific details, experience increased feelings of closeness following memory recollection, and, generally, feel more affected by their romantic relationships (Guilbault & Philippe, 2017).

Doing Evidence-Based Practice

In an age of growing digital presence, the accessibility to popular psychology and self-help resources is expansive. With minimal effort, a simple internet search yields hundreds of self-help books, checklists for improving relationships, tips for strengthening intimacy, and opinions from a range of life coaches, self-proclaimed experts, and social media influencers. Although these resources may lead to desirable outcomes, there are potential drawbacks given the relative ease of accessibility. Individuals and couples may be more inclined to engage in self-help resources in lieu of seeking professional help, even when intervention from a trained professional may be warranted. Furthermore, using resources that lack research and scientific evidence may lead to instances of self-diagnosis and/or misdiagnosis, as well as engaging in techniques that lack empirical support.

It is important for therapists to consider whether empirical support exists for purported claims of readily accessible resources, as well as to better understand the consensus of these resources among the general population. The field of psychology, for example, is represented in American culture by media personalities Phil McGraw and Laura Schlessinger, neither of whom are licensed psychologists (Arkowitz & Lilienfeld, 2009, as cited in Lilienfeld, 2011). The popular magazine, *Psychology Today*, appeals to the interests of society by featuring topics on relationships and love, often written by non-experts and lacking in scientific support (Benjamin & Bryant, 1997, as cited in Lilienfeld, 2011). Given ‘psychology’ is in the title, readers may be susceptible to accepting the magazine’s positions without questioning their validity. These broad societal views of psychology, coupled with the internal critique and discord between researchers and practitioners, create challenges for clinicians who work with couples. Bridging the gap between researchers and practitioners may prove beneficial for couples who seek therapy, as well as society’s view of psychotherapists.

The complexity of couple therapy is widely acknowledged among researchers and practitioners; however, Gurman (2015, p. 17) notes there is a history of disconnection between the two groups surrounding couple therapy. Practitioners claim researchers fail to understand the complexities of working with couples, while researchers suggest practitioners engage in practices that lack empirical support. Even within the field of mental health professionals, divergent opinions exist between the necessary qualifications to provide couple therapy and the most effective treatment modalities. In an international study, Orlinsky and Ronnestad (2005) found 70% of psychotherapists treat couples, despite limited training beyond marriage and family therapy courses (as cited in Lebow, Chambers, Christenson, & Johnson, 2012). This underscores the responsibility of clinicians to understand which approaches are effective for working with couples.

Meta-analyses of efficacious couple therapies found *Emotion-Focused Therapy* and *Behavioral Couple Therapy* (BCT) – the latter of which includes the evolving forms of *Traditional Behavioral Marital Therapy*, *Cognitive BCT*, and *Integrative BCT* – were the only modalities with documented efficacy via randomized controlled trials (Gurman, 2011, p. 282; Halford, Pepping, & Petch, 2016, p. 35; Lebow et al., 2012, p. 159). This finding, however, does not mean other couple therapies are ineffective; rather they have yet to undergo randomized controlled trials (RCTs). Moreover, broad couple therapy approaches have not demonstrated reliable, consistent, and significant differences in terms of efficacy in comparative studies (Gurman & Snyder, as cited in Gurman, 2011, p. 282; Shadish & Baldwin, as cited in Halford et al., 2016, p. 35; Lebow et al., 2012, p. 159).

Halford, Pepping, and Fetch (2016) note that despite research suggesting couple therapy produces large improvements in couple adjustment, longer-term studies examining the effectiveness of couple therapy in clinical practice settings typically yield smaller gains. This gap may be explained in part by the inherent differences between RCTs and clinical practice. RCTs generally have clearly delineated inclusion and exclusion criteria, whereas clinical practice settings are typically less stringent with regard to the couples they see. Despite advances in research on couple therapy outcomes, Lebow, Chambers, Christensen, and Johnson (2012) attribute the limited external validity to a lack of representation in the sample. It is important for clinicians to consider both the outcomes of RCTs, as well as the limitations in terms of the applicability to the couples who present for therapy in natural settings. Furthermore, most empirically supported therapies support an egalitarian view of marriage and generally support a pro-marriage stance given measurements of improvement and divorce rates (Lebow et al., 2012). These perspectives may vary substantially from the couples who present for therapy and the therapists providing services.

Lebow and colleagues (2012) also point to the emergence of a strong evidence-based foundation for the selection of techniques and strategies, such as those found in Gottman's couple therapy and Snyder's *Affective-reconstructive Therapy*. Meta-analyses further the support for a shared base of understanding and strategies that transcend models and attend to cognitive, behavioral, and affective factors (Lebow et al., 2012, pp. 157-158).

Individual pathology and its impact on the couple functioning may account for some of the challenges associated in couple work (Lebow et al., 2012). Distress among couples and individual experiences of depression, anxiety, or substance use may exacerbate one another. In some cases, attending to a partner's individual needs is warranted. Therefore, the clinician should use judgment when determining the best modality to treat a couple's distress, which may include couple therapy concurrent with individual therapy, or recommending partner(s) seek individual therapy prior to seeking couple therapy.

Halford and colleagues (2016) underscore the need for therapists to clarify a couple's goal for treatment at the onset of treatment: whether to continue the relationship or to improve the relationship. Lebow et al. (2012) describe the two types of couples who seek therapy as either "beyond the threshold" (p. 158) or "everyone else" (p. 158), wherein the former are at high risk for factors associated with marital distress, including divorce, and the latter are couples seeking to improve their relationship. The different goals and presentations of couples should guide treatment modality and intervention selection.

Clinicians are encouraged to integrate individual and couple multimodal assessment tools into therapy, systematically monitor progress in therapy, and attend to the therapeutic alliance (Halford et al., 2016; Lebow et al., 2012). Numerous brief and extended measurements exist related to tracking progress in treatment, marital satisfaction, and the therapeutic alliance. Research focused on process-oriented couple therapy emphasizes unique aspects of the therapeutic alliance, which differs from how the therapeutic alliance is experienced within individual therapy. Pinsof and colleagues (Pinsof, 1994; Pinsof & Catherall; 1986; and Pinsof, Zinbarg, & Knobloch-Fedders, 2008, as cited in Lebow et al., 2012, pp. 156-157) identified distinct components of alliance within couple therapy: the alliance between self and therapist, the view of partner's alliance with therapist, the view of couple alliance with therapist, and the alliance between partners about therapy. Factors such as gender, level of distress, and shared views between partners contributed to different facets of alliance (Symonds & Horvath, 2004, as cited in Lebow et al., 2012; Knobloch-Fedders et al., 2004, as cited in Lebow et al., 2012). Consistently, though, sharing feedback between the couple and therapist regarding progress in treatment and the therapeutic alliance positively affected therapy outcomes (Anker, Duncan, & Sparks, 2009, as cited in Lebow et al., 2012).

In a review of couple therapy research, Lebow and colleagues (2012) found positive effects in approximately 70% of couples by the conclusion of treatment (p. 148), though they also reported that many couples became distressed again (p. 160). The difficulty maintaining gains achieved during therapy points to the complexity of couple therapy, as related to both clinical practice and outcome-based research studies. Numerous factors contribute to the complexity associated with couple therapy, including challenges associated with aspects of both research and practice. As clinicians, it is important to consider empirical support when selecting interventions, while simultaneously acknowledging the limitations as applied to populations served beyond outcome-based studies.

CONCLUSION

The purpose of this chapter was to examine the body of research pertaining to working with couples involved in romantic relationships. The majority, but not all, of the studies included participant samples of heterosexual, monogamous, and/or legally married couples. In so doing, a great deal of these findings are limited in applicability to individuals and couples who do not fit that descriptor based on various components of identity, including non-heterosexual orientations, cohabitating couples, long-term and committed couples who are not married, and individuals from more collectivistic societies. It is important to recognize both the limited generalizability to these groups, while also underscoring the need for further research on diverse groups, particularly for clinicians who provide psychotherapeutic services to those underrepresented populations (and see Clarke & Harper, this volume, for specific attention to African American couples).

A 1990s *Consumer Reports* study on psychotherapy revealed marriage counselors to be the single group of therapists with the most dissatisfied clients and negative ratings (Seligman, 1995, as cited in Lebow et al., 2012, p. 159). Despite the number of couples who experience relationship distress and seek professional help, it seems the public holds a somewhat negative view of clinicians who provide couples therapy. Though a majority of couples report positive outcomes following treatment as compared to couples who receive no treatment, opportunities for improved training and development of clinicians remain.

REFERENCES

Alea, N., & Vick, S. C. (2010). The first sight of love: Relationship-defining memories and marital satisfaction across adulthood. *Psychology Press*, *18*(7), 730-742. doi: 10.1080/09658211.2010.506443.

Anderson, S. A., & Sabatelli, R. M. (2007). *Family interaction: A multigenerational developmental perspective* (4th ed.). Boston, MA: Pearson Education, Inc.

Aron, A., & Aron, E. (1991). Love and sexuality. In K. McKinney & S. Sprecher (Eds.), *Sexuality in close relationships* (pp. 25-48). Hillside, NJ: Erlbaum.

Aron, E., & Aron, A. (1996). Love and expansion of the self: The state of the model. *Personal Relationships*, *3*, 45-58. doi: 10.1111/j.1475-6811.1996.tb00103.x

Aronson, E. (2012) *The social animal* (11th ed.). New York, NY: Worth Publishers.

Bandura, A. (1971). *Social learning theory*. New York, NY: General Learning Press. Retrieved from: http://www.asecib.ase.ro/mps/Bandura_SocialLearningTheory.pdf

Berscheid, E., & Walster, E. (1969). *Interpersonal attraction.* Reading, MA: Addison-Wesley.

Berscheid, E., & Walster, E. (1974). A little bit about love. In T. L. Huston (Ed.), *Foundations of interpersonal attraction* (p. 356-382). New York, NY: Academic Press.

Byng-Hall, J. (2001). Attachment as a base for family and couple therapy. *Child Psychology & Psychiatry Review, 6*, 31-36. doi: 10.1017/S1360641700002471.

Gottman, J. M. (2011). *The science of trust: Emotional attunement for couples*. New York, NY: W. W. Norton & Company.

Gottman, J. M., & Silver, N. (2015). *The seven principles for making marriage work.* New York, NY: Random House.

Guilbault, V., & Philippe, F. L. (2017). Commitment in romantic relationships as a function of partners' encoding of important couple-related memories. *Memory, 25*, 595-606. doi: 10.1080/09658211.2016.1197943.

Gurman, A. S. (2011). Couple therapy research and the practice of couple therapy: Can we talk? *Family Process, 50*, 280-292.

Gurman, A. S. (2015). The theory and practice of couple therapy: History, contemporary models, and a framework for comparative analysis. In A.S. Gurman, J. L. Lebow, & D. K. Snyder (Eds.), *Clinical handbook of couple therapy* (5th ed., pp. 1-18). New York, NY: Guilford Press.

Halford, W. K., Pepping, C. A., & Petch, J. (2016). The gap between couple therapy research efficacy and practice effectiveness. *Journal of Marital and Family Therapy, 42*(1), 32-44. doi: 10.1111/jmft.12120.

Harasymchuk, C., & Fehr, B. (2010). A script analysis of relational boredom: Causes, feelings, and coping strategies. *Journal of Social & Clinical Psychology, 29*, 988-1019. doi: 10.1521/jscp.2010.29.9.988.

Harasymchuk, C., & Fehr, B. (2012). A prototype analysis of relational boredom. *Journal of Social & Clinical Psychology, 30*, 627-646. doi: 10.1177/0265407512464483.

Haupert, M. L., Gesselman, A. N., Moors, A. C., Fisher, H. E., & Garcia, J. R. (2017). Prevalence of experiences with consensual nonmonogamous relationships: findings from two national samples of single Americans. *Journal of Sex & Marital Therapy, 43*, 424-440. doi: https://doi.org/10.1080/0092623X.2016.1178675.

Lebow, J. L., Chambers, A. L., Christensen, A., & Johnson, S. M. (2012). Research on the treatment of couple distress. *Journal of Marital and Family Therapy, 38*(1), 145-168. doi: 10..1111/j.1752-0606.2011.00249.x.

LGBT Demographic Data Interactive. (2019). Los Angeles, CA: The Williams Institute, *UCLA School of Law.* Retrieved from: https://williamsinstitute.law.ucla.edu/visualization/lgbt-stats/?topic=SS&compare=total#comparison.

Lilienfeld, S. O. (2011). Public skepticism of psychology: Why many people perceive the study of human behavior as unscientific. *American Psychologist, 67*, 111-129. doi: 10.1037/a0023963.

Meuwly, N., & Schoebi, D. (2017). Social psychological and related theories on long-term committed romantic relationships. *Evolutionary Behavioral Sciences, 11*(2), 106-120. doi: 10.1037/ebs0000088.

Muise, A., Harasymchuk, C., Day, L. C., Bacev-Giles, C., Gere, J., & Impett, E. A. (2018). Broadening your horizons: Self-expanding activities promote desire and satisfaction in established romantic relationships. *Journal of Personality and Social Psychology*. Advance online publication. doi: 10.1037/pspi0000148.

Ogolsky, B. G., Monk, J. K., Rice, T. M., Theisen, J. C., & Maniotes, C. R. (2017). Relationship maintenance: A review of research on romantic relationships. *Journal of Family Theory & Review, 9,* 275-306. doi: 10.1111/jftr.12205.

Reis, H. T., & Aron, A. (2008). Love: What is it, why does it matter, and how does it operate? *Perspectives on Psychological Science*, *3*(1), 80-86. doi: 10.1111/j.1745-6916.2008.00065.x.

Reis, H. T., Aron, A., Clark, M. S., & Finkel, E. J. (2013). Ellen Berscheid, Elaine Hatfield, and the emergence of relationship science. *Perspectives on Psychological Science*, *8*(5), 558-572. doi: 10.1177/1745691613497966.

Rubin, J. D., Moors, A. C., Matsick, J. L., Ziegler, A., & Conley, T. D. (2014). On the margins: Considering diversity among consensually non-monogamous relationships. [Special Issue on Polyamory]. *Journal für Psychologie, 22*(1), 19-37.

Sesemann, E. M., Kruse, J., Gardner, B. C., Broadbent, C. L., & Spencer, T. A. (2017). Observed attachment and self-report affect within romantic relationships. *Journal of Couple & Relationship Therapy, 16*(2), 102-121. doi: 10.1080/15332691.2016.1238794.

Sheets, V. L. (2014). Passion for life: Self-expansion and passionate love across the lifespan. *Journal of Personal and Social Relationships*, *31*(7), 958-974. doi: 10.1177/0265407513515618.

Stepler, R. (2017a). *Number of US adults cohabitating with a partner continues to rise, especially among those 50 and older.* Retrieved from: https://www.pewresearch.org/fact-tank/2017/04/06/number-of-u-s-adults-cohabiting-with-a-partner-continues-to-rise-especially-among-those-50-and-older/

Stepler, R. (2017b). *Led by baby boomers, divorce rates climb for America's 50+ population.* Retrieved from: https://www.pewresearch.org/fact-tank/2017/03/09/led-by-baby-boomers-divorce-rates-climb-for-americas-50-population/

Sternberg, R. J. (1988). Triangulating love. In R. J. Sternberg & M. L. Barnes (Eds.), *The psychology of love* (pp. 119-138). New Haven, CT: Yale University Press.

Wang, W., & Parker, K. (2014). *Record share of Americans have never married.* Retrieved from: https://www.pewsocialtrends.org/2014/09/24/record-share-of-americans-have-never-married/

In: Social Psychology and Counseling
Editors: D. A. Kleiber and E. Delgado-Romero
ISBN: 978-1-53616-548-7

Chapter 21

INTIMACY AND MARITAL STABILITY IN AFRICAN AMERICAN COUPLES

Christina Clarke and Lauren Harper

There is considerable evidence that emotional intimacy is essential to physical and mental wellness, yet there is a significant gap in the literature regarding African American romantic relationships and emotional intimacy. This dearth of knowledge needs to be addressed since facilitating emotional intimacy can help develop healthy couples, who in turn can help bolster the African-American community through collaborative child rearing practices and the mutual support they provide. In *The Consequences of Marriage for African Americans,* Blackman, Clayton, Glenn, Malone-Colon, & Roberts (2005) reported that marriage promotes the economic, social, familial, and psychological well-being of African-American men and women and seems to benefit African-Americans economically more than it does White Americans. Furthermore, they go on to note that Black children seem to benefit more from parental marriage than do White children. Although the benefits of marriage have been questioned by society at large, it is evident that, overall, marriage benefits the African-American community.

Health prospects are known to be better for individuals who are involved in intimate relationships (Dennis, 2011). In a study investigating the connection between social support, intimacy, and health outcomes, Reis and Franks (1994) found that intimate relationships engender higher levels of social support. It is well established in epidemiological studies that social isolation and/or poor-quality relationships are associated with morbidity and mortality (Reis & Franks, 1994). In a meta-analytic review, the risk of death for those with poor social relationships is comparable with well-established risk factors for death, such as smoking and excessive alcohol consumption and exceeds the influence of other risk factors such as physical inactivity and obesity (Holt-Lundstad, Smith, & Layton, 2010). Furthermore, Wilkinson and Pickett (2009) have found that people with strong social support networks are less likely than others to get colds and other common illnesses and are at less risk of death.

The evidence on intimacy and health also supports the value of intimacy in reducing the likelihood of developing mental and physical illnesses, experiencing stress-related symptoms, having accidents, and even staying alive (Holt-Lundstad, Smith, & Layton, 2010; Prager, 1995; Way, 2013). Nevertheless, despite the role intimacy plays in health and wellness, Laurenceau, Barrett, and Rovine (2005) observed that there is a lack of basic research on intimacy *processes* in marriage and how couples derive a sense of connectedness and support in their everyday lives. More recently, Skyler and Bayer (2010) described emotional intimacy as sharing emotions verbally and/or nonverbally and allowing oneself to be vulnerable in another's presence. But this is only one description and it may not apply consistently across racial and ethnic boundaries.

AFRICAN AMERICAN COUPLES

Most of the literature on Black couples focuses on high divorce rates and dysfunction within the community, however there is little discussion on the couples that stay together despite the adversities facing them. Blackman et al., (2005) stated that on average, married African Americans are wealthier, happier, and choose healthier behaviors than their single peers. It is vital to learn how intimacy is expressed in the relationships of these resilient couples and further understand what role emotional intimacy plays in their relationships. Research needs to be done in this area so that the factors that facilitate intimacy and healthy relationships can be understood and potentially taught to others. As Black couples flourish, the Black community will be strengthened and bolstered to further overcome the adversities encumbered in the Black experience.

In the past 22 years the divorce rate in America has tripled and the numbers regarding lasting marriages are worse for African American couples (Revell & McGhee, 2013). In 1986, 44.3% of African American women were never married compared to 70.5% of that same age range in 2009 (U.S. Census Bureau, 2011). Those numbers alone might not be alarming; however, the numbers of single parent households have increased accordingly despite the compelling evidence of the benefits of two parent homes (Revell & McGhee, 2013).

Accumulating evidence indicates that young African American adults experience significant challenges in developing and maintaining stable, satisfying romantic relationships (Burton & Tucker, 2009; Dixon, 2009; Fields 2004; Kogan et al., 2013). The evidence suggests that racial discrimination, a common experience among African Americans, appears to take a toll on couples' relationship quality. Studies link racial discrimination with reduced marital satisfaction and relationship quality (e.g., Riina & McHale, 2010). Black couples being able to effectively partner with each other increases their ability to promote healing and connection in communities that have experienced countless traumas through racism and oppression.

Unfortunately, the majority of literature on African American couples is deficit-based with little research done on the strengths that allow some African American couples to thrive in the face of systemic oppression. Helm and Carlson (2013) provide further insight into barriers to intimacy for African American couples by deconstructing how systemic oppression has led to poverty, disproportionately high incarceration rates for African American men, and internalized stigma derived from pervasive negative stereotypes and racism. They go on to assert key strengths for Black couples including extended family networks, spirituality, religious community support, and community resources that strengthen their relationship over time. But despite their book being titled "Love, Intimacy, and the African American Couple" no definition of intimacy is provided. A review of other literature on emotional intimacy (Clarke, 2019) indicated that most of the research in the area was done with predominantly white samples (cf. Gross, this volume). The following section provides a review of the definitions of emotional intimacy. Then intimacy is explored across different relationships in a multiple case study (Clarke, 2019) which provides descriptions of how three satisfied Black couples define, experience and sustain emotional intimacy. And finally, more general implications for counseling African American couples will be drawn.

Emotional Intimacy

Many Definitions

Erikson (1963) defined intimacy as the ability to commit to concrete affiliations and partnerships and develop the ethical strength to uphold such commitments, despite the probability that it will call for significant sacrifice and compromise. Furthermore, he emphasized that these partnerships require *vulnerability*. In Erikson's (1963) psychosocial theory of development the sixth stage of development is young adulthood, which is when people ages 18 to 35 typically traverse the intimacy versus isolation crisis. This "crisis" is generally resolved with the acquisition of the essential ability to relate one's deepest hopes and fears to another person and to accept in turn the other's need for intimacy (Dacey & Travers, 2006). Erikson (1963) did allow that the qualities developed in each stage are not always consistently and permanently displayed, with recurring conflicts being common, but, with favorable circumstances, a readjustment usually occurs in such cases. This is important to bear in mind when thinking about implications for couples' and individual therapy. If isolation is the experience of one who fails to generate intimacy with another, it alone may lead one to seek counseling.

Sternberg (1986) explored intimacy as a component of his *Triangular* theory of love. He described intimacy as encompassing feelings of closeness, connectedness, and bondedness experienced in loving relationships (see also Gross, this volume). The other two components of his theory are *passion* and *commitment*. Triangular love theory posits that the type of love a person experiences depends on the strengths of these three parts in relation to each other. Sternberg (1986) explains that stronger forms of passion and intimacy are reflected in *romantic love*, while commitment and intimacy combine in *companionate love* and intimacy, passion and commitment intersect in *consummate love*. Reis and Aron (2008) note that strong intimacy is often heavily linked with companionate love, which may be associated with lesser passion. They go on to note that there has been much less research focused on the intimacy and commitment aspects of love as opposed to the passionate side of love.

Birnie-Porter and Hunt (2015) conducted a study exploring sexual satisfaction, intimacy and relationship status and found that intimacy and sexual satisfaction was positively correlated within each relationship type. Furthermore, other research has indicated that when couples have feelings of intimacy, they tend to report high levels of relationship satisfaction (e.g., Greeff & Malherbe, 2001). Despite this evidence Reis and Aron (2008) also note that there has been little focus on understanding the evolutionary significance of the intimacy and commitment aspects of love. Intimacy is an essential component of a satisfying relationship, particularly since partners may find it difficult to communicate if they are struggling to develop and maintain intimacy.

Reis and Shaver (1988) defined intimacy as occurring when one person expresses personal feelings and information to another. It continues when the listener responds supportively and empathetically. For an interaction to become intimate, the discloser must feel understood, validated and cared for. Laurenceau, Barrett and Pietromonaco (1998) conducted two studies to verify Reis and Shaver's (1988) interpersonal process model of intimacy. Their findings strongly supported Reis and Shaver's conceptualization of intimacy as a combination of self-disclosure and partner disclosure at the level of individual interactions with partner responsiveness as a partial mediator in this process. Additionally, in the second portion of Laurenceau and colleagues 1998 study, self-disclosure of emotion emerged as a more important predictor of intimacy than did self-disclosure of facts and information.

The earlier definition of intimacy provided by Erikson set the stage for Sternberg to build upon the concept and for Reis and Shaver to follow up and create a behavioral construct that was measurable. Their definitions complement each other but still leave something to be desired. Others have gone on to provide additional meanings. Mackey, Diemer and O'Brien (2000) note that "to be intimate is to be open and honest about the levels of the self that usually remain hidden in daily life." Baumeister and Bratslavsky

(1999) point out that many definitions of intimacy have involved the mutual expression of affection, warmth, and caring. Reis and Shaver (1988) also took care to include the expression of positive feelings toward the other as part of the realization of intimacy.

This review highlights how the literature about intimacy is broad with no consensus on one specific definition. Yoo, Bartle-Haring, Day and Gangamma (2014) note that the definition of intimacy is not clear in the literature. Each researcher exploring the topic finds new facets to touch on, thus suggesting that a concrete agreed-upon definition is "unobtainable" (Prager, 1995). This is probable since intimacy varies based on the relationship in question and context. Berscheid and Reis (1998) synthesized a large body of research and stated:

> Intimacy has been used variously to refer to feelings of closeness and affection between interacting partners; the state of having revealed one's innermost thoughts and feelings to another person; relatively intense forms of nonverbal engagement (notably, touch, eye contact, and close physical proximity); types of relationships (especially marriage); sexual activity; and stages of psychological maturation. (p. 224)

Whether the result of a lack of one or more of those aspects of intimacy, marriage is a particularly precarious aspect of American life. Bernard (1972) noted that "marriage introduced such profound discontinuities into the lives of women as to constitute genuine emotional hazards." The idea that marriage benefits men more than women while marital *quality* affects women more than men forms the cornerstone of sociological research on gender, marriage, and mental health and continues to drive much of the research conducted in this area today (Williams, 2003). A negative view of marriage permeates current American culture which is supported by the groundbreaking work from Bernard in the 1970s. Her research was an accurate reflection of marriage in the 1900's, however Bernard hoped for a future in which marriage offered equal benefits to women. Women's rights have progressed as the decades have passed and research has been done to detrmine whether the institution of marriage has shifted since Bernard's assessment. Williams' (2003) analysis of three waves of a nationally representative surveys indicated that being in a satisfying, supportive marriage offers similar benefits to women and men, and exiting such a marriage or being in a strained marriage confers similar costs.

Yoo and colleagues (2014) conducted a study that explored emotional and sexual intimacy and found that although wives' relationship satisfaction was not associated with their husbands' sexual satisfaction, husbands tended to report high levels of relationship satisfaction when their wives reported greater sexual satisfaction. The importance placed on the wife's sexual satisfaction in a partnership could indicate a shift in a positive direction when considering women's needs. Cordova, Gee and Warren (2005) stated that many studies have considered only one aspect of couple intimacy, often either emotional intimacy or sexual intimacy. The study of Yoo et al., (2014) sought to address this gap by looking at both emotional and sexual intimacy in relation to communication and relationship satisfaction. Their results suggest that it is important to look at both emotional intimacy and sexual intimacy, rather than separating them when conducting research with couples. Given the variations in experience of intimacy and marriage of men and women, it seems reasonable to consider cultural differences as well, in this case the experience of African American couples.

Cultural Variations in Expressions of Intimacy

The importance of intimacy extends beyond romantic partnerships and is essential for connection in social relationships as well. Closeness is a term that is frequently tied to intimacy, which separates the term from only passionate aspects. A close friend is someone with whom you may share a special bond, thus establishing a degree of intimacy. Numerous studies conducted over the past forty years on children and adolescents, have indicated that positive peer relationships and close friendships are associated with positive outcomes such as emotional and physical well-being as well as academic achievement (Bishop & Inderbitzen, 1995; Nangle et al., 2003; Oldenburg & Kerns, 1997; Thompson, O'Neill-Grace, & Cohen, 2002; Way 2013). Jia and associates (2009) conducted survey studies of middle school students in the United States and in China and found that support from close friends was more predictive of psychological well-being and academic performance than support from parents.

These studies make it clear that the need for relatedness and the ability to build meaningful relationships starts earlier than Erikson's early adulthood phase. But there has been little inquiry into how expressions of intimacy could potentially vary among cultures. The same Westernized definitions of intimacy ranging from Erikson to Sternberg and then Reis are applied to all the studies on intimacy with no question posed as to whether this is the best definition for all cultures. Given the various interpretations of intimacy, a look at Black couples' experience of intimacy (i.e., vulnerability, closeness, trust, etc.) is warranted, with special attention to how such components are encouraged or discouraged in contemporary American society.

Debnam, Howard, and Garza (2014) focused specifically on adolescent African American girls' characterization of healthy dating relationships. Many of the characteristics named overlap with components of intimacy identified earlier such as trust, communication, understanding, and honesty. The study's findings validate that adolescent girls are aware of components of intimacy, but the investigators did not tackle the question of how these traits are learned. However, they do recommend using the findings to develop programming in schools within and between groups that cultivate healthy dating experiences. It is apparent that these same components can also be fostered to develop intimacy across different types of relationships and in preparation of dating relationships. These skills can then be fostered in Black married adults. Conversely, Pleck, Sonenstein, and Ku (1993) discussed the role of masculinity on male heterosexual relationships. The authors note traditional ideas of gender roles and masculinity impact the quality and level of closeness in other male relationships. Additionally, these ideologies influence diminished intimacy and risky sexual behaviors in heterosexual partnered relationships. Tackling ideologies around components of intimacy in same gendered relationships (ie friendships) can foster intimacy-related skills that can be transferred to partnered (ie dating or married) relationships.

Helm and Carlson (2013) offer some explanation in their intriguingly titled *Love, Intimacy, and the African American couple*. In this text they extensively cover the threats to intimacy such as systemic oppression, gender imbalance due to the high incarceration rate of African American men, negative stereotypes of African American men and women, lack of financial/educational/medical resources and lack of positive relationship models within the community. Although it is helpful to learn about the threats to intimacy they never provided a clear definition of intimacy. Helm and Carlson readily noted in the text that they spent a great deal of time on the threats so that the problems are clearly understood for researchers and clinicians. However, this further supports the need for research that would reveal how intimacy is expressed in a marriage-supportive way with cultural factors being considered.

The question, again, is how important is intimacy as a building block to promoting healthy marriages and does this take a different form in African-American couples? The ability to engage intimately does not start with a romantic partner. Way (2013) noted that in her study of minority adolescent boys and their emotionally intimate friendships with other boys she learned that the boys who could engage in intimate friendships with other boys had at least one parent who promoted emotional expression. This helps us to understand how intimacy starts early and is rooted in attachment. Solomon (2009) explained that securely attached individuals are better able than insecure individuals to take emotional risks, reach out to and provide support for others, and cope with conflict and stress. Furthermore, their relationships tend to be happier, more stable, and more satisfying, they can better acknowledge and communicate their needs, and they are less likely to be verbally aggressive or withdraw during problem solving. Understanding that secure attachment starts in early childhood and prepares people to maintain healthy relationships is a reminder that the difficulties in the African American community are systemic and the current trend in low marriage rates and negative stereotypes about Black couples needs to be disrupted and healed with a strengths-based approach.

MULTIPLE CASE STUDY FINDINGS

A multiple case study with three satisfied African American couples (Clarke, 2019) was implemented to explore how they defined, experienced and sustained emotional intimacy. Each person in the couple was interviewed individually and then conjointly for a total of nine interviews. The two themes that reflected couples' definitions of emotional intimacy were *vulnerability* and *connection*. Four additional themes were derived from how the couples experienced and sustained emotional intimacy: 1) embracing community strengths, 2) seeing the relationship as a haven, 3) increasing emotional expression through personal growth, and 4) committing to the work of the relationship. Figure 1 provides a visual conceptualization of the findings:

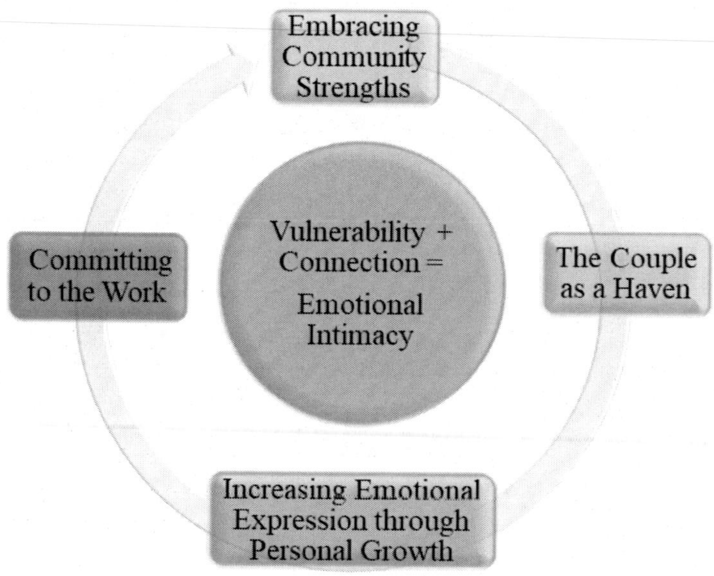

Figure 1. A model of evolving emotional intimacy in three African American couples.

Couples' Definitions of Emotional Intimacy

When defining emotional intimacy each of the six participants cited vulnerability as a necessary component. Women and men all processed vulnerability as someone seeing both strengths and weaknesses fully. Each couple used the term "connection" to convey the importance of experiencing a feeling of togetherness despite emotional or external obstructions. The definition provided by these couples is congruent with the literature and does not seem to heavily indicate how or if Black couples experience emotional intimacy differently. Couples in the study provided cultural context to their experience of vulnerability, which was described in the cross case findings section of the study:

> All three couples discussed how the oppression of the Black community has led to coping styles that are not conducive to vulnerability. In their conjoint interview Michael described how oppression makes it difficult to be vulnerable, "When you are disadvantaged and disenfranchised, you have to sometimes push that emotion deep, deep down to hide it. …under that tough exterior just to suppress." He went on to say that, "we've even been aware enough to go, well, you know, this is kinda how my family was, and I want to kinda change that," to process how he and Camille have shifted from suppressing emotions to taking risks, being vulnerable and expressing emotions more often. The expression of emotions is a form of communication that establishes connection, which is the other primary component the three couples described in emotional intimacy (Clarke, 2019).

Sustaining Emotional Intimacy

The theme of *Embracing Community Strengths* was evident in how the couples described being intentional about identifying role models within their community. Participants whose parents were not together were intentional about looking to extended family or community for examples of "Black love." Furthermore, the couples also emphasized the importance of spending time with other Black couples who are friends to normalize their own relationship and have peer support. The *Couple as a Haven* is a theme that highlights how each couple described viewing their partner and their home as a haven from the world. This encouraged them to be a support to each other and to seek each other out for support. One husband poignantly shared the significance of their relationship as a haven by noting that "We got to be vulnerable with each other. The rest of the world won't let us."

The theme of *Increasing Emotional Expression through Personal Growth* further supported the prior theme. Each person in the study discussed how they engaged in personal growth which enabled them to become more vulnerable and connected through emotional expression. Examples of personal growth practices included therapy, consistent prayer, seeking mentorship from family and community, and utilizing emotional intelligence training offered through professional development training at work. Each participant used multiple personal growth practices. One wife shared why personal growth is a pivotal aspect of her marriage:

> 'cause you have to love yourself. …be comfortable with yourself. You have to be mentally healthy yourself in order.... for the marriage to thrive. …because if you aren't

mentally healthy then you're bringing in everything that you're dealing with into the marriage.

The final theme of *Committing to the Work* was prominent in all the interviews. Each participant emphasized the importance of committing not just to the relationship, but to the work required to be patient with one's partner, navigating adversities while keeping the other in mind and dealing with one's own internal process.

IMPLICATIONS FOR COUNSELING PSYCHOLOGY

Although evidence-based practice is on the rise, Griner and Smith (2006) caution practitioners against presuming that the efficacy of any treatments will translate to clients from diverse backgrounds, particularly when the sample sizes from minority groups tend to be quite small. For example, *Cognitive Behavioral Couple Therapy* (CBCT) is the most widely investigated couples therapy approach (DeLoach, 2013). LaTaillade (2006) notes that treatment tends to emphasize independence and autonomy as optimal outcomes, rather than interdependence and reliance on familial and community support, which are more congruent with African American values. However, DeLoach (2013) noted that CBCT's use of tangible skill development could be helpful in enhancing communication, which is necessary for a healthy couple.

Despite the elevated divorce rate in African American communities, models for couples' therapy that would be especially efficacious with African American couples have not been adequately developed or evaluated. DeLoach (2013) assessed numerous couple's therapy theories and their fit with the needs of African American couples. *Emotion Focused Couple Therapy* (EFT), with its focus on building intimacy and being rooted in attachment theory and systemic perspectives, stood out as being the most promising for addressing the dynamics within African American relationships. Johnson (2008) explained that EFT seeks to understand and disrupt destructive cycles of interaction with others while still centering on the core emotional experiences of each partner to foster the development of healthier intimate responses. EFT's efficacy is empirically supported with the general population but has not been specifically studied with African American couples. However, its emphasis on attachment and adult love may prevent pathologizing the interdependency and close emotional intimacy with one's family of origin and romantic partnerships common in African American family systems (DeLoach, 2013).

As indicated in the literature (Debnam, Howard, & Garza, 2014; Pleck, Sonenstein, and Ku, 1993), components of intimacy such as closeness, understanding, and trust are capable of being fostered or destroyed by early attachments, platonic relationships, and dating experiences. Similarly, counseling requires clients and therapists to be vulnerable in making it a challenging place to re-learn or un-learn early ideologies while also encouraging intimacy. As a result, EFT could be particularly beneficial to African American couples who may need to identify the benefits of vulnerability, which leads to intimacy, and then learning how to incorporate these skills into the relationship. Although EFT may be a good option for some African American couples, general practice guidelines should be considered in the case that this mode of therapy is not the ideal fit. Helm and Carlson (2013) stated that Black couples "respond better to treatment that highlights their strengths and allows them to use these strengths as effective coping tools for problem-solving" (pg. 10). This assertion is congruent with Clarke's 2019 findings that the participants in the study were able to effectively problem solve in their relationships by pulling from the strengths of their community, themselves and each other. Further research needs to be conducted to develop specific modes of therapy that include interventions that can elicit strengths identification and development in the context of the Black experience. Same-sex Black couples also need interventions developed that will meet their context-based needs. Rather than attempting to apply research findings from different-sex couples to same-sex couples, research also needs to be conducted to develop interventions for same-sex Black couples. Umerson, Thomer, Kroeger, Lodge, and Xu (2015) discourage researchers from conducting comparison studies due to same-sex couples being demographically distinct from different-sex couples.

Finally, it is important to consider best practices to reach African American couples and generate trust in the counseling process. There is distrust and stigma toward mental health treatment in the African American community. Fripp and Carlson (2017) noted that African Americans may have low engagement due to less access to resources and a perception that counseling is not effective. These concerns are rooted in the field of psychology's history of skewing science to falsely establish white superiority and Black inferiority (Guthrie, 2004). In focusing on the creation of evidence-based treatment for African American couples it is not likely the interventions will be efficacious if African American people do not feel comfortable seeking treatment, therefore clinicians should be prepared to address building trust and reducing the stigma toward counseling for African Americans.

It seems clear from the research that clinicians would be well advised to work with community partners, other mental health clinics and religious organizations in the communities of African-American couples. Through these community partnerships clinicians can provide psycho-education around counseling to the community and develop an understanding of the cultural context of Black couples. Furthermore, clinicians, themselves need to engage in diversity consultation and continuing education training specific to working with Black couples, while also engaging in reflective practices that aid in processing their own racial identity development and emotional intimacy experience. Regardless of the race of clinicians, their understanding of their own racial identity and ability to understand and experience emotional intimacy is important to more effectively treat the needs of Black couples.

REFERENCES

Baumeister, R. F., & Bratslavsky, E. (1999). Passion, intimacy, and time: Passionate love as a function of change in intimacy. *Personality and Social Psychology Review*, 1, 49-59.

Bernard, J. (1972). *The future of marriage*. New Haven, CT: Yale University Press.

Berschei, E., & Reis, H. T. (1998). Attraction and close relationships. In D. T. Gilbert, S. T. Fiske & G. Lindzey (Eds.), *The handbook of social psychology* (4th ed., Vol 1, pp. 391-445). New York, NY: McGraw-Hill.

Birnie-Porter, C., & Hunt, M., (2015). Does relationship status matter for sexual satisfaction? The roles of intimacy and attachment avoidance in sexual satisfaction across five types of ongoing sexual relationships. *The Canadian Journal of Human Sexuality 24(2),* pp. 174–183.

Bishop, J. H., & Inderbitzen, H. M. (1995). The development of friendship, values and choice. *Adolescence*, 15, 476–489.

Blackman, L., Clayton, O., Glenn, N., Malone-Colon, L., & Roberts, A. (2005). *The consequences of marriage for African Americans: A comprehensive literature review.* New York: Institute for American Values.

Burton, L. M., & Tucker, M. B. (2009). Romantic unions in an era of uncertainty: A post-Moynihan perspective of African American women and marriage. *Annals of the American Academy of Political and Social Scient, 621,* 131-148.

Clarke, C. (2019). *The experience of emotional intimacy in African American couples.* Unpublished doctoral dissertation, University of Georgia.

Cordova, J. V., Gee, C. B., & Warren, L. Z. (2005). Emotional skillfulness in marriage: Intimacy as a mediator of the relationship between emotional skillfulness and marital satisfaction. *Journal of Social and Clinical Psychology*, 2, 218-224.

Dacey, J. S., & Travers, J. F., (2006). *Human development across the lifespan* (6th). New York, NY: McGraw-Hill.

Debman, Howard, & Garza. (2014) "If you don't have honesty in a relationship, then there is no relationship": African American girls' characterization of healthy dating relationships, A qualitative Study. *Journal of Primary Prevention, 35*, 397–407.

DeLoach, C. (2013). Couples therapy with African American Couples: Specific treatment strategies and techniques. In K. M. Helm & J. Carlson (eds.) *Love, intimacy, and the African American couple*. New York, NY: Taylor & Francis.

Dennis, M. R. (2011). Social control of healthy behavior between intimate college students. *Journal of American College Health. 59,* 728-735.

Dixon, P. (2009). Marriage among African Americans: What does the research reveal? *Journal of African American Studies, 13,* 29-46.

Erikson, E. H., (1963). *Childhood and society.* New York, NY: Norton.

Fields, J. (2004). *America's families and living arrangements: 2003* (Current Population Reports, p20-553). Washington, DC: US Census Bureau.

Fripp, J. A., & Carlson, R. G. (2017). Exploring the influence of attitude and stigma on participation of African American and Latino populations in mental health services. *Journal of Multicultural Counseling & Development, 45*, 80–94.

Greeff, A. P., & Malherbe, H. L. (2001). Intimacy and marital satisfaction in spouses. *Journal of Sex & Marital Therapy*, *27*, 247–257.

Griner, D., & Smith, T. (2006). Culturally adapted mental health intervention: A meta-analytic review. *Psychotherapy: Theory, Research, Practice, Training, 43*, 531-548.

Guthrie, R. (2004). *Even the rat was white: A historical view of psychology.* Allyn and Bacon.

Helm, K. M., & Carlson, J. (2013). *Love, intimacy, and the African American couple.* New York, NY: Taylor & Francis.

Hold-Lundstad, J., Smith, T. B., & Layton, J. B. (2010). Social relationships and mortality risk: A meta-analytic review. *PLoS Med, 7.* doi:10.1371/journal. Pmed.1000316.

Johnson, S. M. (2008). Emotionally focused couple therapy. In A. S. Gurman (Ed.), *Clinical handbook of couple therapy, 4th edition* (pp. 107-137). New York: Guilford.

Jia, Y., Way, N., Chen, X., Yoshikawa, H., & Hughes, D. (2009). The influence of student perceptions of school climate on socioemotional and academic adjustment: A comparison of Chinese and American adolescents. *Child Development*, 80, 1514–1530.

Kogan, S. M., Simons, R. L., Gibbons, F. X., Lei, M., Grange, C., Brody, G., Chen, Y. (2013). The contribution of community and family contexts to African American young adults' romantic relationship health: A prospective analysis. *Journal of Youth and Adolescence. 42,* 878-890.

Landis, M., Bodenmann, G., Bradbury, T., Brandstatter, V., Peter-Wight, M., Backes, S., Sutter-Stickel, D., Nussbeck, F. (2014). Commitment and dyadic coping in long-term relationships. *Gerontological Psychology, 27,* 139-149.

LaTaillade, J. J. (2006). Considerations for treatment of African American couple relationships. *Journal of Cognitive Psychotherapy, 20*, 341–358.

Laurenceau, J., Barrett, L. F., & Pietromonaco, P. (1998). Intimacy as an interpersonal process: The importance of self-disclosure, partner disclosure, and perceived partner responsiveness in interpersonal exchanges. *Journal of Personality and Social Psychology, 74,* 1238-1251.

Mackey, R. A., Diemer, M. A., O'Brien, B. A. (2000). Psychological intimacy in the lasting relationships of heterosexual and same-gender couples. *Sex Roles. 43,* 201-227.

Nangle, D. W., Erdley, C. A., Newman, J. E., Mason, C. A., & Carpenter, E. M. (2003). Popularity, friendship quantity, and friendship quality: Interactive influences of children's loneliness and depression. *Journal of Clinical Child and Adolescent Psychology,* 32, 546–555.

Oldenburg, C. M., & Kerns, K. A. (1997). Associations between peer relationships and depressive symptoms: Testing moderator effects of gender and age. *Journal of Early Adolescence, 17,* 319–337.

Prager, K. J. (1995). *The psychology of intimacy.* New York: Guilford Press.

Pleck, R., Sonenstein, & Ku. (1993). Masculinity ideology: Its impact on adolescent males' heterosexual relationships. *Journal of Social Issues. 49.* 11-29.

Reis, H. T., & Aron, A., (2008). Love: What is it, why does it matter, and how does it operate? *Perspectives on Psychological Science. (3) 1.* 80-86.

Reis, H. T., Franks, P. (1994). The role of intimacy and social support in health outcomes: Two processes or one? *Personal Relationships. 1,* 185-197.

Reis, H. T., Shaver, P. (1988). Intimacy as an interpersonal process. In S. W. Duck (Ed.), *Handbook of personal relationships* (pp. 367-389). Chichester, UK: Wiley.

Revell, M. A., & McGhee, M. N., (2013). Evolution of the African American family. *International Journal of Childbirth Education. 27,* 44-48.

Riina, E. M., & McHale, S. M. (2010). Parents' experiences of discrimination and family relationship qualities: The role of gender. *Family Relations, 59,* 283-296.

Skyler, J., & Bayer, C. R. (2010). Eight spheres of intimacy. *American Journal of Sexuality Education*, (3), 290.

Solomon, M. F., (2009). Attachment repair in couples' therapy: A prototype for treatment of intimate relationships. *Clinical Social Work Journal*, 37, 214-223.

Sternberg, R. J. (1986). A triangular theory of love. *Psychological Review*, 93(2), 119–135.

Thompson, M., O'Neill-Grace, C., & Cohen, L. (2002). *Best friends, worst enemies: Understanding the social lives of children.* New York, NY: Ballantine Books.

U.S. Census Bureau. (2011). *Number, timing, and duration of marriages and divorces: 2009.* Retrieved from http://www.census.gov/prod/2011pubs/p70-125.pdf.

Way, N. (2013). Boys' friendships during adolescence: Intimacy, desire, and loss, *Journal of Research on Adolescence, 23,* 201-213.

Wilkinson, R. D., & Pickett, K. (2009). *The spirit level: Why greater equality makes societies stronger.* London: Penguin.

Williams, K. (2003). Has the future of marriage arrived? A contemporary examination of gender, marriage, and psychological well-being. *Journal of Health and Social Behavior. 44,* 470-487.

Yoo, H., Bartle-Haring, S., Day, R. and Gangamma, R. (2014). Couple communication, motional and sexual intimacy, and relationship satisfaction. *Journal of Sex & Marital Therapy, 40,* 275–293.

Section IX.
Perspectives: Cultural, Environmental, and Developmental

In: Social Psychology and Counseling
Editors: D. A. Kleiber and E. Delgado-Romero
ISBN: 978-1-53616-548-7

Chapter 22

ACCULTURATION AND MENTAL HEALTH

Fengkan Zhu

Almost every sojourner or immigrant undergoes the psychological process of acculturation in another culture. The process and quality of acculturation can play a significant role in determining the psychological well-being of people in new cultural contexts. This chapter aims to review the literature on acculturation and the mental health of immigrants and to discuss implications for providing counseling services with these populations and suggestions for improving multicultural competency in the field of professional mental health.

THE MEANING OF ACCULTURATION

With increasing globalization, international communication and travel have become ever more commonplace. What happens to individuals, who have developed and lived in one cultural context when they attempt to travel to and live in a new cultural context? If human beings are social animals who are greatly shaped and influenced by the external sociocultural environment, how do they behave and adjust in a new environment that is different from their original environment? These are the questions that cross-cultural psychology aims to answer. Cross-cultural psychology is a subset of social psychology and has endeavored in the past decades to help understand psychological processes like acculturation.

Acculturation refers to the changes a person experiences in behavior, values, knowledge, and cultural identity, as a result of contact with another culture (Kim & Abreu, 2001). Originally, acculturation was typically defined as one acculturating group being assimilated into the other, which means individuals highly identify with the host culture but devalue the heritage culture (see Flannery, Reise, & Yu, 2001 for a review). In that sense assimilation was synonymous with acculturation. Later, researchers have found that acculturation can manifest in other ways, such as resistance to both groups, creating new cultural forms that did not exist in either heritage or host cultures, or initiating changes that appear more fully years later (Berry, 1997).

Moreover, some researchers suggest distinguishing acculturation by the *levels* on which it takes place. For example, Graves (1967) suggested a distinction between a collective or group-level acculturation and psychological acculturation. Different from a change in the culture of the group, psychological acculturation focuses on a change of experience of the individual. This psychological acculturation has become the focus of cross-cultural psychology studies in recent years (see also Wu & Bathje, this volume).

ACCULTURATION MODELS

Early acculturation theories applied a unidimensional construct in research. That is, acculturation was assumed to occur on a single continuum between one's heritage culture and a host culture (Gordon, 1964). In other words, acculturation is the process of shedding off an old cultural tradition and taking on a new culture. This unidimensional model is also called "unilinear." An individual is placed somewhere between immersion in their heritage culture and being fully acculturated to a new culture.

Different from the unidimensional model of acculturation, bi-dimensional or bidirectional model conceptualizes acculturation in terms of two cultural orientations: one's relation to a host culture and one's relation to a heritage culture. Instead of an "either-or" type relationship between two orientations in a unidimensional tradition, a bi-dimensional model regards these orientations as independent, which makes other interactions between the two cultural orientations possible. When referencing bi-dimensional acculturation, the acculturation strategy model proposed by Berry (1997) is relevant. Berry categorized acculturation strategies into four types based on the combinations of different attitudes towards a host culture and a heritage culture (see Figure 1). *Separation* is the outcome of the combination of positive heritage culture attitudes and negative host culture attitudes; *assimilation* is most often seen on individuals who have negative heritage culture attitudes but have positive host culture attitudes; *integration* most often is the result of positive attitudes toward both cultures; in contrast, negative attitudes toward both cultures are very likely to result in *marginalization*. Similar to proponents of the unidimensional model, proponents of Berry's bi-dimensional model believe that acculturation takes place in many areas or on many layers, such as linguistic, economic, social, and political.

		Identification with host culture	
		Strong	Weak
Identification with heritage culture	Strong	Integration	Separation
	Weak	Assimilation	Marginalization

Figure 1. Four types of acculturation strategies, adapted from Berry (1997).

In addition, Schwartz and his colleagues (2010) developed a multidimensional acculturation model. Their model includes three domains: 1) cultural practices that include language use, food preference, dress, and social affiliations; 2) cultural values that show one's value orientation, for instance, from an individualistic orientation to that of a collectivistic orientation; and 3) cultural identification that demonstrates one's attachment and pride related to a specific cultural group. This multidimensional acculturation model recognizes more than one or two aspects of culture.

The aforementioned bi/multidimensional models of acculturation mainly focus on acculturation at an individual level. However, every sojourner or immigrant lives and acculturates within a broader ecological context of intercultural contact (Stuart & Ward, 2015). Along with increasing globalization, there have been calls for revising and expanding our conceptualization of acculturation (Van Oudenhoven & Ward, 2013). Considering contextual factors, Ward and Geeraert (2016) created an ecological model that conceptualizes acculturation as a dynamic process and this process is affected by its ecological context. The ecological model was created with a goal to examine how contextual factors including the familial, institutional and societal contexts impact acculturation and adaptation.

According to this model, the first layer of acculturation context is familial. While the experience of acculturation occurs at the individual level, the process often unfolds within a family context (Ward & Geeraert, 2016). This family context includes but not limited to variables such as family relations/functioning (Li, 2014), parental expectations (Schachner, Van de Vijver, & Noack, 2014), and acculturation discrepancies between parents and children (Wang, Kim, Anderson, Chen, & Yan, 2012). Familial context can influence individuals who either immigrate as part of a family unit or on their own.

The second layer of acculturation context is institutional and organizational. For example, a study demonstrated that perceived social support from school and peers are more likely to elicit positive attitudes among adolescent immigrants toward the host country and as a consequence, are more likely to lead to cultural integration (Tartakovsky, 2012). Similarly, a work environment with multicultural policies and practices is more likely to foster organizational cohesion and help minority or immigrant employees to achieve engagement and success (Apfelbaum, Norton, & Sommers, 2012).

The most outside layer of acculturation context, according to this model, is societal. Factors such as multicultural policies, diversity, acculturation expectations, and current and historical sociopolitical climates impact acculturation outcomes of all immigrants/sojourners (Ward & Geeraert, 2016). For example, one study found that a more positive attitude toward multiculturalism in the host society may encourage a stronger orientation toward the host culture in immigrants whereas heritage culture orientation remains strong in environments that expect immigrants to be assimilated (Yağmur & van de Vijver, 2012).

Ward and Geeraert's ecological acculturation model helps us to understand and conceptualize acculturation vertically by taking contextual factors into consideration. This model is helpful to recognize that an individual's acculturation is a process that is fluid and is situated in a unique ecological context. To this end, this model is a breakthrough from the previous dimensional and categorical frameworks. The author will discuss the applications of this ecological acculturation model in counseling later in the chapter.

Acculturation and Mental Health

In the course of acculturation, people often experience negative social and psychological consequences, which is often referred to as "acculturative stress." Acculturative stress was defined as "a reduction in health status (including psychological, somatic and social aspects) of individuals who are undergoing acculturation, and for which there is evidence that these health phenomena are related systematically to acculturation phenomena" (Berry, Kim, Minde, & Mok, 1987, p. 491). That acculturative stress may lead to mental health problems in sojourners or immigrants is a common theme in cross-cultural literature. For example, a 3-wave longitudinal study found that greater exposure to acculturative stress predicted significantly more withdrawal, somatic, and anxious/depressed symptoms among immigrant adolescents (Sirin, Ryce, Gupta, & Rogers-Sirin, 2013). Furthermore, different acculturation styles have different impact on the psychological well-being of immigrants. A literature review (Koneru, de Mamani, Flynn, & Betancourt, 2007) found that people who participate in a new society while maintaining their culture of origin (i.e., an integrative style) experience fewer mental illness symptoms in comparison with those using other acculturation strategies. In other words, an integrative acculturation strategy is the most reliable predictor of psychological well-being for immigrants. The preference of integration as the most adaptive acculturation strategy for immigrants in a new society has been supported by research (see Nguyen & Benet-Martínez, 2012; Sam & Berry, 2006, for reviews).

It is also noteworthy that a variety of other factors affect the experience of acculturation of immigrants/sojourners. These include the purpose of immigration, immigration history, the age and generation of immigrants, host-country immigration regulations, length of stay in heritage culture and host culture, income, perceived discrimination, employment and health. For example, a study conducted in the

Netherlands (Nap et al., 2015) found that acculturation status differed among immigrant groups (i.e., immigrants from Morocco, Surinam, and Turkey). They found that their Turkish immigrant participants showed more maintenance toward their original Turkish culture than the other two groups. Surinamese immigrants showed the most participation in the host Dutch society as evidenced by their level of skills and social integration while Moroccan immigrants were situated in between. In their discussion, they hypothesized that this difference could be attributed to factors such as the cultural distance between the host and heritage culture, the overall economic and political status of different immigrant groups in the host society, as well as the relationship between the dominant religious traditions in the host and heritage societies. Moreover, they found that higher cultural adaptation was associated with less need for care, lower mental illness symptom levels, and a higher quality of life.

Acculturation is also reflected in emotional expression among immigrants. Bruner (1996) contended that people embody cultural ideas in the form of emotions. Specifically, the ways individuals express their emotions reinforce the prevalent cultural meanings, values, and practices in their contexts and, therefore, implicitly demonstrate their sociocultural affiliation. Similarly, Markus and Kitayama (1994) contended that whether a person experiences a specific emotion frequently or rarely is systematically influenced by his or her culture and its core meanings and practices. If we take one step further, people's fit with the modal emotional pattern of the culture in which they engage may thus reflect their levels of sharing and participation in the culture's meanings and practices. Therefore, we may wonder for immigrants, how are their emotions regulated and expressed in a new society?

De Leersnyder, Mesquita, and Kim (2011) tried to define and study emotional acculturation among immigrants. They defined emotional acculturation as the changes in emotional patterns due to an immigrant's exposure to and contact with a new or second cultural context. Their studies demonstrated that *emotional concordance* (i.e., the fit or similarity between an immigrant's emotional pattern and the one typical of the host culture) appeared to be higher for those immigrants who spent more time in the new culture or who engaged more in relationships with host group members, even after controlling for the valence of the emotion. De Leersnyder and colleagues, therefore, hypothesized two different paths to emotional acculturation. They thought emotional patterns may change either: (1) because immigrants who are introduced in the new culture will experience different situations or (2) because they start appraising the same situations differently. The mechanisms underlying emotional acculturation are certainly worthy of further investigation.

Another challenge that cross-cultural psychologists are encountering is determining directions of causality between acculturation and mental health. A stressful and problematic acculturation might contribute to the development of mental health issues. On the other hand, immigrants who have previous trauma exposure in their homelands (e.g., war, starvation, torture, terrorism, natural disasters) are more susceptible to certain mental health issues and thus might be more likely to encounter and experience more stress in the process of acculturation and might have more difficulty in adapting to a new society (Pumariega, Rothe, & Pumariega, 2005; see also Perlman, this volume).

In addition, there is a common tendency in public discourse that unsuccessful acculturation is a product of immigrants' reluctance to assimilate or integrate (Triandafyllidou, 2000). However, there is little focus on the responsibility or role of majority groups in the acculturation process (Vasta, 2007). Berry (1997) contended that integration is achieved through mutual accommodation. A successful state of integration where immigrants occupy socio-economic positions comparable with those of majority members cannot be accomplished solely through immigrants' own endeavors but requires majority members' active support (Kurthen & Heisler, 2008; Phelps, Eilertsen, Türken, & Ommundsen, 2011).

It is noteworthy that active support is different from passive tolerance. Under the guise of passive tolerance, there always remains a gap between majority members and immigrants. Immigrants oftentimes hold significantly lower socio-economic positions. And this wide gap is usually one of the main factors that contribute to the damage of psychological well-being of immigrants. Unfortunately, it is not uncommon to hear that immigrants have to face pervasive prejudice and discrimination from majority members in the new society, and prejudice and discrimination are reliable predictors of poor psychological well-being (Finch, Kolody, & Vega, 2000; Kessler, Mickelson, & Williams, 1999). For example, the results of a study conducted in Sweden (Johnsson, Zolkowska, & McNeil, 2015) indicated that immigrants' long-term experiences of great difficulty in adapting to Sweden were explained primarily by exposure to accumulated stressors including discrimination, xenophobia, and racism, rather than by their backgrounds or attitudes toward integrating.

Pumariega and colleagues (2005) summarized some common features of the mental health of immigrant and refugee populations. For example, they noted that in general, immigrant adolescents demonstrate better social functioning than immigrant adults and thus are less symptomatic. They also contended that compared to first-generation immigrants (those who have immigrated to a new country), second-generation immigrants (those who are born and raised in a new country) may face more chronic stressors and thus may be at higher risk for certain mental health issues such as substance abuse. Moreover, other than traumatized immigrants, older first-generation adult immigrants may have the highest risk for mental health issues due to a lack of cultural and cognitive flexibility, isolation from community and family members especially offspring generations, and health risk factors.

ACCULTURATION AND HELP-SEEKING BEHAVIORS

Research suggested that an individual's decision to seek professional mental health services is an interactive process, which is influenced by two main factors: 1) the person's attribution of the cause of specific physical symptoms and/or behavioral changes that beset him/her, and 2) the accessibility to relevant culturally competent treatment and healing practices in the person's community (Fung & Wong, 2007; Hwang, Myers, Abe-Kim, & Ting, 2008; Kleinman, 2004). In some non-Western cultures, stress often manifests itself in somatic symptoms more than psychological symptoms and people prefer to seek advice from significant others, such as family members, spiritual leaders, and indigenous medicine healers when they are under stress (Mori, 2000). Studies indicate that such a mode of help-seeking behavior is prevalent among immigrants of ethnic minority groups in the U.S., and the utilization of Western professional mental health services is often precluded or delayed (Fung & Wong, 2007; Hwang et al., 2008). A study of Chinese international students in the U.S. (Li, Marbley, Bradley, & Lan, 2016) found that those who reported a stronger Chinese ethnic identity were less likely to seek professional counseling services. To many immigrants, the dramatic change in their socio-political-cultural reality in a new culture may lead to an abrupt disruption of the help-seeking pathways with which they were familiar and thus impoverish their established support networks and coping mechanisms (Chung, 2010).

In addition to the stigmas associated with mental health illness, inaccessibility of culturally competent services is another important factor that contributes to the under-utilization of treatment services and subsequent negative repercussions (Zhang, Snowden, & Sue, 1998). In a qualitative study, Chung (2010) interviewed thirty-one Chinese immigrants about their mental healthcare in New York City. She found that most of the participants would seek help from their primary care physicians for help with depressive symptoms; but they did not seem to have received adequate psychoeducation and assistance for psychiatric referral from their practitioners. Some participants became suicidal in those circumstances, and those who didn't nevertheless experienced it as a poignant turning point in their lives. Only after that were they able to find a supportive environment within professional mental health services. In other words, some immigrants turned to formal or informal help-seeking avenues as viable options only after they faced a personal crisis that often included suicidal ideation.

Furthermore, English proficiency may be another barrier to help-seeking for immigrants (Sue & Sue, 2012; Wu, 2012). A client who does not speak English or speaks English as a second language risks being seen as uncooperative, sullen, negative, or repressed due to language expression alone (Sue & Sue, 2012). This language barrier even exists for many international students who are relatively well educated and have access to professional mental health services on campus (Mori, 2000).

In addition to the language barrier, the shortage of culturally knowledgeable and competent services providers and an underrepresentation of diverse cultural backgrounds among providers are also significant obstacles to new immigrants' use of services (Abe-Kim et al., 2007; Mori, 2000;). It is difficult for immigrants to establish solid and trusting relationships with professionals who are uninformed about the history, traditions, value and belief systems, religious practices, family structures, sex role expectations, and language styles of their culture (Uba, 1994). Part of the trust-building process is having culturally- competent therapists, regardless of their own backgrounds; but having providers from the client's background is important as well. However, the current professional mental health services delivery system in the U.S. lacks diversity among practitioners (Abe-Kim et al., 2007). All of the aforementioned factors contribute to an underutilization of mental health services among immigrants first and foremost and a high dropout rate after they seek help (Mori, 2000).

Applications of the Ecological Acculturation Model in Counseling

Mental health professionals are well advised to consider applying Ward and Geeraert's (2016) *Ecological Acculturation Model* in practice and research to understand and address the aforementioned issues of acculturation stress and mental health disparities among immigrants. And clearly the issues do not reside only with the immigrants themselves; as professionals who work with immigrants in the mental health delivery system and as members of the majority group in the host society, mental health professionals need to realize that they are also cultural beings with their own biases as a product of socializing and being educated in their own ecological systems. Cultural competence involves a lifelong commitment to reflection and cultural humility (Hook & Watkins, 2015). Indeed, Gallardo (2014, p. 3) defined cultural humility as a "lifelong process of self-reflection, self-critique, continual assessment of power imbalances, and the development of mutually respectful relationships and partnerships." Although being humble itself cannot prevent one from making mistakes, without cultural humility, professionals are more likely to engage in overgeneralization and stereotypical thinking, which may result in inaccurate assessment, misdiagnosis, harmful treatment, and microaggression in practice and research (Sue et al., 2007). Although it is impossible to become an expert about every culture, routine engagement with and curiosity regarding issues of diversity help mental health professionals challenge their biases and stereotypical thinking (Fields, 2010).

When working with immigrants, mental health professionals need to take their familial context into consideration. For example, when working with adolescents or young adult immigrants in therapy, clinicians need to consider the familial expectations clients have received about acculturation, academic achievement, and religious affiliation as well as how the family will react to therapeutic interventions after clients leaving therapy room, reentering into their familial context. For instance, Western psychology has a tradition of embracing and advocating for independence of individuals; however, mental health professionals need to be aware that this personal value of independence may not be celebrated as much in societies where interdependence is the norm (see Wu & Bathje, this volume; Markus & Kitayama, 1994). Therefore, imposing individualist/independent values onto international students from other cultures in therapy without considering their familial context can potentially cause harm to their relationships with their families.

In community and institutional contexts, one of many factors that mental health professionals need to consider is the availability of resources for immigrants in their communities or institutions. The availabilities and accessibilities of these resources is a significant component of social capital providing immigrants with the tools to build their lives in the host society (American Psychological Association, 2017). For example, by asking about the neighborhood where an immigrant client lives, clinicians can get a sense about the availability of resources such as healthcare services, public schools and their qualities, as well as potential problems that may interfere with any interventions. It might also be helpful for mental health professionals to share such information with their clients. Such consideration of community and institutional contexts would play an important role in mental health professionals' decision making about the services they provide. For example, clinicians working with international students at university counseling centers need to consider cultural competence of community referrals, safety concerns, and accessibilities of local public transportation when referring international students to community agencies for services. Agnew (2009) discussed the importance of empowerment and as mental health professionals, we can help outside of therapy rooms by providing specific resources such as support groups, language classes, and vocational training in local immigrant communities. These resources will help immigrant communities empower themselves and adapt to their host society. Helping a client is only the beginning while helping the community by providing them with resources critical for health helps all (APA, 2017).

When considering the factors that may impact an individual and the effectiveness of interventions, mental health professionals also seek to understand and influence the societal context. In addition, cultural mistrust is another factor that mental health professionals need to keep in mind. Cultural mistrust results when targets of oppression develop a justifiable skepticism to medical, mental health, and research settings due to prior exploitation or oppression (Terrell & Terrell, 1984). Prior mistreatment in health settings can result in cultural mistrust in the future and thus cause underutilization of services (Alegria et al., 2008). Without being aware of this issue, clinicians in psychotherapy with immigrants are likely to prematurely attribute the challenges they encounter in building therapeutic relationships to the lack of commitment or motivation of their clients or simply to a language barrier. "[A] therapist's willingness to engage with sociocultural issues is critical for clients' feelings of safety and comfort in disclosing and exploring painful experiences related to their sociocultural identities and/or experiences of oppression" (APA, 2017, p. 22).

Moreover, attending to and influencing policy making at a societal level is a practice of social justice that mental health professionals need to engage in. One great example is the significant contributions that Mamie Clark and Kenneth Clark (1939) made to desegregation through their research and advocacy work. Their study found that many Black/African American children who were placed in classes for students of intellectual disabilities in New York City were actually above average in intelligence. Their findings contributed to the Supreme Court's decision in 1954 to rule that segregation in public schools by race was unconstitutional (Guthrie, 2003). Most recently, certain states in the U.S. have passed propositions that limit undocumented immigrants' access to health care, welfare, and higher education. Both legal and undocumented immigrants can be impacted by the prejudices behind these actions. As a result, they may experience more difficulties in their acculturation and may develop more psychological distress. Mental health professionals should not be absent in the continuous movements of improving the sociopolitical environment. Instead, they are encouraged to continuously reflect on their social privilege owing to their professional identity and become agents to advocate for social justice at large (APA, 2017).

Another contextual factor about immigrants' life experiences that needs to be considered is the domestic and international political *climate* of both heritage and host countries. For example, in 2018 the Supreme Court upheld the Trump administration's travel ban 5-4, affirming the president's power over matters of national security. This iteration of the ban included restrictions against Iran, Libya, Somalia, Syria, Yemen, North Korea, and Venezuela. How immigrants from these countries in the U.S. and their family members who still live in these countries are affected by the travel ban remains to be studied systemically. However, we can image that an Iranian student's acculturation experience in the U.S. would be more challenging and stressful due to this ban. It will be much harder for them to reunite with their families in Iran compared to international students from other countries.

IMPLICATIONS

It is imperative for mental health professionals to improve their multicultural competency in working with immigrants. Multicultural competency needs to include the awareness of clinicians' own cultural bias, the knowledge of relevant immigration policies as well as immigrants' culture and subjective realities in their ecological context, and culturally appropriate intervention skills in working with immigrants (Sue, Arredondo, & McDavis, 1992). The principles of culturally competent mental health services are particularly applicable to the delivery of mental health services for immigrants (Pumariega, Rogers, & Rothe, 2005). It is crucial to establish a constructive and trusting therapeutic relationship with immigrants by demonstrating acceptance and genuine respect for and sensitivity to cultural and ethnic diversity.

Learning and improving multicultural competency is a lifelong career goal for professionals in mental health. The latest *American Psychological Association Multicultural Guidelines* (APA, 2017) is a document that can be tremendously helpful to psychologists who study and practice psychology about immigrants. Compared to the previous version, the new version of the *Guidelines* embraces a layered contextual model and regards the term "multicultural" more fully, reflecting current trends in research and practice that consider contextual factors and intersectionality among and between reference group identities such as race, ethnicity, gender, sexual orientation, ability status, etc.(APA, 2002). In this regard, the aforementioned ecological acculturation model proposed by Ward and Geeraert (2016) dovetails nicely with the latest *APA Multicultural Guidelines*.

Moreover, academic programs are encouraged to make changes in recruitment and training of diverse counselors and psychologists. These changes should not be limited to recruiting demographically diverse trainees but also those who are invested in working with marginalized populations. Furthermore, training programs need to incorporate more specific training in working with international populations into the curriculum. To achieve this goal, it can be beneficial for the training programs in the U.S. to collaborate with institutions and psychologists from other countries and, if possible, to invite visiting scholars and recruit students from those countries. This can promote cross-cultural communication in the field of counseling or psychology. As a consequence, it may help professionals in the U.S. to better understand cultures outside of the U.S. and thus to better work with clients or students from other cultures. All of these aforementioned endeavors could be a great compliment to the cultural competency training in the U.S., which is currently mostly focused on White, middle-to-upper class female psychology trainees.

Additionally, it is imperative for the field of mental health to recognize the role of language and strive to provide services in languages other than English to the immigrant population. Chen's study (2015) suggested that language embodies the culture and values in which it is spoken. Language holds an intrinsic connection to culture, and thus it reflects the social identity of the person who speaks the language (Chiu & Chen, 2004). Mental health professionals can consult with insiders from immigrant communities to understand the most appropriate terminology related to mental health and use the local terminology in work to help reduce stigma associated with mental health and help seeking (see also Wu & Bathje, this volume).

The U.S. professional mental health services system is also encouraged to train and hire more clinicians who are knowledgeable about other cultures and who can provide services in other languages. Studies have shown that when events occur within a specific language environment, they may have emotions attached to them that are difficult to translate precisely (Javier, 2007). Therefore, when an immigrant whose first language is not English receives counseling in English in which their life experiences were not encoded, the person may feel disconnected from associated emotions. Ideally, it would be most helpful if people receive mental health services in their native language with someone who is knowledgeable about their culture. Therefore, the author of this chapter, who identifies as a Chinese international psychological trainee in the U.S., advocates for hiring more international and sojourner counselors and psychologists to work in the U.S. professional mental health delivery system.

Last, but not least, interventions need to be expanded beyond interview rooms. For example, mental health professionals as social justice advocates may try to advocate a common group identity among the majority members in the host society by actions such as facilitating discussions about common group identity on media, donating money to immigrant-supporting organizations, and personally volunteering in these organizations and/or local immigrant communities. Research has shown that common group identities can improve out-group attitudes and also lead to more favorable behavior toward out-groups (Dovidio, Gaertner, Shnabel, Saguy, & Johnson, 2009). Therefore, majority members with a higher common group identity that "makes room" for immigrants in the in-group will be more interested in adapting active acculturation efforts and helping immigrants to obtain an equitable socio-economic position in society (Kunst, Thomsen, Sam, & Berry, 2015). Mental health professionals also need to think about expanding their roles in helping immigrants. Endeavors might include providing language courses, labor-market training, and other official or unofficial integration programs. In addition to constantly providing immigrant clients with emotional support, mental health professionals may also play significant roles in helping connect clients with various educational, recreational, health care, financial, employment, and legal services and resources as needed.

References

Abe-Kim, J., Takeuchi, D. T., Hong, S., Zane, N., Sue, S., Spencer, M. S., & Alegría, M. (2007). Use of mental health–related services among immigrant and US-born Asian Americans: results from the National Latino and Asian American study. *American Journal of Public Health*, *97*, 91-98. doi:10.2105/AJPH.2006.098541.

Agnew, V. (2009). Immigrant women and health. In V. Agnew (Ed.), *Racialized migrant women in Canada: Essays on health, violence and equity* (pp. 95–97). Toronto, Canada: University of Toronto Press.

Alegría, M., Canino, G., Shrout, P. E., Woo, M., Duan, N., Vila, D., Torres, M., Chen, C. H. & Meng, X. L. (2008) Prevalence of Mental Illness in Immigrant and Non-Immigrant U.S. Latino Groups. *The American Journal of Psychiatry, 165*, 359-369. doi:10.1176/appi.ajp.2007.07040704.

American Psychological Association (2002). *Guidelines on multicultural education, training, research, practice, and organizational change for psychologists.* Washington, DC: Author.

American Psychological Association. (2017). *Multicultural Guidelines: An Ecological Approach to Context, Identity, and Intersectionality*. Retrieved from: http://www.apa.org/about/policy/multicultural-guidelines.pdf.

Apfelbaum, E. P., Norton, M. I., & Sommers, S. R. (2012). Racial color blindness: Emergence, practice, and implications. *Current Directions in Psychological Science, 21*, 205-209. doi:10.1177/0963721411434980.

Berry, J. W. (1997). Immigration, acculturation, and adaptation. *Applied Psychology: An International Review, 46*, 5-34. doi:10.1080/026999497378467.

Berry, J. W., Kim, U., Minde, T., & Mok, D. (1987). Comparative studies of acculturative stress. *International Migration Review, 21*, 491–511. doi:10.1177/019791838702100303.

Bruner, J. (1996). Frames for thinking: Ways of making meaning. In D. R. Olson, N. Torrance, D. R. Olson, N. Torrance (Eds.), *Modes of thought: Explorations in culture and cognition* (pp. 93-105). New York, NY, US: Cambridge University Press.

Chen, S. X. (2015). Toward a social psychology of bilingualism and biculturalism. *Asian Journal of Social Psychology, 18*, 1–11. doi:10.1111/ajsp.12088.

Chiu, C. Y., & Chen, J. (2004). Symbols and interactions: Application of the CCC Model to culture, language, and social identity. In S. H. Ng, C. N. Candlin, & C. Y. Chiu (Eds.), *Language matters: Communication, culture, and identity* (pp. 155–182). Hong Kong: City University of Hong Kong Press.

Chung, I. (2010). Changes in the sociocultural reality of Chinese immigrants: Challenges and opportunities in help-seeking behaviour. *International Journal of Social Psychiatry, 56*, 436-447. doi:10.1177/0020764009105647.

Clark, K., & Clark M. (1939). The development of consciousness of self and the emergence of racial identification in Negro preschool children. *Journal of Social Psychology, 10*, 591–599.

De Leersnyder, J., Mesquita, B., & Kim, H. S. (2011). Where do my emotions belong? A study of immigrants' emotional acculturation. *Personality and Social Psychology Bulletin, 37*, 451-463. doi:10.1177/0146167211399103.

Dovidio, J. F., Gaertner, S. L., Shnabel, N., Saguy, T., & Johnson, J. (2009). Recategorization and prosocial behavior: Common in- group identity and a dual identity. In S. Stürmer & M. Snyder (Eds.), *The psychology of prosocial behavior* (pp. 191-207). West-Sussex, UK: Wiley-Blackwell.

Fields, A. J. (2010). Multicultural research and practice: Theoretical issues and maximizing cultural exchange. *Professional Psychology: Research and Practice, 41,* 196–201. doi:10.1037/a0017938.

Finch, B. K., Kolody, B., & Vega, W. A. (2000). Perceived discrimination and depression among Mexican-origin adults in California. *Journal of Health and Social Behavior, 41*, 295–313. doi:10.2307/2676322.

Flannery, W. P., Reise, S. P., & Yu, J. (2001). An empirical comparison of acculturation models. *Personality and Social Psychology Bulletin, 27*, 1035-1045.

Fung, K., & Wong, Y. R. (2007). Factors influencing attitudes towards seeking professional help among East and Southeast Asian immigrant and refugee women. *International Journal of Social Psychiatry, 53*, 216-231. doi:10.1177/0020764006074541.

Gallardo, M. E. (2014). *Developing cultural humility: Embracing race, privilege and power*. Thousand Oaks, CA: Sage.

Gordon, M. M. (1964). *Assimilation in American life: The role of race, religion and national origins*. Oxford University Press.

Graves, T. D. (1967). Acculturation, access, and alcohol in a tri-ethnic community. *American Anthropologist, 69*, 306-321. doi:10.1525/aa.1967.69.3-4.02a00030.

Guthrie, R. (2003). *Even the rat was White: A historical view of psychology* (2nd ed.). New York, NY: Pearson.

Hook, J. N., & Watkins Jr., C. E. (2015). Cultural humility: The cornerstone of positive contact with culturally different individuals and groups? *The American Psychologist, 70*, 661–662. doi:10.1037/a0038965.

Hwang, W., Myers, H. F., Abe-Kim, J., & Ting, J. Y. (2008). A conceptual paradigm for understanding culture's impact on mental health: The cultural influences on mental health (CIMH) model. *Clinical Psychology Review, 28*, 211-227. doi:10.1016/j.cpr.2007.05.001.

Javier, R. A. (2007). *The bilingual mind: Thinking, feeling, and speaking in two languages*. New York, NY: Springer.

Johnsson, E., Zolkowska, K., & McNeil, T. F. (2015). Prediction of adaptation difficulties by country of origin, cumulate psychosocial stressors and attitude toward integrating: A Swedish study of first-generation immigrants from Somalia, Vietnam and China. *International Journal of Social Psychiatry,61*, 174-182. doi:10.1177/0020764014537639.

Kessler, R. C., Mickelson, K. D., & Williams, D. R. (1999). The prevalence, distribution, and mental health correlates of perceived discrimination in the United States. *Journal of Health and Social Behavior, 40*, 208-230. doi:10.2307/2676349.

Kim, B. K., & Abreu, J. M. (2001). Acculturation measurement: Theory, current instruments, and future directions. In J. G. Ponterotto, J. M. Casas, L. A. Suzuki, C. M. Alexander, J. G. Ponterotto, J. M. Casas, C. M. Alexander (Eds.), *Handbook of multicultural counseling* (2nd ed., pp. 394-424). Thousand Oaks, CA: Sage.

Kleinman, A. (2004). Culture and depression. *The New England Journal of Medicine, 351*, 951-953. doi:10.1056/NEJMp048078.

Koneru, V. K., de Mamani, A. G. W., Flynn, P. M., & Betancourt, H. (2007). Acculturation and mental health: Current findings and recommendations for future research. *Applied and Preventive Psychology, 12*, 76 –96. doi:10.1016/j.appsy. 2007.07.016.

Kunst, J. R., Thomsen, L., Sam, D. L., & Berry, J. W. (2015). 'We are in this together': Common group identity predicts majority members' active acculturation efforts to integrate immigrants. *Personality and Social Psychology Bulletin, 41*, 1438-1453. doi:10.1177/0146167215599349.

Kurthen, H., & Heisler, B. S. (2009). Immigrant integration: Comparative evidence from the United States and Germany. *Ethnic and Racial Studies, 32*, 139-170. doi:10.1080/01419870802298439.

Li, J., Marbley, A. F., Bradley, L. J., & Lan, W. (2016). Attitudes toward seeking professional counseling services among Chinese international students: Acculturation, ethnic identity, and English proficiency. *Journal of Multicultural Counseling and Development, 44*, 65-76. doi:10.1002/jmcd.12037.

Li, Y. (2014). Intergenerational conflict, attitudinal familism, and depressive symptoms among Asian and Hispanic adolescents in immigrant families: A latent variable interaction analysis. *Journal of Social Service Research, 40*, 80–96. doi:10.1080/01488376.2013.845128.

Markus, H. R., & Kitayama, S. (1994). A collective fear of the collective: Implications for selves and theories of selves. *Personality and Social Psychology Bulletin, 20*, 568-579. doi:10.1177/0146167294205013.

Mori, S. (2000). Addressing the mental health concerns of international students. *Journal of Counseling & Development, 78*, 137-144. doi:10.1002/j.1556-6676.2000. tb02571.x.

Nap, A., van Loon, A., Peen, J., van Schaik, D. F., Beekman, A. F., & Dekker, J. M. (2015). The influence of acculturation on mental health and specialized mental healthcare for non-Western migrants. *International Journal of Social Psychiatry, 61*, 530-538. doi:10.1177/0020764014561307.

Nguyen, A. D., & Benet-Martínez, V. (2013). Biculturalism and adjustment: A meta-analysis. *Journal of Cross-Cultural Psychology, 44*, 122-159. doi:10.1177/0022022111435097.

Phelps, J. M., Eilertsen, D. E., Türken, S., & Ommundsen, R. (2011). Integrating immigrant minorities: Developing a scale to measure majority members' attitudes toward their own pro- active efforts. *Scandinavian Journal of Psychology*, *52*, 404-410. doi:10.1111/j.1467-9450.2011.00876.x.

Pumariega, A. J., Rogers, K., & Rothe, E. (2005). Culturally competent systems of care for children's mental health: Advances and challenges. *Community Mental Health Journal, 41*, 539-555. doi:10.1007/s10597-005-6360-4.

Pumariega, A. J., Rothe, E., & Pumariega, J. B. (2005). Mental health of immigrants and refugees. *Community Mental Health Journal, 41*, 581-97. doi:10.1007/s10597-005-6363-1.

Schachner, M. K., Van de Vijver, F. J., & Noack, P. (2014). Family-related antecedents of early adolescent immigrants' psychological and sociocultural school adjustment in Germany. *Journal of Cross-Cultural Psychology*, *45*, 1606-1625. doi:10.1177/0022022114543831.

Schwartz, S. J., Unger, J. B., Zamboanga, B. L., & Szapocznik, J. (2010). Rethinking the concept of acculturation: implications for theory and research. *American Psychologist*, *65*, 237. doi: 10.1037/a0019330.

Sirin, S. R., Ryce, P., Gupta, T., & Rogers-Sirin, L. (2013). The Role of Acculturative Stress on Mental Health Symptoms for Immigrant Adolescents: A Longitudinal Investigation. *Developmental Psychology, 49*, 736–748. doi:10.1037/a0028398.

Stuart, J., & Ward, C. (2015). The ecology of acculturation. In P. Pedersen, J. G. Draguns, W. J. Lonner, J. E. Trimble, and M. Scharrón-del Rio (Eds), *Counselling across cultures* (7th ed., pp. 383–405). *Thousand Oaks*, CA: Sage.

Sue, D. W., Capodilupo, C. M., Torino, G. C., Bucceri, J. M., Holder, A. M. B., Nadal, K. L., & Esquilin, M. (2007). Racial microaggressions in everyday life: Implications for clinical practice. *American Psychologist, 62*, 271–286. doi:10.1037/0003-066X.62.4.271.

Sue, D. W., & Sue, D. (2012). *Counseling the culturally diverse: Theory and practice* (6th ed.). Hoboken, NJ, US: John Wiley & Sons Inc.

Sue, D. W., Arredondo, P., & McDavis, R. J. (1992). Multicultural counseling competencies and standards: A call to the profession. *Journal of Multicultural Counseling and Development, 20*, 64-88. doi:10.1002/j.2161-1912. 1992.tb00563.x.

Tartakovsky, E. (2012). Factors affecting immigrants' acculturation intentions: A theoretical model and its assessment among adolescent immigrants from Russia and Ukraine in Israel. *International Journal of Intercultural Relations*, *36*, 83–99. doi:10.1016/j.ijintrel.2011.02.003.

Terrell, F., & Terrell, S. (1984). Race of counselor, client sex, cultural mistrust level, and premature termination from counseling among Black clients. *Journal of Counseling Psychology, 31*, 371–375. doi:10.1037/0022-0167.31.3.371.

Triandafyllidou, A. (2000). The political discourse on immigration in southern Europe: A critical analysis. *Journal of Community & Applied Social Psychology*, *10*, 373-389. doi:10.1002/1099- 1298(200009/10)10:5<373::AID-CASP595>3.0.CO;2-R.

Uba, L. (1994). *Asian Americans: Personality patterns, identity, and mental health*. New York, NY, US: Guilford Press.

van Oudenhoven, J. P., & Ward, C. (2013). Fading majority cultures: The implications of transnationalism and demographic changes for immigrant acculturation. *Journal of Community & Applied Social Psychology*, *23*, 81–97. doi:10.1002/casp.2132.

Vasta, E. (2007). From ethnic minorities to ethnic majority policy: Multiculturalism and the shift to assimilationism in the Netherlands. *Ethnic and Racial Studies*, *30*, 713-740. doi:10.1080/01419870701491770.

Wang, Y., Kim, S. Y., Anderson, E. R., Chen, A. C.-C., & Yan, N. (2012). Parent–child acculturation discrepancy, perceived parental knowledge, peer deviance, and adolescent delinquency in Chinese immigrant families. *Journal of Youth and Adolescence*, *41*, 907–919. doi:10.1007/s10964-011-9705-z.

Ward, C., & Geeraert, N. (2016). Advancing acculturation theory and research: The acculturation process in its ecological context. *Current Opinion in Psychology, 8,* 98-104. doi:10.1016/j.copsyc.2015.09.021.

Wu, I. (2012). Acculturation, coping, and attitudes toward seeking professional psychological help among Chinese international college students. *Dissertation Abstract International: Section B. Science and Engineering*, *73*, 636.

Yağmur, K., & van de Vijver, F. J. (2012). Acculturation and language orientations of Turkish immigrants in Australia, France, Germany, and the Netherlands. *Journal of Cross-Cultural Psychology*, *43*, 1110-1130. doi:10.1177/0022022111420145.

Zhang, A. Y., Snowden, L. R., & Sue, S. (1998). Differences between Asian and White Americans' help seeking and utilization patterns in the Los Angeles area. *Journal of Community Psychology, 26*, 317-326. doi:10.1002/(SICI)1520-6629(199807)26:4<317::AID-JCOP2>3.0.CO;2-Q.

In: Social Psychology and Counseling
Editors: D. A. Kleiber and E. Delgado-Romero
ISBN: 978-1-53616-548-7

Chapter 23

Global Climate Change, Environmental Psychology, and Weather Justice

Alan E. Stewart

While many of the chapters in this book have examined interpersonal, social, and cultural influences on psychological functioning and mental health, an often overlooked category of influences comes from the physical environments in which people live, work and travel (Moser & Uzzell, 2003). The study of the ways in which the environment affects psychological functioning encompasses environmental psychology (Bechtel, 1997; Fleury-Bahi, Pol & Navarro, 2017; Stokols & Altman, 1987). Environmental psychology matters because the natural environment may affect behavior directly or may moderate the effects of the interpersonal, social, and cultural variables (Gifford, 2014).

Environmental influences on psychological functioning and behavior matter especially at this time in the history of the United States because of the possibilities and threats that are posed by global climate change (Intergovernmental Panel on Climate Change [IPCC], 2014). Environmental psychologists have been working on two fronts, the first of which involves efforts to mitigate greenhouse gas emissions that stem from anthropogenic sources. The second, and arguably broader, front for environmental psychology involves adaptation to a changed global climate (Grothmann & Patt 2005; Swim et al., 2011). The mitigation of greenhouse gases and adaptation to climate change intersect with issues of social, environmental, and climate justice in that people of different socioeconomic, racial, ethnic, regional, and cultural groups will be disproportionately affected by global climate change (Walker, 2012). Further, routine and severe weather conditions, whether they stem from global climate change or not, also can disproportionately affect marginalized communities such as economically disadvantaged groups and ethnic and racial minorities. Yet, such inequities from weather and the topic of weather justice have not been examined previously in the literature.

The author has four purposes in this chapter, the first of which is to review briefly the nature and scope of global climate change. Second, because global climate change will affect people in developing countries to a greater extent than people in the countries that most contributed to the problem of global warming, the author examines the concepts of environmental and climate justice. Third, the author explores and discusses several topics from environmental psychology that directly bear upon climate justice including the psychological attachments to places for living and working and the effects of environmental stress, especially as it may arise from the natural hazards that are possible with global climate change and severe weather (drought, wildfires, floods, hurricanes, severe storms, and so forth). This exploration leads to the author's fourth purpose, which is to propose the new concept of *weather justice* to describe the disproportionate risks and impacts of routine and severe weather events on diverse groups of people with respect to the places where they live and work.

Global Climate Change

For nearly 30 years the IPCC has evaluated the prospects for global climate change and attempted to assess the likely impacts and ways that humans and ecosystems may need to adapt (Houghton et al., 1990). Many of the consequences of climate change that were anticipated within the initial IPCC report have been borne out in terms of decreases in polar ice sheets and glaciers, the poleward-expansion of warm tropical air from the equator, and changes in weather patterns due to the shifting jet streams (IPCC).

The IPCC reports concerning the impacts of climate change have consistently maintained that agrarian, non-industrialized countries (e.g., those member countries of the G77; Vihma, Mulugetta, & Karlsson-Vinkhuyzen, 2009) will experience greater hardships resulting from climate change. These challenges may take the form of altered growing seasons, changes in the availability of food sources (from land or water), changes in the habitability of land, and shortages in food, water, and energy among other resources (IPCC, 2014a). Heath-related impact disparities also will exist because changes in vector borne diseases will follow from an altered global climate (Caminade, McIntyre, & Jones, 2019). Impoverished regions along with people living in poverty within G20 countries will be disproportionately affected by the continued increase of global temperatures and the greater frequency and variability of extreme weather events (IPCC, 2014a, b). Thus, due to ocean level rise, the loss of food or water sources, or because of destruction from extreme weather events, places will become uninhabitable, as discussed previously. This will create stresses due to the loss of place and the necessity to relocate.

Similarly, severe and extreme weather events will pose greater risks to physical and psychological health.

CLIMATE JUSTICE

The concept of climate justice has its roots in global activism, post-colonial arguments, and environmental justice (Meikle, Wilson & Jafry, 2016). Environmental justice provides an orienting framework for understanding climate justice. In this regard, environmental justice originated in the United States within the last 30 years and has since become a global movement with many different emphases (Walker, 2012). Although different movements and organizations have developed their own conceptions of environmental justice, one of the most common definitions is that of the United States Environmental Protection Agency (US, EPA). The EPA (2019) definition states:

> Environmental Justice is the fair treatment and meaningful involvement of all people regardless of race, color, national origin, or income with respect to the development, implementation, and enforcement of environmental laws, regulations, and policies. EPA has this goal for all communities and persons across this Nation. It will be achieved when everyone enjoys the same degree of protection from environmental and health hazards and equal access to the decision-making process to have a healthy environment in which to live, learn, and work.

Climate justice emphasizes the idea of distributional justice of the EPA definition above, while also emphasizing the more specific hazards that may exist with longer-term changes in the climate. Bruno, Karliner, and Brotsky (1999) first used the term *climate justice* (Meikle, Wilson, & Jafry (2016). Bruno and colleagues emphasized the needs for mitigation of greenhouse gas emissions and attempted in their description of climate justice to discuss the roles of oil companies, the World Bank, and transnational corporations in jeopardizing the climate through the growth of a carbon-based economy. More recently, the Mary Robinson Foundation (MRF, 2015) has provided a conception of climate justice that embraces both mitigation and adaption while addressing issues of distributional, procedural, and relational justice. The introduction to the MRF definition of climate justice states:

> Climate Justice links human rights and development to achieve a human-centred approach, safeguarding the rights of the most vulnerable and sharing the burdens and benefits of climate change and its resolution equitably and fairly. Climate justice is informed by science, responds to science and acknowledges the need for equitable stewardship of the world's resources. (MRF, 2015, p. 1).

The MRF statement then articulates seven principles that specify the values and procedures of climate justice. These include: (a) respecting and protecting human rights, (b) supporting the rights of people on developing countries to use their resources and to develop economically, (c) sharing equitably in the benefits and burdens of climate change, (d) ensuring that decisions about climate change issues are made in ways that are participatory, transparent, and accountable, (e) highlighting gender equality and equity, (f) realizing the transformative role of education about climate change, and (g) using effective partnerships to secure climate justice (MRF, 2015, pp. 1-3).

Several authors have used Sens' (2009) theory of social justice and Nussbaum's (2011) capabilities approach to emphasize additional important facets of climate justice in addition to those that involve distributional and procedural justice (Alves & Mariano, 2018; Schlosberg, 2012; Sovacool, 2013). Principally, the emphases of Sens and of Nussbaum have been more applicable in adapting to climate change. Their framework asks how the freedom of people can be increased so that they can pursue choices that they value. How can freedoms of agency and well-being be increased or ensured in the light of climate change (Alves & Mariano, 2018)? A capabilities approach also is more flexible and locally applicable to different kinds of weather or climate challenges that communities may face. Environmental psychology provides a framework for addressing some of the questions that arise from the capability perspectives of Sens and Nussbaum. Environmental psychology also provides a way to understand some of the psychological challenges that global climate change may bring.

ENVIRONMENTAL PSYCHOLOGY

The study of person-environment relationships arose in the 1960's as a relatively circumscribed field that originally addressed a variety of practical problems in architecture and design (Holahan, 1986). The scope of inquiry in environmental psychology expanded rapidly to include topics such as: (a) attitudes, values, belief and affective processes concerning the environment, (b) territoriality, personal space, and the effects of crowded environments, (c) stressful environments, (d) behavioral settings, school, and work environments, (e)home environments and place attachment, (f) extreme, isolated, or contained environments, (g) environmental risk perceptions and risk-taking, (h) environmental assessment, and (i) global climate change among other areas (Bechtel, 1997; Clayton 2012; Gifford, 2014; Stokols & Altman, 1987). The topics of place attachment, environmental stressors, and the perception of environmental risks are relevant in an examination of adaption to climate change and to issues of climate justice.

Place Attachment and Rootedness

A growing body of scholarship in environmental psychology has examined peoples' attachment to the various places (e.g., homes, communities, and towns) in which they live or work. Place attachment broadly refers to the affective connections that link people to specific places or behavior settings (Altman & Low, 1992; Giuliani & Feldman, 1993; Hidalgo & Hernandez, 2001; Manzo & Devine-Wright, 2014). Investigators have identified three facets of place attachment, the first of which involves bonding to a place via the social attachments and relationships associated with the setting (Riger & Lavrakas, 1981). From this perspective, people become attached to places because they form attachments to the setting inhabitants and consequently perceive themselves as *insiders* with respect to the setting and social group (Altman & Low, 1992).

Rootedness is the second facet and refers to attachments to the physical attributes of settings. Rootedness represents attachment to place that is unmediated by peoples' social relationships (Fried, 1982; Gustafson, 2001; Hidalgo & Hernandez, 2001; McAndrew, 1998). Some researchers have additionally conceptualized rootedness stemming from the long-term habitation in one locality that involves a relative incuriosity about the world beyond the locality as well as a more immediate focus on the present time frame compared to a past or future-focus (McAndrew, 1998; Tuan, 1980).

The third facet, sense of place, embodies elements of both bondedness and rootedness. Sense of place involves a kind of optimal *psychological distance* between self and place that gives rise to a heightened appreciation for the place, to a sense of security, and of being *at home* (Hay, 1998; Manzo & Devine-Wright, 2014; Tuan, 1980). Importantly, sense of place also involves feelings of belonging within the physical and social realms of a place.

In an extensive qualitative study of New Zealand residents, Hay (1998) observed that there were various types of sense of place and that developmental stages characterized the relative maturity of one's sense of place. Regarding type, Hay distinguished between superficial, partial, personal, ancestral, and cultural senses of place. A recurring theme in Hay's (1998) study was that sense of place, especially involving personal, ancestral, or cultural types, was rather inextricably woven into peoples' accounts of interpersonal relationships. That is, recollections of the family and home life were imbued with elements of the physical place in which such life experiences occurred. Overall, Hay's work suggested that *places* are an important part of peoples' life experiences.

Sense of place especially may be challenged when relocations to new or distant geographical locations are mandated by economic (e.g., to keep one's job), civil/militaristic (e.g., war refugees or reassignment to new bases), or natural (floods, hurricanes, etc.) forces. Such displacements can uproot peoples' connections with the physical places of their homes, neighborhoods, and towns. Similarly, people may mourn their lost sense of place as ties with other significant people in the settings are broken and sources of social support are no longer available. Fullilove (1996) maintained that geographical displacement may give rise to disorientation, alienation, and a lack of belonging, all of which could diminish general psychological health and well-being.

The attachment to the place of one's home and daily activities means that events that threaten the nature of those places or perhaps their very existence necessarily pose psychological challenges. Global climate change and the extreme weather events stemming from climate change may require adjustments to a changed or altered landscape and the opportunities that the place affords (i.e., affordances). Alternatively, global climate change may so alter some places that people have to relocate and may thus grieve the loss of their home places (Cunsolo & Landman, 2017; Devine-Wright, 2014).

The empirical study of the relationships of global climate change with place attachment has yielded an interesting mixture of results. Generally, for cultures and communities with longstanding relationships with place – lands and bodies of water – sense of place and place attachment are high (Adams 2016; Willox et al., 2012). In addition, distress about the disruptions that can be attributed to a changed climate have negatively affected place attachment such that both mental and physical health have arisen. This was the case in an Inuit community in Canada that has experienced many lifestyle changes due to the physical alteration of their homelands (Willox et al., 2012). Similarly in Peru, despite the current and future changes that this region of the central Andes will experience, people tend not to migrate to places that are more socially or climatologically safer because of either satisfaction with place or attachment to place (Adams, 2016). In a sample of people living in Australia, Walker, Devine-Wright, Price, and Leviston (2015) observed that attachment to place was related to pro-environmental behaviors and weakly to perceptions of environmental degradation of the place. Retreat from the effects of climate change and resettlement in new, safer places will be psychologically challenging (Agyeman, Devine-Wright, & Prange, 2009).

Socioenvironmental Stress

Many social or interpersonal environment stressors are related to the density of people in a given space and the ways that person spaces are negotiated. Four types of stressors are pertinent here: crowding, privacy, personal space, and territoriality. Baum and Paulus (1987) further conceptualized crowding as involving excessive stimulation (i.e., noise, movements, etc.), intimacy that is overly intense, or restrictions on behavioral freedom and control. The negative effects of crowding have been reported in several studies when the density of people has exceeded approximately 1.0 to 1.5 people per dwelling room (Evans & Lepore, 1993; Regoeczi, 2003; Zuravin 1986). Privacy refers to "the selective control of access to the self or to one's group" (Altman, 1975, p. 18). The lack of privacy may occur in physical settings where it is difficult or impossible to regulate the degree of exposure to others and social interactions with others, resulting in stress or distress (Gatersleben & Griffin, 2017; Pedersen, 1999). Personal space or proxemics concerns the control and management of the immediate physical space around one's body. Researchers still rely upon estimates from the classic work of Hall (1959, 1966) for evaluating normal or appropriate personal space according to social settings. That is, intimate distances are less than 1.5 feet apart while social distances of 4 to 12 feet are considered the norm. Infractions of these distances may result in stress or distress. Finally, territoriality extends the notion of personal space to wider areas and to objects that a person or group claims some degree of ownership (Altman, 1975). At least three types of territories exist, one of which is primary (e.g., one's apartment), secondary (a church), and public (a city square) (Gatersleben & Griffin, 2017). Conflicts over territories or the location of territorial boundaries can result in stress or even physical aggression.

Within the context of global climate change and severe weather, socioenvironmental stressors may affect behavior in several ways. First, if people evacuate from their homes to temporary shelters, issues of crowding and the stress associated with it can occur. Second, some people decide not to evacuate their homes out of concerns for crowding, sufficient spaces or places for the pets at evacuation shelters, and out of a need to protect their homes (i.e., their territories) from looting while an area is under an evacuation (Blendon et al., 2007). Third, if homes or communities are damaged to the extent that temporary or permanent relocation is required, then the process of finding or negotiating new spaces, places, and home "territories" may also become stressful for people who have evacuated (Blendon et al., 2007).

Physical Environmental Stress

Evans and Cohen (1987) delineated four categories of physical environmental stressors that vary both with respect to severity and to size or scope. The first two of these, ambient environmental stressors and daily hassles, tend to be smaller-scaled in nature and more personal in their effects (Evans & Cohen, 1987). Daily environmental hassles could involve a rainy or foggy drive that is stressful (Resnick, 2000) or encountering dust of pollen while outside such that breathing is difficult or respiratory conditions are triggered (Grundstein, Shephard, Miller & Sarnat, 2017). Environmental psychologists also have studied ambient stressors of noise level and extremes of temperature (Gatersleben & Griffin, 2017). Especially when it is unpredictable and uncontrollable, unwanted sound (noise) can increase stress levels. A wide range of individual differences and sensitivities to noise exist (Gatersleben & Griffin, 2017). Another ambient stressor concerns the contribution of air temperature to the performance of aggressive behaviors. Dexter (1903) was among the first to study these relationships which have garnered regular interest from environmental psychologists. In a broad review of the literature and from the assimilation of multiple data sets, increasing temperatures have been reliably associated with increases in aggression and interpersonal violence (Anderson, 1989). Although some researchers differ in their characterization and in the theories that may explain this relationship, the general shape of the relationship appears to be that of an inverted U. That is, at lower temperatures aggressive behavior occurs infrequently. At extremely high air temperatures aggression decreases, while at moderately hot temperatures aggression is at its peak (Bell, 2005).

The third and fourth types of challenging physical environmental stressors involve stressful life events and cataclysmic events (Evans & Cohen, 1987). Beyond an ambient stressor or hassle, stressful life events emanating from the environment, for example, may involve damage from severe storms (i.e., downed trees, hail damage to roofs or vehicles, loss of power or smartphone service). Similarly, weather-related motor vehicle crashes (MVC) may not only be stressful life events but also give rise to acute stress disorder or to MVC-related posttraumatic stress disorder (Blanchard & Hickling, 1997). Sometimes the weather or climate become stressful because of what it *does not do*. Here, the author is referring to the stresses growers may experience during periods of heat and drought when needed rains do not occur (Quinn et al., 2011).

Cataclysmic events include natural hazards such as wildfires, hurricanes, tornadoes, floods, earthquakes, tsunamis, and so forth (Cutter, 2006). Within the United States, the greatest numbers of injuries and deaths annually occur from excessive heat, tornadoes, and floods (National Weather Service, 2019). Such events may result in extreme stress or posttraumatic stress in several ways that include: (a) exposure to the extreme conditions (e.g., howling, destructive hurricane or tornado winds, inundation by flood waters, shaking and damage of structures during an earthquake, etc.), (b) injury from the natural hazard, (c) exposure to the property damage and/or losses resulting from natural hazards, (d) exposure to death (i.e., dead bodies of people or animals), (e) loss or damage to infrastructure (i.e., water, food, and power supplies) that prolongs a return to normal functioning in the aftermath of a disaster, and (f) the stresses and adjustments following the relocation and resettlement processes (some of which were discussed above). These characteristics of natural disasters ("cataclysmic events" for Evans & Cohen, 1987) also may result in other symptoms associated with psychological distress or disorders.

Researchers have documented the traumatizing effects of weather-related disasters and their role in creating or worsening psychopathology in people who survive disasters. In this regard the effects of hurricane Katrina have been investigated extensively. King et al., (2016) observed that for people who fled Hurricane Katrina, approximately 10% met the diagnostic criteria for posttraumatic stress disorder (PTSD), over 25% met the criteria for major depressive disorder, with 15% of the people reporting depression specific to the effects of hurricane Katrina. Lai et al., (2015) observed that in a sample of children who experienced hurricane Katrina, posttraumatic stress symptoms decreased over time, however, the presence and persistence of such symptoms reduced the positive effects of social support. David et al. (1996) observed somewhat higher rates of PTSD 36% in south Florida residents who were affected by hurricane Andrew. The incidence rate of major depression following hurricane Andrew was 30% while the rate for anxiety disorders was 20%.

Floods also are associated with negative psychological consequences. In a ten-year follow-up after a flood in China, researchers found that the prevalence of PTSD was 9.5%; the prevalence was 9.2% for anxiety disorders. Low levels of emotional support and emotional instability were predictors of persisting symptoms over time (Dai et al., 2017). Shortly after a flood in southern Spain in 2012, researchers documented that people within the flood zone were approximately eight times more likely to develop PTSD symptoms compared to nearby residents who were unaffected by flooding (Fontalba-Navas et al., 2017).

Regarding other natural hazards that can produce destruction and trauma, a follow-up investigation of adolescents in Alabama and Missouri following the devastating tornado outbreaks in the spring of 2011 revealed a prevalence rate of 3.5% for PTSD and 3.2% for a major depressive episode (Adams et al., 2015). Most commonly, PTSD for this group was comorbid with either depression (3.7%) or with substance use disorders (1.1%). Following wildfires in Greece in 2007, researchers observed a high rate of 46.7% of people met the criteria for PTSD while 63% of the victims met the criteria for a sleep disorder (Psarros et al., 2017).

Weather-related motor vehicle collisions (MVCs) occupy a unique position among stressful life events and those that are disastrous (Blanchard & Hickling, 1997). While MVC's in inclement weather may be stressful to the extent that vehicles or property are damaged, crashes that result in injury, disability, death, and /or traumatization exceed that which is merely stressful – such events may result in PTSD. Norris (1992) noted that the MVC's were unique in their impact and severity in contributing to PTSD. She observed that 11.5% of people who experienced a MVC met all of the diagnostic criteria for PTSD. Stein et al., (2016) examined the effect of severe MVC's across 13 epidemiological studies and observed a 2.5% prevalence rate of PTSD. Investigators in several studies have observed that rainfall increases the frequency of crashes and of injuries (Caliendo, Guida, Parisi, 2007; Omranian, Sharif, Sessouky, & Weissmann, 2018). Although MVC's occur more frequently during inclement weather, most frequently on pavement made wet by rain, fewer crash fatalities occur in bad weather (i.e., snow, ice, fog). From 2006 to 2017, there were over 5,891,000 vehicle crashes each year on average. Of these MVC's, 1,235,000 (21%) were weather-related (U. S. Department of Transportation, Federal Highway Administration (2019).

In summary, environmental psychology is relevant for understanding and responding to the challenges people may face with global climate change. Place attachment is significant because weather events stemming from climate change may bear upon the quality of life in different places or ultimately affect the habitability of different places. In this regard because places are significant, so is the weather and changing climate that affect places. Routine weather and climate conditions may create ambient stresses or hassles that demand coping resources and adjustment. Impacts from ordinary or severe weather may create stressful life events that eventuate in PTSD or other psychological problems such as depression or anxiety. The perception and awareness of environmental risks that come from the weather may help people to anticipate and prepare for the risks that the weather or future climate presents.

The ubiquity of specific climate and weather-related risks and stressors as revealed in this section suggests an extension of the construct of climate justice. Just as climate refers to a broad area over a given time, climate justice is concerned with the effects of global climate change on people within regions who must cope with the cumulative challenges brought by climate change. Single weather events – whether routine or extreme in nature – may disproportionately affect people living or working in particular places. This implies the need for a corresponding conception of weather justice. The final section of this chapter explores this concept and provides some empirical justification for its value and potential uses.

WEATHER JUSTICE

The concept of weather justice is concerned with examining the extent to which disparities or inequities exist in the exposure to severe or routine weather events and in the extent to which these disparities matter along multiple dimensions (moral/philosophical, psychological and physical health, economic, and so forth). Similarly, with respect to a capabilities approach on social justice (Nussbaum, 2011; Sens 2009), to what extent do disparities exist in the exposure to specific weather conditions or events that promote agency, growth, development, and psychological health? Disparities and inequities may exist across a range of demographic variables such as socioeconomic status, region, race, culture, ethnicity, religion, language community, among others, taken singly or in combination.

The author intends weather justice to augment and extend the concept of climate justice – not to replace it. Weather justice is additive in several ways. First, whereas climate justice focuses upon the inequities that exist over regions for larger groups of people and that accumulate over time, weather justice downscales this emphasis so that it could apply to a community or city whose members experienced weather-related inequities from a single event or set of related events, much as was the case with the flooding of the lower ninth district in New Orleans with Hurricane Katrina (Cutter et al., 2014). Second, climate justice is inextricably connected with global climate change (Bruno, Karliner, & Brotsky, 1999; Mielke, Wilson & Jafry, 2016; Schlosberg, 2012).

Such is not the case with weather justice – the concept can apply to the inequitable and significant effects of a rather routine event (e.g., a flooding rain, cold and uncomfortable conditions) as well as to those extreme weather events that are determined to have occurred because of climate change. This points to the third and most significant feature of the weather justice concept, which is the realization that there are many impactful weather events have nothing to do with climate change that have very disparate effects on people who have been marginalized in some way and/or who live in poverty. Empirical research that documents some weather-based inequities is presented below.

Temperature

These features of weather justice find support in the literature that show the different ways in which people of different races have experienced a greater degree of exposure and the ensuing social and psychological impacts of weather events. With respect to heat and hot conditions, Wilson, Richard, Joseph and Williams (2010) used data from geographical information systems (GIS), the Behavior Risk Factor Surveillance System of the US EPA, and from the National Center for Health Statistics to examine at the county-level the risks to people for heat-related health problems (e.g., heat stroke, breathing problems, and so forth). When comparing the vulnerability to high air temperatures and heat-related health problems, Wilson et al., (2010) observed that many of most vulnerable counties contained a higher proportion of African Americans. These regions included concentrations in urban and suburban areas in South Carolina, Louisiana, Arkansas, Florida, Missouri, Maryland, Delaware, New Jersey, New York, Arizona, and California. Although not included in their analyses, Wilson et al., (2010) conjectured that many of these same areas also included higher proportions of Hispanic or Latino/a residents.

Flooding

Other researchers have examined the extent to which disparities may exist in peoples' likelihoods of experiencing flooding. Qiang (2019) also used a geographic information approach and US Census data to examine the demographic characteristics of people who live in zones that may flood according to the Federal Emergency Management Agency (FEMA). Although people of higher socioeconomic status were more prone to coastal floods (e. g, from hurricanes or tropical storms), a much larger proportion of the US population was vulnerable to inland flooding from rivers, creeks and streams. The characteristics of people most likely to live in a region prone to flooding included: single mothers, people living at or below the poverty level, people who were unemployed, and those who did not possess insurance. In addition, Qiang (2019) also identified older people who are experiencing higher vulnerability for flooding risks.

Montgomery and Chakraborty (2015) performed a similar analysis for the Miami, Florida metropolitan statistical area (MSA) to examine the vulnerabilities of people to coastal and inland flooding. These researchers also looked at communities according to the residents' national origins. Montgomery and Chakraborty observed that inland flood risks are higher for neighborhoods that included greater proportions of non-Hispanic African Americans, Hispanics, and subgroups of people from Colombia or Puerto Rico. People from Mexico were inequitably exposed to flooding along the coastal regions around Miami. Maldonado, Collins, Grineski and Chakraborty (2016) compared the Miami and Houston MSA's for flood risks and observed that Hispanic immigrants, compared to non-Hispanic Whites, were much more likely to live in flood prone areas in and around Houston.

Weather-Related MVC's

The evidence for weather-related MVC's disparities is more tentative, but noteworthy nonetheless. Generally, the risk for crashes increases during rainfall events by 57%; rainfall intensity also increases the likelihood of MVC occurrence (Omranian et al., 2018). Hilton (2006) in studying data from fatal MVC's in the United States reported that Native American and Hispanic people had a disproportionately higher likelihood of death from a MVC compared to other ethnic or racial groups. Further, African American children in rural or urban setting also experienced disproportionately higher rates of fatal MVC's. Although only suggestive at this point, these results would seem to imply that African Americans, Hispanic Americans, and Native Americans may also experience disproportionately higher risks for weather-related MVC's (and for MVC fatalities) than people in other ethnic groups.

Occupational Exposure to Outside Conditions

To what extent might disparities exist in peoples' exposure to outside weather conditions as a function of their occupation? Although the opportunity to be outside, especially in natural settings, can be restorative and promote psychological health (Kaplan & Kaplan, 1989), the necessity to work outside in built or urban settings, sometimes despite the weather conditions, could be stressful and also carry risks for physical health (Evans & Cohen, 1987). Similarly, some occupations depend upon favorable weather conditions for the work to occur. Thus, longer stretches of unfavorable weather (e.g., extremes of temperature, dust, or rainfall), may present economic disadvantages for some occupations

The author consulted the Bureau of Labor Statistics website (BLS, 2019; https://www.bls.gov/data/; Torpey, 2017) to examine exposure to outdoor working conditions by occupation and race. The most frequent occupations held by people identifying as Hispanic, especially men, were in construction and agriculture fields (e.g., roofers, painters, planters, and harvesters). Approximately 78.6% of the occupations, on average, involved extensive outside exposure – and presumably to the prevailing weather conditions. The most frequently reported occupations for African Americans spanned a wider range of fields (e.g., postal service workers, nurses, barbers, bus/taxi divers, healthcare support, bailiffs or corrections officers). On average, there were 51.0% of these occupations that involved outside exposure. These results should be interpreted carefully because occupations are partly a choice that people make. Sometimes, however, people go into particular occupations because they do not have choice or opportunities for other vocational paths.

DISCUSSION AND IMPLICATIONS

People have physical and psychological relationships both with the places of their residence and work and also with the weather and climate of those places. Increasing, it is likely that these relationships will be affected by different weather regimes associated with global climate change. It is just as likely that routine weather events also may affect psychological functioning. Within this chapter the author has reviewed selected topics from environmental psychology that are becoming increasingly relevant as the climate changes: place attachment and environmental stressors. Everyone will not experience stress and the risks of climate change equitably. This relates to the still-developing concept and work around climate justice. Climate justice is responsive to the efforts to mitigate greenhouse gases as well as in preparing diverse and underserved people to adapt to a changed climate. Weather justice is a downward extension of climate justice and encompasses both the weather under climate change and more ordinary weather with respect to the disparate and inequitable risks and stresses that the weather may bring.

Several implications follow from this review. First, in addition to the psychological challenges posed by social, cultural, economic, and political influences, the emergence of global climate change and the enhanced potential for severe and extreme weather that will accompany it strongly implies that peoples' mental health burdens will increase. It follows that the mental health infrastructure also will need to expand to accommodate this greater demand for psychological services (Hayes et al., 2018; Watts et al., 2018). It especially is important that the emerging social and health policies and the health care infrastructure not perpetuate existing disparities in the provision of services. As this review emphasized, some of the same groups that would be disproportionately affected by climate and weather events are those underserved by the current health care delivery systems in the United States (Cook et al., 2017). A second implication is that although extreme climate or weather events may be temporally and geographically bounded, their psychological impacts may persist in time and accumulate within individuals, families, and communities. This means that the provision of psychological services, rather than being temporary or piecemeal with respect to the weather event, should become a more enduring feature of community mental health care. It is likely that anxiety, depression, or trauma that stems from a weather event may exacerbate a person's preexisting psychological difficulties or emerge as new disorders (Hayes et al., 2018). Third, because diverse ethnic and cultural groups may be disproportionately exposed to climate and weather events, it is imperative that mental health providers be skilled in the diagnosis, assessment, and provision of services to culturally diverse clients. This will involve not only skill in treating particular symptoms from culturally sensitive perspectives, but also understanding the greater vulnerability to weather events and the lack of treatment resources that people from underserved groups have experienced in the past. Rather than viewing culturally different persons as victims without initiative or agency to help themselves, those who provide disaster mental health services should strive to empower people as survivors who can recover from disasters (Louis & Stewart, 2017). Finally, the prevention of physical and psychological harm may help many people to become more resilient to severe weather events when they do occur. Here, early and regular education at the K-12 levels about the nature of severe weather, ways to remain safe during extreme events, and then how to cope and to rebuild in the aftermath may help to reduce the psychological challenges of climate change (Stewart, Knox, & Schneider, 2018).

References

Adams, H. (2016). Why populations persist: mobility, place attachment and climate change. *Population and Environment, 37*, 429–448. doi: 10.1007/s11111-015-0246-3.

Adams, Z. W., Danielson, C. K., Sumner, J. A., McCauley, J. L., Cohen, J. R., & Ruggiero, K. J. (2015). Comorbidity of PTSD, major depression, and substance use disorder among adolescent victims of the spring 2011 tornadoes in Alabama and Joplin, Missouri. *Psychiatry, 78*, 170–185. doi:10.1080/00332747.2015.1051448.

Agyeman, J., Devine-Wright, P., & Prange, J. (2009). Close to the edge, down by the river? Joining up managed retreat and place attachment in a climate changed world. *Environment and Planning A: Economy and Space, 41*(3), 509–513. https://doi.org/10.1068/a41301.

Altman, I. (1975). *The environment and social behavior: Privacy, personal space, territory, crowding*. Monterey: Brooks/Cole.

Altman I. & Low, S. M. (Eds.). (1992). *Place attachment: Human behavior and environment. Advances in theory and research*. New York, NY: Plenum Press.

Alves, M. W. & Muriano, E. B. (2018). Climate justice and human development: A systematic literature review. *Journal of Cleaner Production, 202,* 360-375.

Anderson, C. A. (1989). Temperature and aggression: Ubiquitous effects of heat on occurrence of human violence. *Psychological Bulletin, 106,* 74-96.

Baum, A. & Paulus, P. B. (1987). Crowding. In D. Stokols and I. Altman (Eds.), *Handbook of environmental psychology*. (pp. 533-570). New York: John Wiley & Sons.

Bechtel, R. B. (1997). *Environment and behavior: An introduction*. Thousand Oaks, CA: Sage Publications.

Bell, P. A. (2005). Reanalysis and Perspective in the Heat-Aggression Debate. *Journal of Personality and Social Psychology, 89*, 71–73. doi: 10.1037/0022-3514.89.1.71.

Blanchard, E., & Hickling, E. (1997). *After the crash: Assessment and treatment of motor vehicle accident survivors* (1st ed.). Washington, DC: American Psychological Association.

Blendon, R. J., Benson, J. M., Desroches, C. M., Lyon-Daniel, K., Mitchell, E. W., & Pollard, W. E. (2007). The Public's preparedness for hurricanes in four affected regions. *Public Health Reports, 122*(2), 167–176. https://doi.org/10.1177/003335 490712200206.

Bruno, K., Karliner, J. and Brotsky, C. (1999), *Greenhouse gangsters vs climate justice.* Transnational Resource & Action Center and CorpWatch, San Francisco, CA, http://s3.amazonaws.com/corpwatch.org/downloads/greenhousegangsters.pdf.

Caliendo, C. Guida, M., & Parisi, A. (2007). A crash-prediction model for multilane roads. *Accident Analysis and Prevention, 39,* 657-670. doi:10.1016/j.aap.2006. 10.012.

Caminade, C., McIntyre, K. M., & Jones, A. E. (2019). Impact of recent and future climate change on vector-borne diseases. *Annals of the New York Academy of Sciences, 1436*(1), 157–173. https://doi.org/10.1111/nyas.13950.

Cook, B. L., Zuvekas, S. H., Chen, J., Progovac, A., & Lincoln, A. K. (2017). Assessing the individual, neighborhood, and policy predictors of disparities in mental health care. *Medical Care Research and Review, 74*(4), 404–430. https://doi-org.proxy-remote.galib.uga.edu/10.1177/1077558716646898.

Cunsolo, A., & Landman, K. (Eds.). (2017). *Mourning nature: Hope at the heart of ecological loss and grief*. Montreal: McGill-Queen's University Press.

Cutter, S. L. (2006). *Hazards, vulnerability, and environmental justice*. Sterling, VA: Earthscan.

Cutter, S. L., Emrich, C. T., Mitchell, J. T., Piergorsch, W. W., Smith, M. M. & Weber, L. (2014). *Hurricane Katrina and the forgotten coast of Mississippi*. New York: Cambridge University Press.

Dai, W., Kaminga, A. C., Tan, H., Wang, J., Lai, Z., Wu, X., & Liu, A. (2017). Long-term psychological outcomes of flood survivors of hard-hit areas of the 1998 Dongting Lake flood in China: Prevalence and risk factors. *PLoS ONE, 12*(2), 1-14. doi: 10.1371/journal.pone.0171557.

David, D., Mellman, T. A., Mendoza, L. M., Kulick-Bell, R., Ironson, G., & Schneiderman, N. (1996). Psychiatric morbidity following Hurricane Andrew. *Journal of Traumatic Stress, 9*(3), 607–612. doi: 10.1002/jts.2490090316.

Devine-Wright, P. (2014). Dynamics of place attachment in a climate changed world. In L. C. Manzo & P. Devine-Wright (Eds.), *Place attachment: Advances in theory, methods and applications*. (pp. 165–177). London: Routledge.

Devine-Wright, P., Price, J., & Leviston, Z. (2015). My country or my planet? Exploring the influence of multiple place attachments and ideological beliefs upon climate change attitudes and opinions. *Global Environmental Change, 30*, 68–79. https://doi.org/10.1016/j.gloenvcha.2014.10.012.

Dexter, E.G. (1903). *Weather Influences*. New York: Macmillan.

Evans, G. W., & Cohen, S. A. (1987). Environmental stress. In D. Stokols & I. Altman (Eds.), *Handbook of environmental psychology* (Vol. 1), (pp. 571-610), New York: Wiley.

Evans, G. W., & Lepore, S. J. (1993). Household crowding and social support: A quasiexperimental analysis. *Journal of Personality and Social Psychology, 65,* 308-316.

Fleury-Bahi, G., Pol, E., & Navarro, O. (Eds.) (2017). *Handbook of environmental psychology and quality of life research.* (International Handbooks of Quality-of-Life). Cham, Switzerland: Springer International Publishing.

Fontalba-Navas, A., Lucas-Borja, M. E., Gil-Aguilar, V., Arrebola, J. P., Pena-Andreu, J. M., & Perez, J. (2017). Incidence and risk factors for post-traumatic stress disorder in a population affected by a severe flood. *Public Health, 144*, 96–102. doi: 10.1016/ j.puhe.2016.12.015.

Fried, M. (1982). Residential attachment: Sources of residential and community satisfaction. *Journal of Social Issues, 38,* 107-119.

Fullilove, M. T. (1996). Psychiatric implications of displacement: Contributions from the psychology of place. *American Journal of Psychiatry, 153,* 1516-1523.

Gatersleben, B., & Griffin, I. (2017). Environmental stress. In G. Fleury-Bahi, E. Pol, & O. Navarro (Eds.), *Handbook of environmental psychology and quality of life research.* (pp. 469–485). Cham: Springer International Publishing. https://doi-org.proxy-remote.galib.uga.edu/10.1007/978-3-319-31416-7_25.

Gifford, R. (2014). Environmental psychology matters. *Annual Review of Psychology, 65*, 541-580. Doi: 10.1146/annurev-psych-010213-115048.

Giuliani, M. V., & Feldman, R. (1993). Place attachment in a developmental and cultural context. *Journal of Environmental Psychology, 13,* 267-274.

Grothmann, T., & Patt, A. (2005). Adaptive capacity and human cognition: The process of individual adaptation to climate change. *Global Environmental Change, 15*, 199-213, doi: 10.1016/j.gloenvcha.2005.01.002.

Grundstein, A., M. Shepherd, P. Miller, & Sarnat, S. E. (2017) The role of mesoscale-convective processes in explaining the 21 November 2016 epidemic thunderstorm asthma event in Melbourne, Australia. *Journal of Applied Meteorology and Climatology, 56*, 1337–1343. doi: 10.1175/JAMC-D-17-0027.1.

Gustafson, P. (2001). Roots and routes: Exploring the relationship between place attachment and mobility. *Environment and Behavior, 33,* 667-686.

Hall, E. T. (1959). *The silent language*. New York: Doubleday.

Hall, E. T. (1966). *The hidden dimension*. New York: Doubleday.

Hay, R. (1998). Sense of place in developmental context. *Journal of Environmental Psychology, 18*, 5-29.

Hayes, K., Blashki, G., Wiseman, J., Burke, S., & Reifels, L. (2018). Climate change and mental health: risks, impacts and priority actions. *International Journal of Mental Health Systems, 12*, 28. doi:10.1186/s13033-018-0210-6.

Hidalgo, M. C., & Hernandez, B. (2001). Place attachment: Conceptual and empirical questions. *Journal of Environmental Psychology, 21*, 273-281.

Hilton J. (2006). *Race and Ethnicity in Fatal Motor Vehicle Traffic Crashes 1999 – 2004*. Technical Report: DOT HS 809 956. National Highway Transportation Safety Administration, U. S. Department of Transporation, Washington, DC.

Holahan, C. J. (1986). Environmental psychology. *Annual Review of Psychology, 37,* 381-407.

Houghton, J., Jenkins, G., Ephraums, J., & Intergovernmental panel on climate change. Working group I. (1990). *Climate change: The IPCC scientific assessment*. Cambridge; New York: Cambridge University Press.

Intergovernmental Panel on Climate Change. (2014). Summary for policymakers. In: *Climate Change 2014: Impacts, Adaptation, and Vulnerability. Part A: Global and Sectoral Aspects*. Contribution of Working Group II to the Fifth Assessment Report of the Intergovernmental Panel on Climate Change [Field, C. B., V. R. Barros, D. J. Dokken, K. J. Mach, M. D. Mastrandrea, T. E. Bilir, M. Chatterjee, K. L. Ebi, Y. O. Estrada, R. C. Genova, B. Girma, E. S. Kissel, A. N. Levy, S. MacCracken, P. R. Mastrandrea, and L. L. White (eds.)]. Cambridge, United Kingdom and New York, NY: Cambridge University Press.

Kaplan, R., & Kaplan, S. (1989). *The experience of nature: A psychological perspective*. New York: Cambridge University Press.

King, R. V., Polatin, P. B., Hogan, D., Downs, D. L., & North, C. S. (2016). Needs assessment of Hurricane Katrina evacuees residing temporarily in Dallas. *Community Mental Health Journal, 52*, 18-24. https://10.1007/s10597-015-9938-5.

Lai, B. S., Kelley, M. L., Harrison, K. M., Thompson, J. E., & Self-Brown, S. (2015). Posttraumatic stress, anxiety, and depression symptoms among children after Hurricane Katrina: A latent profile analysis. *Journal of Child and Family Studies, 24*, 1262–1270. doi: 10.1007/s10826-014-9934-3.

Louis, E. F., & Stewart, A. E. (2017). *Minority Perceptions of Natural Disaster Victims and Survivors Based Upon Race and Gender.* Poster presented at the National Multicultural Conference and Summit, Portland Oregon, January 2017.

Maldonado, A., Collins, T. W., Grineski, S. E., & Chakraborty, J. (2016). Exposure to flood hazards in Miami and Houston: Are Hispanic immigrants at greater risk than other social groups? *International Journal of Environmental Research and Public Health. 13*(8), 1-20. doi:10.3390/ijerph13080775.

Manzo, L., & Devine-Wright, P. (Eds.). (2014). *Place attachment: Advances in theory, methods, and applications*. New York: Routledge.

Mary Robinson Foundation (2015). *Principles of climate justice*. https://www.mrfcj.org/wp-content/uploads/2015/09/Principles-of-Climate-Justice.pdf. Accessed 2 April 2019).

McAndrew, F. T. (1998). The measurement of rootedness and the predictions of attachment to home towns in college students. *Journal of Environmental Psychology, 18*, 409-417.

Meikle, M., Wilson, J., & Jafry, T. (2016). Climate justice: Between mammon and mother earth. *International Journal of Climate Change Strategies and Management, 8*(4), 488-504. doi: http://dx.doi.org.proxy-remote.galib.uga.edu/10.1108/IJCCSM-06-2015-0089.

Montgomery, M. C. & Chakraborty J. (2015). Assessing the environmental justice consequences of flood risk: a case study in Miami, Florida. *Environmental Research Letters, 10*, 1-12. doi:10.1088/1748-9326/10/9/095010.

Moser, G. and Uzzell, D. L. (2003). Environmental psychology. In Millon, T., & Lerner, M. J. (Eds.), *Comprehensive handbook of psychology, Volume 5: Personality and social psychology*, New York: John Wiley & Sons. Pp. 419 – 445.

National Weather Service (2019). *NWS Fatality, injury, and damage statistics*. NOAA, National Weather Service. https://www.nws.noaa.gov/om/hazstats.shtml (Accessed 4.2.2019).

Norris, F. H. (1992). Epidemiology of trauma: Frequency and impact of different potentially traumatic events on different demographic groups. *Journal of Consulting and Clinical Psychology, 60*, 409–418. doi: 10.1037/0022-006X.60.3.409.

Nussbaum, M. (2011). *Creating capabilities: The human development approach.* Cambridge, Mass.: Belknap Press of Harvard University Press.

Omranian, E., Sharif, H., Dessouky, S., & Weissman, J. (2018). Exploring rainfall impacts on the crash risk on Texas roadways: A crash-based matched-pairs analysis approach. *Accident Analysis and Prevention, 117*, 10-20. doi: 10.1016/j.aap. 2018. 03.030.

Pedersen, D. M. (1999). Model for types of privacy by privacy functions. *Journal of Environmental Psychology, 19*, 397–405.

Psarros, C., Theleritis, C., Economou, M., Tzavara, C., Kioulos, K. T., Mantonakis, L., Soldatos, C. R., & Bergiannaki, J. D. (2017). Insomnia and PTSD one month after wildfires: evidence for an independent role of the "fear of imminent death." *International Journal of Psychiatry in Clinical Practice, 21*, 137-141. doi:10.1080/ 13651501.2016.1276192.

Qiang, Yi. (2019). Disparities of population exposed to flood hazards in the United States. *Journal of Environmental Management, 232*, 295-304. Doi: 10.1016/j. jenvman.2018.11.039.

Quinn, C. H., Ziervogel, G., Taylor, A., Takama, T., & Thomalla, F. (2011). Coping with Multiple Stresses in Rural South Africa. *Ecology & Society, 16*(3), 1–20. doi: 10.5751/ES-04216-160302.

Resnick, A. (2000). *Due to the weather: Ways the elements affect our lives*. Westport, CT: Greenwood Press.

Regoeczi, W. C. (2003). When context matters: A multilevel analysis of household and neighborhood crowding on aggression and withdrawal. *Journal of Environmental Psychology, 23,* 457-470.

Riger, S. & Lavrakas, P. J. (1981). Community ties: Patterns of attachment and social interaction in urban neighborhoods. *American Journal of Community Psychology, 9*, 55-66.

Schlosberg, D. (2012). Climate justice and capabilities: a framework for adaptation policy. *Ethics & International Affairs, 26*(4), 445-461. doi:10.1017/ S0892 679412000615.

Sen, A. (2009). *The idea of justice*. Cambridge, Mass.: Belknap Press of Harvard University Press.

Sovacool, B. K., 2013. Adaptation: the complexity of climate justice. *Nature Climate Change 3*, 959-960. doi: 10.1038/nclimate2037.

Stein, D. J., Karam, E. G., Shahly, V., Hill, E. D., King, A., Petukhova, M., … Kessler, R. C. (2016). Post-traumatic stress disorder associated with life-threatening motor vehicle collisions in the WHO World Mental Health Surveys. *BMC Psychiatry, 16*, 257-271. doi: 10.1186/s12888-016-0957-8.

Stewart, A. E., Knox, J. A. & Schneider, P. (2018). Reaching students and parents through weather science and safety workshops for teachers. *Bulletin of the American Meteorological Society, 99*, 1545–1555, doi: 10.1175/BAMS-D-17-0114.1.

Stokols, D. (1979) A congruence analysis of human stress. *Stress and Anxiety*, In I. G. Sarason and C. D. Spielberger (Eds.) Vol. 6, *Hemisphere,* 27-53.

Swim, J. K., Stern, P. C., Doherty, T. J., Clayton, S., Reser, J. P., Weber, E. U., Howard, G. S. (2011). Psychology's contributions to understanding and addressing global climate change. *American Psychologist*, 66, 241-250. doi: 10.1037/a0023220.

Torpey, E. (2017). Jobs for people who live being outdoors. *Career Outlook*. U. S Bureau of Labor Statistics. Available online: https://www.bls.gov/careeroutlook/2017/article/outdoor-careers.htm (accessed March, 22, 2019).

Tuan, Y. (1980). Rootedness versus sense of place. *Landscape, 24,* 3-8.

US Department of *Transportation, Federal Highway Administration* (2019). Road weather management program. https://ops.fhwa.dot.gov/weather/q1_roadimpact.htm (accessed 4.2.2019).

US Environmental Protection Agency (2019). *Definition of environmental justice. US Environmental Protection Agency*, Environmental Justice web page: https://www.epa.gov/environmentaljustice. (Accessed 3.20.2019).

Vihma, A., Mulugetta, Y., & Karlsson-Vinkhuyzen, S. (2011) Negotiating solidarity? The G77 through the prism of climate change negotiations, *Global Change, Peace & Security, 23*(3), 315-334, doi: 10.1080/14781158.2011.601853.

Walker, G. (2012). *Environmental justice: Concepts, evidence and politics*. London: Routledge.

Walker, I., Leviston, Z., Price, J., & Devine, W. P. (2015). Responses to a worsening environment: relative deprivation mediates between place attachments and behaviour. *European Journal of Social Psychology, 45*, 833-846. https://doi.org/10.1002/ejsp.2151.

Watts, N., Amann, M., Ayeb-Karlsson, S., Belesova, K., Bouley, T., Boykoff, M., Costello, A. (2018). The Lancet Countdown on health and climate change: From 25 years of inaction to a global transformation for public health. *The Lancet, 391*(10120), 581–630. https://doi.org/10.1016/S0140-6736(17)32464-9.

Willox, A. C., Harper, S. L., Ford, J. D, Landman, K., Houle, K., & Edge V. L. (2012). 'From this place and of this place:' climate change, sense of place, and health in Nunatsiavut, Canada. *Social Science & Medicine, 75,* 538-547. https://doi.org/10.1016/j.socscimed.2012.03.043.

Wilson, S. M., Richard, R., Joseph, L., & Williams, E. (2010). Climate change, environmental justice, and vulnerability: An exploratory spatial analysis. *Environmental Justice, 3,* 13-19. doi: 10.1089=env.2009.0035.

Zuravin, S. J. (1986). Residential density and urban child maltreatment: An aggregate analysis. *Journal of Family Violence, 1*, 307-322.

In: Social Psychology and Counseling
Editors: D. A. Kleiber and E. Delgado-Romero ISBN: 978-1-53616-548-7

Chapter 24

SOCIAL PSYCHOLOGY OF AGING AND MENTAL HEALTH

Elizabeth A. Stewart and Douglas A. Kleiber

THE NATURE OF LATER LIFE IN THE NEW MILLENNIUM

Many social scientists believe we, in industrialized countries, are experiencing an aging of the population that is having a critical impact on society (e.g., Torres-Gil, 2017). It's not that today's older people are entirely different than those in the past; but there are a lot more of them! The redistribution of the population is partly due to improvements in health care that have enabled people to live longer, with individuals who get to 65 years old adding an additional 19.5 years to their age (Administration on Aging, 2018). The increased birth rate in the years 1946 to 1964 created a "baby boom" of epic proportions, and these "Boomers" are now retiring. In a little over a decade, 20% of American residents will be over 65 years old and within the next fifteen years these residents will exceed the number of children aged 18 years and younger (U.S. Census Bureau, 2018). Of course, more older people and greater longevity does not equate to better *quality* of later life, and aging well is an art that science has not entirely clarified. Furthermore, the benefits of aging will continue to be elusive to those with social and economic difficulties; life may even be shortened for the poor and ethnic minorities who lack social and financial security (Torres-Gil, 2017).

In this chapter, we explore the dynamics of aging around the mostly predictable life events of retirement and widowhood, adaptive and maladaptive responses to them, and other social psychological processes that may be affected as a result of biological and social aspects of aging. Practical implications for clinicians are considered along with interventions for mental health. We examine aging in general and address aging as one aspect of developmental diversity,[1] beginning with the situational factors that affect both social regard and self-regard of older adults in ways largely consistent with the role-related influences and changes.

SIGNIFICANT AND SOMETIMES STRESSFUL LIFE EVENTS

While the biological, and especially cognitive, changes that affect child and adolescent development are not as dramatic after the age of 20, the suggestion that development thus plateaus and there is relatively little change has been largely refuted with evidence of significant change throughout adulthood. While many of those changes come about in accidental and serendipitous ways, some are predictable with role changes, graduation, employment, marriage, parenting, and retirement being among the most obvious. To the extent that behavior and mental health status are affected by such changes, both the acquisition and loss of these roles are worthy of closer scrutiny. Three events very common to later life are retirement, widowhood, and loss of physical capacity.

Retirement

Retirement has been reconceptualized (e.g., Dychtwald & Flowers, 1990; Freedman, 1999, 2007; Sterns & McQuown, 2015; Weiss, 2005). With the demographic trends noted above, related changes like extension of the age at which social security benefits can be sought, decline of company pensions, and near elimination of a mandatory retirement age, retirement now holds many different opportunities and challenges than it did decades ago. Individuals move toward the next phase of their life in an individualized and often more gradual manner (Sterns & McQuown, 2015). Transitions from work can be one time and final or over several times, a "blurred" exit (Mutchler, Burr, Pienta, & Massagli, 1997) while reasons for leaving may be related to having a stable financial position, unfulfilling job, alternate interests, or physical and/or mental health problems (Berk, 2018; Vaillant, 2002; Weiss, 2005). Those continuing to work may do so to realize different needs: fulfilling a passion, finding meaning, changing directions with an "encore career," or pursuing a "bridge" position (Freedman, 1999; 2007; James, Matz-Costa, & Smyer, 2016; Weiss, 2005).

---

[1] Notable with respect to the research on aging – including that which we draw on here – is that there is insufficient attention to sources of diversity, including race, ethnicity and sexual orientation. Further analysis is warranted in those areas.

Looking at the exit process for workers can reveal a good bit about how they fare psychologically; however, research hasn't provided consistent data on the subject. Some researchers find no effect on mental health when one's exit is voluntary, whereas, an involuntary exit is associated with poorer mental health (Mosca & Barrett, 2014). With blurred exits, the reason for leaving along with success or lack thereof in obtaining a bridge position can impact level of life satisfaction. When individuals want to work again and are unable to secure employment, life satisfaction decreases. When individuals seek bridge positions for their intrinsic value, life satisfaction rises but decreases if the motivation for working the position is financial. In other words, even if workers find a bridge position to mitigate the losses associated with an involuntary exit, there are typically other factors at work that limit life satisfaction (Dingemans & Henkens, 2014).

Negative and positive stereotypes about retirement impact mental and physical health. Regarding psychological well-being, one may expect to have a life filled with purpose or, in contrast, just exist without any meaningful relationships or engagements. These stereotypes, though typically overdrawn, nevertheless appear to relate to one's adjustment while those associated with one's physical health relate to physiological issues (Ng, Allore, Monin, & Levy, 2016).

As people transition, they may shed various responsibilities and roles, and the question becomes, how does one now see oneself as a result? And when individuals create new roles, how meaningful are they? The needs to belong, engage, and contribute to society are well established (Ryan & Deci, 2000; Varley & Zito, this volume) and this does not typically change with age (James et al., 2016). Even those well beyond retirement age continue to pursue new possibilities for constructing a meaningful life (cf. Laslett, 1989). For example, formal volunteering provides individuals with a major role identity absent another way to develop a sense of purpose (Greenfield & Marks, 2004). Maintaining and strengthening current social connections along with developing new relationships can address emptiness without the constancy of workplace friends (Vaillant, 2002). Experiencing time to pursue meaningful leisure activities may also contribute to a newly crafted identity. One retiree noted that where she previously identified herself through her work, now her different activities gave her new roles and opportunities for engagement (Castel, 2018).

Still, self-esteem and/or self-efficacy associated with being a competent worker is commonly diminished (Weiss, 2005). Having a sense of purpose may be missing. Feelings of detachment from valued work friends can bring about loneliness. Questions about what the future holds over the long term (Rubin, 2007) or uncertainty about one's altered role may lead to the need for some self and social reconstruction. According to George Vaillant (2002, p. 200), the "happy-well" were distinguished from the "sad-sick" in his longitudinal study by the new ways they found to engage, be creative, and find new friends. For some, though, this adjustment may be elusive, with mental health at risk.

Widowhood

Spousal loss in later life is not uncommon. Women over 65 years old are more affected as there are three times the number of widows as widowers (Administration for Community Living, 2018). For all gender orientations, loss of a spouse or intimate partner is one of the most serious and challenging events to occur across the lifespan. Widow/ers are likely losing one of the most significant people in their lifetime (Belsky, 2018; June & Marty, 2018).

It is common to hear the words "untethered" and "unmoored" as the experience of widow/ers for a good while after the death of a spouse, with grief and social disintegration almost inevitable. That feeling is addressed to a great extent in turning to other relationships, and social support is essential to coping, whatever reconstruction of self-conception may be required. Connecting with family and particularly friends can be very beneficial (de Vries, Ulz, Caserta, & Lund, 2014).

Initial emotions may consist of shock and loss, sadness, and even anger or a sense of betrayal (June & Marty, 2018). Physical sequelae are not uncommon, and individuals may struggle with sleep and appetite problems among others. But the emotion that is most prevalent and acutely felt is loneliness. Eating by oneself, sleeping in a double bed alone or celebrating holidays without one's loved one seem to accentuate this feeling (Nauf, Ward, Mahrer-Imhof, & Grande, 2013). Men may feel this more than women as they don't maintain the same social networks outside of work that women typically do, nor do they necessarily reach out to friends. They may fail to express their emotions or seek help regarding household tasks (Bennett, 2007). When looking at re-partnered widows and widowers and their experience of widowhood prior to re-partnering, research shows the tendency for women to cope through the use of resilience while men struggle and fail to cope as well, even with social support, before engaging in a new relationship (Koren, 2016).

Loss of Physical Capacity

With popular models of successful aging (cf. Rowe & Kahn, 1998) indicating that one is not aging well if she or he is disabled in some way or ill, it is understandable to think that depression would inevitably accompany loss of health and physical well-being. There are, however, alternative models of effective adaptation that recognize adaptability and resilience in aging well such as the *Selective Optimization with Compensation* (SOC) model (Baltes & Baltes, 1990; Baltes & Carstensen, 1996). This framework, in particular, acknowledges a gradual but inevitable reduction in the range of activities that comes with biological aging but suggests that healthy adaptation recognizes some the value of instrumental dependence (M. Baltes, 1996) and being wisely discriminating about what to do and how to do it, taking advantage of accommodations, to live a rich and satisfying life. Contrary to popular stereotypes, older adults are not mired in the past but instead are more commonly focused on enjoying the present, what Carstensen, Fung, and Charles (2003) refer to as "socioemotional selectivity," while maintaining a sense of purpose with some immediate goals. Their *Socioemotional Selectivity* model is an advance on the SOC model in describing successful adaptation in later life in ways that may be useful, both preventively and palliatively, for counselors and other mental health practitioners.

Social Psychological Dynamics That Change with Age

Identity Reconstruction

Identity has been characterized as having more of a social aspect than self-concept alone. According to Erikson (1980) and others it evolves through a dialectic of individuation, where one seeks uniqueness and autonomy (a basic need identified by Ryan & Deci, 2000; see also Varley & Zito, this volume), and identification, where self-naming is associated with group belonging and the intrinsic need for relatedness (also described by Varley & Zito). Levinson and colleagues (1978) suggested that midlife brings a kind of "detribalization" that attenuates those social bonds required for becoming established as an adult; while individuation in the form of self-expression must also yield, ultimately, to the potential for dis-integration that Erikson sees resulting in despair. Especially with role constriction - when children move out, a marriage may be dissolved, and jobs come to an end - identification with others such as in the family and work settings is diminished. For newer cohorts of retirees, "Third Agers" (Rubenstein, 2002), the effect can be liberating, but it is inevitably isolating and may lead to loneliness and depression.

Ultimately, strong bonds with others become part of the consolidation and integration of later life, also ushering in some natural conservatism (or perhaps "cautiousness" is a better word) stylistically. But as innovation theorists have learned (e.g., Nimrod & Kleiber, 2007) individuation/self-expression motives do not go away, especially among the 'young old' Third Agers, as new opportunities are embraced and growth continues, for some into their 80s and beyond. While it is safe to say that these patterns vary considerably across culture (e.g., with collectivist cultures putting more emphasis on identification) and gender (e.g., with women seeking communality more than men) and are affected by social class and other conditions, individuation and identification are important in later life as well as earlier in adult life, albeit in new ways.

Ageism: Stereotyping, Prejudice, and Age Discrimination

Ageism, as first defined by Robert Butler in 1969, is stereotyping and discriminating against someone based on their age; and it comes in many forms: personal, institutional, intentional, and unintentional. Stereotypes often label older adults as unhappy, frail, unattractive, inappropriately interested in sex, and memory deficient, all while failing to contribute to society (The Anti-Ageism Taskforce at The International Longevity Center, 2006). Older adults engage in ageism themselves (Applewhite, 2016; Nelson, 2016a) though their self-effacing humor seems to help rather than undermine their mental health (Ivan & Schiau, 2017). Others reject the use of humor as a defense mechanism (Applewhite, 2016).

These and other myths of aging are generally not supported by available research (see Applewhite, 2016; Nelson, 2016a; Nelson, 2016b; The Anti-Ageism Taskforce at The International Longevity Center, 2006 for a data-based review). As examples, happiness *increases* across the lifespan (Yang, 2008) and mental health problems decrease in prevalence (Byers, Yaffe, Covinsky, Friedman, & Bruce, 2016). Older adults as a group are not a drag on societal resources or the economy (Applewhite, 2016).

Nonetheless, as noted, there is often a diminishment of self-regard in the course of aging as a product of ageism that affects many aspects of life. For example, when exposed to negative stereotypes, older adults perform more poorly on memory recall tasks and do so over long periods of time (Hess, Hinson, & Statham, 2004; Levy, Zonderman, Slade, & Ferrucci, 2012). The risk for depression increases the more that older adults believe that they are a burden on their family and society (Bai, Lai, & Guo, 2016). Older adults who attribute their illnesses entirely to old age experience poorer health outcomes. When they don't believe they have control over health outcomes, they often fail to use preventive health care or pursue appropriate care when needed (Nelson, 2016b). Older adults bear the burden of others' negative stereotyping in medical and behavioral health settings. Physicians may favor seeing younger patients than older ones reasoning that older ones can't be treated or that illnesses are part of the aging process and unimportant. Behavioral health providers may erroneously believe older adults seek help because they want someone to talk with due to loneliness (Nelson, 2016b).

Discrimination of older people in the workplace may be prevented by law to some extent, but if the climate always favors youth based on those myths, older people will be discriminated against in spite of evidence that they are no less productive. Burtless (2013) looked at this and found that because of higher levels of education combined with longer work lives, older adults were among the most productive workers. Additionally, researchers suggest that the greater day to day consistency displayed by older adults relative to younger adults could be a significant asset that adds to their productivity (Schmiedek, Lovden, & Lindenberger, 2013). This research also indicated that older workers have lower error rates than younger workers because, while they may work a little more slowly, they tend to work more carefully.

When older adults do resist and reject negative stereotypes, taking a more positive outlook enhances physical health while decreasing the likelihood of mental health decline (Nelson, 2016a). Support systems including one's family serve an important role in fostering a sense of security regarding the older adult's aging process. The perception that assistance will be available if needed allows the older adult to maintain a feeling of control (Nelson, 2016a), reflecting what Margaret Baltes (1996) referred to as "instrumental dependence."

Conservatism and Rigidity

The popular notion that older people are inevitably and irretrievably stuck in the past has not been abandoned despite evidence to the contrary. A preference for continuity, stability, and "doing things the old way" is indeed a prevailing inclination for older people and likely affects attitudes toward society more generally, but older people are increasingly aware that adaptation is necessary for survival, quality of life and happiness, and that even with diminishing capacity people remain capable of optimizing their lives as well as growing and changing.

The *Selective Optimization with Compensation* (SOC) model, referred to earlier with respect to coping with loss and disability, emphasizes adaptability. Rigid independence is problematic for older people and puts them at risk, whereas the pattern of compensating to allow optimal engagement is associated with physical and psychological well-being. The critical factor is to identify opportunities for engagement for which there is continuing capacity, using whatever means are necessary to compensate and optimize that engagement and releasing what is no longer satisfying or available. Clinicians working with older adults can help clarify values, identify activities that no longer hold interest while problem-solving constraints to engagement in those still desirable, and find adaptive mechanisms to optimize the potential experience.

The SOC model continues to have relevance even as society and aging are changing in ways that make conservatism and rigidity less likely. As noted earlier, given the number of years available now after retirement, people in their 60s and early 70s are inclined to be experimental and innovative rather than rigid and unchanging and will approach aging with greater awareness that growth is still possible until the end of life.

Prosocial Behavior

In the course of maturation through adulthood, according to Erik Erikson (1963), the principle challenge is to resist stagnation after midlife by being generative. Generativity is ''working for the well-being of future generations through various kinds of activities and enterprises in churches, schools, neighborhoods, communities, organizations, and society writ large'' (McAdams & Logan, 2004, p. 16), and is most essentially looking after the next generation, whether with one's own progeny or others. The jobs of parenting and teaching are thus essentially generative but having or teaching children as an obligation may be done in a manner that lacks that quality of true prosocial, generative interest. Nor is either role necessary to be generative, that is to care about the young and generations to follow.

Generativity includes both agentic and communal aspects according to McAdams and others, the former quality being concerned with having an impact that will serve as a legacy of sorts as one outlives the self (Kotre, 1996) while the latter, which is best reflected in care-giving and social support, is prosocial in a more altruistic way. According to McAdams and Logan (2004), both aspects are necessary to be truly generative, but without the second aspect, a concern with legacy alone is less prosocial than ego oriented. Vaillant (2002) went a little farther with Erikson's ideas in identifying a subsequent stage of "Keeper of the Meaning," (pp. 48-49) as taking responsibility for cultural preservation. Continuing a generativity orientation, this is less about the next generation than the culture at large but involves assuming roles, such as volunteer coordinator or historian for a local charitable organization, that are for the good of the order. There is considerable debate as to whether older people become more conservative as they age, but the impulse toward conservatism is consistent with the idea of preserving the best of life, nature and one's community. The fact that it sometimes morphs into resistance to progressive change and cultural diversification should be understood as deriving in most cases from that same impulse.

Finally, while volunteerism can have multiple meanings and instrumental, extrinsic values – such as learning new skills, being "credited" for good works or simply making new friends - it is clearly prosocial behavior in its purpose. The Stanford Center on Longevity research (The Sightlines Project, 2016) finds that about 26% of Americans volunteer, those with a college education more than others. What is also important to note as well about volunteerism is the evidence for its consistently positive impact on mental health (Musick & Wilson, 2003; Okun & Michel, 2006). And while women are more inclined, men benefit just as much. Indeed, because it is less expected of men and they may have neglected the more nurturant aspects of the personalities in early life in favor of the more agentic, they may stand to gain even more by way of compensatory value.

ISSUES AND SOLUTIONS

Of the many events that may be disruptive in later life and the circumstances that could seem disabling, most are manageable with a little resilience and adaptation. One must be careful not to pathologize later life and its variations simply on the basis of decline in capacity. Nevertheless, it is noteworthy that some of the issues, if not addressed, can become pathological. Thus, rolelessness and loss of companionship and relatedness (loneliness) may lead to depression, complicated grief or even suicidal inclinations. Consequences may be minimized through counseling and psychotherapy. Within such counseling, application of the *Selective Optimization with Compensation* (Baltes & Baltes, 1990) and the *Socioemotional Selectivity* (Carstensen et al., 2003) models referred to earlier, might be helpful with respect to coping with physical and emotional distress.

Worklife Change

About 30% of retirees find the adjustment to retirement to be stressful (Bosse, Spiro, & Kressin, 1996). Psychologists can help individuals plan an effective transition from work or adjust to retirement if the process or outcome is different than expected. How individuals fare can be linked to pre-planning for retirement, marriage status, finances, mental and physical health, the way in which they retired, and feeling of control (Sterns & McQuown, 2015). A lack of meaningful relationships has been associated with unsatisfactory adjustment to retirement (Vaillant, 2002; Weiss, 2005). Psychologists help clients through this transition particularly when addressing obstacles whether they involve readiness to retire, adjustment to a new life role, or mental health issues. Readiness to retire may depend, in part, on variables outside of one's control. Checklists have been developed to identify other important areas of preparation before leaving the work world (Sterns & McQuown, 2015).

Another way to conceptualize the common issues in this context is using a *transition* model. In looking at a work transition, the approach by Anderson and associates (2012) suggests that the clinician might start by exploring with the client issues including how and when the change came about, the amount of control the client has, feelings of stress, and any prior history the client has with a similar change. Clinician may also elicit information on work salience (the importance of the work role in combination or contrast with other life roles), sense of resilience, areas of self-efficacy, and sources of meaning. This helps the clinician understand what priorities a client places on which roles as well as where one sees oneself in the role. As part of the transition model described by Anderson et al., (2012), Schlossberg has created "A model of worklife transitions" (p. 184) that structures the clinical work to be done when someone is transitioning in as a new employee, "moving through" (for example, on a "fast track" p. 184), exiting a job including "leaving, grieving, and striving" (p. 184), or again trying to become employed.

For those experiencing psychological issues, psychologists use standard protocols to assess for common disorders such as anxiety, depression and substance use. Addressing personal orientations that are implicated, including self-efficacy, mastery, and locus of control, may be helpful in promoting one's adjustment around retirement issues (Sterns & McQuown, 2015).

Living with Loneliness

Loneliness is now considered a public health issue for older adults (Gerst-Emerson & Jayawardhana, 2014). The causes are varied but secular, historical changes may be partly responsible. There is currently less probability of baby boomers participating in community-based (including religious) activities than 20 years ago (Alpert, 2017; The Sightlines Project, 2016). Nor do they feel they have significant exchanges with partners or close ties with family and friends. Given that just being older is a risk factor for experiencing loneliness, the statistics that there is less individual and community engagement and connection with others appears to predict the potential for much increased loneliness in the foreseeable future (Alpert, 2017).

Different from depression, "…loneliness is the unpleasant experience that occurs when a person's network of social relationships is significantly deficient in either quality or quantity" (Perlman & Peplau, 1984, p. 15). Predictors for loneliness in older adults include physical health, socioeconomic status, social relationships, and personality. Loneliness increases with age in both genders. The increase in women is consistent and steady while there is a U shaped curve for men with levels of loneliness highest at ages 40 and 80. Relationships are important, and those without a spouse, widowed or who fail to maintain regular contact with friends are at risk (von Soest, Luhmann, Hansen, & Gerstorf, 2018). The size of one's social network and relationship with one's spouse are significant with quality of the relationship being most important (Hawkley et al., 2008). Those who exhibit extroversion and emotional stability experience less loneliness (von Soest et al., 2018). Serious suicidal ideation is associated with loneliness (Stravynski & Boyer, 2001).

Exploring the qualitative experience of loneliness, Kitzmüller and colleagues, (2017) found "the overriding meaning of the existential human core of loneliness in old age expressed through the metaphor 'trapped in an empty waiting room' " (p. 1). In their study, older adults experienced losses encompassing physical loss, functional capacity, connectivity, and meaning. Interconnecting themes included negative feelings of loneliness, loss of meaningful relationships, influences of self-perception, and actions taken in response to loneliness. Some of their participants felt trapped or abandoned and insignificant. Lost relationships created a hole that couldn't be replaced, and due to a lack of commonality, new relationships did not fill the gap. "Useless," "rejected," and "disconnected," were among other feeling descriptors used by these individuals.

While aging is a natural part of human existence and reduced responsibility can be an opportunity for growth, it seems many things go into the experience of the lonely life of an older adult in addition to the above-named risk factors, including earlier life experiences and personal resources (Vaillant, 2002). Feeling that lack of connection to someone who shares common experience, unable to articulate purpose and meaning in one's life, and/or believing one is burdensome to others (even family) appear to engulf one in a way that depresses self-esteem. Kitzmüller et al. (2017) propose the idea that individuals are filled with angst and distress without meaning or connection in their life and thus experience the inability to move forward. The "waiting room" (p. 222) offers the possibility that with desire on the part of the individual and an opportunity for meaningful connection extended from genuine others, such feelings of being stuck can be ameliorated. By focusing on the provision of genuine interactions and relationships (through home health care workers, family, and important others), implementation of activities relating to one's life story, strengthening familiar connections and perhaps trying to support spirituality may all have transitional value (Kitzmüller et al., 2017).

Death Anxiety

As was discussed earlier, most of adult life, at least in a social psychological sense, is directed more by social changes than biologically directed ones. Physical decline or other losses in later life, however, may raise the level of awareness of death, what psychologists refer to as *mortality salience*. According to *Terror Management Theory* (TMT; Maxwell, Pyszczynski, Greenberg, Pepin, & Davis, 2012), as people age they become increasingly aware of impending death which is associated with existential angst and defensiveness. They then may become more susceptible to anxiety, depression, and related problems. Anxiety about death can reach disabling proportions. Older Chinese individuals experiencing stressors and a higher level of psychological problems expressed more death anxiety (Wu, Tang, & Kwok, 2002). Individuals who showed less ego integrity and more global physical and mental health problems also appear to hold more anxiety regarding death (Fortner & Neimeyer, 1999).

Nevertheless, over the course of one's adult life, anxiety regarding death tends to decrease (Cicirelli, 2006) and many older adults continue to experience psychological well-being through the end of their life (Baltes & Balters, 1990; Vaillant 2002). Older adults regulate their emotions more effectively and thus cope better with fears (Berk, 2018). The concept of generativity appears to buffer death anxiety (Major, Whelton, Schimel, & Sharpe, 2016). The achievement of ego integrity allows one to look back on life with a sense of fulfillment and satisfaction. Being at peace with one's past, finding meaning in how one lived, and not dwelling on regrets or wishing things were different increases the likelihood that one will not experience death anxiety (Parker, 2013).

It is also reasonable to assume that fear of dying would be attenuated for those with a strong belief in life after death, whether in a religious or spiritual sense. Research indicates lower death anxiety among religious people although other studies reflect the opposite--that those with higher religiosity experience higher death anxiety (June & Marty, 2018). In a review, Berk (2018) found that those with steadfast beliefs and consistent religious practices held less fear of death, whereas when such beliefs and actions were not in alignment, individuals feel a higher level of anxiety. Individuals who perceive death as a natural part of life and one that satisfies life goals hold less fear of death. When one has a comprehension and exposure to what is involved in the death process, anxiety seems to lessen, even among the non-religious (McClatchey & King, 2015; see also Tornstam, 2005).

Rando (2000) addresses ways clinicians can work with those experiencing anticipatory grieving related to a variety of illnesses and other losses. As people near the end of their life, Carpenter (2015) suggests that psychological "treatments can enhance quality of life more broadly by helping patients clarify goals and values, adopt beneficial coping skills, use effective communication strategies, maximize remaining abilities, and grapple with questions about identity and meaning in the face of mortality" (p. 581). Older adults generally bring considerable contextual experience that informs their thinking and coping styles around death and dying. Being around the deaths of others or bearing the burden of chronic illness in oneself or as a caregiver for a significant other may inoculate one to some extent from severe death anxiety (Carpenter, 2015).

Appropriate psychological interventions depend on the individual's goals. Two helpful approaches include *Meaning Centered Group Psychotherapy* and *Dignity Therapy*. The first was designed by Breitbart and colleagues (2010) for individuals with cancer to address spiritual well-being and sustain or enhance a sense of meaning, peace and purpose as they approach the end of their lives. *Dignity Therapy*, created by H. M. Chochinov and colleagues (2011) is a brief psychotherapy intervention to address psychosocial and existential distress among individuals terminally ill with cancer. The goal gives clients opportunities to talk about things that matter most to them. Conversations are recorded and form the basis of a "generativity document" (p. 754) clients can give to loved ones.

Grief

While individuals experience grief and distress, most do not become clinically depressed and, instead, show enhanced well-being over time. In general, widow/ers find that they are resilient (Neimeyer & Holland, 2015). Meeting various challenges related to creating a new life can allow one to feel efficacious (Cheek, 2010). Neimeyer and Holland (2015) summarize literature that reflects how conventional thinking held that people work through stages of grief with a final goal that one is no longer attached to the deceased while theorists now believe it is normative to progress through a series of tasks while reconstructing a bond that survivors will maintain with their loved one.

For those grieving, the *Dual Process Model* (Stroebe & Schut, 1999, 2010) conceptualizes how individuals cope with a focus on the stressors that exist and must be addressed. In this model, individuals oscillate between two orientations: (1) one of loss in which one grieves for the deceased, experiences unwanted reminders of grief, and tries to re-situate their bond, and, alternately, (2) a restoration orientation in which one engages with the world, attending to necessary daily activities, engaging in activities that are different or move oneself away from grief, working to see oneself and establish one's life anew without the loved one. This is a dynamic process where individuals both grieve and work to construct a new identity, but not without periods of avoidance or denial in each.

Another model of adjusting to loss that focuses on meaning-making (Neimeyer, 2001) suggests that in the wake of a loved one's death, survivors are challenged to understand the death and what life afterwards will mean for them. Individuals have a self-narrative that underlies who they are, what they feel and strive for, and how they act in a social world. When either the deceased was at the center of the survivor's life or when the beliefs upon which one's world was built or one's sense of self are destroyed, there is a desperate seeking to understand (Neimeyer & Holland, 2015). Working through the narrative of the death and the story of the relationship to solidify the bond is important work to be done. Identity construction can either move forward or revert. With positive movement, one's identity can be "integrated into a (subtly or profoundly) changed self-narrative" (Neimeyer & Holland, 2015 p. 650).

Bereavement requires a reorientation in one's social world. There are varied challenges, yet this also presents as an opportunity to develop and take on new roles (Naef et al., 2013). The reconstruction of one's new identity, in part, appears to relate to finding a sense of balance during this process. Holtslander, Bally, and Steeves (2011) looked at older adults taking care of their partners before death and found the theme to be how one effectively straddled intense mourning and constructed a new life without one's spouse. The significant difficulty that survivors face is trying to maintain a tenuous position such that they don't lose control of the balance when challenging thoughts, emotions, and fears arise. Some of the goals of keeping this fine line include learning "to walk alone" and "to find a new identity" (Holtslander et al., page 256).

Changes in caregiver identity can start before one's spouse dies and extend through to widowhood. A qualitative study (Cheek, 2010) showed that modest changes reflected through social and cognitive domains enhanced identity reconstruction. Social support let widows in the study know they were liked for themselves. Widows learned that they were self-determining as they used formerly dormant or unknown talents to manage various issues. As they restructured their lives and identities, these widows were assertive in acting on their preferences such as deciding about living arrangements. Ultimately, each woman felt like a whole individual again. Cheek noted the importance of considering the totality of one's environment in how small details are used as resources to help with one's transition.

MENTAL HEALTH RISKS AND IMPLICATIONS FOR PSYCHOTHERAPY

Addressing Complicated Grief

Most bereaved individuals do not require therapeutic intervention. Those who continue to feel distress and related symptoms may be experiencing *complicated grief.* According to the *Diagnostic and Statistical Manual of the American Psychiatric Association* (2013), several features of this diagnosis, also called "Prolonged Grief Disorder," include, among other things, a feeling that one has lost part of oneself and is having difficulty in engaging with social or other activities. Interventions grounded in several different theoretical perspectives include challenging dysfunctional thoughts, behavioral activation, and doing life review (Neimeyer & Holland, 2015). Others involve narrative therapies that allow for meaning-making related to the death and to the survivor's life afterward. Some specific areas of focus may include individuals sharing the story of the death in a way that is restorative, determining meaning as they move forward with their lives, and reconstructing the attachment they had with their loved one in a healthy way (Neimeyer & Holland, 2015).

Restating the story of the death in a therapeutic manner is one way to make new meaning and help the survivor become more empowered (Neimeyer & Holland, 2015). Meaning-based grief therapy supports different creative interventions including "analogical listening to probe the felt sense of grief-related emotions in the body" (Neimeyer & Holland, 2015, p. 655) and journaling. Clinical interventions that help the survivor reflect, recreate meaning and rework the bonds they share with the deceased include looking at family pictures as a way to pull together good memories, sharing stories about, and communicating with one's loved one (Neimeyer & Holland, 2015). Another approach is "…a dialogical self model [which] might appropriately be viewed as an elaboration of a meaning-focused narrative approach…" (Neimeyer, 2011, p. 338). This conceptualization adds to the therapist's ability to listen to and finely deconstruct the survivor's story in various ways including how one may be limiting or weakening oneself. Neimeyer (2011) also uses evocative visualization in which the survivor talks with other internal selves.

Depression

Late life used to be equated with discouragement and depression. Most often, though, older adults experience positive emotions as their usual state with depression not being a normal, much less inevitable, part of aging (Blazer, 2014). Although less prevalent in older adults than younger ones, individuals over 65 years old do experience depression. For a significant number, symptoms don't rise to the level of a diagnosis but still impact social functioning or otherwise negatively affect one. Additionally, in many older adults, health providers fail to diagnose depression. Later life depression presents a complicated picture given an older adult's cognitive changes, physical (and possible multiple) health challenges, and new social roles (Edelstein, Bamonti, Gregg, & Gerolimatos, 2015; Power, Greene, & Lawlor, 2017).

Symptom presentation differs for older adults as they report more psychomotor changes, sleep and appetite problems, anhedonia, and poor mood in the morning (Edelstein et al, 2015). Older adults don't express sadness or guilt the way younger people do. The role of loneliness is often missed and not considered (Power et al., 2017). Cognitive impairment can lead to depression (Blazer, 2014). Strong associations exist between depression and physical illness such as cardiovascular disease and Parkinson's disease, among others (Hegeman, 2018; Power et al., 2017). Cognitive characteristics and personality traits may also influence whether a response to adversity is protective or maladaptive. Combining a triggering event such as physical illness, loneliness or bereavement with a maladaptive response can lead to a depressive episode (Power et al., 2017). Risk factors for late life depression include physical illness and functional incapacity, pain, insomnia, personality traits, loss of loved ones, loneliness, and stress among others (Edelstein et al., 2015; Power et al., 2017).

Notwithstanding the challenges of accurate diagnosis, depression in older adults is treatable, and psychosocial and biomedical therapies are efficacious. To address variables contributing to and sustaining depressed mood, therapeutic interventions focus on participating in enjoyable activities, negative thoughts, relationship differences, and developmental issues (Edelstein et al, 2015).

Another evidence-based treatment for older adults with depression is *Reminiscence Therapy* (Edelstein et al., 2015). Robert Butler, an eminent gerontologist, introduced the idea of reminiscence and life review activities suggesting they were normal and essential to personal growth and well-being (Butler, 1963). Use of reminiscence, life review, and autobiography has been identified as a trend of this era, brought on by many things including research on the cognitive and emotional impact of such activities (Birren & Svensson, 2013). Reminiscence plays several roles including social, instrumental, and integrative. Interventions that utilize the functions of each of these have been categorized into three types: reminiscence, life review, and life review therapy. The first type which serves an instructional purpose and is social in nature allows one to share good memories with others, thus facilitating bonding and elevating one's mood. Interventions involving life review allow the older adult to see how they have coped with challenges in the past and/or examine and incorporate memories that are positive and negative across their lifespan. Lastly, the goal of life review therapy attempts to change one's beliefs and emotions about one's past, particularly those in which the individual has identified with negative experience, thereby improving psychological symptoms and allowing one to move forward in development (Westerhof & Bohlmeyer, 2014).

Suicidality

Suicidality is a significant concern for those 85 years and older, second only to the 45 to 54 age group (American Foundation for Suicide Prevention, 2019). The baby boomer cohort is likely to contribute to an increase in the rate of later life suicides due to a historically elevated propensity for suicide (Conwell, Van Orden, & Caine, 2011). To understand late life suicide, Fiske, Smith, and Price (2015) utilize Joiner's *Interpersonal Theory of Suicide* within a life span developmental framework. Joiner (2005) conceptualized suicide from an interpersonal theory in which suicide risk is the interaction between the wish to die and the capability to engage in lethal self-harming behavior. Feelings of failed or thwarted belongingness and perceived burdensomeness lead one to a desire for death. Across the lifespan individuals experience vulnerabilities, stress, and protective factors of varying frequency that impact on one's desire to die. Some risk factors are continuous through one's life (such as psychopathology) while others happen more often in later life (such as physical illness). Other components that may present more of a risk in later life include low openness to experience and high significance placed on independence. Those who are resistant to change may experience more challenges in responding to shifting circumstances. Suicidal capacity may be impacted by a number of factors occurring over the lifespan that differ with age such feeling isolated (Fiske et al., 2015).

While the most significant risk factor for late life suicide is depression (Fiske et al., 2015), others include social exclusion, loneliness, bereavement, cognitive impairment or alterations, physical illness and pain, and psychological pain (Conejero, Olie, Courtet, & Calati, 2018). Reasons associated with relationships with family and friends, one's faith and beliefs, and moral objections serve as protective factors against suicide (Fiske et al., 2015). In the face of late life stressors including death of one's partner or lack of new romantic partner, social support that is significant can be protective (Conejero et al., 2018).

Unfortunately, while interventions have been developed for suicidal behavior, few are targeted toward use with or validated with older adults. Because older adults have a higher likelihood of death during a suicide attempt, using universal and selected interventions may increase in importance (Fiske et al., 2015). There are only a limited number of evidence-based studies directed at the prevention of suicidal behavior and reduction of suicidal ideation. Primary care-based collaborative depression care management interventions have been found effective because they reduce risk factors as they assess and treat depression and decrease social isolation (Okolie, Dennis, Simon Thomas, & John, 2017).

CONCUSION

The upcoming decades will be full of change with a very different demographic group occupying the world. In this chapter we saw some of the issues that individuals face in later life that don't change, like loss, whether it is one's partner, one's role/s in society, or one's physical capacity. One also sees, though, that opportunities abound with "third age" thinking and a blurred retirement that let people reach out for what holds meaning and purpose for them. Nevertheless, these reasonably healthy developments are troubled as well. We see that underlying the context of all the events and processes described is the subtle and not so subtle prejudice and discrimination of ageism. The impact of ageism permeates our culture and is significant and tangible. Where resilience has been demonstrated in response to age and ageism, perhaps there is little required of counselors and other mental health providers, but more is needed where, among other possibilities, loneliness leads to depression and suicide is a considered alternative. With respect to psychological disorders and treatments, counselors can utilize qualitative information for a deeper understanding of such painful feelings, including research projects such as *Sightlines* to learn to enhance social engagement of older clients and work with other medical and health professionals to reduce the impacts of cognitive decline while enhancing quality of life.

REFERENCES

Administration for Community Living. (2018). 2018 Profile of Older Americans. Retrieved from https://acl.gov/sites/default/files/Aging and Disability in America/2018OlderAdmericansProfile.pdf.

Alpert, P. T. (2017) Self-perception of social isolation and loneliness in older adults, *Home Health Care Management & Practice*, *29*, 249–252.

American Foundation for Suicide Prevention. (2019). *Suicide statistics*. Retrieved from https://afsp.org/about-suicide/suicide-statistics/.

American Psychiatric Association. (2013). Prolonged grief disorder. In *Diagnostic and statistical manual of mental disorders* (5th ed.). Washington, DC: Author.

Anderson, M. L., Goodman, J., & Schlossberg, N. K. (2012). *Counseling adults in transition: Linking Schlossberg's theory with practice in a diverse world.* New York, NY: Springer.

Applewhite, A. (2016). *This chair rocks*. New York: Celadon Books.

Bai, X., Lai, D. W. L., & Guo (2016). Ageism and depression: Perceptions of older people as a burden in China, *Journal of Social Issues*, *72*, 26-46.

Baltes, M. M. (1996). *The many faces of dependency*. Cambridge, U.K.: Cambridge University Press.

Baltes, M. M., & Carstensen, L. L. (1996). The process of successful aging. *Aging and Society, 16*, 398-404.

Baltes, P., & Baltes, M. (1990). Psychological perspectives on successful aging: The model of selective optimization with compensation. In P. Baltes & M. Baltes (Eds.), *Successful aging* (pp. 1-34). New York: Cambridge University Press.

Belsky, J. (2018). *Experiencing the lifespan*. New York, NY: Worth Publishers.

Bennett, K. M. (2007). "No sissy stuff": Toward a theory of masculinity and emotional expression in older widowed men. *Journal of Aging Studies*, 21, 347-356.

Berk, L. E. (2018). *Exploring lifespan development* (4th ed.) Boston, MA: Pearson.

Birren, J. E., & Svensson, C. (2013). Reminiscence, life review, and autobiography: Emergence of a new era. *The International Journal of Reminiscence and Life Review*, *1*, 1-6.

Blazer, D. G. (2014). Editorial: Late life depression: a historical perspective upon a maturing field of inquiry, *Aging & Mental Health, 18*, 538-539.

Bosse, R, Sprio, A., III, & Kressin, N. R. (1996). The psychology of retirement. In R. T. Woods (Ed.), *Handbook of the clinical psychology of ageing* (pp. 141-157).

Breitbart, W., Rosenfeld, B., Gibson, C., Pessin, H., Poppito, S., Nelson, C., Tomarken, A., Timm, A. K., Berg, A., Jacobson, C., Sorger, B., Abbey, J., & Olden, M. (2010). Meaning-centered group psychotherapy for patients with advanced cancer: a pilot randomized controlled trial. *Psychooncology, 19*, 21–28.

Burtless, G. T. (2013). The impact of population aging and delayed retirement on workforce productivity. Retrieved from https://papers.ssrn.com/sol3/papers.cfm?abstract_id=2275023.

Butler, R. N. (1963). The life review: An interpretation of reminiscence in the aged. *Journal of Psychiatry*, *26*, 65-76.

Butler, R. (1969). Age-ism: Another form of bigotry. *The Gerontologist, 9*, 243-doi:10.1093/geront/9.4_Part_1.243.

Byers, A. L., Yaffe, K., Covinsky, K. E., Friedman, M. B., & Bruce, M. L. (2010). High occurrence of mood and anxiety disorders among older adults: The National Comorbidity Survey Replication. *Archives of General Psychiatry, 67*, 489-496.

Carstensen, L. L., Fung, H. H., & Charles, S. T. (2003). Socioemotional selectivity theory and the regulation of emotion in the second half of life. *Motivation and Emotion, 27*, 103-123.

Carpenter, B. D. (2015). Geropsychological practice with people near the end of life. In P. A. Lichtenberg and B. T. Mast (Eds.), *APA Handbook of Clinical Geropsychology: Vol. 2. Assessment, Treatment, and Issues of Later Life*, (pp. 579-599). Washington, DC: American Psychological Association.

Castel, A. D. (2019). *Better with age: The psychology of successful aging.* New York: Oxford.

Cheek, C. (2010). Passing over: Identity transition in widows, *The International Journal of Aging and Human Development, 70*, 345-364.

Chochinov, H. M., Kristjanson, L. J., Breitbart, W., McClement, S., Hack, T. F., Hassard, T., & Harlos, M. (2011). The effect of dignity therapy on distress and end-of-life experience in terminally ill patients: a randomized controlled trial. *Lancet Oncology, 12(8)*, 753-762.

Cicirelli, V. G. (2006). Fear of death in mid-old age. *Journal of Gerontology: Psychological Science, 61B(2),* 75-81.

Conejero, I., Olie, E., Courtet, P., & Calati, R. (2018). Suicide in older adults: current perspectives. *Clinical Interventions in Aging, 13*, 691-699.

Conwell, Y., Van Orden, K., & Caine, E. D. (2011). Suicide in older adults, *Psychiatric Clinics, 34*, 451-468.

de Vries, B., Utz, R., Caserta, M., & Lund, D (2014). Friend and family contact and support in early widowhood, *Journal of Gerontology*, *69B*, 75-84.

Dingemans, E. & Henkens, K. (2014). Involuntary retirement, bridge employment, and satisfaction with life: A longitudinal investigation, *Journal of Organizational Behavior*, *35*, 575–591.

Dychtwald, K., & Flower, J. (1990). *Age wave: The challenges and opportunities of aging America*. New York: Bantam.

Edelstein, B. A., Bamonti, P. M., Gregg, J. J., & Gerolimatos, L. A. (2015). Depression in later life. In P. A. Lichtenberg and B. T. Mast (Eds). *APA Handbook of Clinical Geropsychology: Vol. 2. Assessment, Treatment, and Issues of Later Life (pp. 3-47).* Washington, DC: American Psychological Association.

Erikson, E. (1963). *Childhood and society*. New York: Norton.

Erikson, E. (1980). *Identity and the life cycle*. New York: Norton.

Fiske, A., Smith, M. D., & Price, E. C. (2015). Suicidal behavior in older adults. Geropsychological practice with people near the end of life. P. A. Lichtenberg and B. T. Mast (Eds.), *APA Handbook of Clinical Geropsychology: Vol. 2. Assessment, Treatment, and Issues of Later Life*, *(pp. 145-172).* Washington, DC: American Psychological Association.

Fortner, B. V. & Neimeyer, R. A. (1999). Death anxiety in older adults: A qualitative review, *Death Studies, 23, 387-411.*

Freedman, M. (1999). *Prime time: How Baby Boomers will revolutionize retirement and transform America*. Cambridge MA: Perseus.

Freedman, M (2007). *Encore: Finding work that matters in the second half of life*. Cambridge, MA: Perseus.

Gerst-Emerson, K. & Jayawardhana, J. (2014). Loneliness as a public health issue: The impact of loneliness on health care utilization among older adults, *American Journal of Public Health*, *105,* 1013-1019.

Greenfield, E. A., & Marks, N. F. (2004). Formal volunteering as a protective factor for older adults' psychological well-being. *The Journals of Gerontology: Series B: Psychological Sciences and Social Sciences, 59,* S258-S264.

Hawkley, L. C., Hughes, M. E., Waite, L. J., Masi, C. M., Thisted, R. A., & Cacioppo, J. T. (2008). From social structural factors to perceptions of relationship quality and loneliness: The Chicago health, aging, and social relations study, *Journal of Gerontology: Social Sciences, 63B*, No. 6, 375–384.

Hegeman, A., Schutter, N., Comijs, H., Holwerda, T., Dekker, J., Stek, M., & van der Mast, R (2018). Loneliness and cardiovascular disease and the role of late-life depression, *International Journal of Geriatric Psychiatry*, *33*, 65–72.

Hess, T. M., Hinson, J. T., & Statham, J. A. (2004). Explicit and implicit stereotype activation effects on memory: Do age and awareness moderate the impact of priming? *Psychology and Aging*, *19,* 495-505.

Holtslander, L. F., Bally, J. M. G., & Steeves, M. L. (2011). Walking a fine line: An exploration of the experience of finding balance for older persons bereaved after caregiving for a spouse with advanced cancer, *European Journal of Oncology Nursing, 15*, 254-259.

Ivan, L. & Schiau, I. (2017). Fighting ageism: Older people self-deprecating humor in everyday online conversations, *Innovation in Aging*, Vol. 1, No. S1,72.

James, J. B., Matz-Costa, C., & Smyer, M. A. (2016). Retirement Security: It's Not Just About the Money. *American Psychologist, 71*, 334–344.

Joiner, T. (2005). *Why people die by suicide.* Cambridge, MA: Harvard University Press.

June, A., & Marty, M. A. (2018). Death and the dying process, bereavement, and widowhood. In B. P. Yochim, & E. L. Woodhead (Eds.), *Psychology of aging* (pp. 273-298). New York: Springer.

Kitzmüller, G., Clancy, A., Vaismoradi, M., Wegener, C., & Bondas, T. (2018) "Trapped in an Empty Waiting Room"—The Existential Human Core of Loneliness in Old Age: A Meta-Synthesis, *Qualitative Health Research*, *28*, 213–230.

Koren, C. (2016). Men's vulnerability-women's resilience: From widowhood to late-life repartnering, *International Psychogeriatrics*, *28*, 719-731.

Kotre, J. N. (1996). *Outliving the self: Generativity and the interpretation of lives*. New York: Norton.

Laslett, P. (1989). *A fresh map of life: The emergence of the third age*. London, UK: Weidenfeld & Nicolson.

Levinson, D. Darrow, C., Klein, F. Leviinson, M., & McKee, B. (1978). *The seasons of a man's life*. New York: Alfred Knopf.

Levy, B. R., Zonderman, A. B., Slade, M. D., & Ferrucci, L. (2012). Memory shaped by age stereotypes over time. *The Journals of Gerontology Series B, Psychological Sciences and Social Sciences, 67*, 432-436.

Major, R. J., Whelton, W. J., Schimel, J., & Sharpe, D. (2016). Older Adults and the fear of death: The protective function of generativity, *Canadian Journal on Aging, 35*, 261–272.

Maxwell, M., Pyszczynski, T., Greenberg, J., Pepin, R., & Davis, H. P. (2012). The moderating role of executive functioning in older adults' responses to a reminder of mortality, *Psychology and Aging*, *27*, 256–263.

McAdams, D. P., & Logan, R. L. (2004). What is generativity? In E. de St. Aubin, D. P. McAdams, & T.-C. Kim (Eds.), *The generative society* (pp. 15–31). Washington, D.C: American Psychological Association.

McClatchey, I. S. & King, S. (2015). The impact of death education on fear of death and death anxiety among human services students. *Omega: Journal of Death and Dying*, *71*, 343-361.

Mosca, I., & Barrett, A. (2014). The impact of voluntary and involuntary retirement on mental health: Evidence from older Irish adults. *IZA Discussion Paper No. 8723.* Available at SSRN: https://ssrn.com/abstract=2543918.

Musick, M. A., & Wilson, J. (2003). Volunteering and depression: The role of psychological and social resources in different age groups. *Social Science and Medicine, 56*, 259–269.

Mutchler, J. E., Burr, J. A., Pineta, A. M., & Massagli, M. P. (1997). Pathways to labor force exit: Work transitions and work instability. *The Journals of Gerontology, Series B: Psychological Sciences and Social Sciences, 52B,* S4-S12.

Nauf, R., Ward, R., Mahrer-Imhof, & Grande, G. (2013). Characteristics of the bereavement experience of older persons after spousal loss: An integrative review. *International Journal of Nursing Studies, 50,* 1108–1121.

Neimeyer, R. A. (Ed.). (2001). *Meaning reconstruction and the experience of loss*. Washington, DC: American Psychological Association.

Neimeyer R. A., & Holland, J. M. (2015). Bereavement in later life: Theory, assessment, and intervention. In P. A. Lichtenberg and B. T. Mast (Eds.), *A handbook of clinical geropsychology, Vol. 2: Assessment, Treatment, and Issues of Later Life* (pp. 645-666). Washington, DC: American Psychological Association.

Neimeyer, R. A. (2011). Reconstructing the self in the wake of loss: a dialogical contribution. In H. J. M Hermans and T. Gieser (Eds.), *Handbook of Dialogical Self Theory*, (pp. 332-345). New York: Cambridge University Press.

Nelson, T. D. (2016a). The age of ageism, *Journal of Social Issues*, *72*, 191-198.

Nelson, T. D. (2016b). Promoting health aging by confronting ageism, *American Psychologist*, *71,* 276-282.

Ng, R., Allore, H. G., Monin, J. K., & Levy, B. R. (2016). Retirement as meaningful: Positive retirement stereotypes associated with longevity, *Journal of Social Issues*, *72*, 69—85.

Nimrod, G. & Kleiber, D. A. (2007). Reconsidering change and continuity in later life: Toward an innovation theory of successful aging. *International Journal of Aging and Human Development, 65*, 1-22.

Okolie, C., Dennis, M., Simon Thomas, E. & John, A (2017). A systematic review of interventions to prevent suicidal behaviors and reduce suicidal ideation in older people, *International Psychogeriatics, 29*, 1801-1824.

Okun, M. A., & Michel, J. (2006). Sense of community and being a volunteer among the young-old. *Journal of Applied Gerontology, 25*, 173–188.

Parker, D. W. (2013). The relationship between ego integrity and death attitudes in older adults, *American Journal of Applied Psychology, 2*, 7-15.

Perlman, D. & Peplau, L. A. (1984). Loneliness Research: A survey of empirical findings. In L. A. Peplau & S. Goldston (Eds.), *Preventing the harmful consequences of severe and persistent loneliness. (pp. 13-46*). U.S. Government Printing Office, DDH Publication No. (ADM) 84-1312.

Power, C., Greene, E., & Lawlor, B. A. (2017). Depression in late life: Etiology, presentation, and management. In H. Chiu and Kenneth Shulman (Eds.), *Mental health and illness of the elderly* (pp. 187-218). Singapore: Springer Nature.

Rando, T. A. (Ed). (2000). *Clinical dimensions of anticipatory mourning: Theory and practice in working with the dying, their loved ones, and their caregivers.* Champaign, IL: Research Press.

Rowe, J. W. & Kahn, R. L. (1998). *Successful aging*. New York: Pantheon Books.

Rubin, B. A. (2007). Workplace temporalities. *Research in the Sociology of Work, 17*, 437-464.

Rubinstein, R. L. (2002). The third age. In R. S. Weiss & S. A. Bass (Eds.), *Challenges of the third age; Meaning and purpose in later life* (pp. 29-40). New York: Oxford University Press.

Ryan, R. M., & Deci, E. L. (2000). Self-determination theory and the facilitation of intrinsic motivation, social development, and well-being. *American Psychologist*, *55*, 68-78.

Schmiedek, F., Lovden, M., & Lindenberger, U. (2013). Keeping it steady: Older adults perform more consistently on cognitive tasks than younger adults, *Psychological Science, 24*, 1747-1754.

Sterns, H. L., & McQuown, C. K. (2015). Retirement redefined. In P. A. Lichtenberg and B. T. Mast, (Eds.), *A handbook of clinical geropsychology, Vol. 2: Assessment, Treatment, and Issues of Later Life* (pp. 601-616). Washington, DC: American Psychological Association.

Stravynski, A., & Boyer, R. (2001). Loneliness in relation to suicide ideation and parasuicide: A population-wide study, *Suicide & Life-Threatening Behavior, 31*, 32-40.

Stroebe, M., & Schut, H. (1999). The dual process model of coping with bereavement: Rationale and description. *Death Studies, 23*, 197-224.

Stroebe, M., & Schut, H. (2010). The dual process model of coping with bereavement: A decade on. *Omega: Journal of Death and Dying, 61*, 273-289.

The Anti-Ageism Taskforce at the International Longevity Center. (2006). Ageism in America. Retrieved from https://aging.columbia.edu/sites/default/files/Ageism_in_America.pdf.

The Sightlines Project. (2016). Retrieved from longevity.stanford.edu/the-sightlines-project/.

Torres-Gil, F. M. (2017). The evolution of gerontology and geriatrics in an era of a politics of aging, *Gerontology & Geriatrics Education, 38*, 438-442.

Tornstam, L. (2005). *Gerotranscendence: A developmental theory of positive aging*. New York City: Springer Publishing.

U.S. Census Bureau (2018). Older people projected to outnumber children for first time in U.S. history. https://www.ensus.gov/newsroom/press-releases/2018/cb18-41-population-projections.html.

Vaillant, G. (2002). *Aging well.* Boston: Little Brown and Company.

von Soest, T., Luhmann, M., Hansen, T., & Gerstorf, D. (2018). Development of loneliness in midlife and old age: Its nature and correlates. *Journal of Personality and Social Psychology*. Retrieved from http://dx.doi.org/10.1037/pspp0000219.

Weiss, R. S. (2005). *The experience of retirement*. Ithaca, NY: Cornell University Press.

Westerhof, G. J., & Bohmeijer, E. T. (2014). Celebrating fifty years of research and applications in reminiscence and life review: State of the art and new directions. *Journal of Aging Studies, 29,* 107-114.

Wu, A. M. S., Tang, C. S. K., Kwok, T. C. Y (2002). Death anxiety among Chinese elderly people in Hong Kong. *Journal of Aging and Health, 14*, 42-56.

Yang, Y. (2008). Social inequities in happiness, *American Sociological Review, 73*, 204-226.

ABOUT THE EDITORS

Douglas A. Kleiber, PhD, is an emeritus professor of Counseling and Human Development Services, Psychology, and Gerontology at the University of Georgia. He received an A.B in Psychology from Cornell University and a PhD in Educational Psychology from the University of Texas at Austin. He is the author of *Leisure Experience and Human Development* (Basic Books, 1999) among other works. Among his continuing research interests are coping with negative life events and optimizing developmental transitions. He is a charter member of the Association of Psychological Science and a past president of the Academy of Leisure Sciences.

E-mail: dkleiber@uga.edu

Edward A. Delgado-Romero, PhD, is Professor in Counseling and Human Development Services, and Associate Dean for Faculty and Staff Services in the College of Education of the University of Georgia. His research interests are in the development of Latina/o Psychology and the connections between ethnic minority psychology and other aspects of multicultural psychology. He runs an integrated research/service/outreach research program with an emphasis on the provision of services to the Spanish speaking population of Georgia and a Spanish language psychology clinic in the community. He is a founding member of the National Latina/o Psychological Association (NLPA), a past-president of NLPA (2007-2009), and an associate editor of *The Journal of Latinx Psychology*.

E-mail: edelgado@uga.edu

About the Authors

Ruben Atilano, MA, is a fourth-year doctoral student in counseling psychology at the University of Georgia. Atilano earned a BA in Cognitive Psychology at the University of California, Irvine and an MA in Counseling Psychology at the University of Missouri-Columbia. His research interests include the analysis of factors that influence Latinx students' adaptability to navigate and succeed in college, social justice, multiculturalism, and psychological well-being. Currently working as a graduate research assistant in the Center for Latino Achievement and Success in Education (CLASE), he is helping to develop an enrichment program targeting third- to fifth-grade English learners.

E-mail: ruben.atilano25@uga.edu

Geoff J. Bathje, PhD, is a licensed psychologist and Associate Professor in Clinical Mental Health Counseling at Adler University. He also engages in policy work and community organizing related to mental health justice and drug policy in addition to coordinating counseling services for Chicago Recovery Alliance. His clinical work focuses primarily on people who use drugs, people experiencing chronic mental illness, and trauma. He is particularly interested in understanding and addressing the systemic roots of social problems.

E-mail: gbathje@adler.edu.

Lauren Bigham, PhD, is a Health Psychology Fellow in Psycho-Oncology at Augusta University's Cancer Center. She received her doctorate in Counseling Psychology from the University of Georgia, with an emphasis in health psychology and completed an APA-accredited clinical health psychology pre-doctoral internship at the Medical College of Georgia – Charlie Norwood Veterans Affairs Medical Center in Augusta, Georgia. She previously received a Masters of Kinesiology in sport psychology from Georgia Southern University in Statesboro, Georgia. Research interests include health behavior change, physical activity, and hazing.

E-mail: laurenebigham@gmail.com

Ashley Britton, PhD, is a licensed psychologist and Clinical Assistant Professor in the Department of Psychiatry and Behavioral Medicine at East Carolina University's Brody School of Medicine. Dr. Britton is an attending psychologist on the Consultation-Liaison Service and provides multidisciplinary, medical, inpatient clinical work as well as teaching and supervision of medical students, psychiatry residents and psychology trainees. Prior to her position at ECU, Dr. Britton earned a PhD in Counseling Psychology from the University of Georgia, with a concentration in clinical health psychology. She completed a clinical psychology internship at Henry Ford Hospital in Detroit, Michigan and a clinical psychology/behavioral medicine postdoctoral fellowship at the Medical University of South Carolina (MUSC).

E-mail: brittona19@ecu.edu

Clair Cassiello-Robbins, PhD, is a Research Postdoctoral Fellow at Duke University in the Center for Misophonia and Emotion Regulation where she conducts research designed to better characterize and assess misophonia. She completed her graduate training in Clinical Psychology at Boston University and her pre-doctoral internship at the Durham VA Healthcare System. Her research focuses on understanding and treating dysregulated anger. In addition to research, Clair enjoys training and supervising clinicians. She is a certified trainer for the Unified Protocol Institute and trains clinicians to provide the Unified Protocol for Transdiagnostic Treatment of Emotional Disorders.

E-mail: ccassiel@bu.edu

Christina Clarke, PhD, is a Postdoctoral Resident in the Emory University School of Medicine Psychology Postdoctoral Residency Program in Health Service Psychology in Atlanta, Georgia. She completed her APA-Accredited doctoral internship at Georgia State University's Counseling and Testing Center. Dr. Clarke earned her PhD in Counseling Psychology and a certificate in Interdisciplinary Qualitative Studies from the University of Georgia. She conducts research in the areas of diversity, emotional intimacy, human connection, and the African American community.

E-mail: christinaclarke68@gmail.com

Benjamin J. Edner, PhD, is a Clinical Psychology Fellow at Atlanta Psychological Services, Atlanta, GA, and a researcher for the Juvenile Counseling and Assessment Program (JCAP) at the University of Georgia. Prior to fellowship, Dr. Edner earned a PhD in Counseling Psychology from the University of Georgia with a concentration in psychological assessment. He completed a clinical psychology internship at the Durham VA Health Care System, Durham, NC.

E-mail: Benjamin.edner25@uga.edu

Rebekah (Bekah) Ingram Estevez, MEd is a doctoral candidate in Counseling Psychology at the University of Georgia. She previously completed her master's in counseling also at the UGA. Her research interests include resilience, the impact of intersecting marginalized identities on mental health, best counseling practices for working with the LGBT community, and the lived experience of partners to trans persons of color. Estevez is the co-founder of the University of Georgia's College of Education Trans-Affirming Practices Taskgroup, provides individual counseling services for a wide range of presenting concerns as a psychologist in training, and is involved in advocacy for the LGBT community as a Student Representative for APA's Division 44.

E-mail: bingram@uga.edu

Brittany Field, PhD, is a staff psychologist at the United States Penitentiary-McCreary. Dr. Field earned her doctoral degree in Counseling Psychology from the University of Georgia in August 2018. During her doctoral program, she provided services to adjudicated youth in juvenile detention facilities. She currently works for the Federal Bureau of Prisons and provides mental health services to adult male offenders.

E-mail: brittany.field2011@gmail.com

Catherine Stamateris Flaherty, PhD, is a licensed psychologist in private practice in Hockessin, Delaware. In her current position, Dr. Flaherty provides psychotherapy and neurodevelopmental testing to children and adolescents with complex cognitive, learning, and emotional needs. Dr. Flaherty received her doctorate from the University of Georgia in 2017. She completed her internship at Cambridge Health Alliance/Harvard Medical School and her postdoctoral fellowship in neurodevelopmental and autism spectrum disorders at Nemours/A.I. DuPont Hospital for Children.

E-mail: catherinesflaherty@gmail.com.

Dontavious Ford, MEd, is a predoctoral psychology intern at Tuscaloosa VA Medical Center and a doctoral student in Counseling Psychology at the University of Georgia. His interests include working with children with disabilities, individuals with health disparities, and assessment. He is currently researching how headaches affect children with disabilities.

E-mail: dontavious.ford25@uga.edu

Katherine Crosby Gross, PhD, is a postdoctoral fellow in private practice in Athens, Georgia. She is a graduate of the Counseling Psychology program at the University of Georgia and completed her predoctoral psychology internship at Momentous Institute in Dallas, Texas. Katherine's research interests include the training and supervision of clinicians.

E-mail: crosbyk@uga.edu

Anthony W. Hansen, PhD, is a graduate of the Counseling Psychology program at the University of Georgia and is currently a licensed psychologist at Kennesaw State University's Counseling and Psychological Services. He completed his pre-doctoral internship at the University of North Carolina at Chapel Hill followed by a postdoctoral fellowship at Emory University. He also holds a Pre-Professional certificate in Marriage and Family therapy from the University of Georgia. His clinical interests include working with relationships and other relational problems, trauma and recovery, identity concerns (including but not limited to sexuality, diversity in gender, atheists and other types of secular individuals), and with veterans and other non-traditional students.

E-mail: anthony.wayne.hansen@gmail.com

Lauren Simone Harper, PhD, is a Psychology Resident in Primary Care Behavioral Health with Providence Medical Group near Portland, Oregon. She completed her APA-Accredited doctoral internship with the George Fox Integrated Care Consortium also near Portland, Oregon. Dr. Harper earned her PhD in Counseling Psychology and a certificate in Interdisciplinary Qualitative Studies from the University of Georgia. Her research areas of interest are in doctoral education and training of Black women, interventions for mental health treatment of Black people, and clinical training in integrated healthcare.

E-mail: drlaurensimone@gmail.com

Amelia Hoyle, PhD, received her doctorate in Counseling Psychology at the University of Georgia. She completed a pre-doctoral internship at Emory University's Counseling and Psychological Services (CAPS). She is currently a postdoctoral fellow at Emory CAPS. Amelia's clinical interests include working with students in undergraduate and graduate education with an emphasis on disordered eating and trauma.

E-mail: amelia.lynn.hoyle@emory.edu

Cindy Joseph, PhD, is the Executive Director & Licensed Psychologist of Solèy Psychological & Consulting Services. She is dually licensed in the states of Georgia and Texas. She specializes in providing culturally aware psychological services to individuals of diverse backgrounds. Her clinical interests include depression, anxiety, trauma, racial identity, and life transition issues. She attended Florida A&M University where she received her bachelor's and master's degrees and trained in African Psychology. She also received her doctorate in Counseling Psychology at the University of Georgia where she was also trained in Multicultural Psychology. Her professional interests include increasing mental health awareness in minority communities, providing mental health support to minority entrepreneurs and early career professionals, and providing culturally conscious psychotherapy, consulting, and psychological assessments.

E-mail: cindy@soleypcs.com

Reisha E. Moxley, PhD, is a licensed psychologist and currently an Assistant Professor of Physical Medicine and Rehabilitation at Vanderbilt University Medical Center. Prior to her current position, Dr. Moxley coordinated the group programs in counseling centers at Emory University in Atlanta, GA and at Johns Hopkins University in Baltimore, MD. Moxley earned her doctoral degree in Counseling Psychology from the University of Georgia and completed her doctoral internship in Health Service Psychology at the Johns Hopkins University Counseling Center. Dr. Moxley has over a decade of experience as a mental health practitioner for high achievers. Her current research, clinical and training interests converge around cultural identity development and awareness as well as advocacy and promotion of social justice and equity.

E-mail: reisha.e.moxley@vumc.org

Bailey J. Nevels, PhD, is a Licensed Psychologist and Coordinator of Psychological Health Services for Student-Athletes at Clemson University where she delivers clinical, outreach, consultation and educational services to Clemson's student-athletes. She earned her doctoral degree in counseling psychology from the University of Georgia in 2014 and completed her psychology internship at Clemson in 2014. Her professional interests include student-athlete mental health, multiculturalism and diversity, assessment, mindfulness and eating disorders.

E-mail: bnevels@clemson.edu

Paloma Ocampo, PhD, LPC, is a postdoctoral resident at Burrell Behavioral Health in Springfield, Missouri where she performs psychological evaluations. She earned her doctoral degree in counseling psychology from the University of Georgia and completed an internship in integrated behavioral health at Jordan Valley Community Health Center in Springfield, Missouri. Her professional and research interests include Latinx psychology, bilingual therapy, and multiculturalism.

E-mail: ip_ocampo@yahoo.com

JungSu Oh, MA, is a doctoral student in counseling psychology at the University of Georgia. His research interest is at advancing the psychotherapy research and practice by adopting innovative methodologies and technologies. Before starting his doctoral program, JungSu completed his master's degree in educational counseling, at the Seoul National University in Korea.

E-mail: js.oh@uga.edu

Amy Perkins, PhD, received her doctorate in counseling psychology from the University of Georgia. Currently Dr. Perkins is an intensive outpatient therapist for Focus Healthcare in Chattanooga, TN.

E-mail: amp.larocca@gmail.com

Beth L. Perlman, PhD, received her doctoral degree in Counseling Psychology from The University of Georgia in 2018 and is currently the Crisis Therapist/Care Manager at Monsour Counseling and Psychological Services at the Claremont Colleges. During her doctoral program, Beth completed her pre-doctoral internship at the University of Washington Counseling Center and successfully defended her dissertation on how immigration-related media depictions and policy influence aspects of well-being.

E-mail: blp1188@gmail.com

Bret A. Ringdahl, PhD, is a Postdoctoral Health Psychology Fellow in Health Promotion and Behavior at the University of Georgia's College of Public Health and The Recovery Center in Athens, GA. He earned his doctorate in Counseling Psychology from the University of Georgia, with an emphasis in health psychology and completed his pre-doctoral clinical psychology internship at the Washington DC Veterans Affairs Medical Center with an emphasis in behavioral medicine and trauma. Dr. Ringdahl previously earned a Masters in Counseling Psychology from the University of St. Thomas in Minneapolis, MN. His clinical and research interests include health disparity, behavioral medicine, diabetes, adherence, trauma and health, and the psychology of men and masculinity. Contact: dr.bret@outlook.com

Katie K. Robinson MA, RDT, is a doctoral student in Counseling Psychology at the University of Georgia. She serves a member of UGA's Juvenile Counseling and Assessment Program, serving adjudicated youth and their families, and is a graduate instructor in the College of Education. Prior to beginning her doctoral studies, Katie worked as a child and adolescent therapist in a nonprofit organization serving survivors of domestic and sexual violence in Virginia's Shenandoah Valley. Contact: katie.robinson@uga.edu

Alan E. Stewart, PhD, is a weather and climate psychologist at the University of Georgia. He works in the College of Education as a full professor and teaches in the Community Counseling master's program and the Counseling Psychology doctoral program. He is an adjunct faculty member in the Department of Geography and a member of the Atmospheric Science program. Dr. Stewart conducts interdisciplinary research at the intersection of weather, climate, and psychology. He has conducted research and published in areas relating to education and preparation of K-12 students for severe and extreme weather. He also has published on hurricane risk perceptions and the likelihood of evacuation. Dr. Stewart's other research in this area includes personological bases of weather salience and the latent linguistic dimensions that underlie weather and climate perception.

E-mail: aeswx@uga.edu

Elizabeth A. Stewart, PhD, is engaged as an adjunct faculty member at Athens Technical College in Athens, Georgia where she teaches Introductory Psychology and Human Development. She has also served as adjunct faculty at The University of Georgia where she received both masters and doctoral degrees in counseling psychology. Dr. Stewart has worked at a variety of settings including a state psychiatric hospital where she was a Senior Staff Psychologist for two geriatric units. At Northeast Florida State Hospital, she also served as the Director of Training for their doctoral internship program. She has worked as an administrator for a Community Service Board and as an Executive Director at an assisted living facility. She has provided training for professionals, students, and lay audiences on topics including neurocognitive disorders, issues related to older adults, suicide assessment, psychopathology, and substance use. Her professional interests include working with older adults and with individuals who have severe and persistent mental illness, and teaching/training.

E-mail: betsy100@bellsouth.net

Matthew S. Varley, PhD, is a postdoctoral fellow at Lepage Associates in Durham, North Carolina. He completed a doctorate in Counseling Psychology at the University of Georgia. Previously, he earned a master's in mental health counseling at Georgia State University and a bachelor's in religious studies at Brown University. Matthew's research interests include ethics in psychology and the role of moral values in clinical and educational settings.

E-mail: msvarley@gmail.com

Marjory Vazquez, PhD, received her undergraduate degree from the University of California, Irvine with majors in sociology and criminology. She subsequently received a master's degree from the University of Missouri- Columbia and completed her doctoral work at the University of Georgia in Counseling Psychology. Marjory also completed a pre-doctoral internship at Salud Family Health Centers, a primary care clinic in Commerce City, Colorado. Her clinical and research interests center on Latinx psychology, bilingual therapy, integrated health settings, and trauma. Marjory recently began a psychology postdoctoral residency at a Kaiser Permanente Hospital in Northern California doing therapy in Spanish in a bilingual clinic within Kaiser.

E-mail: mv22559@uga.edu

Courtney Williams, PhD, received her doctorate degree from the Department of Counseling and Human Development Services at the University of Georgia. Her research addresses the impact of culturally adapted group interventions for African American middle school girls. Ms. Williams obtained her M.A. in general psychology from North Carolina Central University and her B.A. in psychology from the University of North Carolina at Greensboro, NC. She has worked in university counseling centers and other agencies including an eating disorder inpatient center and a community mental health agency. Ms. Williams completed her APA-accredited internship at the University of Memphis' counseling center and is currently a post-doctoral fellow at Vanderbilt University's student counseling center.

E-mail: cw67401@uga.edu

Yi-Chen (Jenny) Wu, PhD, is an assistant professor in Department of Educational Psychology and Counseling at National Tsing Hua University (NTHU) in Hsinchu, Taiwan. She is also a licensed psychologist in Taiwan and an associate director at the NTHU university counseling center. Her research interest is in cross-cultural psychology and multicultural issues in counseling. She is dedicated to multicultural counseling training in Taiwan and services to international students on campus. She also has experience working as a substance abuse counselor at the Laure Carter Memorial Hospital in Indianapolis, IN.

E-mail: y.c.jenny.wu@gmail.com

Fengkan Zhu, PhD, earned his doctorate in Counseling Psychology from the University of Georgia. He is currently a Postdoctoral Resident at the University of Georgia Counseling and Psychiatric Services in Athens, Georgia. He completed his APA-accredited pre-doctoral internship at the University Counseling Center at the University of Oregon. Fengkan was born and raised in China. His research and clinical interests are immigration acculturation and their mental health as well cross-cultural psychology.

E-mail: zhufengkan1989@gmail.com

Ashlee E. Zito, PhD, is a Licensed Psychologist who earned her doctoral degree in Counseling Psychology from the University of Georgia. Dr. Zito completed her predoctoral psychology internship at the Federal Correctional Complex – Petersburg, VA in 2016 and her postdoctoral residency in Health Service Psychology (Forensics) at Emory University School of Medicine in 2017. She has since worked as a Forensic Psychologist for the Georgia Department of Behavioral Health and Developmental Disabilities.

E-mail: ashleezito@gmail.com

INDEX

A

B

C

D

H

I

J

L

M

N

O

P

Q

R

S

T

U

V

W

Y

Related Nova Publications

Understanding the Risk Factors for Suicidal Behavior

Editor: Horace N. Ballou

Series: Psychology of Emotions, Motivations and Actions

Book Description: In this compilation, the authors provide a literature review of the relationship between hormones including testosterone, prolactin, leptin, hypothalamus-pituitary-adrenal axis hormones, hypothalamus-pituitary-thyroid axis hormones, oxytocin, ghrelin, estradiol and progesterone, insulin, melatonin and suicidal behavior, which has potential public health and clinical significance.

Softcover ISBN: 978-1-53616-468-8
Retail Price: $82

The Psychology of Self-Control

Editor: August van Looij

Series: Psychology of Emotions, Motivations and Actions

Book Description: *The Psychology of Self-Control* reviews evidence that indicates low self-control is among the most important individual risk factors for criminal offending. A developmental pathway that begins with this risk factor and leads to criminal offending is presented, and treatment recommendations for reducing the risk that low self-control poses for criminal offending are discussed.

Softcover ISBN: 978-1-53616-576-0
Retail Price: $82

To see a complete list of Nova publications, please visit our website at www.novapublishers.com